T0150636

PRAISE FOR
PAUL'S WRITING

An Inordinate Fondness for Beetles

"Alfred Russell Wallace, who is best known as a naturalist and co-discoverer of the theory of natural selection, was a classic explorer in the Victorian mold. He was largely self-taught yet erudite, curious, brave and outspoken. This is the first book that structures his adventures and ideas by themes which resonate with contemporary challenges. Paul Sochaczewski, an explorer of ideas, offers informed, sometimes edgy, always accessible illustrations of issues Wallace cared about deeply: the natural dignity of tribal peoples, the role of colonialism, threats to our natural environment, why boys leave home to seek adventures and collect, how women will determine mankind's future, and how difficult it is to eliminate ego and greed from people in positions of power. This book should make everyone want to explore and experience the rainforests of Asia before they are all gone."

ROBIN HANBURY-TENISON
Explorer and author of *Mulu: The Rainforest*, *The Oxford Book of Exploration*, and *The Great Explorers*

"A natural storyteller, Paul Sochaczewski has created something much bigger than an "in the footsteps of" book. He has produced a work that looks at the themes Wallace wrote about and lived through – women's power, why boys leave home, the need to collect, our relation with other species, nature destruction, arrogance, the role of ego, white-brown and brown-brown colonialism, serendipity, passion, mysticism – and interpreted them through his own filter. He is a gifted storyteller and the layers of thought, humor, history, commentary and outrageousness Sochaczewski has given us provides a very special view of Wallace that goes beyond biography, beyond travelogue, beyond memoir."

DANIEL NAVID
International environment and development law expert, former UN diplomat, and secretary general of the International Wetlands Convention

"This book occupies a new category of non-fiction – part personal travelogue, part incisive biography of Wallace, part unexpected traveller's tales, which coalesce into an illuminating, sometimes bizarre and always entertaining volume. And running through the book is a deep respect for the natural world and the corner of Asia that Wallace and Sochaczewski spent years exploring. After reading this book my enthusiasm for this fascinating and little known part of the world was renewed – I eagerly anticipate my next visit to those amazing islands."

JEFFREY SAYER
Professor of conservation and development at James Cook University and founding director general of the Centre for International Forestry Research

"Woven around the adventures of Alfred Russel Wallace and of the author, *An Inordinate Fondness for Beetles* is a fascinating view of culture, biology and nature conservation in both historic as well as contemporary Malaysia, Indonesia and Singapore. Wallace, the unsung co-discover of evolution, is brought to life in a new and informative way here."

SIR GHILLEAN PRANCE
Former president of the Linnean Society and former director of the Royal Botanic Gardens, Kew

"Many of us dream about how exciting it must have been back in the days when Charles Darwin and Alfred Russel Wallace were discovering new ways to think about life. Paul Sochaczewski has shown us that the dreams can go live, if one just heads out and looks for the kinds of intriguing, bizarre, exciting, and mind-bending stories that he writes so well. As Wallace might have said, "diversity is the spice of life," and Paul's adventures with Wallace will make your mental curry taste like a party in your brain."

JEFFREY A. MCNEELY
Chief scientist at IUCN (International Union for Conservation of Nature)

"This is a classic hero's journey – actually a double hero's journey – which amuses, entertains and surprises us as Wallace and Sochaczewski both experience life-changing adventures in Southeast Asia. Wallace was one of science's great over-achievers, and by following his trail, Sochaczewski explores, with ample wit and sardonic insight, Wallace's extraordinary breakthrough in 19th-century evolutionary thinking, and reveals how this relates to contemporary Southeast Asian society, politics and the conservation of life on earth."

ANDREW W. MITCHELL
Founder and director of the Global Canopy Programme, Oxford, and author of *The Enchanted Canopy*

"We all owe Wallace a great debt of gratitude for helping us to understand how biological diversity resonates with and is inseparable from cultural diversity, something anthropologists and others are only recently documenting systematically. Likewise we are greatly indebted to Sochaczewski for adding his own observations and insights about how the human relationship with nature is changing in ways that Wallace suggested might occur. It's rare to find such a captivating book like this one, which so creatively combines hard science, passion, whimsy and travel adventures of a very special kind."

LESLIE E. SPONSEL
Author of *Spiritual Ecology: A Quiet Revolution*

"One of the best books about Alfred Russel Wallace's adventures, insights and impact, coupled with Sochaczewski's tales of modern mysticism, corruption, arrogance, courage, greed and inspiration in Southeast Asia. All combined in a startlingly innovative literary form that I've never come across previously."

JOHN G. WILSON
Author of *The Forgotten Naturalist: In Search of Alfred Russel Wallace*

"I've visited many of the places Alfred Russel Wallace and Paul Sochaczewski write about in this exceptional travelogue. *An Inordinate Fondness for Beetles* does something rare and wonderful – takes us back in time to the mid-19th century when Wallace was collecting and exploring, and forward to the present with insights about Indonesia and our relationship with nature that few people have thought of. This is a true adventure book; it provokes on many levels; it makes me want to dust off my backpack and follow the trail of Wallace once again."

ARISTIDES KATOPPO
Editor of *Sinar Harapan*

"Alfred Russel Wallace isn't widely known in Indonesia, which is a pity since his passion for the natural world and insights about our relationship with nature (and with each other) contain messages that will help contemporary Indonesians learn how to best respect, protect and manage our vast natural resources. But the book never lectures, never becomes boring. Just the opposite, it is a joy to read, filled with fascinating stories that bring Wallace to life. I intend to insist that my students read this book and consider its messages thoughtfully."

JAMALUDDIN JOMPA
Director of research and development at the Center for Marine, Coasts and
Small Islands, Hasanuddin University, Makassar, Indonesia

"After suffering years of neglect, the life and times of Alfred Russel Wallace – the 'Grand Old Man of Science' – have been enjoying somewhat of a revival over the last decade or so. But lest one is tempted to think that Paul Sochaczewski has written yet another book on Wallace, take a peek inside, sense the 'campfire conversations', read a chapter, and then start at the beginning and enjoy the whole book. Sochaczewski takes us not on a chronological or geographic adventure with Wallace, but on a much more thoughtful journey in which Wallace himself is explored through his writings, compared and shared by Sochaczewski's own travels and experiences (by turn fun, weird, and somber) in many of the same places Wallace knew. Many of us who have read Wallace and have seen his specimens will discover much here, not just about him, but also, perhaps, ourselves."

TONY WHITTEN
Asia director of Fauna & Flora International and author of various *Ecology of Indonesia* volumes

"Sarawak figured prominently in the explorations of Wallace and Sochaczewski, and this is one of the most incisive and entertaining books I've come across for anyone who wants to understand the nature and people of Sarawak. It's a guidebook for seekers of ideas, for people who want a different way of viewing one of the most surprising, rich, hospitable and dynamic parts of Asia. The orangutan chapter alone contains insights rarely expressed and could easily be expanded into a book on its own. *An Inordinate Fondness for Beetles* is also wonderfully irreverent and opens the curtains on happenings which some people would be happier to leave unexposed."

PETER KEDIT
Former director of the Sarawak Museum (founded by Charles Brooke at the suggestion of Alfred Russel Wallace)

"This book represents a high point in Sochaczewski's series of Asian-themed books; he couldn't have written it without having explored the hidden corners of Malaysia, Singapore and Indonesia for forty-plus years. It's simultaneously funny, sardonic, and insightful. Sochaczewski isn't afraid to shake Wallace's pedestal once in a while, and doesn't take himself too seriously either. What I particularly like is its unusual structure – it's not chronological but thematic – brown-brown colonialism, why boys leave home and collect insects, the joy of solitude, speaking with spirits, how ego stymies nature conservation. The book is like a pizza with everything – Sochaczewski throws in curious facts and anecdotes which enhance the narrative. Reminds me of Bruce Chatwin's *The Songlines* and Redmond O'Hanlon's *Into the Heart of Borneo*. I think he might even have created a new genre – part biography, part travel adventure, part commentary, part something new and refreshing."

JIM THORSELL
Senior advisor on world heritage to IUCN

"A classic hero's journey that amuses, entertains and surprises us as Wallace and Sochaczewski experience life-changing moments in their travels through Southeast

Asia. Working on several fronts as a coming-of-age book, a travelogue, a bonding of minds, and a good page-turning yarn, the book is compelling with enlightening insights woven into an engrossing narrative."

Mo Tejani
Author of *Global Crossroads: Memoirs of a Travel Junkie*

"A fascinating journey through the tropics of Southeast Asia, Sochaczewski not only follows in the footsteps of Alfred Russel Wallace but engages in a dialog with him for the whole journey. Thought-provoking about change and constancy, and a delight to read."

Peter H. Raven
President emeritus at the Missouri Botanical Garden

"A modern-day adventurer in his own right, Sochaczewski retraces the physical and intellectual journey of Alfred Russel Wallace, the great explorer, naturalist, humanist and pioneering theoretician on evolution by natural selection. The reader, in turn, is swept along on a quest to discover the dynamics that shape our natural world. In a virtual dialogue, both explorers bring their individual experiences to bear. Wallace's steps preceded those of the author by 150 years, yet the enigmas that bewildered and beguiled both, recent science notwithstanding, remain eminently topical, controversial and poignant. Any soul-searcher will find sustenance for thought in this book which touches upon those inescapable, eternal questions: 'Who are we?' 'Why is there such a complexity of life?' 'What is humanity's place in the great order of the universe?'"

Javed Ahmad
Former director of communication, environmental education and publications at IUCN

"Alfred Russel Wallace, co-originator with Charles Darwin of the theory of evolution by natural selection, has been called 'the forgotten naturalist', yet during his lifetime and afterwards he has been among the most widely read scientific and social writers. Wallace declared that the eight years he spent collecting in the Malay Archipelago 'constituted the central and controlling interest of my life'. For Paul Spencer Sochaczewski, this man and that region have had an equally powerful attraction. In his new book, *An Inordinate Fondness for Beetles*, rich anecdotes from his own encounters on the track of Wallace through the lands that are now three nations, Malaysia, Singapore and Indonesia, mingle with quotations from *The Malay Archipelago* and contemplation on Wallace's thoughts and attitudes of more than a century earlier. The product has the rhythm and magic of a verbal fugue. Words, phrases and even whole passages recur, focussing the reader back from lively diversions to the central theme. Two minds, moulded by contrasting background and upbringing, are reflected in reaction to people and places of the region, geographically linked but chronologically divided. Neither man eschews controversy, nor hesitates to express an opinion on current policies and events. Read, laugh and, in the light of impacts during the past century and a half, ponder with Sochaczewski on the uncertain future of the people and the wildlife of land and sea in this gloriously biodiverse archipelago."

DATO SRI GATHORNE, Earl of Cranbrook
Author of *Mammals of Borneo*, *Mammals of Southeast Asia*, and *Wonders of the Natural World of Southeast Asia*

"A fascinating exploration of the people and places that touched Wallace, and insights into his mind seen through the author's personal journey retracing those epic journeys. A deeply personal telling of Southeast Asia's character and nature, through the eyes of a naturalist, and a traveler. An enticing read."

TONY SEBASTIAN
Past president of the Malaysian Nature Society

"This is an audacious book in which Paul Sochaczewski talks with Alfred Russel Wallace, bridging 150 years of change in ecology, geography and demographics. Sochaczewski entertainingly discusses Wallace's views on the natural history of the Malay Archipelago side-by-side with his own reflections on contemporary twenty-first-century Southeast Asia."

NATARAJAN ISHWARAN
Director of ecological and earth sciences at UNESCO

"This is a Really Good Book! Paul Sochaczewski has written a scholarly personal travel book that is much, much more. He follows Alfred Russel Wallace to little-visited corners of Asia, discussing Wallace's views and discoveries combined with the author's erudite insights and musings into history, philosophy, people, and natural history. Extremely well written with nice touches of humor, this book is hard to put down."

LEE M. TALBOT
Professor of environmental science and policy at George Mason University, former director general at IUCN, and environmental advisor to three U.S. presidents.

"A cabinet of curiosities, both astounding and delightful. This is a marvelous book that all travelers through Asia should carry with them."

THOMAS BASS
Author of *The Eudaemonic Pie* and *The Spy Who Loved Us*

OTHER BOOKS BY THE AUTHOR

Distant Greens

"*Distant Greens* is an intimate golfing tour that travels to all corners of the planet and brings us into the heart, mind and soul of the game that we all love."

RICK LIPSEY
Sports Illustrated Magazine

"*Distant Greens* reminds us why we play the game. These enthralling stories take us to some of the world's strangest golf courses. They are more than travel stories; they are insightful, funny, and often touching human tales that provide new insights on why we play the game. Proves the adage that the quality of sports writing is inversely proportional to the size of the ball."

MICAH WOODS
Director of the Asian Turfgrass Center

"Travels to golf courses where they oughtn't be, visits with some of the most intriguing golfic characters the world over, and never strays far from the reader's heart. A quirky, funny, layered, insightful, beautifully written collection for golfers who ponder the meaning of this ever-fascinating, eternally-frustrating, always-satisfying game."

DANIEL NAVID
President of the International Golf and Life Foundation

"More than a golf travel book; more than a discourse on the spiritual nature of the game, this collection of insightful (and funny) essays and exceptional reportage explores new vistas about some of golf's most interesting people and places, and gets to the heart of the very reason so many of us love this game."

FRED SHOEMAKER
Coach, author, and founder of Extraordinary Golf

"*Distant Greens* gets to the core of golf's eco-spiritual essence with a collection of charming, insightful and often amusing stories, anecdotes and commentary that traverse the globe yet reside happily in the realm of 'good heart.'"

STEVE COHEN
President of the Shivas Irons Society (which promotes community, discovery, and transformation through golf)

"An impressive volume that links reportage on golf around the world with insights on the personal aspects of the game. But what makes *Distant Greens* so important, and a must-read, is how Sochaczewski addresses the role of golf in environmental destruction and, surprisingly for some, how golf can be a force for conservation. He offers new directions that golfers, and golf course owners and managers, should heed, for the good of the game and for the good of nature."

JEFFREY A. MCNEELY
Chief scientist at IUCN

"Paul brings insight, awareness, vision and clarity to the unconventional and unsung parts of this historic game. His writing informs and illuminates while drawing attention to the importance of environment to the integrity and future of golf. Indeed, this is big writing."

RON FREAM
Golf architect (has designed golf courses in sixty-five countries)

The Sultan and the Mermaid Queen

"The spirit of Kipling in contemporary Asian journalism. Paul Spencer Sochaczewski is an old Asia hand of incomparable experience and penetration. In these essays and stories you will discover perceptions and details that rarely find their way into any travel guide. This collection is essential reading for anyone who wishes to pass beyond even the unbeaten track, right to the heart of Asia."

JOHN BURDETT
Author of *Bangkok Eight*, *Bangkok Tattoo*, and *Bangkok Haunts*

"Paul Sochaczewski skips about Asia like a Monkey God hopping from mountain to mountain, bringing back life-prolonging peaches while annoying the gatekeepers. Whatever you do, follow him on this journey!"

LEE CHOR LIN
Director of the National Museum of Singapore, former curator of the Asian Civilisations Museum in Singapore, and author of *Batik: Creating an Identity*

"In nearly forty years of exploring Asia's forgotten corners, Paul Sochaczewski has investigated some of the most important and not-often reported issues in nature conservation. He delves into the disappearance of a Swiss Robin Hood-type character who helped local tribespeople in Borneo fight for their rainforest homes. He examines the ecological foundation of modern ethnic headhunting, the plight of mother-of-pearl divers in Indonesia who drown because they are given poor equipment by Chinese traders, how 'miracle rice' ruins Bali's coral reefs, why Indian religious leaders teamed up with conservationists to re-green Krishna's birthplace, and whether the concept of 'green golf' is an oxymoron. All his tales are important, all filled with humor, drama and insight; you won't find anything else like this on the bookshelf."

JEFF A. MCNEELY
Chief scientist at IUCN

"Sochaczewski is a world-class searcher, reporter, and observer who has criss-crossed Asia for thirty years, pausing in the most unlikely places, finding extraordinary people, and along the way has gathered and shaped an insightful, witty chronicle. His essays are filled with a rich tapestry of eclectic, original nobles, wannabe royalty, naturalists, Hindu gods, and Buddhist monks. He is a knowledgeable guide to an often obscure world, revealing Asian cultures often themselves on the brink of extinction. In a hundred years, books like *The Sultan and the Mermaid Queen* may be our only reference to belief systems and a way of life that have gone extinct."

CHRISTOPHER G. MOORE
Author of the Vincent Calvino novels, and *Heart Talk*

"The Sultan and the Mermaid Queen is proof positive that a writer/traveler can immerse himself in Asian cultures and yet remain objective enough to write extremely entertaining articles and colorful stories about what he has experienced. From Indonesian mysticism to a Hawaiian would-be Chinese emperor, the descriptions are spot-on. There is something in these articles and stories that reminds me of the writing of Paul Theroux – not as cynical, perhaps, but the author is just as able to look at events with a clear, unsentimental and yet sympathetic eye. You won't regret a moment spent reading these tales which perfectly capture the allure and spice of the places visited."

DEAN BARRETT
Author of *Memoirs of a Bangkok Warrior*

"Having grown up in Asia, I am deeply indebted to Paul Sochaczewski for his unique ability to reawaken the memories of the humanity and humor, wonder and reality of this magical part of the world. These stories leap off the pages and head straight into your heart. *The Sultan and the Mermaid Queen* is one of the finest gifts you could possibly give to yourself and to your best friends."

ANDY SUNDBERG
U.S. presidential candidate (1988), former worldwide chairman of Democrats Abroad, founder of American Citizens Abroad, U.S. Naval officer, and co-founder of Burlamaqui Society.

"In my line of work, I've been to a lot of places, met a lot of people and done a lot of things. Yet I never tire of living vicariously through Paul Sochaczewski and his writing adventures. He keeps finding these wonderful details that miraculously open up entire worlds to be explored. Paul is the last of the Great Hunters, only, instead of trophies, it is stories he brings home for our admiration, wonder and delight."

MARK OLSHAKER
Filmmaker, author of *Einstein's Brain*, *The Edge*, and *Mind Hunter*

"Sochaczewski is blessed with a relentlessly probing curiosity, an easy-to-read writing style and a sensitive soul. His explorations of the remote jungles, far-flung archipelagoes and quirky characters of Asia leave us with fascinating accounts that mix natural history and modern-day reporting to investigate old fables and inspire new ones."

JAMES FAHN
Executive director of the Earth Journalism Network and author of *A Land on Fire: The Environmental Consequences of the Southeast Asian Boom*

"What a discovery! Paul Sochaczewski is that rarest of writers, who knows that the real 'Asian miracle' isn't malls or computer geeks. In his years traveling the continent he has discovered an eternal assemblage of arcane explorers, putative emperors, frivolous mystics, sacrosanct elephants and, yes, miracle workers. When Sochaczewski finds them, in Javanese palaces or mile-high golf courses, they are caviar (or sweetened bird's nest) for his fascinating portraits. A book for everyone who knows that the Mysterious East is alive and well."

HARRY ROLNICK
Author of *The Chinese Gourmet*, *The Complete Book of Coffee*, and *Spice Chronicles: Exotic Tales of a Hungry Traveler*

"This is travel writing with a quirky difference. Admirers of Paul Spencer Sochaczewski's serio-comic novel *Redheads*, set in the jungles of Borneo, will already know him as a dedicated environmentalist with a taste for off-beat characters and exotic settings. This collection of personal essays introduces a fascinating collection of real-life figures, ranging from a homeless man in Hawaii who claims to be the true last emperor of China to a group of Burmese monks who have trained cats to perform acrobatic tricks.

WILLIAM WARREN
Author of *Jim Thompson: The Unsolved Mystery* and *The Tropical Garden*

"In the great tradition of Asian reporting. The humanity of Somerset Maugham, the adventure of Joseph Conrad, the perception of Paul Theroux, and a self-effacing voice uniquely his own."

GARY BRAVER
Bestselling author of *Skin Deep*

"For three decades Paul Sochaczewski has been trawling Asia for lost white tribes, Hobbits, dancing ghosts, the Last Emperor of China and dancing temple cats, reporting back with tales of hilarity and insight. He's also been at the forefront of efforts to raise awareness of Asia's great environmental diversity, documenting the struggle of indigenous tribes in Borneo to save their precious forest, and has championed 'Darwin's shadow', that other great of evolution, Alfred Russel Wallace. This collection captures the diversity of Asia in all its colorful, and often funny, glory."

JOHN CLEWLEY
Bangkok Post columnist

"Rich pickings from the unexpected corners of the Far East. What makes *The Sultan and the Mermaid Queen* outstanding must surely be the inquisitive mind, the compassionate tone and openhearted admiration of the author towards his subjects. Whatever landmarks you already have on Asia, this book sweeps you to new frontiers."

CYNTHIA WEE-HOEFER
Daughter of Asia, freelance writer

"A wonderful book about traditions and beliefs in Asia. Sochaczewski has that rare gift to bring history and fable to life with respect and affection. This book should be required reading for politicians and people in NGOs concerned with Asia – indeed for anyone seeking a better understanding of life and culture in this most fascinating part of the world."

DANIEL NAVID
International environment and development law expert, former UN diplomat, and secretary general of the International Wetlands Convention

"Among this book's fascinating stories about the people and natural history of South East Asia, we learn that the naturalist Alfred Russel Wallace may have a better claim to the theory of natural selection than Charles Darwin."

JOHN G. WILSON
Author of *The Forgotten Naturalist: In Search of Alfred Russel Wallace*

"Only a lifetime of ambling through Asian cultures could enrich a writer to this degree and enable him to infuse his writing with local lore and wisdom in the manner Paul Sochaczewski has done in this colorful and insightful collection."

JOHN EVERINGHAM
Photographer, and publisher at Artasia Press and Dragon Art Media

"Having seen at least a thousand films from Hollywood, France, Italy, England, Germany, Japan, China, and Russia during my seventy-odd years of life, I had come to assume that I had a pretty good idea of what goes on in the world. This delightful book, *The Sultan and the Mermaid Queen*, has completely (and thankfully) demolished that naive notion. It is a vast tapestry embroidered with real peoples, places, and customs far more exotic than any of the quaint 'travelers tales' of ancient times, and any reader who takes it home is a lucky one!"

DANIEL QUINN
Author of *Ishmael*

"Paul has the extraordinary ability to find hidden and overlooked stories and reveal them as meaningful and profound."

R. IAN LLOYD
National Geographic photographer.

"As a mystic healer I understand the spiritual power of the Mermaid Queen, and have on occasion merged with her strong presence. In this book Sochaczewski has managed something quite extraordinary – he has taken exotic, sometimes esoteric subjects and made them interesting and accessible. His writing peels back the layers of myth and reality, revealing a sensitive, humorous and insightful core of humanity."

AMA LIA WAI-CHING LEE
Pemangku Maha Jeroh Sandat, mystic healer, dancer, chronicler

"Storytelling with a heart of adventure in mind and spirit, unveiling many unknown aspects of Asia "

ARISTIDES KATOPPO
Editor of *Sinar Harapan*

"Paul Sochaczewski's writing combines good travel writing, humor, and environmental consciousness. His stories focus on the human and natural phenomena which make Southeast Asia arguably the most interesting part of the world to live in; he writes about the unusual characters and situations which he encounters with gentle irony. He wears his deep familiarity with the region lightly, smoothing the path into this dauntingly complex area for the reader with no previous experience here."

JOHN MIKSIC
Associate professor at the National University of Singapore and author of *Borobudur: Golden Tales of the Buddhas*, *Indonesian Heritage Encyclopedia*, *Encyclopedia of Malaysia*, *Kraton Surakarta*, and *Icons of Art: The Collections of the National Museum of Indonesia*

"*The Sultan and the Mermaid Queen* is delightful and fascinating – a fun, and funny, introduction to some of the most interesting people, places and sights of Southeast Asia. Never met a real-life hobbit? Come search for them on the Indonesian island of Flores. Worried that your golf game is beyond human redemption? Meet a Japanese monk who uses Zen to unlock the secrets of a supernatural putt. Think a white elephant can only be found in Disneyland? Let Sochaczewski show you how the military autocrats of Burma are seeking out a rare beast to balance out their bad karma. If you can't travel to the rainforests of Borneo and the minefields of Cambodia, pick up a copy of *The Sultan and the Mermaid Queen* and come along for the ride!"

JONAH BLANK
Chief policy advisor on Asia to the U.S. Senate Committee on Foreign Relations and author of *Arrow of the Blue-Skinned God: A Classic Journey through India*

"Sochaczewki is obsessed with were-tigers, seductress mermaids, tiny forest men and one particular beetle-loving Victorian naturalist who changed the way we look at the place of man in the universe. Ho hum. But as you read these fabulous stories, you realize that he has another, higher, obsession: getting to know people. Whether they're from

Brooklyn, Burma or highland Borneo, Sochaczewski shares with us their voices and their stories. And afterwards he goes golfing."

PETER SCHOPPERT
Author of *Java Style* and head of external relations for McKinsey & Company

"This book is full of 'good heart' and surprising news from parts of the world that don't always play by Cartesian rules. Paul Sochaczewski wears his knowledge as lightly as an invisible cloak, but there is a lot to be learned from these finely-wrought tales of faraway places. I recommend you buy this book and savor it."

THOMAS BASS
Author of *The Eudaemonic Pie* and *The Spy Who Loved Us*

Soul of the Tiger

(co-authored with Jeffrey A. McNeely)

"A timely, revealing, delightful and yet totally unsentimental look at the relationship between our own and other species which must lie at the heart of all successful conservation."

LYALL WATSON
Author of *Supernature* and *The Dreams of Dragons*

"Provocative and engrossing . . . a solid combination of natural history and anthropology."

Publishers Weekly

"A rich exotic kettle of myths, origin tales, ritual dances, blood sports, natural history oddities, human animal soul transfers and transformations. . . . A lush ecocultural travelogue of myth and ritual."

Kirkus Reviews

"A marvelous book, unique, intelligent, attuned to cultures and filled with stimulating ideas . . ."

GEORGE SCHALLER
Director of Wildlife Conservation International

"In one fascinating account after another, the authors explain the folklore in which animals are an everyday part of community life as mythological symbols or ancestors incarnate, as well as being sources of meat, leather and medicine. The tales are told with humor, but without condescension. They look with favor on the harmony of human-wildlife relations and conclude that these traditional approaches to conservation should be encouraged in a third world that seeks to balance economic growth and environmental preservation. They note, 'The belief in universal souls means that we are all veritable soul brothers.'"

JOHN NOBLE WILFORD
The New York Times

"*Soul of the Tiger* is a book that travels through space – from the upbeat bustle of Bangkok to rich traditions in the Malaysian countryside – as well as through time, charting significant 'ecocultural revolutions' that have shaped Southeast Asia."

Los Angeles Times

Redheads

"*Redheads* does for the struggle to save the rain forests of Borneo what *Catch* 22 did for the struggle to stay alive in World War II."

DANIEL QUINN
Author of *Ishmael*

"*Redheads* is a roaring tale of tropical suspense, an eco-thriller that is witty and smart and altogether a wonderful treat. It is the perfect example of a new genre, an eco-thriller so suspenseful that you learn about this strange world while sitting on the edge of your seat."

THOMAS BASS
Author of *The Eudaemonic Pie* and *The Spy Who Loved Us*

"A fast-paced novel, at once very funny and deeply serious, about a subject that should be of concern to everyone in today's world."

WILLIAM WARREN
Author of *Jim Thompson: The Unsolved Mystery* and *The Tropical Garden*

"An absorbing story, reminiscent of the social commentary of Somerset Maugham and Evelyn Waugh. Everyone working in conservation should read it and heed it."

JIM THORSELL
Senior advisor on world heritage to IUCN

"*Redheads* is a terrific book about apes and people, do-gooders and do-badders, science and superstition, ecology and psychology, nature and nurture, and how we all fit together in this old world."

MARK OLSHAKER
Filmmaker, author of *Einstein's Brain*, *The Edge*, and *Mind Hunter*

"A ribald, engrossing novel with a deeper message regarding the clash of cultures and our relation to the environment."

EDWIN BERNBAUM
Author of *Sacred Mountains of the World*

"*Redheads* combines the witty insights of George MacDonald Fraser with the realism of Thomas Hardy – a real Asian treat."

JEFFREY A. MCNEELY
Chief scientist at IUCN

This rambunctious romp through the Borneo jungles is both fun and deceptively insightful. If this is how the world *really* works in the realm of nature protection, then where do we go from here? The story reveals important realities about the way things can be in the hurley-burley world of nature protection and environmentalism. Noble-intentioned jetsetting environmentalists: Take Heed!"

SIR RUSSELL BETTS
Former director of the WWF Indonesian program

"Each page carries the scent, the musk even, of tropical Asia – whether enveloped in vanishing rainforests or in the drama of full blooded characters whose courage, or cowardice, has become entwined in the greatest and most tragic story of our age – the catastrophic and irreplaceable loss of primeval forest."

JAMES CLAD
Professor of Asian studies at Georgetown University, U.S. assistant secretary of defense, and author of *Behind the Myth: Business, Money and Power in Southeast Asia*

"Ringing endorsement . . . [in] Sochaczewski's tale of ambition and corruption, sex and compassion, he moves delightfully quirky, flawed characters around a fantastic plot like a clever puppeteer. Action, action and more action . . . readers feel his tongue firmly planted in his cheek, strikes a delicate balance between acutely funny and genuinely serious."

PAIGE RISSER
Peace Corps Writers

"A great read. *Redheads* accurately and entertainingly captures the cynical reality of today's conservation conflicts. This entertaining book is a must for anyone interested in learning how the global environment movement really works."

DANIEL NAVID
International environment and development law expert, former UN diplomat, and secretary general of the International Wetlands Convention

"With the trained eyes and sensitivity of someone who lived among the orangutans in the wilds of Borneo, Sochaczewski tells a captivating story of the struggle to save the rainforests. *Redheads* reads like a fast-paced high-powered movie script that makes the issue of environmental devastation come alive and demand reforms."

ROBERT A. PASTOR
Professor at Emory University and former National Security Council staffer

"Sochaczewski, author of *Soul of the Tiger* and an 'old Asia hand', displays both his extensive knowledge of rainforest politics and a real ability to tell an entertaining story."

CHRIS ELLIOTT
Director of the Forests for Life Campaign of the WWF

"*Redheads* pits the ideals of science and biodiversity conservation against the real world of nasty politics, reductionist thinking, and economic 'imperatives'. The engaging spell of the author weaves the impression that indigenous peoples and other primate inhabitants of the forest are the only hope we have left of saving the tropical ecosystems of the world."

DARREL ADDISON POSEY
Oxford Centre for the Environment, Ethics and Society

Eco-Bluff Your Way to Instant Environmental Credibility
(co-authored with Jeffrey A. McNeely)

"Here we have a hilarious romp through the lexicon of eco-babble, replete with gentle but telling jabs at the people, institutions and jargon of the Green world. But even a book this light-hearted powerfully signals the sweeping breadth of the authors' knowledge about environmental affairs, and the intensity of their caring about the planet's fate. Learn while you laugh, kind reader. Then go forth and spread the Word."

ROGER D. STONE
Author of *Dreams of Amazonia* and *The Voyage of the Sanderling*

"What a book! I couldn't cry . . . I was laughing too much! Well done, Paul and Jeff. You've managed to cover insights into potentially disastrous global issues in a bright and (dare I say) enjoyable way. You've opened our eyes to a new and more effective vision of the pathway to environmental sanity."

NOEL VIETMEYER
U.S. National Academy of Sciences

To Apsara, explore, question, laugh at your own foibles and at folks who think they have the answers.

AN
INORDINATE
FONDNESS
FOR
BEETLES

AN
INORDINATE
FONDNESS
FOR
BEETLES

*Campfire Conversations with
Alfred Russel Wallace on People
and Nature Based on Common Travel
in the Malay Archipelago,
The Land of the Orangutan
and the Bird of Paradise*

PAUL SPENCER SOCHACZEWSKI

EDITIONS
DIDIER
MILLET

First published in 2012 by
Editions Didier Millet Pte Ltd
121 Telok Ayer Street #03-01
Singapore 068590
www.edmbooks.com

Printed in Singapore

Reprinted in 2013

ISBN: 978-981-4385-20-6

THAILAND

CAMBODIA

VIETNAM

SOUTH CHINA SEA

MALAYSIA

Peninsular
Malaysia

• Kuantan

BRUNEI

Sa

• Kuala Lumpur

Gunung Mulu
National Park •

STRAIT OF MALACCA

• Gunung Ledang
• Malacca

Sarawak

SINGAPORE

Santubong •

Batang Ai National Park

• Kuching

SUMATRA

Siujunjan • • Perinjau

EQUATOR

BORNEO

Kalimantan

Kerinci Seblat
National Park

Tanjung Putting
National Park •

• Lubuk Raman

JAVA SEA

INDONESIA

• Jakarta

JAVA

Solo •

• Yogyakarta

Sanghurnih

Buleleng •

BALI

Sanur •

LOMBOK

LOMBOK STRAIT

Legend

-▪-▪-▪-	International boundary
BRUNEI	Country
Sabah	Region/Province
JAVA	Major Island
FLORES	Island
• Jarkata	City/Area

0	180	360	540 km
0	112	224	336 miles

Map of the Malay Archipelago,
with place names mentioned in this book

PHILIPPINES

WALLACE LINE

ARU

Manado •
Bobale • HALMAHERA
Dodinga •
Kotamobagu TERNATE • • Tidore

Sorong • • Manokwari
Minyambou • Arfak Mountains

BACAN

SULAWESI
• Morowali

BURU SERAM
AMBON

WALLACEA
BANDA ISLANDS

NEW GUINEA

• Makassar

KAI ISLANDS
• Dobo
ARU ISLANDS

MODO
FLORES

SUMBA

ROTI

N

Table of Contents

"NOT EVERYTHING THAT CAN BE COUNTED COUNTS, AND NOT EVERYTHING THAT COUNTS CAN BE COUNTED." [1]

THE 19TH CENTURY BRITISH BIOCHEMIST J. B. S. HALDANE, AN ARDENT MARXIST WHO QUIT ENGLAND FOR INDIA, WAS ONCE APPROACHED BY A DISTINGUISHED THEOLOGIAN TO ASK WHAT INFERENCES ONE COULD DRAW ABOUT THE NATURE OF THE CREATOR FROM THE STUDY OF HIS CREATION. HALDANE REPLIED, WITH HIS USUAL TERSENESS, THAT "GOD HAS AN INORDINATE FONDNESS FOR BEETLES."

---

[1]   Attribution uncertain. The quote (with reversed parallel phrases) is often attributed to Albert Einstein; some sources say it was written on a sign in his Princeton office, but it does not appear in his published writing. William Bruce Cameron wrote these well-known words, eight years after Einstein's death, in his 1963 textbook *Informal Sociology: A Casual Introduction to Sociological Thinking*.

London, United Kingdom
A century after his death, there is a growing re-recognition of Wallace's achievements.

I
DEPARTURE

SHIVA'S BEACH — DAWN

Pulau Enu, Aru Islands, Indonesia

A milky sunrise on a deserted beach, watching a miracle.

As the sun rises, a bunch of just-hatched turtles, each shorter than my thumb, scamper like reptilian puppies to the sea. After they all reach the ocean safely, I strip and swim in new-turtle water to wash off the sand. Alfred, I half expect to see you straggling out of the scraggly forest, in need of a bath and English-speaking company.

Back at the nest site, a straggler is emerging from the quickly heating sand half an hour behind his nest-mates. Call it biology, or call it a minor miracle, his appearance is both startling and comforting.

This curious birthing ground I dub Shiva's Beach. A site of creation.

The laggard baby green turtle marches clumsily but with determined flipper steps into the sea. He swims aggressively, sticking his little head out of the water every few seconds. The water is clear and warm and benign, free of hungry fish or crabs, the sky blue and free of turtle-loving gulls.

The little fellow swims toward a group of seven fishing boats anchored a hundred meters offshore. I tell him not to, but he doesn't listen. But the sea is big, and perhaps he will pass his life free of hassle. Eventually he paddles out of sight. A boy. He doesn't really know where he is going, but he knows *he has a journey to make. I wish him well, as much for my sake as for his.*

From chaos
Shiva creates
Trident aloft

BOYS' STUFF

Natural History Museum, London, United Kingdom

In the Zetland Arms pub, which smells of stale beer and has a carpet so threadworn that I sense perhaps Wallace spilled ale on it a hundred and fifty years ago.

In 1854, after an uneventful sea passage from England, Alfred Russel Wallace, a nearly broke, self-taught British naturalist, arrived in Singapore and began an eight-year exploration of Southeast Asia. He traveled some 22,400 kilometers (14,000 miles) and collected 125,660 specimens of insects, birds and animals, including hundreds of new species. But ideas interested him more than taxonomic numbers, and during Wallace's Asian sojourn he elaborated theories of biogeography (the study of the distribution of living things in space and time) and island biology. He opined on man's social quirks and racial distinctions, and developed a theory of natural selection and the evolution of species that he mailed to Charles Darwin, who had been pondering the same questions for many years. Wallace's letter to Darwin spurred the older scientist into publishing his famous *The Origin of Species*. Some conspiracy theorists say that Darwin and his well-placed friends in the British scientific hierarchy deliberately sidelined Wallace, who was in Indonesia during the critical period when the theory of natural selection was presented in London. Darwin today is a household name; Wallace isn't.

In 1969, fresh out of university and motivated by Kennedy-inspired ideals and a reluctance to fight in Vietnam, I joined the United States Peace Corps and was sent to Sarawak, a Malaysian state on the island of Borneo, where I advised rural teachers, slashed and burned the forest, hunted crocodiles and wild pigs, and debated whether I should adorn my body with Iban tattoos. I then moved to Singapore, talked my way into an advertising job, and saw Asia from the other side – the side with the money and power. I eventually moved to Indonesia, traveling through most of the country's twenty-seven provinces in the process of producing TV commercials, writing news stories, feasting on roast bat and cassava leaves and rice wine, breathing volcanic sulphurous air, and swimming with dolphins.

Back in Europe on a foggy winter day, I have to dig deep to remember the emotions of Shiva's Beach. That hot isolated island, so real then, has taken on a Brigadoon-like quality. Shiva's Beach now seems no more real than a museum diorama. I have the notes and the photos, but the dawn of the turtles has taken on a dreamlike quality. Did it happen?

I can't get Alfred Russel Wallace out of my head. He's an insistent presence, a biographical version of malaria or athlete's foot or the smell of durian on my hands or the last song I hear on the radio before going to bed. He's the first person I would invite to a fantasy dinner party.

But my decades in Asia, and Wallace's eight years there, are real because we both have physical souvenirs. When Wallace finally returned home, he wrote:

> When I reached England [after eight years in Southeast Asia] in the spring of 1862, I found myself surrounded by a room full of packing-cases, containing the collections that I

had from time to time sent home for my private use. These comprised nearly three thousand bird-skins, of about a thousand species; and at least twenty thousand beetles and butterflies, of about seven thousand species; besides some quadrupeds and landshells. A large proportion of these I had not seen for years; and in my then weak state of health, the unpacking, sorting, and arranging of such a mass of specimens occupied a long time.[1]

This prodigious collection was amassed while Wallace endured malaria, poverty, and loneliness. Why would a grown man voluntarily suffer to simply collect insects? Wallace could have, after all, stayed in England and worked as a surveyor like his brother.

[As a boy] I possessed a strong desire to know the causes of things, a great love of beauty in form and colour, and a considerable but not excessive desire for order and arrangement in whatever I had to do.[2]

What makes someone a passionate collector? Sigmund Freud, who was born in 1856 while Wallace was in eastern Indonesia, might have analyzed that a chronic gatherer and organizer is locked in an anal-retentive mode, unwilling to let go, unable to touch his emotions.

Psychologist Werner Muensterberger had a different spin: "Observing collectors, one soon discovers an unrelenting need, even hunger, for acquisitions," he wrote. "This ongoing search is a core element of their personality. It is linked to far deeper roots. It turns out to be a tendency which derives from a not immediately discernible sense memory of deprivation or loss or vulnerability and a subsequent longing for substitution, closely allied with moodiness and depressive leanings." Too convoluted for my taste, and sloppily

---

1   *The Malay Archipelago: The Land of the Orang-utan and the Bird of Paradise; A Narrative of Travel With Studies of Man and Nature*, Vol. 1 & 2. 1989. Singapore: Oxford University Press. (original edition: 1869. London: Macmillan & Co.), 5.

2   *My Life: A Record of Events and Opinions*, Vol. I. 1905. London: Chapman & Hall, 224.

written to boot. I think the likely explanation is simpler. I figure this collecting business was simply a way to keep the boy in Alfred Russel Wallace alive.

Like all interesting people Wallace was a bundle of contradictions: a scientist and a believer in spirits, a hard-nosed hunter who shot seventeen orangutans and a soppy surrogate father to an orangutan baby he had orphaned. He saw dignity in the indigenous people he met but he neither refrained from calling them "savages" nor called for an end to colonialism. His collections of birds of paradise fed an increased demand in Europe, which caused various species of those birds to become threatened in the wild. He correctly predicted environmental havoc and the need for personal and governmental environmental responsibility.

Why did he travel far and dirty? I can only speculate – one can decipher only so much from reading another person's books, even an autobiography. We are rarely honest, particularly when our writing will be exposed to the coarse air of scrutiny.

Wallace had a Jack Kerouac-like wanderlust. He was a collector of the most avaricious kind, a taxonomist who both enjoyed and saw the basic need to assign things their proper place in the scheme of things, a scientist who measured the boiling point of water when ascending a mountain, an anthropologist and social reformer. He was a remarkably lucid, provocative, and prolific writer (he wrote 769 publications, including 508 scientific papers and 22 books, totaling some 10,000 pages of printed matter). A Victorian Leonardo in great need of da Vinci's public relations agency.

I put the question of why Wallace collected to Martin Brendell, who works in the beetle section at the British Museum, a generous, easy-to-smile man who bought the first round at the Zetland Arms.

Brendell and I went through the possible explanations. For one, the nineteenth-century British collecting public was fascinated by beetles, and Wallace was paid well – he excitedly wrote that, "[The second shipment of insects sent] from Singapore produced

£1000 gross!"

Wallace was never shy about admitting that he went to Asia to earn some money. But the money was a means to a fuzzy end. He didn't want the cash to buy a new home (as much as he was always in need of a new home); he needed the cash to let him continue his explorations.

Similarly, Martin Brendell has never been in it for the money.

I had first met Brendell in 1980 during the Operation Drake expedition in Sulawesi, a large, orchid-shaped and biologically curious island in eastern Indonesia. My initial image of him will stay with me – it was night, and he had set up a white bed sheet with a gas pressure lamp behind it. Insects of all descriptions, attracted by the light, slammed into the cloth while Brendell nudged them into collecting trays. The parts of Brendell that were not protected by swimming trunks were covered with moths and beetles and flies and god-knows-what.

"I've got some new species here, I'm sure," I remember him telling me, trying hard not to swallow one that was emerging from his scraggly beard. "But there aren't enough taxonomists around so I may never know what I've got." He's not doing too badly, however, with some thirty new species to his credit.

Is *that* it? The immortality that comes with discovering new species? Or are beetles merely stepping stones to the big questions of evolution and natural selection, on which Wallace's current reputation rests?

"I imagine Wallace spent an awful lot of time standing around with his mouth open saying 'this is unbelievable,'" Brendell suggested, sipping on a pint of lager. Beetles are pretty and dramatic and colorful and easy to collect and don't take up a lot of space. A guy could begin a reasonable collection in a couple of afternoons.

> It is a melancholy fact that many of our fellow creatures do not know what is a *beetle*! They think cockroaches are beetles! Tell them that beetles are more numerous more varied and even more beautiful than the birds or beasts or fishes that inhabit the earth and they will hardly believe

you; – tell them that he who does not know something about beetles misses a never failing source of pleasure and occupation and is ignorant of one of the most important groups of animals inhabiting the earth and they will think you are joking; – tell them further that he who has never observed and studied beetles passes over more wonders in every field and every copse than the ordinary traveller sees who goes round the world and they will perhaps consider you crazy, – yet you will have told them only the truth. [italics Wallace][3]

I admire Wallace for maintaining his ability to marvel at the diversity of life. For spending all those years alone, eating rotten food, writing letters to people back in England who might have died since he last saw them, hassling with a dozen porters just to move his camp from one damp location to another, negotiating permission to enter the territory of self-important sultans and officials. A weaker man would have become bitter. Wallace instead rejoiced in small victories.

I had the good fortune to capture one of the most magnificent insects the world contains, the great bird-wing butterfly, Ornithoptera poseidon [now *Ornithoptera priamus poseidon*]. I trembled with excitement as I saw it coming majestically toward me and could hardly believe I had really succeeded in my stroke till I had taken it out of the net and was gazing, lost in admiration. . . . The village of Dobbo [Dobo, in Aru] held that evening at least one contented man.[4]

The Natural History Museum's beetle collection today numbers

---

3   Notebook (unpublished) 1855–59, 148.

4   *The Malay Archipelago*, 434.

some eight to ten million specimens neatly kept in twenty-two thousand flat drawers.[5] The beetles range in size from the top of this exclamation point: ! to an Amazonian species as large as a songbird. The beetles Wallace collected – thirty drawers full – are identified by circular white labels, often written in his own hand. They sometimes share a drawer with beetles adorned with square printed labels, which were collected by Charles Darwin. These are historic creatures that have attained some form of immortality merely by being under the right rotting log at the right time. During eight years in Southeast Asia Wallace collected an astonishing 125,660 specimens, and when these got sorted out he had discovered among them 900 new species of beetles, 200 new species of ants, 50 new species of the Pieridae and 96 of the 130 known species of the Papilionidae families of butterflies.[6] He was the Joe DiMaggio of naturalists, based just on his Asian collections. And we'll never know how many he collected during his four years in the Amazon, since most of his collection, along with most of his notebooks, was lost at sea.

Yet the odd thing is that even late in life, when Wallace and the establishment grudgingly made peace with each other, he considered himself a bit of an upstart, a pretender in Darwin's shadow.

> *I* was then (as often since) the 'young man in a hurry:' *he* [Darwin], the painstaking and patient student, seeking ever the full demonstration of the truth that he had discovered, rather than to achieve immediate personal fame. [italics Wallace][7]

---

5   The museum, in some form, dates to the mid-eighteenth century. Notoriously ill-managed, it legally remained a department of the British Museum with the formal name British Museum (Natural History). In 1866, Wallace, Darwin, Huxley, and other noteworthies petitioned the chancellor of the exchequer, asking that the museum gain independence from the board of the British Museum. In 1963, the British Museum (Natural History) became an independent museum with its own board of trustees, although – despite a proposed amendment to the act in the House of Lords – the former name remained. Only with the Museums and Galleries Act 1992 did the museum's formal title finally change to the Natural History Museum.

6   He collected multiple specimens of the same species, not simply for commercial sale but also to identify the variation among individuals, an important insight into his theory of natural selection.

7   "Acceptance speech on receiving the Darwin-Wallace Medal." July 1, 1908. In *The*

The circular and the square-labeled beetles in the museum's collection represent Alfred Russel Wallace's close but sometimes uncomfortable relationship with Charles Darwin, a touchy area for fans of both men. In the 1840s and 1850s both Darwin and Wallace, living half a world apart, became correspondents. Wallace recalled his first meeting with Darwin: "I was, in 1854, preparing for my visit to the Malay Archipelago by a study of the insects and birds of that region, when one day, I think very early in the year, I was introduced to Darwin in the Insect-room of the British Museum, and had a few minutes' conversation with him, but I cannot recollect that anything of importance passed between us."[8]

Darwin claimed he had no recollection of having met Wallace. Each had been independently grappling with the question of whether species change and, if so, how. While living in Sarawak, on the island of Borneo, and then in Ternate, in eastern Indonesia, Wallace came up with *his* evolutionary theories and sent his thoughts to Darwin, the famous thinker and one-off explorer (Darwin never again left England following the voyage of the *Beagle*, his only overseas trip). Here is where history gets sticky. Darwin had been pretty certain that species evolved, had been working on the question of origin of species for many years, but was missing the key piece of the puzzle – the mechanism for change. Darwin procrastinated over writing up his ideas for many years until the postman surprised him with Wallace's now-famous Ternate Paper of 1858. Imagine Darwin's surprise. There he was, sitting in Down House, working on his theory but afraid to publish it, either because he wasn't sure of his data or because he was afraid of antagonizing the British social order (not to mention his devout wife) with such a revolutionary idea that challenged the Biblical concept of creation. Out of the blue, Wallace, a younger, less-acclaimed scientist of no particular social standing, seemingly lost in the Asian jungles, sent Darwin a significant part of the answer, the mechanism of natural

Darwin-Wallace Celebration Held on Thursday, 1st July, 1908. 1909. London: Burlington House, Longmans, Green & Co., 6.

8   "The Dawn of a Great Discovery (My Relations With Darwin in Reference to the Theory of Natural Selection)." *Black and White* 25, No. 624 (1903): 78–79.

selection as proven by the concept that "the fittest would survive," with the humble entreaty that if Darwin felt the paper had merit, could he please pass it on to Charles Lyell, doyen of the British scientific establishment. In this paper, conceived during a malarial fever, Wallace presented a theory of natural selection that uncannily resembled Darwin's ideas.

Then, according to some historians and writers, Wallace got sidelined. The conspiracy theorists say that due to the prodding of his friends Joseph Hooker and Charles Lyell, well-known botanist and geologist respectively, Darwin rushed to dust off a piece of unpublished correspondence and some unpublished notes, which were presented on July 1, 1858 at a meeting of the Linnean Society in London. Although Wallace's paper was also read into the record at the same meeting by J. J. Bennett, secretary of the Linnean Society, Hooker and Lyell had clearly made the evening Darwin's by ensuring that the elder scientist received top billing.

In the 1980s, when I first began following Wallace seriously, I went to the bookshop of the British Museum (Natural History). I saw rows upon rows of books by and about Darwin. I asked the man in charge whether he had any books by Alfred Russel Wallace.

"What subject might that be then, sir?" he asked.

"Natural history, I suppose."

"No. I don't think so. What did he write?"

I showed the man my dog-eared copy of *The Malay Archipelago*.

"No, we don't have that. Sorry."

The situation has since changed considerably, and Wallace is enjoying a minor renaissance.[9] Nevertheless, he is still a distant second to Darwin: today's arbiter of recognition, Google, offers some nineteen million hits for "Charles Darwin" against fewer than seven hundred thousand for "Alfred Russel Wallace."

Strangely, Wallace never admitted to harboring a grudge against Darwin. In the dedication to *The Malay Archipelago*,[10] which Wallace

---

9   At least eleven Wallace biographies have been published since 2002, plus reissues of most of Wallace's major books and collections of his shorter writings.

10   Full title, in four typefaces: *The Malay Archipelago: The Land of the Orang-Utan, and the Bird of Paradise. A Narrative of Travel, with Studies of Man and Nature.*

wrote in 1869, well after that famous meeting of the Linnean Society, he gushed (in three different type faces): "To Charles Darwin, author of 'The Origin of Species,' I dedicate this book, not only as a token of personal esteem and friendship, but also to express my deep admiration for his genius and his works." Wallace wrote a major work titled *Darwinism*. Wallace was a pallbearer at Darwin's funeral. It was only much later in his life that Wallace sardonically referred to the way things worked out. For his part, Darwin, some historians claim, suffered lifelong angst over what he termed the "delicate situation" he had entered into with respect to Wallace's unspoken claim to immortality.

It's funny how public perceptions change. Most educated people today have at least heard of Darwin, while only folks interested in science know Wallace. However, Charles H. Smith, professor of Library Public Services and science librarian at Western Kentucky University, who runs the best website devoted to Wallace, notes that Wallace was lauded during his lifetime and immediately thereafter, and his relative anonymity is a modern phenomenon.

Smith says: "At the time of his death in 1913 he may well have been the most famous scientist in the world . . . [observers referred] to him in the following glowing terms: 'England's greatest living naturalist'; 'the acknowledged dean of the world's scientists'; '[one of the two] most important and significant figures of the nineteenth century'; 'the Grand Old Man of Science.' "[11]

Although Wallace never sought honoraria, Smith points out that Wallace was awarded the Darwin-Wallace and Linnean Gold Medals of the Linnean Society of London; the Copley, Darwin and Royal Medals of the Royal Society (Britain's premier scientific body); and the Order of Merit (awarded by the ruling monarch as the highest civilian honor of Great Britain; as Smith notes, "quite

---

11 Nevertheless, Wallace was often broke. He seldom got the jobs he applied for, he worked (quietly) for Charles Lyell for five shillings an hour, and Darwin had to pull some strings to get Wallace a government pension.

an honor for such an anti-establishment radical"). He was granted honorary doctorates from the University of Dublin and Oxford University. "After his death, however, he soon fell into what might be termed 'relative obscurity,' and the road back has been slow."

One thing Wallace had in common with scientists of today was the reliance on grants. This is how Wallace referred to himself in the third person in a request to the Royal Geographical Society:

> Mr. Alfred R. Wallace begs leave to lay before the Council of the Geographical Society an outline of his proposed Expedition & to solicit its support and interest.

> He proposes leaving England in the Autumn or Winter of the present year, and, making Singapore his head quarters, to visit in succession Borneo, the Phillippines [sic], Celebes, Timor, the Moluccas and New Guinea, or such of them as may prove most accessible, remaining one or more years in each as circumstances may determine.

> His chief object is the investigation of the Natural History of the Eastern Archipelago in a more complete manner than has hitherto been attempted; but he will also pay much attention to Geography, & hopes to add considerably to our knowledge of such of the Islands as he may visit.

> The expense however of the journey from England is so considerable, that he finds himself unable to make the necessary outlay, & he would therefore wish to know, whether the Council of the Royal Geographical Society will feel justified in recommending her Majesty's Government to *grant him a free passage* to any convenient port in the Archipelago, and thereby enable him to supply

himself with the necessary instruments. [italics Wallace][12]

It worked; Wallace got a first-class ticket to Singapore and spent eight years shooting, grabbing, grubbing, plucking, and scavenging anything alive and remotely interesting. Birds of paradise. Maleo fowl. Orangutans. Pitcher plants. Butterflies. Ants. Flying squirrels. And an inordinate number of beetles.

Asia was Wallace's second great adventure. Some six years earlier, in 1848, Wallace and his friend Henry Walter Bates, both 23, left England for the Amazon, where Wallace spent four years, Bates eleven. Wallace began his Southeast Asia trip in 1854, when he was 31. Adolescence isn't necessarily definable by age. I think Wallace sought a rite of passage. Boys love to travel dirty, to sleep under the stars, to put themselves in ridiculous situations, and then brag about how they outwitted the pirates. Isn't that what he did? An adolescent itch. Boys leave home, go into voluntary exile. Always have. Huck Finn stuff. Sir Lancelot. Odysseus. Jack Kerouac. Joseph Campbell and Luke Skywalker. The search for adventure or the Holy Grail, a quest for a wife or fortune. A self-imposed test. Or maybe to give him a leg up at stuffy dinner parties.

> I believe I am the only Englishman who has ever shot and skinned (and ate) birds of Paradise, and the first European who has done so alive, and at his own risk and expense; and I deserve to reap the reward, if any reward is ever to be reaped by the exploring collector.[13]

When I started my ongoing Asian journey, in 1969, I had not

---

12 Application to the Royal Geographical Society.

13 Letter to Samuel Stevens concerning collecting in Dobbo, Aru Islands, March 10 and May 15, 1857.

heard of Alfred Russel Wallace. In the late 1960s, the memorable years of lunar landings, Bobby Kennedy, and marches on the Pentagon, I chose to join the Peace Corps as an honorable and fun alternative to the Vietnam-era draft. I was sent to Sarawak, one of two Malaysian states on the island of Borneo.

Had I the foresight to read his books at that time, I am certain Wallace could have helped me understand the bewildering situations I encountered in Borneo. What got to me, what kept me in Asia so long, was that every morning I would wake up knowing that I would see something that I might never be able to explain. For me it was a tame version of Indiana Jones. For my Asian hosts, of course, it was real life in high humidity. Never mind that I almost died a couple of times. I played soccer without shoes. I crawled through bat guano-filled caves. I slept in the rainforest and joined the gibbons in their morning whoop for joy. It was boys' stuff, and I don't regret a minute of it.

I then went on to create advertising campaigns in Singapore, Malaysia, and Indonesia. Sounds like a grown-up job, but it wasn't really. Every day I was surprised that managers of multinational companies would give my Sri Lankan partner and me thousands of dollars so that I could do things like write a TV commercial that brought to life the rabbits, goats, and genies that appeared on the packs of one client's mosquito coils (sawdust impregnated with chemicals used to keep the insects at bay). Our tiny agency, barely kept afloat by juggling the creditors and living by our wits, sold lots of candy, cosmetics, airline seats, and hotel rooms. We also helped a company sell cigarettes, an act of which I am not proud.

I wish I could have traveled with Wallace. He had passion. He loved nature. He was broke. He had guts. He was self-taught. He was a scientist who believed in spirits. He was not well-connected, a weird loner who could be charming in the right company. He thought big thoughts and, as a result, became a celebrity of sorts.

Wallace was probably done wrong, like a country-and-western song. And he asked major league questions. G. K. Chesterton, British essayist, novelist, critic, and poet, said that he knew of no one else who was a leader of both a major revolution in thought (the materialistic tendency encouraged by evolutionary theory) and a leader of its counter-revolution (anti-materialistic ideas, which he espoused through his interest in spiritualism and social changes). Wallace's theory of natural selection changed the way we view our place in the cosmos. Humans related to apes. Imagine.

Wallace admitted he could access both his left and right brain.

> The determination of the direction in which I should use these powers [reasoning] was due to my possession in a high degree of the two mental qualities usually termed emotional or moral, an intense appreciation of the beauty, harmony and variety in nature and in all natural phenomena, and an equally strong passion for justice as between man and man – an abhorrence of all tyranny, all compulsion, all unnecessary interference with the liberty of others.[14]

I know I would have had good intellectual conversations with Wallace. But what about the emotional buzzes? I *know* he had them. Isn't that why boys *really* run away? To put ourselves in strange situations that help us construct a sense of self that is robust enough to last a lifetime?

Wallace alluded to the line that separates logic from emotion. I was brought up as a secular Jew, and my parents encouraged me to celebrate as many holidays as I wished. One Christmas morning – I must have been six or seven – I was overjoyed to get a personal note from Santa, thanking me for leaving him some refreshment. The next year, as Christmas Eve approached, my father suggested that perhaps Mr. Claus might be tired from all that sleighing around northern New Jersey and would appreciate a beer instead of milk and cookies. I wasn't too sure about all that Santa business, but

---

14 *My Life*, Vol. 1, 224.

it worked for me and I accepted it. I've got the letter to prove it.

Am I talking too much? With beer I get voluble, then fall asleep. But see if this makes sense. As adults, while we are encouraged to "grow up" and kill the Santas in our life mythologies, we ironically do our absolute best, as Jesse Jackson would say, to "keep hope alive" in our children. In Steven Spielberg's movie *Hook*, Peter Pan has grown up into that most grown-up of jobs – a lawyer – and when his children are kidnapped by Captain Hook, Peter Pan requires the combined prodding of Tinkerbell, Wendy, and the Lost Boys before he can recapture the ability to "believe." Imagine, letting the ability to fly lapse like a library card.

Wallace, like most scientists, preferred to show his "logical" face to the world, rather than his "emotional" side.

> If I had one distinct mental faculty more prominent than another, it was the power of correct reasoning from a review of the known facts in any case to the causes or laws which produced them, and also in detecting fallacies in the reasoning of other persons.[15]

But I wonder whether sometimes in Asia Wallace found that our Western logic, of which we are so proud, just didn't work. I spend more time than most of my contemporaries searching for tiger magicians. I don't know whether tiger magicians exist. I don't expect to ever have proof that they exist. But I'm willing to *believe* that they exist, not simply because thousands of people in Indonesia believe in these men who go alone into the forest and sing to man-eating tigers in order to entice them into traps, but because I *choose* to hope that they exist. Some would call this a boyish reaction, a return to a juvenile state akin to when I collected fireflies (beetles, those) on a summer's night and imprisoned them in a glass jar to capture the flicker that I hoped would last forever. A boy's thing, perhaps. But also a man's thing, I think more and more, this willingness to accept that there are more things out there than we can easily explain.

---

15 Ibid., 223–4.

Fireflies and tiger magicians. Whether one calls these unexplained phenomena the frontiers of science or poppycock simply depends on which side of the line one chooses to stand.

This was brought home to me when I spoke with the late sultan of Yogyakarta in Java about his reverence for the Mermaid Queen, who is the matriarch of his royal line. Sultan Hamengkubuwono IX told me stories that challenged my Western, Cartesian, left-brain way of looking at the world. When I expressed skepticism he told me not to ask a Western question in the context of a Javanese situation. "You either believe it, or you don't," he explained. "Sometimes it doesn't pay to be too analytical."

There are lines in life. Some lines are easy to understand and visualize. The biogeographic line Wallace delineated (and which subsequently was named after him) roughly divides the Malay Archipelago: monkeys and tigers to the West, tree kangaroos and birds of paradise to the East.

Other lines are murkier, such as the distinction between "us" (civilized, handsome, smart) versus "them" (none of the above). I got a taste of this while searching for tiger magicians in Sumatra. When I enquired of a coastal dwelling, wet-rice growing Muslim farmer in Palembang about people who can sing to the souls in animals, he replied that good folks like him had no knowledge of such goings-on. Pointing to the distant hills he added, somewhat conspiratorially, that he heard that the people *up there* are, well, practitioners of magic and are rougher and somehow less sophisticated and, well, not like us good old coastal boys who grow wet rice, are well educated, wear stylish clothes, follow a politically powerful religion, and have the ability to name every player on Manchester United.

But when I went upriver I found, not surprisingly, that these "wild" people, simple though they might be, are certainly human enough, capable of generosity and greed, expressing concern for their families, having the ability to laugh and cry and sing and tattoo and plant vegetables and lust after their neighbor's spouse. But, if pressed, these upriver folks might say that the people over the *next* hill, in the distant valley *way over there* are the ones who get up to some strange practices. "Be careful," they warn. I continued this line of investigation and ultimately reached the people who have their backs against the jungle – Southeast Asian tribes such as the Penans, the Wana, the Rimba. They live at the end of the line, and, because they have few people to feel better than in order to define *their* humanity, they have no option but to find solace by viewing themselves as both part of nature, but somehow different. They may see a vague glimmer of distant kinship in the orangutan and the never-proven "small people" of the forest, but not necessarily brotherhood. The folks in the deepest dead-end alleys of Southeast Asia are people, albeit perhaps at the bottom of the social totem pole. They aren't animals or creatures of the night. You define yourself by what you are and what you are not.

Minyambou, Arfak Mountains, West Papua, Indonesia
Four Modern Religions - Government, Evangelical, Consumer and Nature Conservation - fight for
the hearts and minds of local people.
Photo: Paul Sochaczewski

II

INITIATION

Shiva's Beach – Mid-Morning

Pulau Enu, Aru Islands, Indonesia

Too hot to walk, too hot to think, too hot to sleep.

I've been thinking about many things on this trip. How is it, Alfred, that we human beings will do the following: travel halfway around the world and suffer physical discomfort in order to reach a beach where green turtles come ashore to lay their eggs. Why would we – human beings – watch another creature's life cycle – laying and hatching – with such emotional intensity and intellectual curiosity? Why would it disturb us that others of our race – the Buginese from south Sulawesi – hunt these scarce creatures and why others – the Balinese in this case – pay good money for turtle flesh and enjoy eating this ancient reptile? Why do we have such protective thoughts about another species?

Scampering
Gobbling
Shiva nods, and moves on

TEARS FOR TOSCA

Batang Ai National Park, Sarawak, Malaysia

Scrambling through old secondary forest to catch a glimpse of the few remaining orangutans, about a hundred and fifty kilometers upriver from where Wallace shot seventeen of the big red apes.

One of Wallace's prime objectives in visiting Southeast Asia was to collect orangutans. As it had throughout his life, serendipity blessed his endeavors. Wallace met James Brooke, the White Rajah of Borneo (who Wallace described as "a gentleman and a nobleman in the truest and best sense of those words"). Brooke invited Wallace to visit Sarawak. The eighteen months (November 1, 1854 to January 25, 1856) Wallace spent in northwest Borneo was groundbreaking – in this territory, later to become a Malaysian state, Wallace collected more than some twenty-five thousand specimens, including "two thousand distinct kinds" of beetles. He learned to value the elegance and wisdom of "savages," and explored a region he described as the "Himalayas in miniature." At the White Rajah's beach house in Santubong Wallace wrote the "Sarawak Law," which Wallace described as "my first contribution to the great question of the origin of species." And he had numerous orangutan encounters, which resonate with two discoveries of the period. In 1856 a skeleton, found in the Neander Valley near Dusseldorf, was identified as belonging to an early human race we now call the Neanderthals, a unique subspecies of *Homo sapiens* that flourished in the ice ages. And in 1861 French physician and anthropologist Pierre-Paul Broca first demonstrated that a particular region in the brain (Broca's area) is connected to a particular ability, in this case the faculty of speech.

I'm a sucker for places with evocative names. Mandalay. Luang Prabang. Makassar. Irawaddy and Mekong, Pondicherry and Kathmandu. And Borneo.

I was 22 and off on an adventure with the United States Peace Corps, which had assigned me to Sarawak, a Malaysian state on the island of Borneo. I had no idea what to expect: I only half-facetiously wrote in my journal that I didn't know whether I should bring beads and mirrors to trade. Instead, I found all the clichés and charms of backwater Asia. Rural folk who lived simply, often unhealthily, but with great character. Towns of commercial energy and warm, somewhat wary people. I was constantly asked whether I was a CIA agent; people couldn't quite grasp the notion that my government would send an inexperienced kid halfway around the world simply to assist non-American primary school teachers. I added to the confusion by being a not-particularly adept advisor of primary school teachers. I enjoyed the travel in longboats. I adored the sweaty, leechy treks in the rainforest. I savored life in the longhouse, but I was better suited to after-school amusements – hunting wild boar, fishing with a throw net, taking all the class's handmade wooden desks down to the river to ostensibly wash them but really to give all of us kids a chance to paddle around on these makeshift and not terribly seaworthy craft and reenact the great sea battles of World War II. I return regularly to Sarawak. While I find the people as hospitable as ever, it angers me to see the lushness of the forested land that was home to people and orangutans being ripped open to the unforgiving sun.

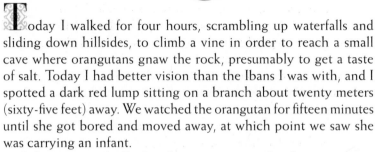

Today I walked for four hours, scrambling up waterfalls and sliding down hillsides, to climb a vine in order to reach a small cave where orangutans gnaw the rock, presumably to get a taste of salt. Today I had better vision than the Ibans I was with, and I spotted a dark red lump sitting on a branch about twenty meters (sixty-five feet) away. We watched the orangutan for fifteen minutes until she got bored and moved away, at which point we saw she was carrying an infant.

I always get a thrill when I see orangutans. Similar in intensity to the rush when Tosca stabs Scarpia and then places a lighted candle on his chest.[1]

> The whole circle of the arts and sciences are ultimately dependent on our possession of [the brain], without which we could hardly have become truly human.[2]

Humans are not alone in having brains. But all brains are not created equal.

I was sitting under a tree at the Sepilok Nature Reserve, in Sabah, Malaysia, and a seven-year-old orangutan named BJ wandered over. He was a "rehabilitant," an unfortunate word that describes the dozens of apes at Sepilok that were captured for the pet trade and then confiscated by Malaysian officials, or who were orphaned when their forest home was cleared for oil palm plantations. Shuffling upright with his red arms hanging almost to his ankles, BJ sat down and leaned over my shoulder and watched

---

1   Giacomo Puccini, composer of *Tosca*, was born in 1858.

2   "Sir Charles Lyell on Geological Climates and the Origin of Species." *Quarterly Review* 126, no. 252 (April 1869): 392.

me scribble notes.

"I can teach you to write, BJ," I optimistically said, half expecting him to respond. I engaged BJ in a deep, meaningful stare. "This is how you write your name." I wrote the initials "BJ" and said the letters. "BEE-JAY." BJ's chin was on my shoulder. Before I could repeat the exercise, BJ ripped the notebook out of my hands, stuck it in his mouth, and scampered up a tree.

To Wallace the chance to shoot an orangutan in a tree was one of his main objectives in coming to Asia.

> One of my chief objects in coming to stay at Simunjon [in Sarawak] was to see the orang-utan (or great man-like ape of Borneo) in his native haunts, to study his habits, and obtain good specimens of the different varieties and species of both sexes, and of the adult and young animals. In all these objects I succeeded beyond my expectations.[3]

BJ returned and we had a tug of war over my notebook, now minus a cover, which might have found a home in the ape's stomach. I don't think this was literary criticism, and I should have been grateful that BJ's energies took such a benign form, since wild male orangutans have been known to attack people. BJ, however, having been raised by people and treated as a surrogate son, had most of the wildness taken from him, and when I scolded him he eventually relinquished the notebook. *I* was the alpha male; *I* was the orangutan equivalent of the gorilla silverback. BJ took his place again at my side, as docile as a golden retriever, his chin leaning on my shoulder, his arm casually draped around my neck. He reached for the pen. Ah, I thought. He's going to try to write. Instead, he chewed the Bic like a candy cane. I snatched it back and dried the pen on his red hair. He matched my action by grabbing a twig and rubbing it on my salt-and-pepper chest hair.

This is a tricky business, attributing human emotions, not to mention intelligence, to "lesser" animals. Wallace didn't seem

---

3   *The Malay Archipelago*, 51.

to worry too much about this. Orangutans were primarily a big paycheck.

> I heard that one was feeding in a tree in the swamp just below the house, and, taking my gun, was fortunate enough to find it in the same place. As soon as I approached, it tried to conceal itself among the foliage; but I got a shot at it, and the second barrel caused it to fall down almost dead, the two balls having entered the body. This was a male, about half-grown, being scarcely three feet high.[4]

I went to Simunjan, where Wallace had had a camp. The town is one of the most attractive in Sarawak, with the usual mixture of Chinese hotels and shops, government buildings, neat *kampong* houses painted in bright colors, and a central market square. The countryside is mostly comprised of small farms set in rolling hills. Like farmers everywhere, these rural folks are not enamored when wild animals such as orangutans eat their fruit, although I doubt they actively kill the animals these days.[5] Nevertheless, the land that used to belong to orangutans now belongs to people, and there is little original lowland forest to which the big apes can escape. Zoologist George Schaller estimated in the late 1950s that some two hundred to three hundred orangutans lived in this area. Biologist Elizabeth Bennett thought there may be no more

---

4   Ibid.

5   The problems farmers in Simunjan face these days are more serious than big apes eating their fruit. In another heated dispute over Native Customary Land Rights in Sarawak, police, in early 2012, arrested five Iban villagers in Simunjan for allegedly setting fire to 13 excavators of an oil palm company. This latest spate of arrests recalls the detention of the "Sebangan Seven" on October 22, 2010, for setting fire to machinery and buildings at a Loyal Billion timber camp, also in Simunjan. Loyal Billion was the logging contractor operating on a timber concession belonging to Quality Concrete, a consortium whose director was Raziah Mahmud, sister of Sarawak Chief Minister Abdul Taib Mahmud. As minister for land and forests, Taib Mahmud had awarded the land to his sister's outfit, despite the local Iban villagers claiming Native Customary Rights to the area.

than thirty to one hundred in the vicinity, and that was back in the 1990s. The only orangutan population with a chance of survival is in Batang Ai, some two hundred and twenty kilometers (one hundred miles) east.

Wallace took up page after page with accounts of shooting orangutans.[6]

> On April 26th I was out shooting with two Dyaks [now commonly spelled Dayaks; he was here referring to Sea Dayaks, generally called Iban], when we found another about the same size. It fell at the first shot, but did not seem much hurt, and immediately climbed up the nearest tree, when I fired, and it again fell, with a broken arm and a wound in the body. The two Dyaks now ran up to it, and each seized hold of a hand, telling me to cut a pole, and they would secure it. But although one arm was broken, and it was only a half-grown animal, it was too strong for these young savages, drawing them up toward its mouth notwithstanding all their efforts, so that they were again obliged to leave go, or they would have been seriously bitten. It now began climbing up the tree again, and, to avoid trouble, I shot it through the heart.[7]

Each time I gaze into an orangutan's eyes I am reminded of a comment made by Malcolm MacDonald, former governor-general of colonial Malaya and Borneo, who thought that "these members of the order Primates contemplate you, when you meet them, with melancholy eyes, as if they had just read Darwin's *The Origin of Species* and were painfully aware of being your poor relations who have not done so well in life."

I can imagine Wallace smirking and thinking "They're *not* aware." He probably would have agreed with John Locke: "Beasts

---

6 Tom Harrisson, former curator of the Sarawak Museum, noted that in Wallace's time "natural history was not done by observation but by assassination." He called such practice "apeicide."

7 *The Malay Archipelago*, 51–2.

abstract not."

I *want* them to be aware, but they don't make it easy. BJ settled down and I continued writing for the third time. "Watch me, BJ. Bee-JAY." I looked at his eyes. He looked at me. We had made contact. I had a protégé. "Bee-Jay. B–" Faster than the downstroke of the "J," BJ had nipped off the button on the epaulette of my pretentious, multi-pocketed, quick-drying jungle shirt and darted up a nearby tree, all the while making shrill whistling noises through the button.

> On May 2 I again found one on a very high tree, when I had only a small 80-bore gun with me. However, I fired at it, and on seeing me it began howling in a strange voice like a cough, and seemed in a great rage, breaking off branches with its hands and throwing them down, and then soon made off over the tree-tops. I did not care to follow it, as it was swampy, and in parts dangerous, and I might easily have lost myself in the eagerness of pursuit.[8]

I had similar experiences in Gunung Leuser National Park in Sumatra, and also in Batang Ai in Sarawak, when I "threatened" mother orangutans with my camera's telephoto lens, and they broke off branches and bombarded me until I gave them space.

> Some Dyaks saw another mias [local name for orangutan] near the same place, and came to tell me. We found it to be a rather large one, very high up on a tall tree. At the second shot it fell, rolling over, but almost immediately got up again and began to climb. At a third shot it fell dead. This was also a full-grown female, and while preparing to carry it home, we found a young one face

8   Ibid., 52.

downward in the bog. This little creature was only about a foot long [thirty centimeters], and had evidently been hanging to its mother when she first fell. Luckily it did not appear to have been wounded, and after we had cleaned the mud out of its mouth it began to cry out, and seemed quite strong and active.[9]

This is the same method that poachers use to get orangutans for trade. Shoot the mother and take the infant. And for the same reason. Hard cash. Wallace wrote that the South Kensington Museum offered him "one hundred pounds in gold for an adult male [orangutan] skin and skeleton to be properly preserved and mounted [and] seventy-five pounds for a female."

He was tough when collecting adult specimens, but turned mushy when he came across the aforementioned infant, even though he had made it an orphan.

I must tell you of the addition to my household of an orphan baby, a curious little half-nigger baby, which I have nursed now more than a month. . . . I am afraid you would call it an ugly baby, for it has dark brown skin and red hair, very large mouth. . . . It has powerful lungs, and sometimes screams tremendously, so I hope it will live.

Don't be alarmed; I was the cause of its mother's death . . . . I can safely say, what so many have said before with much less truth, 'There never was such a baby as my baby,' and I am sure nobody ever had such a dear little duck of a darling of a little brown hairy baby before.[10]

Most people who work with orangutans have made similar

---

9   Ibid., 53.
10   *My Life*, Vol. 1, 343–5.

emotional connections.

Biruté Galdikas, who has spent more than three decades living with orangutans at Camp Leakey, at Tanjung Puting, in Kalimantan, Indonesian Borneo, tells of how one of her "rehabilitant" charges reacted to human mothering. In doing so, she also provides insight into how the human-ape contact brought out her own mothering instincts.

"I had raised Sugito from infancy," Galdikas recalled in a 1980 National Geographic article. "I had cuddled him, called him endearing names, and handed him tidbits of food. Taking my cue from the wild orangutan mothers I was observing, I had let him cling to me night and day."

Wallace also mothered his baby orangutan. In a passage of tenderness and humor he wrote:

> When handled or nursed, [the baby orangutan] was very quiet and contented, but when laid down by itself [in this, and other passages, he never mentions the animal's gender] would invariably cry; and for the first few nights was very restless and noisy. I fitted up a little box for a cradle, with a soft mat for it to lie upon, which was changed and washed every day, and I soon found it necessary to wash the little mias as well. After I had done so a few times, it came to like the operation, and as soon as it was dirty would begin crying, and not leave off till I took it out and carried it to the spout, when it immediately became quiet, although it would wince a little at the first rush of the cold water and make ridiculously wry faces while the stream was running over its head. It enjoyed the wiping and rubbing dry amazingly, and when I brushed its hair seemed to be perfectly happy, lying quite still, with its arms and legs stretched out, while I thoroughly brushed the long hair of its back and arms. For the first few days it clung desperately with all four hands to whatever it could lay hold of, and I had to be careful to keep my beard out of its way, as its

fingers clutched hold of hair more tenaciously than any thing else, and it was impossible to free myself without assistance. When restless, it would struggle about with its hands up in the air trying to find something to take hold of, and, when it had got a bit of stick or rag in two or three of its hands, seemed quite happy. For want of something else, it would often seize its own feet, and after a time it would cross its arms and grasp with each hand the long hair that grew just below the opposite shoulder . . . . Finding it so fond of hair, I endeavored to make an artificial mother, by wrapping up a piece of buffalo-skin into a bundle, and suspending it about a foot from the floor. At first this seemed to suit it admirably, as it could sprawl its legs about and always find some hair, which it grasped with the greatest tenacity. I was now in hopes that I had made the little orphan quite happy; and so it seemed for some time till it began to remember its lost parent and try to suck. It would pull itself up close to the skin, and try about everywhere for a likely place; but, as it only succeeded in getting mouthfuls of hair and wool, it would be greatly disgusted, and scream violently, and, after two or three attempts, let go altogether. One day it got some wool into its throat, and I thought it would have choked, but after much gasping it recovered, and I was obliged to take the imitation mother to pieces again, and give up this last attempt to exercise the little creature.[11]

He also noted, in a style both touching and perceptive, how helpless the orangutan infant was compared to a monkey of similar age.

After I had had the little mias about three weeks, I fortunately obtained a young hare-lip monkey (Macacus cynomolgus), which, though small, was very active, and

11 *The Malay Archipelago*, 53–5.

could feed itself. I placed it in the same box with the mias, and they immediately became excellent friends. The little monkey would sit upon the other's stomach, or even on its face, without the least regard to its feelings. While I was feeding the mias, the monkey would sit by, picking up all that was spilt . . . and as soon as I had finished would pick off what was left sticking to the mias's lips, and then pull open its mouth and see if any still remained inside. The little helpless mias would submit to all these insults with the most exemplary patience, only too glad to have something warm near it.[12]

It was curious to observe the different actions of these two animals, which could not have differed much in age. The mias, like every young baby, lying on its back quite helpless, rolling lazily from side to side, wishing to grasp something, but hardly able to guide its fingers to any definite object and expressing its wants by a most infantine scream; the little monkey, on the other hand, in constant motion, seizing hold of the smallest objects with the greatest precision.[13]

But no amount of loving can replace basic nutrition, and Wallace's pet orangutan, which he had planned to take back to England, fell ill.

After five weeks [the mias] cut its two upper front teeth, but in all this time it had not grown the least bit . . . no doubt owing to the want of milk [it suffered] an attack of diarrhoea . . . but a small dose of castor-oil operated well, and cured it. A week or two afterward it was again taken ill, and this time more seriously. The symptoms were exactly those of intermittent fever, accompanied by

12   Ibid., 55–6.
13   Ibid., 56.

watery swellings on the feet and head . . . after lingering for a week a most pitiable object, died, after being in my possession nearly three months. I much regretted the loss of my little pet, which I had at one time looked forward to bringing up to years of maturity, and taking home to England. Its weight was three pounds nine ounces [1.6 kilograms], its height fourteen inches [thirty-five centimeters], and the spread of its arms twenty-three inches [fifty-eight centimeters]. I preserved its skin and skeleton, and in doing so found that when it fell from the tree it must have broken an arm and a leg, which had, however, united so rapidly that I had only noticed the hard swellings on the limbs where the irregular junction of the bones had taken place.[14]

So much for unproductive sentimentality.[15] The baby orangutan's corpse earned him £6 from the British Museum.[16]

Just as Wallace let his mias "child" play with the monkey, Biruté Galdikas too encouraged cross-species fraternization between her biological son Bin-Bin and the rehabilitant orangutans at her isolated camp in the swamp forest. Having few human children to play with, Bin-Bin naturally made friends with the juvenile red apes. One particular playmate was Princess, a young orangutan that

14 Ibid., 56–7.

15 This episode is reminiscent of Wallace's monkey breakfast in the Amazon, when he wrote: "The poor little animal was not quite dead, and its cries, its innocent-looking countenance and delicate little hands were quite child-like. Having often heard how good monkey was, I took it home, and had it cut up and fried for breakfast." Wallace noted the taste "resembled rabbit." Elsewhere, he said that jaguar meat was "very white, and without any bad taste."

16 This sale, like all of the transactions made on behalf of Wallace, was handled by Samuel Stevens in London, about whom Wallace wrote: "During the whole period of our business relations, extending over more than fifteen years, I cannot remember that we ever had the least disagreement about any matter whatever." Thanks to Stevens' foresight, Wallace's South American collection that was lost at sea was insured for £150, enough for Wallace to survive in London for a year.

researcher Gary Shapiro was trying to teach to speak American Sign Language. Bin-Bin and Princess communicated in basic sign language, which probably included gestures of their own creation. Ultimately, Bin-Bin's father Rod Brindamour decided that California might be a better place for his son than a sticky black river campsite overrun by red apes, and father and son moved to the United States.

Galdikas's surrogate orangutan-child, who was allowed to run free while her biological son Bin Bin was sometimes kept caged for his own protection, developed human-like psychoses. "Now Sugito was 7," she writes, "and I faced the dreadful consequences of inadvertently raising an orangutan as a human being – an adolescent who was not only incredibly curious, active, and tool using, but one who killed." For, despite Galdikas's best mothering efforts, Sugito had picked up a bad habit – he held baby orangutans under the water until they drowned. Perhaps even worse, he had tried the same trick with a human visitor to the research camp.

Biruté Galdikas, like any mother with a child turned criminal, was puzzled and distraught, since wild orangutans are normally not killers. "Sugito was something different," she rationalized. "Perhaps the biblical analogy was apt: Raised by a human mother and exposed to human culture, he had eaten of the 'tree of knowledge' and lost his orangutan innocence. Now, in a very non-orangutan way, he was acting out his jealousy of the infants who had seemingly replaced him in my affection."

The first Westerner to describe the orangutan was Dutchman Jacob de Bondt (Bontius). In the early seventeenth century he presented a drawing of a female who hid "her secret parts with no great modesty from unknown men, and also her face with her hands (if one may speak thus), weeping copiously, uttering groans, and expressing other human acts so that you would say nothing human was lacking in her but speech. The Javanese say, in truth, that they can talk, but do not wish to, lest they should be compelled to labor. The name they give to it is Ourang Outang, which means a man of the woods, and they affirm that they are born from the lust of the Indian women, who mix with apes and monkeys with detestable sensuality."

The designation of the orangutan during Wallace's time as *Simia satyrus* (satyr monkey),[17] refers to the Greek mythological satyrs, male companions of Pan and Dionysus, who are generally shown in classical art as pipe-playing creatures with the upper body of a man and the lower body of a goat. The satyrs of myth show contradictory behaviors – roguish but faint-hearted, subverse and dangerous but shy and cowardly. And as pals of Pan and Dionysus they seek sensual pleasures; in particular, they love to dance with the nymphs (with whom they are obsessed).

Orangutans, too, certainly are sexually opportunistic and free-spirited.

At Biruté Galdikas's Camp Leakey, schizophrenic orangutans jump the animal/human line. They murder. They rape. They steal. They vandalize. They refuse to pay attention in class. They put dirty things in their mouths. They beg. They act like people.

Male orangutans have been known to sexually assault women. Galdikas tells of how Gondul, a rehabilitant orangutan she had raised from infancy (for a while, Gondul slept with Galdikas and her husband Rod Brindamour), grabbed the cook, ripped off her sarong, and tried to rape her.

For a cinematographic parallel, one might look at the closing sequence in the film *Tarzan the Ape Man*,[18] in which actress Bo Derek came dangerously close to being sexually assaulted by an orangutan. Miles O'Keeffe, her leading man, was tossed aside by the enamored, seemingly tame, ape. *Playboy* magazine, in a picture

---

17 Currently, the Bornean orangutan is called *Pongo pygmaeus*, the Sumatran orangutan *Pongo abelii*.

18 This film takes some poetic license – it features an orangutan, which is found only in Malaysia and Indonesia, in a movie allegedly set in Africa, which was shot in Sri Lanka.

spread showing the incident, noted that during a love scene: "C.J., the jealous orangutan, didn't much like the idea of Tarzan and Jane having fun without him. In a totally impromptu move, he pulled 195-pound (88-kilogram) Miles O'Keeffe off Bo Derek, interrupting one of the movie's steamier scenes . . . 'We wrestled with him for an hour and a half,' recalls Derek. 'Orangutans are several times stronger than people and have four things to grab you with.' "

Just as male orangutans can be as aggressive as men, female orangutans can be victimized like women. John MacKinnon, one of the few scientists who has studied three of the great ape species,[19] has reported that several Dayak longhouses in central Kalimantan keep female orangutans in the longhouse for use as primate equivalents of inflatable dolls. In an article in *New Scientist*, he called the world's attention to the danger that Dayak men, tempted by a long evening's revelry, might spread venereal disease through at least part of the wild orangutan population by infecting captive female orangutans, which are later released in the wild.

Sue Savage-Rumbaugh, who has studied pygmy chimps and other apes, argues that they should be eligible for "semi-human" legal status. She is convinced that their emotions, intellect, and consciousness are at least "morally equivalent" to those of profoundly retarded children. "We certainly would not put these children in a zoo to be gawked at as examples of nature," she says, "nor would we permit medical experimentation to be conducted on them."[20]

Or, as Carl Linnaeus, the Swedish botanist who developed the modern scheme of binomial nomenclature, put it: "It is remarkable that the stupidest ape differs so little from the wisest man, that

---

19 The great apes include animals in these genera: chimpanzees – including bonobos (*Pan*), gorillas (*Gorilla*), humans (*Homo*), and orangutans (*Pongo*).

20 The Great Ape Project advocates a UN Declaration of the Rights of Great Apes that would confer basic legal rights on non-human great apes. The rights suggested are the right to life, the protection of individual liberty, and the prohibition of torture. In 2008 the Spanish parliament passed a resolution that makes the killing of an ape a crime and bans their use in medical experiments, circuses, films, and television commercials. Joan Herrera, congressman for the Initiative for Catalonia Greens, argued the measure before parliament, saying that the primates "are capable of recognizing themselves, and have cognitive capabilities."

the surveyor of nature has yet to be found who can draw the line between them."

People living in rural Southeast Asia tell tales about half-ape, half-human creatures, and while Wallace was hanging out in Sumatran villages, he must have heard late-night stories about the tropical equivalent of the yeti.

In the Kerinci Seblat National Park, in southern Sumatra, about two hundred kilometers (one hundred and twenty-five miles) northwest of Wallace's base at Lobo Raman (now called Lubuk Raman), researcher Debbie Martyr claims to have sighted, and obtained plaster casts of footprints of, a previously undiscovered large primate, known locally as *orang pendek*, or "short person." The creature, which she insists is not a misplaced orangutan (orangutans today are limited to northern Sumatra, some seven hundred kilometers away), distantly resembles a chimpanzee or juvenile gorilla, but with long arms, and body-to-head proportions suggestive of a giant, bipedal, terrestrial gibbon. The animal seems to be extremely heavy for its height, and Martyr has estimated that an adult *orang pendek* of one hundred and fifteen centimeters (forty-five inches) in height may weigh in excess of fifty kilograms (one hundred and ten pounds).

In our book *Soul of the Tiger*, Jeff McNeely and I dubbed creatures like these "untrahoms," for "unidentified tropical Asian hominoids." These are ape-like humans (or human-like apes); one of the most productive places to look for them may well be the Kerinci Seblat area in the mountains that form the spine of Sumatra. The 13,791-square-kilometer (4,000-square-mile) Kerinci-Seblat National Park, which includes Sumatra's highest peak, the active 3,810-meter (12,500-foot) Mount Kerinci volcano, has been called "the attic of Southeast Asia" by British naturalist Ivan Sanderson because it holds so many strange plants and animals.[21, 22]

One of many curious descriptions of the *orang pendek* (also called *sedapa*) by local villagers, Dutch farmers, and modern researchers was provided in 1923 by a Dutch planter named van Herwaarden: "The very dark hair on its head fell almost to the waist. . . . The eyes were . . . like human eyes. The nose was broad . . . but in no way clumsy. . . . Its canines . . . were more developed than a man's. I was able to see its right ear which was exactly like a little human ear. . . . Had it been standing, its arms would have reached to a little above its knees. . . . This specimen was of the female sex and about 5 feet [152 centimeters] high."

Yet van Herwaarden, who had an excellent opportunity to shoot

---

21 If *orang pendek* exist in Kerinci Seblat National Park, how many would have to be alive to maintain a viable, genetically robust breeding population? I asked a handful of biologist friends; their replies – all prefaced with "it depends on their habitat and social structure" and "we really can't be sure" – ranged from two hundred and fifty to one thousand individuals.

22 And what would be the maximum carrying capacity for *orang pendek* in Kerinci Seblat National Park? Malaysian conservation biologist Tony Sebastian walked me through his analysis. "We know this beast is a hominid and bipedal," Sebastian says, indicating that it is terrestrial and more suited to open environments – that's why it would develop bipedalism. "Although most sightings have occurred in tall forests, I suggest these tall forest sightings are food related, or crossings.

"A hominid would have an omnivorous but primarily vegetarian diet, with a highly developed sense of spatial distribution of food resources.

"The *orang pendek* is smaller than an orangutan and would need a social structure that provides adequate protection against predation from tigers and leopards. If it sleeps in the open (like gorillas), then its group size would be reasonably large; I would guess twenty to thirty animals. They could also live in caves, in which case their group sizes would be smaller, say three to seven animals; this would allow effective use of natural features for shelter. Kerinci Seblat National Park has many such natural shelters resulting from steep mountainous terrain, volcanic activity, and escarpments; this would be consistent with the other area where they are frequently reported – Ulu Temburong in Brunei.

"Although Kerinci Seblat is a huge area [bigger than Yosemite and Yellowstone National Parks combined], not all habitats will be suitable for the *orang pendek*. In addition, people intrude into many parts of the protected area, damaging habitat and disturbing the reclusive animals.

"My guess is that in Kerinci Seblat they would primarily frequent the subalpine zone – it's rough open shrublands with a fractured landscape. But their food source might be elsewhere, for example, in the submontane forests."

Sebastian assumes a home range of thirty square kilometers per family group of five animals, with overlapping ranges covering thirty percent of the available habitat within the park, or some four and a half thousand square kilometers. That results in one hundred and fifty blocks; each block can support four overlapping groups, giving a total maximum population of six hundred.

the *sedapa* and thereby end the controversy about whether such creatures exist, refused to pull the trigger: "When I raised my gun to the little female I heard a plaintive 'hu-hu,' which was at once answered by similar echoes in the forest nearby. I laid down my gun and . . . the *sedapa* dropped a good ten feet to the ground . . . before I could reach my gun again, the beast was almost 30 yards away. It went on running and gave a sort of whistle. Many people may think me childish if I say that when I saw its flying hair in the sight I did not pull the trigger. I suddenly felt that I was going to commit murder."[23]

Did Wallace feel he was committing murder when he shot all those orangutans? Was it a different feeling to when he shot a pheasant or a floppy huge butterfly in the treetops? Untrahoms, probably like orangutans in Wallace's day, clearly evoke visceral reactions in many people. For rural villagers, they might represent man's rejection of his animal nature, an age-old internal conflict of a species whose culture sets it apart from its closest relatives. Yet this separation is always somewhat ambivalent, as people both deny their jungle essence and secretly savor it. Untrahoms are the Mr. Hyde to our Dr. Jekyll.

Wallace's contemporaries weren't overly willing to explore the question of man's connections with other species.

Spencer St. John, private secretary to James Brooke, recorded Wallace's arrival in late 1854. "We had at this time in Sarawak the famous naturalist, traveller and philosopher, Mr. Alfred Wallace, who was then elaborating in his mind the theory which simultaneously was worked out by Darwin – the theory of the origin of species; and if he could not convince us that our ugly neighbours, the orang-outangs, were our ancestors, he pleased, delighted, and instructed us by his clever and inexhaustible flow

---

23 Do they exist? I want them to exist; I would be thrilled if they exist; I think we should assume they exist and set up appropriate conservation measures, but I think they're in the same category as Santa Claus.

of talk – really good talk."

I imagine Wallace prodded and provoked, excited by the chance to debate ape intelligence and human supremacy with a character who later starred in a Flashman novel.

> The Rajah [was] one of the few of his countrymen to have seen this great ape living in the wild, to have seen its similarities to man. Yet he obviously held, as most others did, to the comforting belief that God had created the human species in His own image. The orangutan was but a highly organized species of animal to which it had pleased God to give some passing similarities to man.

Isn't it ironic that the White Rajah, a brave, bigger-than-life man who pushed the envelope on personal exploits, wasn't willing to buck the Victorian notion of Creationism. Perhaps he felt that if he were to acknowledge the inherent worth of the orangutan this would, in some way, diminish his own stature as a human being.

I cry for Tosca. I wonder if Wallace thought about orangutan emotions, orangutan art.

When Wallace went to Southeast Asia, people were not sure whether the orangutan was a big monkey or a lower form of human being. He pondered the differences between people and other animals and asked whether orangutans have egos.

> If man is but a highly intellectual animal developed from a lower animal form under the law of the survival of the fittest, how did this "second-self," this "unconscious ego," come into existence? Have the mollusk and the reptile, the dog and the ape, "unconscious egos"? And if so, why? And what use are they to these creatures, so that they might have been developed by means of the struggle for

existence?[24]

The question of whether other forms of life have consciousness has challenged philosophers and scientists for millennia. And the orangutan, because of its similarities to a human in so many ways, has always been a particularly provocative subject.

We have a relationship with other species. But how close a relationship? Various studies claim that we share between 95 percent and 99.4 percent of our DNA with chimpanzees, depending on which genetic differences are looked at and a significant but lesser amount with gorillas and orangutans.[25, 26]

But it's not a few percentage points of DNA difference between humans and orangutans that conceals a vast abyss of speculation.

Wallace predicted that fossils intermediate between ape and man would surely be uncovered, and in 1891 Eugène Dubois, a Dutch anatomist and geologist, unearthed in central Java the fossilized femur and parts of the skull of what became widely known as the "Java ape-man," *Pithecanthropus erectus*, the erect ape-man.

24 "What Are Phantasms, And Why Do They Appear?" Arena 3, no. 15 (February 1891): 263.

25 How close is that? The number of genetic differences between humans and chimps is ten times smaller than that between mice and rats. This type of genetic comparison is an evolving science; a study published in 2012 by the Wellcome Trust Sanger Institute noted that although, on average, we are closest to chimps, many of our individual genes are more like those of gorillas. Among them is a gene that enables us and gorillas to hear better than other apes. Fifteen percent of the human genome is closer to the gorilla than the chimpanzee.

26 There are other ways to slice this. Jeffrey H. Schwartz, professor of anthropology at the University of Pittsburgh, and John Grehan, director of science at the Buffalo Museum, claim that humans most likely share a common ancestor with orangutans, as opposed to chimps or gorillas. The scientists scrutinized the hundreds of physical characteristics often cited as evidence of evolutionary relationships among humans and other great apes – and selected sixty-three that could be verified as unique within this group (i.e., they do not appear in other primates). Of these features, the analysis found that humans shared twenty-eight unique physical characteristics with orangutans, compared to only two features with chimpanzees, seven with gorillas, and seven with all three apes (chimpanzees, gorillas, and orangutans). Gorillas and chimpanzees shared eleven unique characteristics.

How did these now fossilized ancient hominids become *Homo sapiens?*

This is where Wallace broke ranks with Darwin, and it remained the main source of disagreement between the two men in later years.

Wallace and Darwin both accepted and promoted natural selection as the mechanism for evolution and the development of new species. But – and it's a very large "but" – Darwin steadfastly believed that man's rise to the top of earth's pecking order was *solely due to the process of natural selection* and that "Man still bears in his bodily frame the indelible stamp of his lowly origins."

Wallace, however, felt that the mechanism of natural selection alone accounted for everything *up to but not including Homo sapiens.*[27]

Wallace was clear in his criticism of Darwin.

> [Darwin concluded that] Man's whole nature – physical, mental, intellectual, and moral – was developed from the lower animals by means of the same laws of variation and survival; and, as a consequence of this belief . . . there was no difference in *kind* between man's nature and animal nature, but only one of degree. [italics Wallace][28]

And he was equally clear in promoting his own theory invoking the intervention of a "different agency."

> [I believe] that there is a difference in kind, intellectually; and morally, between man and other animals; and that while [man's] body was undoubtedly developed by the continuous modification of some ancestral animal form, some different agency, analogous to that which first produced organic *life,* and then originated *consciousness,*

---

27 Put another way: Wallace agreed with Darwin's principle of utility (the cornerstone of natural selection that says attributes in an organism will only develop when they accord the organism a survival advantage), but Wallace insisted that where no clear survival advantage can be found, some teleological (purposive) and intelligent agency must be the cause.

28 *My Life,* Vol. 2, 16.

came into play in order to develop the higher intellectual and spiritual nature of man. [italics Wallace][29]

On what evidence did Wallace base his theory?

Basically, he considered man's wondrous (and not immediately "useful") physical and moral/emotional/intellectual characteristics.

Wallace first used our physical attributes as evidence – none of which, he said, could be attributed to natural selection.

He asked why we have naked skin.

> In the case of the naked skin, [our ancestors] were at first at a positive disadvantage – we know [this characteristic] could not have been produced by natural selection.[30]

He wondered why we evolved some physical abilities that were not immediately useful, like speech.

> The . . . faculty [of human speech] can hardly have been physically useful to the lowest class of savages; and if not, the delicate arrangements of nerves and muscles for its production could not have been developed and co-ordinated by natural selection. This view is supported by the fact that, among the lowest savages with the least copious vocabularies, the capacity of uttering a variety of distinct articulate sounds, and of applying to them an almost infinite amount of modulation and inflection, is not in any way inferior to that of the higher races. An instrument has been developed in advance of the needs of its possessor.[31]

---

29 Ibid., 16–7.

30 "Geological Climates," 392.

31 Ibid., 393.

And he pondered the development of the human hand and foot, as well as the size and abilities of the human brain.

> The brain of the lowest savages, and, as far as we yet know, of the pre-historic races, is little inferior in size[32] to that of the highest types of man, and immensely superior to that of the higher animals. . . . They possess a mental organ beyond their needs. Natural Selection could only have endowed savage man with a brain a little superior to that of an ape, whereas he actually possesses one very little inferior to that of a philosopher.[33]

And then he delved into the realm of non-physical attributes.

According to Wallace, man has countless abilities and skills that go beyond mere evolutionary needs and are so beyond what even our closest animal relatives are capable of that Wallace thought there must be an outside agency, an "overruling intelligence," in action.

An extrapolation of Wallace's list might include: man's ability to reason, to make jokes (is Groucho Marx necessary for our survival?). Beethoven. Calculus. The ability to recognize ourselves in a mirror, the creation of moral codes. The conceptions of eternity and infinity. Abstract notions of form, number, and harmony. Construction of grand temples to imagined gods. Cooking Peking duck and chocolate brownies. Electricity and photography and the Internet. Laws. Reality TV. Crying at Italian opera.

> Neither natural selection nor the more general theory of evolution can give any account whatever of the origin of sensational or conscious life. They may teach us how, by chemical, electrical, or higher natural laws, the organized

---

32 We now know that brain size is not the only, or even a reliable, measure of intelligence.

33 "The Limits of Natural Selection as Applied to Man." In *Contributions to the Theory of Natural Selection: A Series of Essays.* 1870. London and New York: Macmillan & Co., 355–6.

body can be built up, can grow, can reproduce its like; but those laws and that growth cannot even be conceived as endowing the newly-arranged atoms with consciousness. But the moral and higher intellectual nature of man is as unique a phenomenon as was conscious life on its first appearance in the world, and the one is almost as difficult to conceive as originating by any law of evolution as the other. We may even go further, and maintain that there are certain purely physical characteristics of the human race which are not explicable on the theory of variation and survival of the fittest. The brain, the organs of speech, the hand, and the external form of man, offer some special difficulties in this respect.[34]

If I don't switch radio stations quickly, right after the morning news from Radio 74 here in Geneva, I get "Today's Good News." This morning Ron, the mellifluous announcer and founder of what local cynics call "Radio Jesus," told listeners: "An idea that's still taught in some schools [voice-sneer] is that men evolved from [double voice-sneer] lower forms of life. The God *I* believe in created all creation in six days. That includes man in God's own image. It says so right here in Genesis . . ."

Science, and religion, blogs today are awash with discussion of the question: "If Wallace were alive today, would he be a proponent of Intelligent Design? Would he be a Creationist?

Intelligent Design in today's discourse is not a neutral phrase; it is a hot-button issue intimately entwined with the Christian evangelical movement. Wallace had no time for organized religion and no doubt would have rejected any perceived links with such a church-based belief.

Charles H. Smith adamantly denies that Wallace believed in Intelligent Design. "No, no, and no. Assuming that Intelligent

---

34 "Geological Climates," 391.

Design leans on the operation of first causes as Creationism does, that is. Don't fall for the facile understanding being promoted by some agenda-driven observers who argue that, just because Wallace was a spiritualist and believed that "higher intelligences" were influencing events here on earth, that he also believed in miraculous, non-law-based kinds of godly intervention."

Was Wallace talking about God-in-sheep's-clothing? Or was he talking about scientific forces that are provable but beyond the ken of most normally educated people, like the theories of particle physics and the hard-to-grasp concept that all matter is energy?

Wallace deliberately never mentioned God, indeed he was adamantly areligious and had little patience for organized faiths, but he nevertheless employed a bunch of euphemisms that sound suspiciously God-like, at least in the context of the three stern desert religions: "Overruling Intelligence, [upper case Wallace]" "some other power," "some intelligent power," "a superior intelligence," "a controlling intelligence," "higher intelligences," "different individual intelligence," and "one Supreme Intelligence. [upper case Wallace]"[35]

Did the "superior intelligence" manipulate man's development just as we breed toy poodles and square tomatoes?

> The inference I would draw . . . is that a *superior intelligence* has guided the development of man in a definite direction, and for a special purpose, just as man guides the development of many animal and vegetable forms. [italics added][36]

---

35 When Wallace went off on these kinds of spiritual musings he sounded suspiciously New Agey – recall what James Redfield, the author of the wildly successful (and miserably written) *The Celestine Prophecy*, wrote: "I [saw] in one flash the entire story of evolution," Redfield writes of an epiphany that followed a narrow escape from nasty Peruvian soldiers. "[I saw] the story of matter coming into being and then evolving, as if under some guiding plan, toward ever higher vibrations, creating the exact conditions, finally, for humans to emerge . . . for each of us, as individuals, to emerge."

36 "Limits of Natural Selection," 359.

And is a "higher intelligence" beyond our current level of understanding?

> Some *higher intelligence* may have directed the process by which the human race was developed, by means of more subtle agencies than we are acquainted with. [italics added]³⁷

Finally, are the variously described intelligences "a necessary part" of the "great laws which govern the material universe?"

> At the same time I must confess, that this theory has the advantage of requiring the intervention of some distinct *individual intelligence*, to aid in the production of what we can hardly avoid considering as the ultimate aim and outcome of all organized existence – intellectual, ever-advancing, spiritual man. It therefore implies, that the great laws which govern the material universe were insufficient for his production, unless we consider (as we may fairly do) that the controlling action of such *higher intelligences* is a necessary part of those laws, just as the action of all surrounding organisms is one of the agencies in organic development. [italics added]³⁸

He suggests that not only did these "higher intelligences" influence the development of man, but they were responsible for the very act of creation. Wallace wrote that the "higher intelligences" are "probably connected with the *absolute origin of life and organization*. [italics added]"³⁹

---

37 Ibid.

38 Ibid., 359–60.

39 Ibid., 360.

The conundrum is that Wallace was, and actively positioned himself as, a scientist, not a theologian or philosopher. He strove for scientific proof of various phenomena, not only his "higher intelligences" concept but also such slippery ideas such as spiritualism and the ability to communicate with the dead.

He recognized that sometimes truths, as he saw them, might be difficult to prove, but they nevertheless exist.

> It is more probable, that the true law lies too deep for us to discover it; but there seems to me, to be ample indications that such a law does exist,[40]

Wallace was sensitive (and perhaps saw himself as vulnerable) to criticisms that he was invoking the Christian idea of Creationism.

> Some of my critics . . . have accused me of unnecessarily and unphilosophically appealing to 'first causes' in order to get over a difficulty – of believing that 'our brains are made by God and our lungs by natural selection;' and that, in point of fact, 'man is God's domestic animal.' An eminent French critic, M. Claparède, makes me continually call in the aid of – 'une Force supérieure,' the capital F, meaning I imagine that this "higher Force" is the Deity. I can only explain this misconception by the incapacity of the modern cultivated mind to realise the existence of any higher intelligence between itself and Deity. Angels and archangels, spirits and demons, have been so long banished from our belief as to have become actually unthinkable as actual existences, and nothing in modern philosophy takes their place. Yet the grand law of 'continuity,' the last outcome of modern science, which seems absolute throughout the realms of matter, force, and mind, so far as we can explore them, cannot surely fail to be true beyond the narrow sphere of our vision, and leave

---

40 Ibid.

an infinite chasm between man and the Great Mind of the universe. Such a supposition seems to me in the highest degree improbable.[41]

And again he argues in favor of "natural and universal laws."

Now, in referring to the origin of man, and its possible determining causes, I have used the words 'some other power' – 'some intelligent power' – 'a superior intelligence' – 'a controlling intelligence,' and only in reference to the origin of universal forces and laws have I spoken of the will or power of 'one Supreme Intelligence.' These are the only expressions I have used in alluding to the power which I believe has acted in the case of man, and they were purposely chosen to show, that I reject the hypothesis of 'first causes' for any and every *special* effect in the universe, except in the same sense that the action of man or of any other intelligent being is a first cause. In using such terms I wished to show plainly, that I contemplated the possibility that the development of the essentially human portions of man's structure and intellect may have been determined by the directing influence of some higher intelligent beings, acting through natural and universal laws. A belief of this nature may or may not have a foundation, but it is an intelligible theory, and is not, *in its nature*, incapable of proof; and it rests on facts and arguments of an exactly similar kind to those, which would enable a sufficiently powerful intellect to deduce, from the existence on the earth of cultivated plants and domestic animals, the presence of some intelligent being of a higher nature than themselves. [italics Wallace][42, 43]

---

41 "Notes," In *Contributions to the Theory of Natural Selection: A Series of Essays*, 2nd edn. 1871. London and New York: Macmillan & Co., 372.

42 Ibid.

43 Wallace also noted that the very creation and maintenance of life depends on close tolerances of temperature, solar light, water, and so on, and that "all life

So, was Wallace a proponent of Intelligent Design? Would he be today? How would he reconcile his arguments in favor of a scientifically based "one Supreme Intelligence," while distancing himself from folks who believe in an Almighty and All-Knowing Creator? What about nature's difficult-to-analyze-but-nevertheless-real laws? Cosmic Muffin or Hairy Thunderer? Or just part of the (sometimes unfathomable) fabric of life? How many angels dance on the head of a pin?

But I would have told Wallace one thing. I've been with orangutans. I've seen orangutans in cages, and I *know* that they can temporize – they recognize, I think, that yesterday they were in a cage and that tomorrow they're going to be in a cage. Surely *that's* some indication of higher intelligence.

So, can we agree that orangutans are intelligent and "human-like" in some ways? Is that as far as it goes? Perhaps an orangutan will never shudder when Maria Callas, the ultimate Tosca, asks Scarpia his price by which her lover may be saved. Perhaps an orangutan will never cry when Cavaradossi, gazing upon the last stars he ever will see, sings *"E lucevan le stelle ed olezzava la terra."* More interesting to ponder though, would Wallace have thought there is an equally romantic orangutan art form that we humans will never comprehend? Perhaps it's an orangutan love song aimed at that cute red-headed juvenile orangutan eating durian across the valley? Is there an orangutan aria?

development – all organic forces – are due to mind-action." Wallace used the example of the bird's wing and feathers, and the complexity of the cell to conclude "there is intelligent and conscious direction; in a word, there is Mind."

I WANT TO BE ALONE

Batang Ai National Park, Sarawak, Malaysia

Far upriver from the nearest habitation, sliding down waterfalls.

In 1851 Wallace ascended and mapped the Rio Negro/Uaupés River in South America farther than any previous European.

During a similar time period, adventurous (and sometimes quite mad) men were leaving the comforts of Britain to investigate the earth's unexplored corners.

Between 1850 and 1854 Robert McClure transited the Northwest Passage by boat and sledge; he and his men also charted some 2,736 kilometers (1,700 miles) of new coastline.

And from 1853 to 1856 David Livingstone became the first man to traverse Africa from west to east, traveling from Angola to Mozambique; he also became the first European to explore, and name, Victoria Falls. Meanwhile, in 1862, John Hanning Speke reached the source of the Nile.

What drove these men (and I include Wallace in the list of guys who traveled far, endured hardships, and risked their lives)? Why did Wallace put up with bedbugs and alienation and upset stomachs and frustration and privation and loneliness and malnutrition and risk of drowning and malaria? Why travel far? And why travel alone? Curiosity? An escape from the mundane? A search for glory? Missionary zeal?

How often are we truly alone?

A psychiatrist friend, who espouses a school of treatment in which people physically confront their pent-up tensions, told me he encourages his patients to shout as loudly as they can to exorcise their inner demons. It works in his soundproofed therapy room. But where should a person do her shouting homework? Most people spend their entire lives within sight of other people. Even when they go for a walk in the countryside, most people will never venture far enough off the trail to enable them to feel sufficiently alone to cry like a wolf, even though they may be a great distance from another person. Real or not, we always feel the presence of other people and adjust our behavior accordingly. Only the brain-damaged really let go.

I am camping, riverside, with my old friend Bill Stone, several hours upstream from the most isolated Iban longhouse. Our campsite is simply a large sheet of plastic sheltering an uncomfortable platform of boughs.[1] Last night a bat invaded our shelter as we were getting ready to sleep; its musky smell is still with me. The river near camp is clear, rarely deeper than half a meter, just wide enough for an Olympic athlete to leap across.

---

1   Interesting that Old World forest dwellers, like the Ibans we were with, sleep on the ground, while New World forest dwellers, like the Amazon Indians, sleep much more comfortably in hammocks.

This morning I left my Iban and British companions behind and climbed for an hour to a ridge, looking for primary rainforest I was told was "somewhere over there." All I saw was old secondary growth that had cropped up in the thirty years since the Ibans, who were fearful of conflicts with Indonesians during Confrontation with Indonesia (the border is just several kilometers away), moved out of this region.

I have been gone half the day and have not brought food. Time to go back. I take a shortcut into a ravine that my inner mind-map tells me will connect to a tributary of my campsite river.

I soon come to a series of streams and small waterfalls. I jump into the pools and head downstream, almost giddy with the fun of splashing in a nameless stream.

I slide down a small waterfall and suddenly find myself in a pool in the streambed inside a gorge, with rocky walls two stories tall blocking my lateral escape. Should I leave the streambed and try to climb the walls of the gorge and try to find a trail? Or should I continue downstream, which means negotiating the falls? The falls don't look too serious, and I slide down the first waterfall, only to find it leads into hidden falls so steep that I can't safely look over the edge. No way back. I have put myself in this modest predicament and I have to get myself out. Half-sliding, half-crawling, singing "Va, pensiero" from *Nabucco*, I alternately hug the slippery rocks and eventually fall a couple of meters and plop into a deep pool, silly with adrenaline. I should be cautious, I suppose, since no one knows where I am and a broken leg would be troublesome, but my overwhelming feeling is exhilaration. Perhaps stupidly, I am secure in the knowledge that I am a great distance beyond where people live, alone, with just myself to rely on.

I survive the waterfalls and realize I'm not far from camp. Butterflies accompany me the rest of the way along the stream.[2]

2 Wallace had butterfly-schizophrenia. A particularly rare or beautiful specimen would send him into ecstasy, but at the end of the day butterflies were chattel, specimens to be sold. Perhaps there's another way to view butterflies. They like to congregate near clear, running water. Might butterflies be Tinkerbell-like water sprites? I say this in half-seriousness. Waterfalls, like crashing waves and just-finished thunderstorms, produce an abundance of negative ions, which are feel-good ions. They are sacred places of energy. And they are devoid of mosquitoes, which makes them doubly sacred.

Here's a situation that has happened to everyone who has spent long periods away from "home." I visit with friends and family in America, who are nice, intelligent, educated people. I start to talk about my life and, in many cases, their eyes glaze over. My friends and I, by mutual unspoken consent, revert to baseball, or politics, or gossip of the sort "whatever happened to so and so?"

Wallace wrote about this frustration of being unable to share his adventures with stay-at-home friends. In *The Malay Archipelago* he tried, as thousands of writers before and after have attempted, to describe the durian.[3] Durian-describing might just be the most challenging writing exercise anyone can attempt.

> A rich butter-like custard highly flavoured with almonds
> gives the best general idea of it, but intermingled with
> it comes wafts of flavour that call to mind cream-cheese,
> onion-sauce, brown sherry, and other incongruities.[4]

That's not bad, but it falls short of conveying the true essence (the smell, the taste, the heft, the spikes, the cultural importance, the ritual of finding a "good" fruit at the market, the bonds created by eating it with friends, the smell that lingers on your fingers and clothes for days.) He's sort of described it, but I guarantee that he could not *really* share the durian experience with a friend who had never left England.

Similarly, in reading Wallace's letters, it seems that he deliberately skated on the surface with old friends, perhaps because he realized that the depth of his experience would have been unfathomable to them.

I [wrote] to my oldest friend, Mr. George Silk. 'I have

---

3   Which he wrote as "durion." He said "to eat durions, is a new sensation worth a
    voyage to the East to experience." He further raptured that the durian and the orange
    are "the king and queen of fruits."

4   *The Malay Archipelago*, 85.

just received yours of August 3 with reminiscences of Switzerland. To you it seems a short time since we were together, to me an immeasurable series of ages! In fact, Switzerland and the Amazon now seem to me quite unreal – a sort of former existence or long-ago dream. Malays and Papuans, beetles and birds, are what now occupy my thoughts, mixed with financial calculations and hopes for a happy future in old England, where I may live in solitude and seclusion, except from a few choice friends. You cannot, perhaps, imagine how I have come to love solitude.'[5]

Wallace said he had "come to love solitude." Is "solitude" the right word? What Wallace experienced was a form of self-imposed exile from the mundane, the expected, the *vie quotidienne*. Exile from our peers, our friends, our cultural milieu.

I seldom have a visitor but I wish him away in an hour. I find [seclusion] very favourable to reflection.[6]

Reflection? Perhaps. He needed time and space (and evidence) to try to figure out his theories about man's place in the universe.

Often, when people urge me to return home (although that's a slippery concept since I'm not sure where home is), they do it less out of concern for my well-being and more out of selfishness tinged with discomfort, in the realization that I am out there doing things and they're not.

Your [George Silk's] ingenious arguments to persuade me to come home are quite unconvincing. I have much to do yet before I can return with satisfaction of mind; were I to leave now I should be ever regretful and unhappy. That alone is an

---

5   *My Life*, Vol. 1, 365.

6   Ibid.

all-sufficient reason.[7]

Repeatedly, Wallace offers arguments to his friends and family in England that he likes being in exile, makes more money in Asia than he could in England, and is having a ball doing so.

> Besides these weighty reasons there are others quite as powerful – pecuniary ones. I have not yet made enough to live upon, and I am likely to make it quicker here than I could in England. In England there is only one way in which I could live, by returning to my old profession of land-surveying. Now, though I always liked surveying,[8] I like collecting better, and I could never now give my whole mind to any work apart from the study to which I have devoted my life. So far from being angry at being called an enthusiast (as you seem to suppose), it is my pride and glory to be worthy to be so called. Who ever did anything good or great who was not an enthusiast? The majority of mankind are enthusiasts only in one thing – in money-getting; and these call others enthusiasts as a term of reproach because they think there is something in the world better than money-getting. It strikes me that the power or capability of a man in getting rich is in *inverse* proportion to his reflective powers and in *direct* proportion to his impudence. It is perhaps good to *be* rich, but not to *get* rich, or to be always trying to get rich, and few men are less fitted to get rich, if they did try, than myself. [italics Wallace][9]

Perhaps Wallace left something unsaid. I'll put myself into the statement. By leaving home and going off to the distant corners of

---

7   Ibid., 367.

8   Perhaps there's something about surveying that leads to clear thinking; noted surveyors include Henry Thoreau, Leonardo da Vinci, George Washington, Abraham Lincoln, and Herbert Spencer.

9   *My Life*, Vol. 1, 368.

the world, we put down markers. Through the act of leaving, we announce to friends and family that after we have returned (and most of us do return), we will have been changed. It is a desire to move toward individuation. *We* left and did exciting things that our left-behind friends can only dream about; *they* stayed, paid their mortgages, had babies, and worked in the post office. Think of Kipling: "All things considered there are only two kinds of men in the world – those that stay at home and those that do not."

> I really do now think and believe that I am coming home, and as I am quite uncertain when I may be able to send you [George Silk] this letter, I may possibly arrive not very long after it. Some fine morning I expect to walk into 79, Pall Mall, and shall, I suppose, find things just the same as if I had walked out yesterday and come in to-morrow! There will you be seated on the same chair, at the same table, surrounded by the same account books, and writing upon paper of the same size and colour as when I last beheld you. I shall find your inkstand, pens, and pencils in the same places, and in the same beautiful order, which my idiosyncrasy compels me to admire, but forbids me to imitate. (Could you see the table at which I am now writing, your hair would stand on end at the reckless confusion it exhibits!) I suppose that you still walk every morning from Kensington and back in the evening. . . . I fear the stern despot, habit, has too strongly riveted your chains, and as, after many years of torture the Indian fanatic can at last sleep only on his bed of spikes, so perhaps now you would hardly care to change that daily routine, even if the opportunity were thrust upon you.[10]

That's it, perhaps. We go into exile to run away from those stern despots Wallace called habits, which Wallace associates with boredom. Same reason a kid runs away from home. To rebel. To

---

10 Ibid., 380.

draw attention to himself. To march to a different drummer. To feel a buzz.

History treats explorers as individuals who braved the elements alone, stoic, unflappable, and with immense strength of character and fortitude. But, actually, all explorers, the great as well as the ignored, rely on often-unheralded people to assist in their odyssey. Magellan had Enrique of Malacca,[11] Lewis and Clark had Sacagawea.

Alfred Russel Wallace had Ali, and without Ali's assistance it is unlikely Wallace would have been as successful as he was.

Ali accompanied Wallace on most of his Asian travels. Starting out as a cook, Ali learned to collect and mount specimens. He took on more responsibility for organizing travel (just imagine the negotiations with self-important village chiefs, unreliable porters and laborers, and greedy merchants, whose eyes no doubt grew large when they saw a white man like Alfred come to buy supplies). Ali became an invaluable chef de cabinet and friend. Wallace called him "my faithful companion."

Christopher Vogler is a Hollywood screenwriter, whose book *The Writer's Journey* explores how a classical mythic structure is used in iconic films such as *Casablanca*, *The Wizard of Oz*, *Star Wars* and *Close Encounters of the Third Kind*. "All stories consist of a few common structural elements found universally in myths, fairy tales, dreams, and movies," Vogler says. "They are known collectively as The Hero's Journey."

One essential archetype in the hero's journey is the character Vogler calls the Mentor (and which Joseph Campbell refers to as Wise Old Man or Wise Old Woman), who teaches heroes and gives them gifts. In the great epics the Mentor is a sage adult – Merlin

11 Ferdinand Magellan bought the slave Enrique in Malacca and encouraged him (I use the term advisedly) to renounce Islam and convert to Catholicism. Enrique became Magellan's interpreter, guide, and friend; he is also possibly the first person to complete the circumnavigation of the globe (Magellan was killed in the Philippines before finishing the journey, Enrique continued the voyage).

guiding King Arthur, the Fairy Godmother helping Cinderella, or a veteran sergeant giving advice to a rookie cop.

This characterization doesn't fit perfectly, of course. The Mentor archetype is generally related to the image of a parent. In Wallace's case, Ali takes the role of a keen, but initially naive, son, who grows in competence and confidence as the story progresses.

Wallace had only been in the Malay Archipelago for six months when he went to Sarawak, and was undoubtedly wet behind the ears. I figure that James Brooke saw how hapless Wallace was, took him aside, and said: "Look here Wallace, here in Sarawak people know you're my friend, and they will tolerate your odd behavior and not cheat you too much. But out there [no doubt he was pointing south to the wilderness of countless Indonesian islands], they're going to eat you alive." Perhaps Brooke asked one of his Malay assistants if he had a young relative who would be willing to go off on an adventure from which he might not return. The result was Ali.

Here's how Wallace described his engagement of Ali as personal assistant.

> When I was at Sarawak in 1855 I engaged a Malay boy named Ali as a personal servant, and also to help me to learn the Malay language. . . . He was attentive and clean, and could cook very well.[12]

Wallace described how Ali grew into the job.

> He soon learnt to shoot birds, to skin them properly, and latterly even to put up the skins very neatly. Of course he was a good boatman, as are all Malays. . . . He accompanied me through all my travels, sometimes alone, but more frequently with several others, and was then very useful in teaching them their duties, as he soon became

---

12 *My Life*, Vol. 1, 382.

well acquainted with my wants and habits.[13]

Ali was responsible for Wallace's collection of a bird that became a prize in his collection.

> Just as I got home I overtook Ali returning from shooting with some birds hanging from his belt. He seemed much pleased, and said, 'Look here, sir, what a curious bird!' holding out what at first completely puzzled me. I saw a bird with a mass of splendid green feathers on its breast, elongated into two glittering tufts; but what I could not understand was a pair of long white feathers, which stuck straight out from each shoulder. Ali assured me that the bird stuck them out this way itself when fluttering its wings, and that they had remained so without his touching them. I now saw that I had got a great prize, no less than a completely new form of the bird of paradise, different most remarkable from every other known bird . . . . This striking novelty has been named by Mr. G.R. Gray, of the British Museum, Semioptera Wallacei [today *Semioptera wallacii*], or 'Wallace's Standard-wing.'[14]

And eventually Wallace described Ali as "my head man."

> Ali, the Malay boy whom I had picked up in Borneo, was my head man. He had already been with me a year, could turn his hand to any thing, and was quite attentive and trustworthy. He was a good shot, and fond of shooting, and I had taught him to skin birds very well.[15]

After seven years together Wallace said goodbye to Ali in Singapore; thanks to Wallace's generosity the young man was

---

13 Ibid., 383.

14 *The Malay Archipelago*, 335–6.

15 Ibid., 412.

well-off. Wallace took Ali to a photographer; the picture shows a full-mouthed, serious, dark-complexioned lad with wavy hair, thick eyebrows, and a broad nose, dressed in a dark European-style jacket and under-jacket, white shirt, and a white bow tie.

> On parting, besides a present in money, I gave him my two double-barrelled guns and whatever ammunition I had, with a lot of surplus stores . . . which made him quite rich. He here, for the first time, adopted European clothes, which did not suit him nearly so well as his native dress, and thus clad a friend took a very good photograph of him. I therefore now present his likeness to my readers as that of the best native servant I ever had, and the faithful companion of almost all my journeyings among the islands of the far East.[16]

Then what? Where did Ali go?

Did Ali return to Kuching, the city of his birth, where he no doubt had relatives? In Kuching I spoke with leaders of the Malay community and local historians. No one had any idea of who Ali was. More disheartening, the folks I spoke with expressed little initiative to publicize the quest for Ali's relatives among the Malay citizenry.

Or did he stay in Singapore, a city he knew reasonably well and which had a large Malay community?

"Nice story," the historians I spoke with said. But no follow through.

Or, did Ali return to Ternate, where he and Wallace had resided for many years? This seems the most likely; indeed, Wallace refers to Ali having established a family in Ternate.

> During our residence at Ternate he married, but his wife lived with her family, and it made no difference in his accompanying me whenever I went till we reached

16 *My Life*, Vol. 1, 383.

Singapore on my way home.[17]

The other big clue that Ternate was Ali's final residence is based on a 1907 account by American naturalist Thomas Barbour, who visited Ternate and met Ali, who was by then an old man. This is what Barbour wrote: "Here came a real thrill. . . . We were stopped by a wizened old Malay man. I can see him now, with a faded blue fez on his head. He said, 'I am Ali Wallace.' I knew at once that there stood before me Wallace's faithful companion of many years, the boy who not only helped him collect but nursed him when he was sick. We took his photograph and sent it to Wallace when we got home. He wrote me a delightful letter acknowledging it and reminiscing over the time when Ali had saved his life, nursing him through a terrific attack of malaria. This letter I have managed to lose, to my eternal chagrin."[18]

I went to Ternate and spoke to the mayor and various officials. I suggested they could place an article in the local paper; I even volunteered to write it. "Let's show his photo and story to the village elders," I suggested. "Let's get a university student to write a thesis on the search for Ali." I pointed out that this search could generate national, even international news, and be a stimulus for the tourist business. It would certainly help build local pride, which is always a good thing for elected officials to bask in. *"Bagus,"* everyone said. Lots of enthusiasm, no action. Indonesian inertia, the Indonesian dearth of intellectual curiosity, a reluctance to pursue a "foreign" idea? I have no idea. In a fit of frustration I went on what I knew would be fruitless quest. Surely, I thought, someone would have a memory of great-great-great-uncle Ali. With the help of a friend who spoke the local dialect, I strolled through the Malay kampong, showed the photo to every old person I met and asked if they had heard of this guy Ali. The search goes on.

---

17   Ibid.
18   It would have been nice if Wallace had also written a note to Ali.

99

One minor benefit of voyaging to distant places was being able to taunt his stay-at-home colleagues that he was in places they did not know. According to Arnold Brackman, "Wallace liked to twit his friends in London by identifying the place he was at and then challenging his correspondent . . . to find the spot on their maps. 'By-the-by, you do not yet know where I am,' Wallace wrote a friend, 'for I defy all the members of the Royal Geographical Society in full conclave to tell you where is the place from which I date this letter.' In this instance the letter was dated 'Bessir, September 1, 1860.' Bessir is a village on the island of Waigiou, at the northwest tip of New Guinea, then (and now) barely known outside the immediate vicinity."[19]

Regardless of his motives, Wallace was driven. He was a reluctant hero in the Joseph Campbell mold: Odysseus and Rama, Don Quixote and Lancelot, Luke Skywalker, and Bruce Willis in *Die Hard*. He lived and breathed adventure, but, paradoxically, he equally longed for stability and inner peace. Deep down he wanted it all – the excitement of being alone and the security of a Beaver Cleaver existence.

> As to health and life, what are they compared with peace and happiness? and happiness is admirably defined in the *Family Herald* as to be best obtained by 'work with a purpose, and the nobler the purpose the greater the happiness.'[20]

Family Herald? Sounds like one of the women's magazines that offer advice on twenty ways to seduce a man and thirty ways to cook tuna-fish casserole. It's a lazy reference for Wallace, an otherwise fastidious researcher.

---

19 Italian journalist Tiziano Terzani summed up this delectable feeling of taunting the world by his outsiderness. Terzani had been warned by a fortune teller that he would die if he flew during 1993. He heeded the warning, mostly out of curiosity and a desire to be cantankerous; that year he only traveled by car, train, and boat. "Sheer madness, many people already thought," he wrote in his cult classic *A Fortune Teller Told Me*. "But being taken for a madman amused me more and more."

20 *My Life*, Vol. 1, 368.

American neuroscientist Robert Sapolsky discussed self-imposed exile in the context of young male primates leaving the nest. "Another key to our success must have something to do with this voluntary transfer process," he wrote. "This primate legacy of getting an itch around adolescence. How did voluntary dispersal evolve? What is going on with that individual's genes, hormones, and neuro-transmitters to make it hit the road? We don't know, but we do know that following this urge is one of the most resonantly primate of acts. A young male baboon stands riveted at the river's edge; an adolescent female chimp cranes to catch a glimpse of the chimps from the next valley. New animals, a whole bunch of 'em! To hell with logic and sensible behavior, to hell with tradition and respecting your elders, to hell with this drab little town, and to hell with that knot of fear in your stomach. Curiosity, excitement, adventure – the hunger for novelty is something fundamentally daft, rash, and enriching that we share with our whole taxonomic order."

"To hell with tradition." That's the positive analysis of Wallace's exile. Wallace didn't actually use the word "exile," but I think he felt it. "To hell with the British upper class," he might have thought. Sounds admirable, but this go-it-alone attitude cost Wallace valuable contacts later in life. People comfortable in the mainstream aren't too sure how to handle a rebel with a gleam in his eye.

And I'm not convinced that this yearning for adventure and "differentness" doesn't have a flip side. Perhaps this self-imposed search for adventure is a form of running away, an escape for kids who somehow didn't belong or weren't popular or just couldn't find their voices.

Imagine Wallace's lonely nights, thinking concurrently about food, butterflies, money, leaking roofs, and romance. He seems to swing between rival impulses. He wanted to go home to settle down, but he was also dying to keep chasing birds of paradise.

A boy's indecision, this unwillingness to go to sleep and miss something exciting, the reluctance to make a choice, the fear of being bored and boring.

> I look forward with unmixed satisfaction to my visit to the rich and almost unexplored Spice Islands – the land of the Lories, the cockatoos and the birds of paradise, the country of tortoise-shell and pearls, of beautiful shells and rare insects. I look forward with expectation and awe to visiting lands exposed to destruction from the sleeping volcano and its kindred earthquake; and not less do I anticipate the pleasures of observing the varied races of mankind, and of becoming familiar with the manners, customs and modes of thought of people so far removed from the European races and European civilization. The physical privations which must be endured during such journeys are of little importance, except as injuring health and incapacitating from active exertion. Intellectual wants are much more trying: the absence of intimate friends, the craving for intellectual and congenial society, make themselves severely felt, and would be unbearable were it not for the constant employment and ever-varying interest of a collector's life, and the pleasures of looking forward to a time when the stores now amassed will furnish inexhaustible food for study and reflection, and call back to memory the strange beautiful scenes among which they have been obtained.[21]

While gathering "food for study and reflection" was essential in helping Wallace to keep his sanity, he nevertheless wrote about his longings for "real" food: He complained that he "had often to make a small parroquest serve for two meals," and he lusted after the "table d'hote breakfast at ten" at the Hotel des Indes in Jakarta and couldn't wait to return to Ternate where he could enjoy "milk

---

21   "Observations on the Zoology of Borneo," *Zoologist* 14, no. 164 (June 1856): 5117.

[in] my tea and coffee." He had food fantasies about "fresh bread and butter," and "fowl and fish daily for dinner." And he went rhapsodic in thinking about "Oh, beef-steaks" and "Damson tart, a paradise for hungry sinners."

Historian Lloyd Fernando linked Wallace with Joseph Conrad, calling both "well-balanced romantics." Fernando had an interesting spin on how both Wallace and Conrad survived loneliness. "Each possessed twin stabilizers. These were first, pride in being faithful to difficult and taxing routines and thereby earning the respect of their fellow professionals, second, a common-sense recognition of the need to earn a living."

Fernando might have also added a third stabilizer: a sense of humor.

Even on the edge of a forest, curious locals paid him a visit. Wallace writes how a "good-natured savage" scolds him – "we don't know from what country you come. Ung-lung! it can't be; I know that is not the name of your country." And in Batchian [Bacan] he showed a villager "how to look at a small insect with a hand-lens, which caused such evident wonder that all the rest wanted to see it too. . . . Some declared it was a yard long; others were frightened, and all were as much astonished, and made as much shouting and gesticulation, as children at a pantomime."

He was fascinated by the local folks, and they found him similarly curious.

> This was the first time a real white man had come among them, and, said they, 'You see how the people come every day from all the villages round to look at you.' This was very flattering, and accounted for the great concourse

of visitors which I had at first imagined was accidental. A few years before I had been one of the gazers at the Zoolus [sic] and the Aztecs in London. Now the tables were turned upon me, for I was to these people a new and strange variety of man, and had the honor of affording to them, in my own person, an attractive exhibition gratis.[22]

The novelty value of Wallace in a village even affected the animals.

Hardly any of the people appeared to have seen a European before. One most disagreeable result of this was that I excited terror alike in man and beast. Wherever I went, dogs barked, children screamed, women ran away, and men stared as though I were some strange and terrible cannibal monster. Even the pack-horses on the roads and paths would start aside when I appeared and rush into the jungle; and as to those horrid, ugly brutes, the buffaloes, they could never be approached by me – for fear of my own, but of others [sic] safety. They would first stick out their necks and stare at me, and then on a nearer view break loose from their halters or tethers, and rush away helter-skelter as if a demon were after them, without any regard for what might be in their way. Whenever I met buffaloes carrying packs along a pathway, or being driven home to the village, I had to turn aside into the jungle and hide myself till they had passed, to avoid a catastrophe which would increase the dislike with which I was already regarded. If I came suddenly upon a well where women were drawing water or children bathing, a sudden flight was the certain result; which things occurring day after day, were very unpleasant to a person who does not like to be disliked, and who had never been accustomed to be treated as an ogre.[23]

22   *The Malay Archipelago*, 459–60.

23   Ibid., 230–1

I've spent my entire adult life away from "home," which was basically northern New Jersey, where I grew up. I have a little nostalgia for the place, but no great incentive to return to live there. My U.S.-based friends are all over the country. The American city I feel closest to is Washington, D.C., where I went to university.

My expatriate friends, whether in Singapore, Bangkok, Geneva, or Melbourne, are similar wanderers, folks who left their homes to live elsewhere. I put the question of what this self-imposed exile means to friends at a Bangkok dinner party.

Their opinions were varied, but naturally inconclusive. Some friends attributed their wanderlust to a positive quest for freedom or "differentness." Others felt they were escaping from something. Some folks became wanderers due to forces beyond their control – their fathers were in the army, or they were refugees. Some attributed the home-leaving to an overpowering mother; others to a low birth order and the desire to achieve something special out of the shadow of the older brother or sister. Several friends noted that the exploring gene was present in a parent, generally the father. Some bemoaned the lack of roots.

"It's not true we have no roots," my friend Steve said. "We carry our roots with us."

Yet even the most cross-cultural of us – those who have married "foreign" spouses, who speak other languages fluently, who can order a streetside meal in ten countries – have a deep affinity with our original tribe. Tribalism (and I'd add prejudice) is a bit like malaria – you might feel that you're rid of it, but it's always lingering inside.

Geographer Joel Kotkin noted the importance of tribal links in global trade. He quotes Ibn Khaldun, a fourteenth-century Arab historian: "Only tribes held together by a group feeling can survive in a desert." Substitute "globalised economy" for "desert," and this describes the modern world quite well, he suggests. An article on this theme in *The Economist* proposes that "Tribal loyalty fosters trust. Cultural affinity supercharges communication. Reading a contract is useful, but you also need to be able to read people. Even as free trade and electronic communications bring the world closer together, kinship still counts. Indians in Silicon Valley team up with other Indians; Chinese-Americans do business with Taiwan and Shanghai."

Pankaj Ghemawat of IESE, a business school, calculates that two countries that share a common language trade 42% more with each other than two otherwise identical countries that lack that bond. Two countries that once shared imperial ties trade a startling 188% more. In fact, imperial ties affect trade patterns more than membership of a common currency (which boosts trade by only 114%).

I asked Jane – who moved seventeen times before the age of forty, speaks several languages, and has lived outside the United States for decades – whether she maintained a strong link to the United States, her country of origin. She wasn't completely buying the tribal argument. Her analysis resonates: "When I go to the U.S. I'm an imposter. I sound American, look American, but don't fit in." Even if she wants to be tribal she can't go home again.

Is it the dream that catalyzes some people to travel hard? Bruce Chatwin suggested that " 'travel' is the same word as 'travail'" – physical or mental labor, toil, especially of a painful or oppressive nature, exertion, hardship, suffering, a journey.

"We travel to test ourselves, to cleanse, to rejuvenate," he said. "This could be termed 'catharsis,' which is Greek for 'purging' or 'cleansing.'" According to Chatwin, one controversial etymology derives from the Greek *katheiro*, "to rid the land of monsters."

So . . . we want to "rid the land of monsters?" External *and* internal demons? Sounds to me like we're trying to relive the great epics.

Bruce Chatwin tried "the experiment of slotting the career of a modern hero, Che Guevara, on to the structure of the Beowulf epic. The result was, with a bit of tinkering here and there, that both heroes are seen to perform the same set of exploits in the same sequence: the leavetaking, the voyage across the sea, the defeat of the Monster (Grendel-Batista), the defeat of the monster's mother (The water hag-the Bay of Pigs). Both heroes receive their reward: a wife, fame, treasure (in Guevara's case a Cuban wife and the Directorship of the National Bank of Cuba) and so forth. Both end up dying in a distant country: Beowulf killed by the Scaly Worm, Guevara by the Dictator of Bolivia."

So, we travelers see ourselves as heroes. We are smug. Paul Theroux[24] wrote: "The tourist doesn't know where he's been; the traveller has no idea where he's going." Chatwin adds: "The Hero Cycle, wherever found, is a story of 'fitness' in the Darwinian sense; a blueprint for genetic success. Beowulf leaves . . . the young Aboriginal on Walkabout leaves . . . even the antique Don Quixote leaves. And these *Wanderjahre*, and combats with the Beast, are the story-teller's version of the incest taboo; whereby a man must first prove 'fitness' and then must 'marry far.'"

We – modern boys and girls – lack rites of passage, rituals, and ceremonies where we clearly shift from childhood to adulthood. Instead, our rites of passages are fuzzy. Girls in Western societies begin to menstruate many years before they are old enough to bear children in a socially acceptable context. Boys might be old enough to drive but not to drink, old enough to kill/be killed in the army but not to vote, old enough to father children but not old enough to leave school of their own volition.

Most preindustrial societies had distinct rites of passage; today, at best, we get a watered-down, made-for-TV ceremony, like a bar mitzvah.

One classic rite of passage for young men is the Iban concept of *berjalai*. I asked Peter Kedit, former director of the Sarawak Museum (an institution that was created based on a suggestion by Wallace to the second White Rajah of Sarawak, Charles Brooke), whether Wallace's odyssey was comparable to *berjalai*, the coming-of-age ritual for young men, which sometimes ended with the taking of a

---

24 Theroux owes me a book, by the way. We exchanged letters, and on his request I sent him recipes for medicinal animal stews, then sent him my book *Soul of the Tiger* in promised exchange for one of his.

human head.[25] Kedit, an Iban from Sarawak, thought Wallace's drive was more attuned to a combination of English drives: the Protestant work ethic, missionary zeal, socialistic tendencies. I disagree. I think there was a large element of rite of passage involved in Wallace's adventures, the need to prove himself to both the community and to himself. He "failed" in his first rite of passage when most of his Amazon collection was lost at sea. So, back to the sweat lodge.

Maybe Wallace's butterfly-chasing and my waterfall-slushing were simply aspects of our own rites of passage, rituals that we created ourselves because our society gave us few hints and forgot to stage a ceremony just for us. We were denied the vigil in the desert, where we were expected to kill a lion, fast for three weeks, have a vision, return to the village to get circumcised, forced to fast, get tattooed, then blessed and finally reintroduced to the clan as an adult, decorated with feathers and body paint.

The vision, for me, is the most important part of the rite of passage. The illumination of a higher purpose. The dream. Martin Luther King and all that. Although I doubt he had Alfred Russel Wallace in mind when he wrote these lines, T. E. Lawrence's observation seems particularly apt.

All men dream: but not equally.
Those who dream by night in the dusty
recesses of their minds wake in the day
to find that it was vanity: but the dreamers
of the day are dangerous men, for they may act their dreams with open eyes,
to make it possible.

---

25 In the modern version of *berjalai*, which means "wandering," a teenaged Iban wannabe warrior might travel far to Saudi Arabia, and instead of returning with a trophy head, he might bring back more useful souvenirs, a flat-screen TV and a helmet that reads "Bechtel."

DIVERS DO IT DEEPER, THEN DIE

Meror, Aru Islands, Indonesia

Where the Chinese Indonesians get rich and the indigenous Indonesians are shark food.

Around the period that Wallace spent in the Aru Islands, from January 8 to July 2, 1857, France and England declared war on China. This conflict, the Second Opium War, was part of a long period of gamesmanship between Europe and China to expand and control global trading; one element was a desire to legalize the lucrative opium trade. At the same time, Wallace was noting the important role the ethnic Chinese played in buying and selling a wide variety of products from the land and seas of Aru, a group of ninety-five low-lying small islands southwest of the considerably larger island of New Guinea. Wallace was impressed not only by the fact that "five hundred people of various races all met in this remote corner of the East 'to look for their fortune,'" but also that Aru revealed "the genius of Commerce at the work of Civilization."[1]

This ubiquitous trade both fascinated and frustrated Wallace.

---

1   *The Malay Archipelago*, 444.

While he viewed trade as a positive force for keeping the peace, he railed against any form of commercial exploitation that abused the workers. His solution to the ills of worker abuse was socialism. He wrote: "If we review with care the long train of social evils which have grown up during the nineteenth century, we shall find that every one of them, however diverse in their nature and results, is due to the same general cause . . . due, broadly and generally, to our living under a system of universal *competition* for the means of existence, the remedy for which is equally universal *co-operation*." [italics Wallace][2]

In all of Indonesia I have never visited a place where commerce is so directly intertwined with nature as occurs on Aru. On the isolated islands and in the backward villages of this isolated region in far-eastern Indonesia, people eke out a living from hunting and small-scale cultivation. Fishermen from all over Indonesia catch anything in the sea. And through it all, the Chinese make money buying what Wallace called "natural productions" (Wallace noted "pearl-shell and tripang, or 'bêche-de-mer,' with smaller quantities of tortoise-shell, edible birds' nests, pearls, ornamental woods, timber, and birds of paradise") to sell to their compatriots worldwide.

I met a murderer today. Chek Chong is a Chinese merchant in this isolated corner of the isolated Aru Islands, who loans scuba equipment to young men so they can dive for mother-of-pearl and oysters, which he buys by the piece. Some of the men make a decent living. Some wind up as shark food.

Wallace wasn't shy about describing racial and ethnic stereotypes— Malays were "certainly not handsome . . . impassive . . . practical

2   *Social Environment and Moral Progress.* 1913. London, New York, Toronto, and Melbourne: Cassell and Company, Ltd., 166.

joking is utterly repugnant to his disposition," Papuan "boys sing cheerfully as they walk along . . . [have] higher [intellect] than that of the Malays . . . [are deficient] in affections and moral sentiments." The Chinese are not spared.[3]

> The Chinese merchant is generally a fat, round-faced man, with an important and business-like look. He . . . is always clean and neat; and his long tail, tipped with red silk, hangs down to his heels. . . . He is rich, he owns several retail shops and trading-schooners, he lends money at high interest and on good security, he makes hard bargains, and gets fatter and richer every year.[4]

Wallace noted how the Overseas Chinese control much of the trade and business, at all levels, in Southeast Asia.[5]

> The Chinese here [Dobo], as elsewhere, showed their superior wealth and civilization by tombstones of solid granite brought from Singapore, with deeply cut inscriptions, the characters of which are painted in red, blue, and gold. No people have more respect for the graves of their relations and friends than this strange, ubiquitous, money-getting people.[6]

---

3   The only people who are not skewered by Wallace are the Europeans. He thereby violates the basic rule for political incorrectedness – if you make fun of or are critical of one race you have an obligation to be equally critical of *all* races, your own included. And make no mistake, everyone, even the most high-minded philosopher, is riddled with gender, racial, cultural, religious, sexual orientation, political, and ethnic prejudices.

4   *The Malay Archipelago*, 33.

5   Although the Chinese make up less than three percent of Indonesia's population they control some sixty percent of the country's wholesale and seventy-five percent of the retail businesses, as well as controlling three-quarters of all the paid-up investment in finance companies, according to journalist James Clad.

6   *The Malay Archipelago*, 483.

Wallace was impressed by the volume of trade going on in Aru.

> The trade carried on at Dobbo is very considerable. This year [1857] there were fifteen large praus from Macassar, and perhaps a hundred small boats from Ceram [Seram], Goram, and Ké [Kei]. The Macassar cargoes are worth about £1000 each, and the other boats take away perhaps about £3000 worth, so that the whole exports may be estimated at £18,000 per annum. These are purchased with . . . arrack, about equal in strength to ordinary West India rum . . . native cloth from Celebes . . . white English calico and American unbleached cottons, common crockery, coarse cutlery, muskets, gunpowder, gongs, small brass cannon, and elephants' tusks.[7]

It's not uncommon to place blame for environmental villainy on somebody else.

Go to any international conservation conference where most of the delegates come from the South and you will find that the favorite sport is North-bashing. Mahathir bin Mohamad, Malaysia's feisty former prime minister, reckoned that it was better politics for him to be notorious than anonymous. He was a wizard at blaming his country's environmental problems on the industrialized, rich North. "We're doing a good job," he always argued, pointing out that tropical countries like his retain some forty percent of their forests while the North boasts of just five percent. He earned domestic kudos for suggesting that enforced nature conservation is a deliberate ploy of the North to keep the South weak and poor. "What right does the arrogant North have to tell Malaysia not to develop?"[8]

---

7   Ibid., 485.

8   Most tropical countries that actively denude their forests are secretly pleased by international press coverage of northern forest transgressions, like when the old-growth forests of British Columbia are cut. "Finally," the tropical forest destroyers

Picking up on this theme, but taking a slightly different tack, Soeharto, a former president of Indonesia, whined that his country was misunderstood. He argued that Indonesia had good forestry laws and that his government recognized all the conservation arguments for saving the rainforest. But the North should realize that "actually, the current [bad] condition of the [Indonesian] environment is the result of their [the North's] own doings," he said, arguing that the rich countries can afford to buy the timber that Indonesia produces, and that Indonesia, being a poor country that had been unjustly colonized by the North, needed to sell natural resources to join the ranks of wealthy nations.

These circular arguments ignore some basic questions of right and wrong, culpability and greed, not to mention the importance of environmental integrity, but the "we are victims of the North – we just want to develop" arguments play well to the home audience.[9]

Certainly the North's appetite for coffee and oil palm, beef and cocaine, contributes to the current destruction of the world's tropical forests. Paradoxically, few people have the courage to point the finger at the economically powerful Chinese. The Chinese are in the middle of so much of the wildlife trade and forest destruction that if you could single-handedly cut them out of the picture, you'd do a lot to stop the illegal trade in rhino horn, tiger skins, and elephant ivory and a host of other, lesser-known yet economically valuable commodities, like pangolins and birds' nests and shark fins and sea cucumbers.[10]

---

mutter with relief, "so we can show that the North is no better than we are."

9   Environmental crime, which includes wildlife trafficking, illegal logging, dumping of hazardous waste, and smuggling of chemicals that deplete the ozone layer, has become so widespread that it is recognized by the UN Office on Drugs and Crime as the third largest form of global crime, accounting for at least US$3.5 billion a year. Interpol, which has an environmental crime department, says such actions exacerbate deforestation and climate change, threaten the existence of endangered species, and affect the livelihoods of rural communities.

10 Few contemporary writers have been as candid about the Chinese lack of respect for the global commons as James Clad, who notes "nowhere do we find Chinese ethnic fingerprints more in evidence than in Southeast Asia's environmental destruction, still continuing unabated despite fine words from regional governments."
Clad has gone through various incarnations, as a diplomat, foreign correspondent (who earned his journalist's street cred by being imprisoned in Malaysia for refusing

Wallace noted that he was a curiosity, even an aberration, in Aru because he was not buying and selling.

> All [the traders] . . . pay me a visit, to see with their own eyes the unheard-of phenomenon of a person come to stay at Dobbo who does not trade![11]

He observed that the "natural productions" of Aru had little intrinsic value for local people, but enjoy a huge overseas market.

> These islands [Aru] are quite out of the track of all European trade, and are inhabited only by black mop-headed savages, who yet contribute to the luxurious tastes of most civilized races. Pearls, mother-of-pearl, and tortoise-shell, and birds of paradise find their way to Europe, while edible birds' nests and 'tripang,' or sea-

---

to reveal his sources), academic at Georgetown University, U.S. deputy assistant secretary of defense, and consultant to international oil companies. In his 1991 book *Behind the Myth: Business, Money and Power in Southeast Asia*, he documented Chinese domination of the timber trade, a major driver behind galloping deforestation and related environmental calamities. Twenty years later he sees no meaningful change in the trends.

"Just as ethnic Chinese business acumen has had an indispensable and leading part in East Asian economic dynamism, so also do the ethnic Chinese apply the same skill set to any and all activities, licit or illicit, for which they find a market.

"Take your pick," Clad continues. "Whether human trafficking, the drug trade, gem smuggling; shipping of endangered species in deplorable conditions to mainland Chinese and Western "collectors" [and health seekers and diners, he might have added]; vicious prostitution protection rackets; sales of small arms to myriad insurgencies; despoliation of archaeological sites – whatever you choose, the ethnic Chinese dominate these businesses as they do most others."

"The wealth generated by stupendous growth in mainland China simply adds to the momentum. 'Business is business' marks the enduring cultural orientation, signalling a culturally grounded indifference, by a class of ethnic Chinese business families, to individual human misery or the reduction of animal habitats, even to the biggest issue of all, global warming. Formally and diplomatically, the Chinese Motherland signals her indifference as well, arguing that earlier polluting Western industrial practices – puny by comparison to China's gargantuan carbon 'paw print' today – gives China a license to pollute indefinitely."

11   *The Malay Archipelago*, 435.

slug,[12] are obtained by shiploads for the gastronomic enjoyment of the Chinese.[13]

There's a market and the Chinese control it. And now there exists the technology to rip off nature much more efficiently than in years past.

The Chinese don't do the dirty work themselves, of course. They finance and indirectly control the operations of a huge fleet of independent boats that sails from Dobo consisting of more than one hundred diving boats; three hundred fishing boats owned by Buton and Bugis sailors who have migrated from South Sulawesi; and some seven hundred fishing boats manned by local Arunese.

> I asked if [the residents of Dobo] knew when the trade with Aru first began, when the Bugis and Chinese and Macassar men first came in their praus to buy tripang [*teripang*, sea cucumber] and tortoise-shell, and birds' nests, and paradise birds? This they comprehended, but replied that there had always been the same trade as long as they or their fathers recollected.[14]

The divers in this economically impoverished region south of the Indonesian part of New Guinea are generally poorly educated fishermen who are commissioned by the merchants to collect sea products but who are given little or no scuba training. And, because they are paid by the piece, the guys dive deeper and more

---

12 Wallace described them as "looking like sausages which have been rolled in mud and then thrown up the chimney." Other commentators have used more robust descriptors involving the digestive process of canines.

13 *The Malay Archipelago*, 409. For all their well-deserved culinary acumen, the Chinese taste for wild-caught food includes some of the most tasteless food on the planet – shark's fins, birds' nests, and sea cucumbers.

14 Ibid., 459.

frequently than they should.

When I dived with tanks and regulators rented from Chek Chong, I saw first-hand that the equipment is not kind to inexperienced divers. All the equipment was battered and corroded. Four out of five regulators I tested malfunctioned. None had depth or pressure gauges; the tanks lacked reserve pulls.

One recent victim was twenty-two-year-old Daud Karatim from Kampong Sia in southeast Aru. Having no training, he broke the rules of safe diving and died of the bends. I suggested to Chek Chong that perhaps Daud Karatim's death was the merchant's responsibility.

"He chose to go down," Chek Chong said, not at all pleased by the conversation. "They all want the money."

Wallace, ever the social reformer, was voluble on the subject of job-related injuries.

> It is one of the great defects of our law that deaths due to preventable causes *in any profit-making business are not criminal offenses*. [italics Wallace][15]

Wallace criticized the hazardous working conditions in British factories. Toxic chemicals, such as yellow phosphorus, used in the manufacture of matches, were handled without proper safeguards. About these, and other trades, he wrote:

> [the misery] was absolutely needless, since . . . all without exception *could* be made entirely harmless if adequate pressure were brought to bear upon the manufacturers. [italics Wallace][16]

Much of the data concerning diving deaths in Aru is anecdotal, but I spoke to enough Chinese merchants, divers, and officials to believe that the following incidents represent the tip of the iceberg.

---

15 *Social Environment and Moral Progress*, 52.

16 *The Wonderful Century: Its Successes and Its Failures*. 1898. London: Swan Sonnenschein and Co., 356.

- A researcher at the University of Pattimura in Ambon recorded eighteen diving deaths in the Aru Islands during 1992 and four for the month of January 1993.
- A fisherman on board the *Cahaya Laut*, sailing out of Dobo, Aru, said that he knew of seven men who had died during a two-month period in the 1990s.
- On Pulau Baun, two men died during a one-week period in March 1993.

Diving tragedies are not limited to the Aru Islands.
- On the island of Bobale, off Halmahera, six men died in diving-related accidents and another six have been crippled for life.

According to Indonesian law, in the event of an injury the merchant who "commissions" the diver is only required to pay initial medical costs, which are insignificant since there is nothing anyone can do to reverse the permanently crippling effects of even a mild case of the bends.

A diver with the bends cannot be sent to a decompression chamber since the nearest facility is in Surabaya, thousands of kilometers away and a day's journey by (nonexistent) plane. The only choice is to go back down once the cramps start. Ely, who worked on the fishing boat *Cahaya Laut*, explained that when he got the bends – Indonesians call it "rheumatic" – his colleagues brought him back down to about thirty meters (one hundred feet), where he stayed for forty-eight hours while his friends brought fresh tanks and slapped him to keep him awake.

When a diver dies, the merchant is required to pay compensation to the deceased's family. The amount is determined by the Indonesian labor office – generally the equivalent of between US$500 and US$1,000. In Daud's case, Chek Chong paid the man's family US$750.

Wallace argued that employers who cause the deaths of their employees should be guilty of manslaughter.

> Let every death that is clearly traceable to a dangerous
> trade be made manslaughter, for which the owners, or, in
> the case of a company, the directors, are to be punished
> by imprisonment.[17]

This is tricky business, of course, placing a dollar value on a
person's life. What would an American jury have awarded Daud's
family? Wallace, writing in the second half of the nineteenth
century, weighed in on the importance of having a good lawyer.

> The party who can pay the highest fees for the services
> of the most experienced counsel is most likely, through
> the lawyer's skill and eloquence, to secure a verdict in his
> favour.[18]

But, I was wondering, how much *is* a life worth? A 1995 report
on the social cost of global warming by the UN's Intergovernmental
Panel on Climate Change (IPCC) valued the lives of people in the
North up to fifteen times higher than those in the South, ranging
from US$1.5 million for people from the richest countries down to
US$100,000 for those in poorer developing nations. The valuations
are based on assessments of a community's willingness and ability
to pay to avoid risks of death. At the UN conference at which the
report was tabled, delegates from India, China, Brazil, Cuba, and
other countries where the report's economist-authors determined
that life is cheap vetoed the study.

Just or not, Chek Chong's "compensation fine" is a small business
expense, considering the profits involved.

Divers can earn US$5 for a mother-of-pearl shell and anywhere
between US$1.70 and US$15 for an oyster that can be used in
culturing pearls.

---

17 Ibid.

18 *Social Environment and Moral Progress*, 72.

The merchants then sell the mother-of-pearl to overseas craft workshops and the oysters to one of the twenty-six oyster farms in Aru for a profit of three hundred percent to one thousand percent. As they say, the rich get richer . . .

> [The] chief social effect [of man's increased command over the powers of nature], has been the increase of luxury and the widening of the gulf between rich and poor. Although material wealth, reckoned not in money but in things, has increased perhaps twenty or thirty fold in the last century while the population has little more than doubled, yet millions of our people still live in the most wretched penury the whole vast increase of wealth having gone to increase the luxury and waste of the rich and the comfort of the middle classes.[19]

Our group of scientists was stuck in Dobo. The once-weekly Merpati Airlines flight had been cancelled (we later learned it was because the pilot, who didn't particularly like to fly to Aru, simply didn't show up for work). The Chinese merchant who owns PT. Sumber Mas, a company that is the airline's agent, and who is a major trader in threatened species, had as much concern for us as if we had told him we had a mosquito bite. We insisted he try to call the Merpati headquarters in Jakarta for a clarification of whether there might be a replacement flight and so on. He had one of the few phones in Dobo and before he dialed he made us promise to pay for the call. When he saw that we *really* had to get out of Dobo, he offered to help us charter a boat to Kei island, which has more frequent flights, for a usurious sum.

Am I being too hard? Even Wallace, a cynic with rose-colored glasses, had to search hard to see the good in Dobo. But somehow he came to the curious conclusion that ripping off nature has a

19 "Economic and Social Justice." In *Vox Clamantium: The Gospel of the People*. 1894. London: A. D. Innes and Co., 169.

soothing effect on people's souls.

> [Most of the people of Dobo] have the very worst
> reputation for honesty, as well as every other form of
> morality – Chinese, Bugis, Ceramese, and half-caste
> Javanese, with a sprinkling of half-wild Papuans from
> Timor – yet all goes on as yet very quietly. This motley,
> ignorant, bloodthirsty, thievish population live here without
> the shadow of a government, with no police, no courts, and
> no lawyers; yet they do not cut each other's throats, do not
> plunder each other day and night, do not fall into anarchy.
> It is very extraordinary. It puts strange thoughts into one's
> head about the mountain-load of government under which
> people exist in Europe, and suggests the idea that we may
> be overgoverned. Think of the hundred acts of Parliament
> annually enacted to prevent us, the people of England, from
> cutting each other's throats, or from doing to our neighbor
> as we would *not* be done by. . . . Here we may behold in
> its simplest form the genius of Commerce at the work of
> Civilization. Trade is the magic that keeps all at peace,
> and unites these discordant elements into a well-behaved
> community. [italics Wallace][20]

About the only good thing that came out of our enforced stay in Dobo is that I was able to follow Wallace's well-described route circumscribing part of the island.

I was accompanied on the walk by Ahmad, a local Indonesian conservation official, and Gilly, a chattering graduate student in marine biology from Manado, who was a participant in our research expedition. I was impressed by Gilly's ability to avoid going into the water even once during our three-week trip researching turtles, coral reefs, and other wet things. She had overheard me asking one of the

---

20   *The Malay Archipelago*, 443–4.

guys if he wanted to come on the walk, and she asked if she could join me. I couldn't come with a fast enough reason to exclude her.

But even silly, scatterbrained, superficial Gilly couldn't spoil this walk.

Wallace gave us great directions.

[In Dobo] I set off to explore the virgin forests.[21]

Virgin forests? Well, today it's rural, but no virgin forests around town. We pass the Indonesian telecommunications office, which proudly displays a huge satellite dish that enables us to phone Europe. We pass the Muslim cemetery, the police station, and the school, where neat blue-uniformed children – Chinese and Papuan and a smattering of Javanese – run and giggle.

We had to walk about half a mile along the beach.[22]

This beach stroll is most pleasant. We start in a coconut plantation, then cross a stream, where Gilly complains "my shoes will get wet, what will I wear on the [nonexistent] plane?" We then pass through a small, neat village with a modern church featuring a gigantic bible on the roof, before finally arriving at a pleasant bay, where we take a break and Gilly asks if I will give her a copy of my book *Soul of the Tiger*. "No," I reply. She asks why, in a whining voice that I guess helps her get what she wants. I lie and tell her that I only got three free copies as author. What I want to tell her is: "You can barely read traffic signs in English, you have as much in common with me as an Egyptian camel trader, your appreciation of either my incisiveness or wit would be negligible, and, finally, I don't particularly like you."

The path was very little used . . . so that after about a mile we lost it altogether. . . . In the mean time, however, I had

---

21   Ibid., 433.

22   Ibid.

not been idle, and my day's captures determined the success of my journey.[23]

We hadn't come to collect, but using two large floppy hats we catch a floppy birdwing butterfly as large as the span of my hand, which reminds me of a golden retriever in its gawky movements and willingness to get captured. I'm not sure, but it seems to fit the description of one of Wallace's orgasmic butterflies, *Ornithoptera poseidon*. I keep my passion in check, however, and examine the beast and then let it go.

> I had taken about thirty species of butterflies – more than I had ever captured in a day since leaving the prolific banks of the Amazon, and among them were many most rare and beautiful insects, hitherto only known by a few specimens from New Guinea.[24]

We catch some twelve species of butterflies without trying too hard; obviously biodiversity is alive and well in the suburbs of Dobo.

> And then turned into the forest along a path which leads to the native village of Wamma.[25]

We take roughly the same turning and continue to Durjela village, after about two and a half hours of leisurely walking. The kids show us their homemade slingshots, with which they zap anything in sight – butterflies, chickens, the odd bird. The village has had electricity for two years, a fact the elders are quite proud of. People tell us of a whale skeleton further up the coast, and we find several enormous vertebrae of a beached blue whale, which we later calculate might have been some 36 meters (118 feet)

---

23 Ibid.

24 Ibid.

25 Ibid.

long. Near the skull we find a small offering of betel and incense, recognition by some people that this animal represents their tribal ancestor totem.

That night, in Dobo's most popular restaurant, which doubles as a brothel, I strike up a conversation with the chief of police, born and bred in Aru, and tell him about the whale skeleton.

"Do local people here eat whales?" I ask.

"Rarely. And never if the whale is their totem, as it is with the people who placed the offerings you saw."

"Is there anything the *Chinese* don't eat?"

The police chief thinks for a while. "Dugongs. They never eat dugongs."

"I wonder why not?"

The police chief shrugs his shoulders as if to say "who can understand the Chinese?"

KILL MOSQUITOES TILL
THEY'RE DEAD

Gunung Ledang, Malaysia.

Sleeping on a ledge next to one of the world's most beautiful
waterfalls amidst some of the world's most senseless litter.

After spending three months in Singapore, Alfred Russel Wallace headed north to Malacca, in what is now Malaysia. He was to stay for two months, from July through September 1854. This was his first real contact with "wild Asia," although British colonial Malaya was not without creature comforts, and expatriates kept up with the latest trends. This period saw significant developments in marketing and product innovation. The first paid advertising in a newspaper appeared (France 1836), an anonymous London artist printed the world's first Christmas cards (1843), advertising posters were banned on private property (London 1839), Le Bon Marché in Paris was the world's first true department store (1852), French fashion label Louis Vuitton was founded (1854), the first use of the telegraph for mass unsolicited spam occurred (1864), and advertising billboards were rented for the first time (1867). Opposing all this rampant commercialism, in 1854 Charles Dickens wrote *Hard Times*, which campaigned against laissez faire capitalism; in the same year Henry David Thoreau's *Walden* lamented the rise of industrialization and the related destruction of wilderness.[1, 2]

I left the United States partly to get away from rubbish, both literal and emotional. Sarawak was a relatively stuff-free zone, but that changed when I talked myself into a job in Singapore as regional creative director of an advertising agency. Suddenly it became my job to promote consumption, something I did for a decade, first in Singapore and Malaysia, and later in Indonesia. The irony is that I later moved into the field of nature conservation, which actively rants against consumerism as part of the eco-liturgy. Each Northerner, the litany goes, uses as many resources and produces as much waste as thirty-two Nepalese.[3, 4]

At its most extreme, the conservation gurus urge profligate Americans and Europeans to turn themselves into compost by committing suicide in a tropical rainforest using biodegradable poison while wearing natural fiber clothes.

"I'm Super Chicken and I kill mosquitoes till they're dead," I sang. It was late at night, and even if there was anyone within a kilometer, which I doubted, I knew my voice would be drowned out by the rush of the Mount Ophir waterfall.

---

1   Wallace ended *The Malay Archipelago* with a similar warning: "Our mastery over the forces of nature has led to a rapid growth of population, and a vast accumulation of wealth; but these have brought with them such an amount of poverty and crime, and have fostered the growth of so much sordid feeling . . . that it may well be questioned . . . whether the evil has not overbalanced the good."

2   About this time, in 1855 when Wallace was in Sarawak, the term "acid rain" was first used.

3   Be careful with these kinds of statistics; there are lies, damn lies, and statistics. For example, the United States has some thirty times more crime per capita than Nepal (or does the United States simply have better policing or stricter laws?).

4   An even more astonishing statistic: Using data from the International Telecommunications Organization, researcher Tomi Ahonen calculated that eighty-nine percent of households worldwide have television sets.

Mount Ophir was beautiful at night, when I couldn't see the litter. It seems my career has always been linked with garbage.

I found advertising fascinating. I got a quick and shallow education in lots of fun stuff – how one client made a "safe" household insecticide, what goes into candies, and what happens when you look at Indonesian tap water through a microscope (it ain't pretty). I probably peaked with the ad that featured the mosquito-killing heroes – Super Chicken, Double Rabbits, and Invincible Goat – "who kill mosquitoes till they're dead." It was my Cecil B. DeMille moment, a two-minute extravaganza for a client's down-market mosquito coils, with live action mixed with animation and a catchy jingle.[5]

Our advertising agency had a branch office in Kuala Lumpur, and I went up there at least twice a month, often stopping off in Malacca, the historic city that was the center of the great waves of sea exploration.

> Malacca . . . is the market of all India, of China, of the Moluccas, and of other islands round about, from all which places, as well as from Banda, Java, Sumatra, Siam, Pegu, Bengal, Coromandel, and India, arrive ships, which come and go incessantly, charged with an infinity of merchandises.[6]

I helped contribute to the consumer wave through my advertising work. One highlight: I created one of the region's most hummable jingles for a perfume called Lady Gay, the package of which announces: "A happy marriage between Miss English Lavender and Mr. Eau de Cologne."[7] So, for me, the experiences I had in Malaysia, Singapore, and Indonesia were mercantile as much as social and emotional and natural.

---

5   I feel all advertising is improved with jingles.

6   *The Malay Archipelago*, 37.

7   I wish I had written that copy.

It struck me when Wallace wrote:

> Thence it is that all who live in the country [Malacca] pay
> tribute of their health, suffering from a certain disease,
> which makes them lose either their skin or their hair.[8]

This widespread fear of disease kept me in business. We promoted a brand of bottled water called Aqua, marketed by an Indonesian company that curiously called itself Golden Mississippi. This was the first bottled water sold in Indonesia, and we had to convince people to pay lots of money for something they could get free. In our advertising film we started off with microphotography showing the menagerie of miniscule beasties that are found in Jakarta's tap water. Then we showed that *even boiling* doesn't kill all the germs. Big mini-monster close-ups. Then we showed microphotography of purified, filtered, sterilized, tasteless Aqua.

It wasn't always so straightforward. I made a film for another client who manufactured ceramic toilet bowls – in a country where, at the time, I don't know, maybe two percent of the people had flush toilets.

This toilet bowl commercial was choreographed to Rachmaninoff's "Rhapsody on a theme of Paganini." We built two film sets, one in Jakarta and one in Singapore. The star was a white Angora cat – two cats actually, since the Indonesian cat didn't have travel documents for Singapore. The second cat turned out to be as big a bitch as its owner – the cat scratched the cameraman, bit one of the actors, and threw up under the lights. After all that production drama the film never made it to air. The Jakarta TV station rejected it because a segment of the film showed a little girl giving the cat milk. Their logic was "most Indonesians don't drink milk, why should a cat?" We offered to cut out the milk scene. They then rejected the spot because the setting was too luxurious

---

8   *The Malay Archipelago*, 37–8.

and would create unreasonable expectations among the populace.[9]

Malacca guards the strategically vital 900-kilometer- (550-mile-) long Strait of Malacca, which links the Pacific Ocean to the Indian Ocean via the South China Sea to the east and the Andaman Sea to the west. Some fifty thousand ships annually transit the narrow passage; carrying about one quarter of the world's traded goods. Also, about a quarter of the world's oil carried by sea passes through the strait, mainly from Persian Gulf suppliers to Asian markets such as China, Japan, and South Korea.[10]

Malacca has for centuries been the key to wealth and power for outsiders and regional traders alike. First to arrive were Muslim traders, coming from India in the eleventh century. Then came Catholic Portuguese, the first of the European mercenaries who sailed around the Cape of Good Hope to the "Indies." In today's global economy we rarely get excited about exotic commodities, but in centuries past, the arrival of a leaky galleon filled to the gunwales with nutmeg, cardamom, cloves, and pepper generated a frenzy of mercantile excitement in Lisbon, Madrid, Venice, and Amsterdam. Charles Corn, author of *The Scents of Eden: A Narrative of the Spice Trade*, noted, "Spices drove the world economies in those days the way oil does today." So important was this strategic city that Tomé Pires, a sixteenth-century Portuguese apothecary and historian, noted that, "Whoever is lord of Malacca has his hands on the throat of Venice."

---

9   This attitude has changed dramatically, and conspicuous consumption is everywhere in Indonesian cities. I knew the middle class in Jakarta was permanently entrenched when the English-language newspaper in Jakarta published a week-long series of letters from Indonesian readers complaining that a local Pizza Hut outlet had discontinued thin-crust pizza.

10 Historically, piracy has been a problem in the Strait of Malacca. In 2004 the narrow strait accounted for forty percent of piracy worldwide, and some fifty pirate attacks were recorded in 2006. But with better policing the danger has dramatically decreased. According to the International Maritime Bureau, in the first quarter of 2009, for instance, the number of pirate attacks around the world nearly doubled (to 102 incidents) but only one of them occurred in the Strait of Malacca.

I went to Malacca for the history and to enjoy the waterfall; Wallace went to Malacca for the insects.

> The manner in which I obtained one fine insect was curious, and indicates how fragmentary and imperfect a traveller's collection must necessarily be. I was one afternoon walking along a favorite road through the forest, with my gun, when I saw a butterfly on the ground. It was large, handsome, and quite new to me, and I got close to it before it flew away. I then observed that it had been settling on the dung of some carnivorous animal. Thinking it might return to the same spot, I next day after breakfast took my net, and, as I approached the place, was delighted to see the same butterfly sitting on the same piece of dung, and succeeded in capturing it. It was an entirely new species of great beauty, and has been named by Mr. Hewitson Nymphalis calydona. I never saw another specimen of it, and it was only after twelve years had elapsed that a second individual reached this country from the north-western part of Borneo.[11]

Having done what they could to eliminate the real forest around Malacca, the canny Malaysians decided to make money on the *idea* of the forest. Today, roughly along the Malacca–Mount Ophir route Wallace took, the Melaka (the Malaysian spelling of the city) Butterfly and Reptile Sanctuary brags that it is home to "more than 20 different species of butterflies" – about an afternoon's catch for Wallace. "You will feel like Alice in Wonderland watching these magnificent creatures performing their daily routine over the inviting flowers that blooms [sic] by hundreds and filled [sic again] with the magical nectar," the website proclaims.

---

11 *The Malay Archipelago*, 40–1.

Mount Ophir. What a wonderful name. The legendary Mount Ophir of the bible provided Solomon with gold, ivory, sandalwood, peacocks, apes, and precious stones.

The Malaysian Mount Ophir, now renamed Gunung Ledang and designated a national park, is today simple to get to. Wallace walked "through extensive forests, along paths often up to our knees in mud, and were much annoyed by the leeches, for which this district is famous." I took a bus and a taxi, and left my pack with a guy named Ganesh at one of the food stalls at the base of the hill. I carried water, a box of raisins, a couple of chocolate bars, a notebook, and a lightweight sleeping bag.

Wallace's climb was marked by foliage; my climb was marked by garbage. Litter was everywhere, particularly at the level area about two thirds of the way up, which marks the top of the waterfall and which is the preferred camping spot for hundreds of weekend nature lovers. (Following my visit, the Malaysian Nature Society organized a cleanup of Gunung Ledang and collected "several tons" of rubbish.) Was this the modern discounted legacy of Mount Ophir's "gold, sandalwood, ivory and precious stones?"

> We had been told we should find water at Padang-batu [near the top], but we looked about for it in vain, as we were exceedingly thirsty. At last we turned to the pitcher-plants, but the water contained in the pitchers (about half a pint in each) was full of insects, and otherwise uninviting. On tasting it, however, we found it very palatable, though rather warm, and we all quenched our thirst from these natural jugs.[12]

I drank from the descendants of Wallace's pitcher plants. And I drank the water from the waterfall. Maybe I was risking a bad stomach, but I figure that water that seemingly falls from the sky like this waterfall does *can't* be dirty.

---

12 Ibid., 43.

[We] stood on the summit of Mount Ophir, 4000 feet above the sea [actually 1,276 meters, 4,186 feet]. The afternoon was clear, and the view fine in its way – ranges of hill and valley everywhere covered with interminable forest, with glistening rivers winding among them.[13]

I slept next to the waterfall, on a flat rock that formed an overhang above a 40-meter (130-foot) drop-off. It was one of the most perfect evenings of my life – the sky was brilliant with stars, and I was alone with my ghosts, who were benevolent that night. I was a little surprised, actually, by how content I was since earlier I had been furious at the lack of respect people show to nature. I hate litter, and the Gunung Ledang waterfall had more garbage than most places in Asia.

One apologist explanation for litter is that up until the Age of Plastics, all packaging was biodegradable – leaves, baskets, rattan – and local folks are simply jettisoning what they see as (natural) garbage. But I don't buy that. The folks who climb Gunung Ledang are educated Malaysians and Singaporeans who live in towns and cities, and who know very well that a cigarette pack or an instant noodle bag is not the same as a bit of rice and curry wrapped in a banana leaf. I consider it a disrespect, a disinterest in the commons. (In the true spirit of ASEAN solidarity, the Malaysians claim that the Gunung Ledang garbage is the detritus of Singaporean holiday-makers. The logic, one Malaysian told me with a straight face, is that the Singaporeans are such anally compulsive neatniks in their own country that they go wild and litter with abandon on foreign shores). There was so much garbage there I was able to conduct a mini-market research study. The Gunung Ledang hiker prefers to smoke Dunhill, brushes her teeth with Colgate, and enjoys noshing on tapioca chips and instant noodles.

Wallace had a curious relationship with consumer goods. He

---

13 Ibid., 44.

actually looked forward to the day when "the natives" would have the resources and desires to consume European goods, thereby making the people of Europe happy.

> Under such a [colonial] system [good roads, strict justice towards the natives, introduction of a good system of cultivation as in Java, production of sheep, horses, and wheat] the natives would soon perceive that European government was advantageous to them. They would begin to save money, and property being rendered secure, they would rapidly acquire new wants and new tastes, and become large consumers of European goods. This would be a far surer source of profit to their rulers than imposts and extortion.[14]

Well, "the natives" got independence *and* the taste for consumer goods. The irony is that the trail is plastered with "don't litter" signs sponsored by Pepsi. The company might take some solace in the fact that discarded Pepsi cans littering the path outnumbered discarded Coke cans by about three to one. Is litter what Wallace had in mind when he wrote: "A deficient morality is the great blot of modern civilization, and the greatest hindrance to true progress."[15]

My friend Herschell Gordon Lewis started out making satirical exploitation movies – he has been designated as the "Godfather of Gore" and is credited with having invented the nudie-cutie and slasher genres, with such classics as *Goldilocks and The Three Bares*, *The Gruesome Twosome*, and *Blast-Off Girls* (as well as having written and directed America's first lesbian western). But what I admire most about Lewis is that in addition to his filmmaking career he became America's most famous direct marketing expert – he knows more about how to

---

14 Ibid., 206.

15 Ibid., 456.

write junk mail letters (whoops, direct mail communications) than anyone. In his direct marketing seminars he reveals *the* most powerful human emotion in generating direct mail response. Not anger. Not fear. Greed. The *best* way to get a response to whatever it is you're selling is to invoke the Big G. Which Wallace saw coming, even a hundred and fifty years ago.

> During the last century, and especially in the last thirty years, our intellectual and material advancement has been too quickly achieved for us to reap the full benefit of it.[16]

Malaysians are living proof of the power of greed. Sensing that ASEAN solidarity will bring handsome profits, Indonesian developers put up a sign at the entrance to Malaysia's Gunung Ledang Nature Reserve, expressing their desire to improve nature by building holiday chalets, a bird aviary, herbal garden, and parking for eight hundred cars. In fact, in Asia you can even take the good life with you. Wallace must have seen the fake paper money Chinese burn at funerals to give the deceased some cash with which to gamble in the afterlife. In Malacca I passed several shops selling made-to-be-burned paper models of a microwave oven with roasting chicken inside, a Hellevision fake TV, Sanya Hell Video Cassette Recorder, and Hellevideo blank tapes.

But why wait until you're dead? The week I climbed Gunung Ledang, the *New Straits Times* ran a full-page, full-color ad offering homes in Baiduri Villa in the Malaysian city of Johor Bahru: "Designed to impress and overawe," the ad began. "The grandeur of classicism-revisited features water cascades, statues. The evocation of lifestyle at Baiduri Villa is certain to delineate it as the pinnacle of condominium village." The happy owner could choose between Tudor and Georgian architecture.

---

16   Ibid.

Of course, the Americans are no better. One Saturday morning in Honolulu, I zapped between two television channels that ran the following simultaneous ads. The first was an infomercial for a group called Life to the Children, which provided aid to Mozambique famine victims. They showed a girl named Manume, who was three years old and who had lost half her body weight. She was going to die within days if someone didn't help. Horrible images. The announcer said that thirty dollars would feed three children for six months. Their number is 1-800-547-3100.

I flicked the station. The second ad was a segment on QVC, the shopping channel. It was the "doll hour," and they offered Item C-7657, "Crying Jenny," a sixteen-inch porcelain "collectible" doll for only $49.95. You could also buy twelve doll dust covers, Item C-8010, for just $14.50. Phone: 1-800-345-1515.

I have no doubt that the ad for "Crying Jenny" pulled better than "Starving Manume." I think Americans, and British, and all the other rich guys – and that includes well-off people in Hong Kong and Japan and Venezuela and Saudi Arabia and India and Thailand – basically are so caught up in their own little worlds that they become calloused to other people's problems. At WWF we called this "compassion fatigue." People are tired of hearing about other people's problems. And people aren't about to voluntarily give up what they have. That's why George H. W. Bush refused to sign the biodiversity convention at the 1992 Earth Summit in Rio – he said "the American life style is not negotiable."

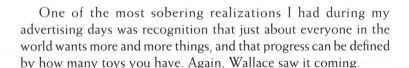

One of the most sobering realizations I had during my advertising days was recognition that just about everyone in the world wants more and more things, and that progress can be defined by how many toys you have. Again, Wallace saw it coming.

> And if we continue to devote our chief energies to the
> utilizing of our knowledge of the laws of nature with
> the view of still further extending our commerce and

our wealth, the evils which necessarily accompany these when too eagerly pursued, may increase to such gigantic dimensions as to be beyond our power to alleviate.[17]

Americans, in spite of their technological achievements and widely distributed wealth and high literacy, are among the most innocent people on earth. When I arrived in Hawaii I was proudly told by any number of people that they considered themselves to be conservationists. I asked them how they had decided that. "Because when I'm in the supermarket I take a paper bag instead of a plastic bag." I was flabbergasted. "Have you considered what junk you put into that paper bag?" I lectured. "What the environmental impact is of the production of that food, the pesticides it uses, the forests that are destroyed, the transport costs, the chemicals to process it, the packaging, the open refrigerators pouring cold air into the aisles?" This is the Jewish Mother mode of conservation – nag people and make them feel guilty. Not a good way to win friends and influence people.

Wallace took on the tone of an Anglican vicar when he railed against the social sins generated by greed.

> Our mastery over the forces of nature has led to a rapid growth of population, and a vast accumulation of wealth; but these have brought with them such an amount of poverty and crime, and have fostered the growth of so much sordid feeling and so many fierce passions, that it may well be questioned, whether the mental and moral status of our population has not on the average been lowered, and whether the evil has not overbalanced the good.[18]

---

17 Ibid., 457.
18 Ibid., 456–7.

This greed business is pervasive, and it is the single biggest obstacle to lasting conservation. A chilling factoid, one of many: In 2011 Jakarta, a city of ten million people, had 3.1 million cars and 8.2 million motorcycles, and *every day* 1,500 new motorcycles and 500 new cars enter the streets. Yet Jakarta's road system expands by only 0.01 percent annually. Experts predict total gridlock by 2014.

Yet I don't want to be naive. The desire to improve our physical living conditions and accumulate "things" is global and seemingly ingrained in virtually all societies. A guy living on the edge of a forest wants electricity for his hut. Then a bicycle. Then a tin roof so his hut doesn't leak. Then a motorcycle. Then a road so he can go to town. Then a better road. Then a car. Or does he want a TV set with a satellite dish before the bicycle? Or does a small fridge come first? Not to forget a few new sarongs for his wife and a ready supply of cigarettes and beer for himself.

I had my personal commercial epiphany while I was sitting in a Baduy resettlement village in West Java. The Baduy are mysterious and proud isolationists who have rejected all forms of authority – they fled into the hills to avoid being subjugated by the Islamic Mataram empire four hundred years ago, and since then the Baduy have refused to have much to do with the Dutch, or even other post-independence Indonesians. They can get away with giving the world the finger because they are perceived to have remarkable magical powers, which they dole out in small quantities to the powers-of-the-moment. But even the Baduys find it hard to resist the momentum of the Jakarta government – somehow the government managed to convince a few dozen families to try life on the outside.

> We should now clearly recognize the fact, that the wealth
> and knowledge and culture of *the few* do not constitute
> civilization, and do not of themselves advance us toward

the "perfect social state." Our vast manufacturing system, our gigantic commerce, our crowded towns and cities, support and continually renew a mass of human misery and crime *absolutely* greater than has ever existed before. [italics Wallace][19]

I got frightened of being one of "the few." It comes to me as I'm drinking tea with a Baduy family. I'm curious how they are adapting to life outside the isolated and strict community[20] in which they grew up. They are trying to figure out the meaning of life. I'm no use at all to them because I'm trying to figure out the same thing myself. We're half-watching the community television when one of my commercials – for Trebor candies – comes on. These good people are watching my commercial, and the kids are very interested. They want to buy the stuff. I could see it in their eyes. My commercial worked. I knew that the next time around they would be humming the jingle that my go-to Singapore composer Horace Wee and I had cooked up: "Trebor sweets taste great with real fruit flavors that sing." And it just didn't make any sense. Advertising had been a boy's trip, but I went cold turkey on the industry. It was time to let Super Chicken, Double Rabbits, and Invincible Goat and their respective mosquito coil brands find their way in the marketplace without me.

---

19 Ibid.

20 The relocated Baduy I visited are "Outer Baduy," cousins of the stricter "Inner Baduy," whose constraints make the Amish look like party animals. No wet rice agriculture, no fertilizers, no modern tools, no four-legged animals. They are forbidden to kill, steal, lie, commit adultery, get drunk, take any form of conveyance, wear flowers or perfumes, accept gold or silver, touch money, or cut their hair.

HAPPY, HAPPY BIRTHDAY ALFRED

Jirlai, Aru, Indonesia

Is a man's most valuable possession his bow and arrow or a butterfly or a memory or simply time? What birthday gift should I give a guy who lived a hundred and fifty years ago?

Birthday presents for the young Alfred Russel Wallace were likely to have been meager. He was the eighth of nine children born to a middle-class family in Usk, in South Wales, and hand-me-downs were his destiny.

Alfred Russel Wallace's father, a devout Anglican, not-practicing lawyer, and not-very-successful businessman, could afford little in the way of material goods.

But one gift his father did give his son was a love of reading and encouragement to use a library, and in this way Alfred Russel Wallace voraciously consumed an inspiring assortment of books on science, natural history, and travel. His eclectic reading list included Defoe's *Robinson Crusoe*, Milton's *Paradise Lost*, Dante's *Inferno*, Fielding's *Tom Jones*, Cervantes' *Don Quixote*, Thomas Paine's *Age of Reason*, all of James Fenimore Cooper's novels, Malthus's *An Essay on the Principle of Population* (of which Wallace said "twenty years later gave me the long-sought clue to the effective agent in the evolution of organic species"), Alexander von Humboldt's dramatic personal account of his travels in Latin America, Darwin's journal of the *Beagle*, and Lyell's *Principles of Geology*. One of the books that stimulated him most was a book on evolution, *Vestiges of the Natural History of Creation*, written by Robert Chambers, another amateur naturalist.[1]

In later life Wallace came to also appreciate how much he owed his older brother William for encouraging pastimes that required no cash, and as a father himself Alfred Russel Wallace deplored the growing craze of giving children elaborate and contrived mechanical toys that called for no creative skill on the part of the recipient.

And from somewhere Wallace received the gift of rebellion, which he used to enthusiastically challenge existing institutions and which gave him the courage to embrace controversial theories.

As a kid I loved to build model airplanes and ships. Up close they revealed my sloppy glue-work, but sitting on the shelf in my room they were the stars of the American defense force.

I had too much stuff. I was an only child and received the beneficence of doting relatives who generally had no idea of the tastes of a young boy. A couple of uncles understood though and slipped me a few bucks whenever they visited. Cash to buy ancient Roman coins for a few dollars each. Cash to buy the new Revell Thunderhawk fighter. Cash to buy a pet parakeet. Cash to buy Robert Sheckley science fiction books. Not quite independence, but a start.

---

1   *Vestiges*, published in 1844, suggested a "law of development" in which one species is transformed into another by external circumstances.

I drink a birthday toast to Alfred Russel Wallace. The eighth of January. I'm trying to figure out what to give him as a present.

I toast Wallace with sweet tea, since this tiny and poor hamlet on this forgotten island in this isolated corner of the archipelago is alcohol-free.

Seems the headman, in what must have been a first in Indonesia, kicked out the Chinese merchant who had stocked a tiny shop in someone's house. The headman was not driven by missionary zeal as much as he was concerned that his cash-poor fellow villagers would walk into the shop intending to buy necessities like batteries and fishing line, but would wind up spending the kid's school fees on beer and cigarettes.

Seems people without stuff want stuff.

What does Wallace want?

My wife and I moved house from Bangkok to Geneva. We had left about thirty boxes of stuff in storage in Geneva. Our Bangkok house, which we thought was not too crowded with junk, resulted in 329 boxes, fitting into a twelve-meter (forty-foot) container.

The shipping company, Crown, includes an annoying sanctimonious message on their emails: "Think of the environment before printing this email." Their packers (who did a good job) used double and triple cardboard boxes, meters of Styrofoam, kilometers of packing tape, huge swaths of plastic and bubble wrap. I wonder if anyone has calculated the environmental footprint of a household move.

We tried to de-junk while in Bangkok. Really we did. We gave things away. We threw things away. We left things for friends. But we still had *too much stuff*. I can't get rid of my Ganesha collection; I really can't. I can't throw away my father's army photos. I can't sell my tribal wooden carvings, or the paintings, or the antique bronzes, or the Chinese porcelain. And the carpets? Might need those some day.

And I *really* can't get rid of books.

What is it about books? They pack up so nicely into small boxes that weigh as much as mercury. There are basically two kinds of people in the world – those with books and those without. The People With Books, probably like you and your friends, acquire but don't discard. Bookshelves groan. Our house in Geneva is smaller than our house in Bangkok, and my study has less shelf space. I had to exile books about entire continents to the garage – South America, be gone, Australia and the Pacific, banished. Not to mention packing into storage whole thematic sections – Ayurveda and traditional medicine, exiled to the darkness of the garage, alongside opera librettos and I forget what else. Boxes of tribal bronzes sit in the basement, as do boxes of Chinese porcelain, a poor man's version of the basement of the Louvre. Of course, I will live just fine without ever opening those cartons again. But I like the idea of having them nearby. Having stuff isn't about the actual stuff; it's about the idea of the stuff being there, just in case.

Wallace was an observer of what kind of stuff people owned. When he was here in Jirlai, he noted:

> [The people of New Guinea] live in the most miserable, crazy, and filthy hovels, which are utterly destitute of any thing that can be called furniture; not a stool, or bench, or board is seen in them, no brush seems to be known, and the clothes they wear are often filthy bark, or rags, or sacking.[2]

In Jirlai I stayed in an unfinished house set over the water, accessible by walking a plank and crawling through a window frame. It was empty, yet it was one of the most comfortable shelters

2   *The Malay Archipelago*, 512.

I have had on the road, particularly after two weeks of trying to sleep on boats. Indonesian boat builders must take special courses in anti-ergonomics. They learn how to put blind lintels at forehead height, how to make decks slippery, and how to eliminate any comfortable nooks.

Wallace relished the creature comforts of a home on terra firma.

> Few can imagine the luxury it was to stretch myself on a sofa, and to take my supper comfortably at table seated in my easy bamboo chair, after having for five weeks taken all my meals uncomfortably on the floor. Such things are trifles in health, but when the body is weakened by disease the habits of a lifetime can not be so easily set aside.[3]

Bugs me too. I've got a bad back, and rotten knees. Can't sit cross-legged for the life of me. Maybe I should give Wallace an inflatable Thermarest mattress for his birthday.

Wallace didn't, couldn't travel light.

In the Amazon, Wallace carried what Henry Walter Bates called "extensive apparatus," which included folding tables, chairs, and camp beds, guns with supplies of powder and shot, collecting nets, pouches, killing bottles, pins, and elaborate and cumbersome corkboard-lined boxes. He also lugged around magnifying lenses, prismatic compasses, thermometers, barometers, a sextant, and tin boxes full of notes.

The Malay Archipelago is filled with lists of the things he carried with him.

> I . . . sent two of my boxes of specimens by a Macassar prau to be forwarded to Ternate, thus relieving myself of a considerable incumbrance. I bought knives, basins, and handkerchiefs for barter, which with the choppers, cloth, and beads I had brought with me, made a pretty good

---

3   Ibid., 231.

assortment. I also bought two Tower muskets to satisfy my crew, who insisted on the necessity of being armed against attacks of pirates; and with spices and a few articles of food for the voyage, nearly my last doit was expended.[4]

He needed these things, but these possessions limited his freedom of movement.

I put up the smallest quantity of baggage possible for a six days' trip, and on the morning of December 18th we left Makariki, with six men carrying my baggage and their own provisions.[5]

Six men to carry his stuff for a six-day trip? Sounds like the trip I just made to Pulau Enu on the other side of Aru. Ating Sumantri, the head of turtle conservation for the Indonesian nature conservation department, had the unenviable task of organizing a trip to the outer reaches of the Aru islands; ten days, ten people. One afternoon Ating and I sat on the beach and made a list of what we had brought:

FOOD
powdered milk, 1 can
coffee, 6 packs
tea, 5 packs
Khong Guan biscuits, 1 box
pineapple biscuits, 4 packs
pumpkins, 2
cucumbers, 5 kg
cabbages, 10 kg
beans, 5 kg
potatoes, 5 kg
onions, 5 kg

---

4   Ibid., 380.

5   Ibid., 360.

water, 20 x 20 L jerry cans
bottled water, 48 bottles
rice, 25 kg
eggs, 50
soy sauce (sweet), 10 bottles
sambal hot sauce, 10 bottles
instant noodles, 24 packs
prawn crackers, 5 packs
sugar, 5 kg
vinegar, 1 bottle
shredded beef, 1/2 kg
dried beef, 2 kg
clove cigarettes, 80 packs

THINGS
firewood, 10 packs
detergent
matches
kerosene, 10 L
rice pots, 2
wok
kettle
radio
rice strainer
plastic plates
mugs
ladle
plastic water jugs, 2
lanterns, 2
raffia, 1 roll
plastic sheets (4 x 6 m), 5

BOAT
gasoline (for onboard generator), 40 L
diesel, 2,000 L

Wallace made some sixty major moves during his Asian travels. Unpacking and packing. He yearned for the stability and sanctuary he found in Ternate.

> The next day we reached Ternate, and I ensconced myself in my comfortable house, to examine all my treasures, and pack them securely for the voyage home.[6]

Bali was for me what Ternate was for Wallace. A retreat. After a month or two on the road I would return to my friend Didier's bungalow in Sanur. There, I would reclaim my modest possessions and spend time with friends. Brent – a talented potter and businessman who was one of five residents in the compound – and I would eat Italian food and play squash. I might be sitting on my terrace and Leonard, across the lotus pond, would play music that uncannily matched both his mood and mine – salsa or *Abbey Road* or Beethoven. I'd wander over, and we would talk about surfing and girls and photography. My mail would be waiting. There was a fax and phone. My mountain bike was there. I could satisfy my food fantasies. Perhaps, best of all, I could sit on the terrace of the thatched bungalow in the early morning following a dawn swim, watch the light play on the lotus pond, pound away on my laptop, nibble on papaya, and recognize that the world is a pretty special place after all.

Wallace cherished his time in comfortable Ternate.

> [In Ternate] a deep well supplied me with pure cold water – a great luxury in this climate. Five minutes' walk down the road brought me to the market and the beach. In this house I spent many happy days. Returning to it after a three or four months' absence in some uncivilized region, I enjoyed the unwonted luxuries of milk and fresh

---

6   Ibid., 354.

bread, and regular supplies of fish and eggs, meat and vegetables, which were often sorely needed to restore my health and energy. I had ample space and convenience for unpacking, sorting, and arranging my treasures, and I had delightful walks in the suburbs of the town, or up the lower slopes of the mountain.[7]

Even when he wanted to travel light he couldn't quite manage it.

As I intended to stay two or three nights on the mountain I engaged two coolies to carry my baggage.[8]

When I travel upriver I tend to leave caches behind. Once I leave the city I no longer need town shoes and socks, which get left, along with the long-sleeved batik shirt that gains acceptance to most Indonesian events. But there's still weight – hiking boots, Keen sandals, mask and fins, maybe a lightweight tent. In my backpacker days I could get by with a daypack and a medium-sized gym bag. Two cannot-travel-without items: a tattered Nature Company hat with a handmade hatband of turtles made by an artist friend in Honolulu and an equally tattered green headband from the Ramsar Convention's global conference in Kushiro, Japan, which identifies me, in faded kanji, as a "festival person."

On one trip to Ternate, Bacan, and Ambon, I took books. Heavy bastards. I brought *The Malay Archipelago*, scribbled on, highlighted, dog-eared, which I kept in a waterproof plastic sandwich bag in case the dugout flipped.

On our way back from Makariki, as on our way there, we had storm and rain at sea, and we arrived at Awaiya late in the evening, with all our baggage drenched.[9]

---

7   Ibid., 314.

8   Ibid., 125.

9   Ibid., 363.

How did Wallace ever keep his specimens dry?

More books. I carried Bill Dalton's guide to Indonesia. Periplus guides to Sulawesi and Maluku.

And I have a fear of being stuck somewhere with nothing to read, therefore: Maugham's *A Writer's Notebook*.

I travel in Southeast Asia with Maugham. In this book I got frustrated by his arrogant youthful insights ("Most people are such fools that it really is no great compliment to say that a man is above the average."). Instead, I skipped to the back of the chronological volume for the solid advice of the mature Maugham. ("the writer should have a distinguished and varied culture, but he probably errs when he puts its elements into his work. It is a sign of naïveté to put into a novel your views on evolution, the sonatas of Beethoven, or Karl Marx's *Das Kapital*.")

Wallace too had his favorite escapist literature.

> When I went to New Guinea, I took an old copy of
> 'Tristam Shandy', which I read through about three times.
> It is an annoying and, you will perhaps say, a very gross
> book; but there are passages in it that have never been
> surpassed, while the character of Uncle Toby has, I think,
> never been equalled, except perhaps by that of Don
> Quixote.[10]

One way to differentiate people is to use my "Yin-Yang Cultural Scale."[11] There are people who travel far versus people who stay at home. People who are curious versus folks who are intellectually

---

10 *My Life*, Vol. 1, 366–7.

11 Put another way, it's a subset of the Equilibrium of Opposites. That's why so many Asian mythological tales and gods are based on conflict – for example, the male, sun-loving, creative Garuda is based on the eagle, which is in eternal opposition to the Naga, a female mytho-snake representing the dark underworld, rain, agricultural productivity, and weaving. There is a biological basis: the Naga is based on the king cobra, a natural prey of the eagle. We need both to keep the world in balance. Nevertheless, black-and-white concepts rarely occur without countless shades of grey.

content with what they already know. People whose homes contain art versus people whose houses contain junk. And, most telling and easy to determine, people whose homes are filled with books versus folks whose shelves are used to hold basketball trophies.

I was sitting in a filthy losman in Bacan, talking to a couple of Indonesians who worked for the electricity board and who were on the island for business. They were fascinated by the guidebooks I carried, rich in detail, full of photos of beautiful people and places. After drinking tea and eating fried bananas with them, I felt I could ask why most of the books about Indonesia were written by foreigners. "Foreigners think differently," one of them replied. I asked him to explain. More or less, he said: "Indonesians are tied to the daily search for ways to stay alive; foreigners look for ideas."

I think he was too hard on his countrymen and certainly too starry-eyed about the noble intentions of the white race. I offered a somewhat different theory. That, basically, the Indonesian vision is inward-directed and therefore focused on family and *bangsa*, which is a person's tribe or race or language group. But foreigners have weaker family structures, not to mention smaller families; therefore they find it easier to extend their vision outward, to other cultures.

I carry more books on my back than can be found in most Indonesian households. My stash includes an Indonesian/English dictionary, which is the most insulting piece of rubbish I have ever seen published.

The dictionary, by Drs Harun Asnawi and Drs Saleh Effendi and Ralph J. E., is partly a work of fiction, partly a compendium of typos that make "Indonesian quality-control" an oxymoron. Under the (English) section "P," for example, we find such Lewis Carrollean words as:

propaedeutic
prsaist
protrct
proximo
predu
psalmody

pundemdum
pubicity
puisne
putrescant
pyxis[12]

Am I wrong to get fed up with sloppiness by people who should know better? These folks have claimed to have published a dictionary! Most of my friends, including Indonesians, would just laugh it off – "Yup, no attention to detail." Why should the standard by which I judge a dictionary be the operative version? I guess because while it's their country, it's my language.

Wallace lived in anxiety about getting ripped off.

> The next day [in Bacan] I received my money, and secured it well in a strong box fastened under my bed. I took out five or six hundred cents for daily expenses, and put them in a small japanned box, which always stood upon my table. In the afternoon I went for a short walk, and on my return this box and my keys, which I had carelessly left on the table, were gone. . . . I immediately gave information . . . to the . . . commandant at the fort, and got for answer that if I caught the thief in the act I might shoot him. . . . I lost my cash and my box, a seal I much valued, with other small articles, and all my keys – the severest loss by far.[13]

Some people I meet wouldn't think of stealing, but they are not above making a play for something I have. Yanas, the Indonesian government nature conservation department officer on Bacan, took me for a long walk through the nature reserve a couple of weeks

---

12 I noted the words, but failed to note the definitions, which would have been insightful. If any reader can help, I would be grateful.

13 *The Malay Archipelago*, 339.

ago. He asked me to pay his airfare to Ambon so he wouldn't have to take the three-day boat. I declined. Then he went lateral. Told me I looked like Sylvester Stallone. Depending on the sobriety of the observer, I have been compared to Harrison Ford, and Omar Sharif, and, when I'm grumpy, to Jack Nicholson, and my bald spot has been likened to that of Sean Connery, and Dustin Hoffman images have been mentioned by others – but Sly Stallone?[14] Yanas was good. He knew what buttons to push. He wanted my boots.

> The constant walking in water, and over rocks and pebbles, quite destroyed the two pairs of shoes I brought with me, so that, on my return, they actually fell to pieces, and the last day I had to walk in my stockings very painfully, and reached home quite lame.[15]

Maybe I'll give Wallace a pair of nylon and leather hiking boots.

It's hard to imagine a world without synthetics. On even the most isolated beaches I see the flotsam of plastic bottles and rubber flip-flops. Worldwide, clothes of hot, sticky synthetic material replace hot, sticky homespun, and plastic buckets and jerry cans replace earthenware pots.

Jirlai is so isolated, and the people so poor, that people still make and use hand-thrown clay pots for storing water. I was invited for tea at Ely's house, and I glanced around and did a quick inventory – the only externally produced things were cooking utensils, plastic buckets, his machete and a few gardening tools, a battery-powered cassette player, and kerosene pressure lamp. Plus a few clothes and one or two pictures of Indonesian movie stars ripped out of a magazine and nailed to the wall.

> The houses and furniture [in Aru] are on a par with the food. A rude shed, supported on rough and slender sticks rather than posts, no walls, but the floor raised to within a

---

14   My golf swing has never been compared to that of Fred Couples or Adam Scott.

15   *The Malay Archipelago*, 363.

foot of the eaves, is the style of architecture they usually adopt. Inside there are partition-walls of thatch, forming little boxes or sleeping-places, to accommodate the two or three separate families that usually live together. A few mats, baskets, and cooking-vessels, with plates and basins purchased from the Macassar traders, constitute their whole furniture; spears and bows are their weapons; a sarong or mat forms the clothing of the women, a waistcloth of the men.[16]

Little privacy in these parts. Ely had watched me unpack in the half-completed house. He had longingly examined my Swiss Army knife and quietly noted my French backpack, Italian trekking shoes, American tent, and Australian pants, complete with the zippered knees that allow them to be turned into shorts. Ely concluded that I was rich.

He was also quick to point out that he was poor.

"You're wrong," I said. "You're not poor at all. You're rich." Ely looked skeptical. Who was this mad man? "You are self-sufficient. You have your family. You breathe fresh air and swim in clear water. Nobody tells you what to do every day."

Ely examined my sunglasses, the same ones I use for skiing in Verbier, and was even more convinced that this was a crazy conversation. "Every day I do the same thing," he said. "I hunt or fish or farm. If I don't work I don't earn any money. As it is I can hardly pay for my children's education."

"But you've got your religion, and community support. People in the West do not have these things anymore."

"You," Ely replied with his trump card, "can afford to travel to Aru. I cannot afford to visit you."

Of course, I had no answer and felt moderately ashamed for leading him on. I told him what he really had that was of great value that I didn't. It was time. He had time, and thought it was worthless. I had things, and valued time more than any physical

---

16 Ibid., 453.

possession I owned.

I asked him what he would really like if he could have anything. "An outboard engine," he said, somewhat hopefully, perhaps thinking that I was about to offer him a present.

I asked this illiterate man what his most valuable possession was. I was expecting, but not looking forward to his saying "My bible." Instead he said the only sensible thing, and he said it immediately. "My bow and arrow." Quickly he added: "And my parang." I asked him why. "With those I can hunt and build a new house."

I couldn't reply as quickly. The house containing everything you own is on fire. What gets saved? What is left behind?

Wallace biographer Arnold Brackman narrated Wallace's reaction when the brig *Helen* caught fire on his return from four years exploring the Amazon. "Wallace raced to his cabin and snatched up a 'small box . . . which [was] luckily at hand.' The box contained a set of pencil drawings of different palm species, together with notes on their distribution and characteristics; a collection of sketches, drawn to scale, of fishes, with notes on their color, dentition, and scale structure and a Portuguese folio notebook containing his Rio Negro diary and notes made while mapping both the Rio Negro and Uaupés. Everything else, [most of his collection] the labor of four years, was smoldering and burning in the hold beneath the cabin. Wallace, who wrote that at the time he was 'still suffering from fever and ague, which had nearly killed me ten months before on the upper Rio Negro,' also grabbed his watch and a purse containing a few sovereigns, the only money he possessed."

I can't imagine what my feelings would be. After an initial relief at being alive, I suppose I would enter a deep despair about the loss.

> I cannot attempt to describe my feelings and thoughts during these events [the burning of the *Helen*]. I was surprised to find myself cool and collected. I hardly thought it possible we should escape, and I remember thinking it almost foolish to save my watch and the little money I had. . . . My collections, however, were in the hold and were irretrievably lost. And now I began to think

that almost all the reward of my four years of privation
and danger was gone. What I had hitherto sent home had
little more than paid my expenses, and what I had with me
in the *Helen* I estimated would have realized about £500.
But even all this might have gone with little regret had not
by far the richest part of my own private collection gone
also. All my private collection of insects and birds since
I left Para was with me, and comprised hundreds of new
and beautiful specimens which would have rendered (I
had fondly hoped) my cabinet, so far as regards American
species, one of the finest in Europe.[17, 18]

It seems our possessions can be divided into three categories.
First are the things people need to survive. Today, if they're near
a store that would simply be cash and, in a city, a credit card.
Otherwise, some clothes, rice, an all-purpose tool, a weapon,
matches, fishing gear.

Then there are things people think they must have but don't
really. The iPod. Electric pasta machine. Tickets to the Knicks. A
government ID card. A bible.[19]

Finally, there are things people covet, which are often the
hardest to give up – birds of paradise, thy neighbor's wife.

I knew how few Europeans had ever beheld the perfect
little organism I now gazed upon [the king bird of
paradise, *Paradisea regia*], and how very imperfectly it was
still known in Europe. The emotion excited in the minds
of a naturalist who has long desired to see the actual

---

17 *My Life*, Vol. 1, 305.

18 For his part, Henry Walter Bates returned from his eleven years in the Amazon with
some eight thousand new insect species.

19 In Tom Wolfe's *Bonfire of the Vanities*, the main character, a self-described Master of
the Universe, faces poverty. "I'm already going broke on a million dollars a year!" he
complains. But he just can't get rid of his Porsche. Just can't. Ditto for the summer
house in Southampton, the three maids and one handyman, the New York Park
Avenue duplex, the country club membership, the private school education for his
kids. Impossible.

thing which he has hitherto known only by description, drawing, or badly-preserved external covering, especially when that thing is of surpassing rarity and beauty, require the poetic faculty fully to express them. . . . I thought of the long ages of the past, during which the successive generations of this little creature had run their course – year by year being born, and living and dying amid these dark and gloomy woods, with no intelligent eye to gaze upon their loveliness – to all appearance such a wanton waste of beauty.[20]

This, by far, is the most interesting choice. Things you covet. Things with an emotional attachment. Things that have big meaning but little monetary value. Things that reflect our dreams and hopes and memories. Would I choose between a charcoal portrait of my father, the briar pipe clenched in his teeth, or the thousands of pages of notes for this book?

I want to give Wallace a present. What would he like from the beginning of the twenty-first century?

A camera? Maybe. I bet he would have been a superb photographer. But he was already manic enough, writing meticulous notes, collecting everything in sight, collecting vocabularies on fifty-seven languages[21] and filling Asian skulls with sand to measure cranial capacities.

This birthday present list is getting unwieldy. Swiss army knife? Bubble gum? Maybe an insect fogger like Terry Erwin used in Panama to collect all those arboreal beetles. I scrutinized *The Malay Archipelago* for some hints.

---

20 *The Malay Archipelago*, 448.

21 Although not on a par with the loss of his South American collection when the *Helen* sank, Wallace lost half of the Asian vocabularies he had painstakingly collected. "These represent about fifty-seven distinct languages . . . more than half of which I believe are quite unknown to philologists. . . . Some years ago I lent the whole series to the late Mr. John Crawford [sic], and having neglected to apply for them for some months, I found that he had in the meantime changed his residence, and that the books, containing twenty-five of the vocabularies had been mislaid. . . . Being merely old and much-battered copy-books, they probably found their way to the dust-heap along with other waste paper."

All the time I had been in Ceram I had suffered much from the irritating bites of an invisible acarus, which is worse than mosquitoes, ants, and every other pest, because it is impossible to guard against them. This last journey in the forest left me covered from head to foot with inflamed lumps, which, after my return to Amboyna [Ambon], produced a serious disease, confining me to the house for nearly two months.[22]

A proper medical kit with mosquito repellant, antibiotics, and antihistamine cream?

I was surprised by the range of products available in Singapore at the time Wallace lived there.

Even then, the Singapore *Straits Times* newspaper published ads promoting perambulators, buggy whips, Irish linen, and horse-hair petticoats. Perhaps Wallace picked up a few bottles of Rolands Macassar Oil, "patronized by Queen Victoria," which "prevents Hair from falling off or turning grey, strengthens weak Hair, cleanses it from Scurf and Dandruff and makes it Beautifully Soft, Pliable and Glossy."

I bet Wallace enjoyed a nightcap. Wallace could have stopped by Cursetjee & Co., which offered Glenlivet whiskey, Johannisberg hock, and a "fine selection of new music and novels."

There were medicines, to be sure. "Sparkling Effervescing Citrate of Magnesia as prepared by Geo. Curling and Compy. Its agreeable flavour and cooling effects upon the System justly cause it to be more highly esteemed and valued (especially in Hot Latitudes) than any other Saline."

Another *Straits Times* ad for Holloway's Pills boasted numerous testimonials, including "an extraordinary cure of dropsy after suffering for eighteen months."

---

22 *The Malay Archipelago*, 363.

Lea and Perrins took out an ad to warn against "spurious imitations" of their famous sauce.

Perhaps Wallace was tempted by "The Greatest Medical Discovery of the Age," which was Perry's Cordial Balm of Syriacum, used to "restore the impaired power of life when exhausted by the follies of youth, maturity or old age."

The Straits Times accepted advertising from Dubarry's "delicious Health Restoring Revalenta Arabica Food." The manufacturers noted that they have fifty-six thousand cures listed in their files, in one of which, cure no. 49,832, Revalenta Arabica Food "helped a patient of fifty years [who suffered] indescribable agony from dyspepsia, nervousness, asthma, cough, constipation, flatulency, spasms, sickness and vomiting."

Back to birthday presents.

Maybe Wallace would have appreciated some detailed maps.

Or maybe a Zippo. Sure, he had matches, but it must have been tough keeping them dry.

Pots and pans?

> I had a great iron pan, in which I boiled the [orangutan] bones to make skeletons.[23]

Okay, forget about kitchen appliances, seems like he was well equipped.

Maybe a lightweight tent. Mine is Sierra Designs, weighs less than three kilos [six pounds], goes up in a flash.

> I preserved the [orangutan] skin of this specimen in a cask of arrack.[24]

He was carrying around full casks of alcohol? That's serious weight. I guess if he had a staff to carry full casks of alcohol, he would be able to hire a few more people to carry lengths of canvas

---

23 Ibid., 67.
24 Ibid., 53.

to make a shelter.

I've decided to give Wallace something rather mundane, but he will appreciate the logic.

I've opted for a gift that is not valuable, not frivolous, not decorative. About as practical as you can imagine. I keep thinking of Wallace moving camp, trying to keep live insects from devouring his dead insects, struggling to keep his sugar and gunpowder dry, trying to keep his fountain pen-inscribed notebooks from disintegrating in the humidity. It must have been hell when the skies opened and rain fell like Thor himself was pissing down on the jungle.

My gift to Wallace: a large selection of plastic bags – ranging from the heaviest-duty, industrial-strength giant-sized garbage bags to small, easily sealable sandwich bags. For his journals. For his butterflies. For his coffee. For his sanity.

TRUST ME

Minyambou, Arfak Mountains, West Papua, Indonesia

*In a mountain village where birds are descended from
paradise and where men seek to follow suit.*

Wallace spent a frustrating three and a half months, from April
to July 1858, near Dorey (now Manokwari) in what is now the
Indonesian province of West Papua (formerly West Irian Jaya)
on the island of New Guinea.

In Dorey, Wallace found few insects, and injured his ankle
which turned septic and "had to be leeched, and lanced, and
doctored with ointments and poultices for several weeks." As
a result, he was unable to move without a crutch, "till I was
almost driven to despair – for the weather was at length fine,
and I was tantalized by seeing grand butterflies flying past
my door, and thinking of the twenty or thirty new species of
insects that I ought to be getting every day. And this, too, in
New Guinea! – a country which I might never visit again – a
country which no naturalist had ever resided in before – a
country which contained more strange and new and beautiful

natural objects than any other part of the globe."[1]

Wallace was too incapacitated to trek into the birds of paradise-rich Arfak Mountains, but he noted ruefully that in the steep and rugged hills, "a few miles in the interior, away from the recently elevated coralline rocks and the influence of the sea air, a much more abundant harvest might be obtained."

He was happy to leave the main island of New Guinea. "We bade adieu to Dorey, without much regret," he wrote, "for in no place which I have visited have I encountered more privations and annoyances. Continual rain, continual sickness, little wholesome food, with a plague of ants and flies, surpassing any thing I had before met with, required all a naturalist's ardor to encounter; and when they were uncompensated by great success in collecting, became all the more insupportable. This long-thought-of and much-desired voyage to New Guinea had realized none of my expectations. [But] Dorey was very rich in ants. They immediately took possession of my house . . . they swarmed on my table, carrying [my insect collection] off from under my very nose . . . they crawled continually over my hands and face, got into my hair, and roamed at will over my whole body . . . they visited my bed also . . . and I verily believe that during my three and a half months' residence at Dorey I was never for a single hour entirely free from them."

New Guinea, another place with an evocative name that evokes visions of high adventure.

I went to Manokwari (which Wallace knew as Dorey) on a

---

1. Wallace was correct in bemoaning his missed opportunity. The Arfak Mountains Nature Reserve is home to fifty-one rare and endemic mountain bird species (out of some 320 bird species in total). The area is also the world's center of biodiversity for birdwing butterflies, holding a large percentage of the estimated five thousand species of butterflies and moths found in Papua.

WWF mission to document conservation efforts involving local tribesmen. It was on this trip that I witnessed the courtship of the bower bird. More to the point, it was on this physically challenging trip that I learned how Four Modern Religions – Government, Evangelical, Consumer, and Nature Conservation – fight for the hearts and minds of local people.

In the isolated mountains of Papua, people search for gold, copper, timber, and adventure. But perhaps the most hotly contested prize is Zakarias Sayori's soul.

Zakarias Sayori is a farmer, hunter, father; a member of the Hatam tribe. He's a prime target for the snake oil salesmen promoting Four Modern Religions in his cold and damp mountain village.

First, the government wants to "Indonesianize" him, that is, to get him to speak the national language, Bahasa Indonesia, and to follow the civic principles of Pancasila, the national feel-good philosophy. This is the Government-Religion.

Second, Protestant preachers want to Christianize him, and by doing so add his tenor voice to the Sunday choir. Let's call this the Evangelical-Religion.

Third, tycoons who manufacture soap and running shoes want to consumerize him, to make him feel the need for things like shampoo and instant noodles that his ancestors had survived without for millennia. This is the Consumer-Religion.

And fourth, conservationists want to "empower" him, to give him a chance to save nature the way the conservationists think best; this is the Nature Conservation-Religion.

Each of these four groups is promoting a faith, a cult, an alien belief system. "Trust us," they seem to say. "We're prophets from the Government/Evangelical/Consumer/Nature Conservation-

Religions. We're here to help you. Believe in us, even though we give you no guarantee, and your life will be improved."

Consider the Government-Religion. The patriotic civil service missionaries have been successful in spots. Most urban people, and an increasing number of rural folk in Irian Jaya, speak Bahasa Indonesia, the national language of Indonesia that originated in distant Sumatra. But the frustrating reality for proponents of the Government-Religion is that Papuans are aggressively lobbying for independence and an end to what they consider to be Javanese colonialism.

I acknowledge that some Christian groups in Papua, particularly the Catholics, who I have found to be the most reasonable and helpful religious folk in the country, have done good works. They have helped stop cannibalism and infanticide, have promoted public health, have helped establish schools and clinics, and have initiated community development projects like water systems and gardens.

But the Evangelical preachers and their Evangelical-Religion are hard to love.

> On catechising evenings the school-master was a great man, preaching and teaching for three hours at a stretch much in the style of an English ranter. This was pretty cold work for his auditors, however warming to himself; and I am inclined to think that these native teachers, having acquired facility of speaking and an endless supply of religious platitudes to talk about, ride their hobby rather hard, without much consideration for their flock.[2]

---

2   *The Malay Archipelago*, 261.

I've seen these "native teachers" and they do go at it. Merciless. They've been taught something and by god they believe it. As do members of their flocks. It is not uncommon for churchgoers in Papua to believe that merely sitting in church will result in immunity from sickness and that forgetting to shut one's eyes during prayers will lead to blindness.

It seems that some societies out here are renegade Cargo Cultists at heart.

An American missionary told me that he had had a disciple, a young man whom he had hoped would go off and undertake God's work in a neighboring valley. The American missionary and his American wife and two obstinately American kids lived in a prefab house that someone (surely not them) had lugged up into the mountains. Although he had known the young Papuan would-be missionary for several years, the American bible-thumper lived aloof from the community and had never invited his protégé into his house. Finally, the American felt the local lad had passed all the hurdles but one. He suggested the man join the family for a Coke, whereupon he asked him: "How will you know that you are the best Christian you can be?" The local man, who had grown up without shoes in a village with no running water, gazed around the inner sanctum, taking in the sight of a television and VCR, a radio-phone, a microwave, a refrigerator, a boom box, all powered by electricity generated by a tiny, state-of-the-art hydroelectric system the missionary had asked the local people to build on the stream behind the village. The young man pondered the question, because it was important for him to get it right. When would he be a Christian success? Finally, he replied. "When I have all the things you have."

Sounds like the Koreri cargo cult hasn't died out completely, in spite of the fact that the good people of Hatam-land deposit a sweet potato in the collection box every Sunday before raising their voices to praise Jesus.

The good folks of Papua share the universal desire for stuff. The first obstacle is to get the cash. The next obstacle is having the infrastructure to use the stuff they buy – no point in having a cell phone if you live outside the cell-phone coverage area, no point in having a refrigerator if you don't have electricity, no need for a motorcycle if you have no roads.

Barter economies give way quickly to cash economies. I saw the Consumer-Religion in action when I developed advertising campaigns for tiny packaging of single-use shampoo, single-meal monosodium glutamate, and four-pack blisters of analgesics, which replaced more expensive ten packs. It's a bit like getting a kid hooked on drugs. Give the kid the first couple of hits at a low price, and before you know it, he's yours.

There's no sign the Consumer-Religion is losing steam. In 2011 hundreds of Indonesians queued all night to buy a new BlackBerry smartphone; dozens were injured in the crush when the shop doors were opened. Sociology professor Sulfikar "Joel" Amir of the Nanyang Technological University in Singapore said that the Blackberry riot is "the materialization of what Marx once called material veneration, in which commodities become like a new God. They are like the people who go to religious temples to worship."

The Nature Conservation-Religion preachers started off with a list of commandments seemingly etched in stone by the Cosmic-Eco-Hairy-Thunderer. "Kill no protected species." "Respect the national park boundaries and enter not therein." "Wear colorful clothings and ornaments and stomp your feet in rhythmic patterns for the benefit of tourists." "Be thankful for whatever crumbs you may receive." "And, in case you weren't paying attention, don't even think about killing that bird of paradise."

But religions, like species, evolve.

Here's the modern gospel of the Nature Conservation-Religion, from a 1980s WWF publication.

First, admire the wisdom of the noble savage: "For centuries, the indigenous inhabitants of Wasur National Park in southeastern Irian Jaya [now Papua province] have actually improved the region's environmental equilibrium. Their practice of burning off dead vegetation in the dry season makes way for new plant growth and traditional hunting doesn't over-exploit species."

Second, in a tactic that has worked for countless religions, find a villain: "Everything was fine until the 1970s, when outsiders began entering the park to hunt and plunder such resources as timber and sand. The interlopers depleted wildlife stocks and degraded Wasur's forests, swamps and mangroves, jeopardizing the survival of many animals and plants, and reducing locals' meat supplies."

Finally, explain the religion: "After a lot of discussion and experiments, the government gave local people sole rights to hunt in the area using only traditional methods and to sell the meat in the nearby provincial capital, and asked them to help prevent outsiders from coming to poach game and fell trees."

I wanted to see this Nature Conservation-Religion at work and went to the Arfak Mountains, south of Manokwari.

> On the other side of the bay rises the great mass of the Arfak mountains, said by the French navigators to be about ten thousand feet high [actually about 7,700 feet maximum, 2,350 meters], and inhabited by savage tribes.[3]

I flew up there with a mission plane – twenty minutes flight instead of three days hard walk. Wallace had heard that the folks in the mountains were dangerous.

> These [Arfak tribes] are held in great dread by the Dorey people, who have often been attacked and plundered by them.[4]

Well, today the folks up in the hills are fine. It's so civilized now

---

3   *The Malay Archipelago*, 504.

4   Ibid.

that part of this area has been designated the Arfak Mountains Strict Nature Reserve. In the village of Minyambou, Zakarias Sayori showed me his garden on the perimeter of the reserve, where he grows carrots and beans. But he would have to carry the produce two days to reach the nearest market, and even then there would be no certainty anyone would want his meager productions or that he could recover his expenses. Where else might he earn some money? The quickest way for him to get cash would be to shoot a few birds of paradise and sell them to the Chinese merchants in the town. This is risky business because it goes against two of the four religions; the Government-Religion and the Nature Conservation-Religion both forbid the killing of the threatened birds.

Zakarias put down his bow and arrows and squatted down next to a shrub.[5] He motioned me to bend down next to him as he showed me a chunky grey caterpillar munching lazily on a skinny heart-shaped leaf, which WWF had encouraged him to grow. Zakarias, a member of the Hatam tribe, knows that the grey caterpillar will soon enter the chrysalis stage and emerge several weeks later as a dramatically colored black-and-yellow birdwing butterfly (*Troides oblongomaculatus*, closely related to varieties Wallace collected further west, in Buru and Sulawesi). Zakarias has been told – and this is where the Nature Conservation-Religion kicks in – that someone will pay him hard cash for that butterfly.

For several years Zakarias had nothing to put in his retirement account but faith. Then WWF and the local community solved the problem of setting up a marketing board and bingo, the 1,500 families participating in the butterfly farming program during 1993 grossed US$11,000 in just five months. The religion worked! Can Jimmy Swaggart claim similar immediate benefit?

Some people who promoted this butterfly/nature/cash-in-hand religion had second thoughts about it. "How will this change their behavior?" I found a similar attitude among people who promoted the community cooperative in Batang Ai in Sarawak. They whine,

---

5   He says he carries them because he's afraid of being ambushed by the bad guys from the next valley. That may have been true, and certainly people still kill each other. But I think most guys carry bows and arrows because they look cool.

"Have we introduced these simple people too abruptly to the cash economy? Have we built up unreasonable expectations? What have we wrought?" These people make lousy missionaries. A missionary should have no doubts.

The Nature Conservation-Religion is not this simple, of course. WWF has also actively promoted the concept of "management committees," made up of Hatam elders who decide where the nature reserve boundaries should be located and who should control access to the reserve. It is the Hatam who have decided the "eleven commandments" of the reserve (no construction of houses, only hunting with bow and arrows, no hunting of protected species, only small cooking fires allowed, and so on). This approach may well be the only way to achieve lasting conservation. But it is based on the assumption that people will change their behavior in fundamental ways. "Don't collect birds of paradise," the Nature Conservation-Religion outsiders say, offering vague arguments about biodiversity, national heritage, and so on. Change your behavior and earn eco-karma points. "Don't clear land on top of steep hillsides" is a related injunction, partly because it makes sense, but mostly because various powers from outside ask the local folks to follow this commandment.[6] "Trust us," the conservation-preachers say. "Believe in what we tell you and change your behavior. We can't prove that we're right. But have faith. You'll be rewarded. Well, maybe not you, but surely your children. Do it for your children."

Wallace was comfortable with such guided paternalism.

> I believe there is no example elsewhere of such striking results being produced in so short a time – [due to the system] which may be called a 'paternal despotism.' Now we Englishmen do not like despotism – we hate the name and the thing, and we would rather see people ignorant, lazy, and vicious, than use any but moral force to make

---

6   While it's hard to imagine there not being water in Manokwari, that's the argument. In order to save the caterpillars you have to save the forest. By doing this you ensure rainfall and prevent erosion, thereby keeping the streams flowing and so on. It's a favorite of the Nature Conservation-Religion priests.

them wise, industrious, and good. And we are right when we are dealing with men of our own race, and of similar ideas and equal capacities with ourselves. . . . Children must be subjected to some degree of authority, and guidance; and if properly managed they will cheerfully submit to it, because they know their own inferiority, and believe their elders are acting solely for their good. They learn many things the use of which they can not comprehend. . . . Under the best aspect of education, children are subjected to a mild despotism for the good of themselves and of society.[7]

Tough sell, this business of treating indigenous people like children.

WWF found this out to its dismay when it ran an ad featuring an Amazon Indian chopping a tree. "He's destroying his own rainforest. To stop him, do you send in the army or an anthropologist?" the headline read. The ad's body copy noted that "native peoples . . . are not the problem. They're the victims." "Native people," in this model, are children who need outside guidance and protection.

The perceived arrogant tenor of the ad spurred protests from a large number of indigenous-sensitive pressure groups. The Asia Indigenous Peoples Pact, for example, condemned the ad as "racist, misleading, inaccurate and cheap. We are angry that we are being used in such a way to make money, through this advertisement, which demonstrates the eco-colonialist character of the WWF."

Similarly, an ad by UK-based Survival International showed a befeathered South American Indian with the headline: "He'd have a better chance if he was a panda."[8]

---

7   *The Malay Archipelago*, 261–2.

8   British singer Sting generated visibility for his "Save the Amazon" campaign when he paraded Raoni, a Kayapo Indian chief, around Europe and the United States. Raoni sat stoically in European TV studios barechested, decked with beads, pig fat in his hair, proudly speaking garbled Portuguese. The reason for his lack of elocution was not that he was uneducated, but because he had a photogenic twenty-centimeter (eight-inch) wooden saucer implanted in his lower lip. Raoni's earnest pleas for conservation of nature and traditional lifestyles owe everything to a gentleman named Chief Seattle, the poster boy for traditional knowledge and conservation

They're heroes, even if they don't realize it. The conservation rhetoric now is that such indigenous folk "hold in trust for the world" the birds of paradise that foreigners care so much about conserving.

> Many of my journeys were made with the express object of obtaining specimens of the birds of paradise, and learning something of their habits and distribution; and being (as far as I am aware) the only Englishman who has seen these wonderful birds in their native forests, [I] obtained specimens of many of them.[9]

Wallace explained why they are called by that name.

> When the earliest European voyagers reached the Moluccas in search of cloves and nutmegs, which were then rare and precious spices, they were presented with the dried skins of birds so strange and beautiful as to excite the admiration even of those wealth-seeking rovers. The Malay traders gave them the name of 'Manuk dewata,' or God's birds; and the Portuguese, finding that they had no feet or wings, and not being able to learn any thing authentic about them, called them 'Passaros de Sol,' or Birds of the Sun; while the learned Dutchmen, who wrote in Latin, called them 'Avis paradiseus,' or Paradise Bird.

wisdom. Chief Seattle (a sharp eco-bluffer can score points by using his real name, Seathl) was a nineteenth-century chief of the North American Suwamish tribe who is reputed to have made an eloquent plea (in 1854, the year Wallace arrived in Asia) that the white man should leave the red man alone, since the Indian alone knows how to live as part of nature. Some skeptics claim that Chief Seathl's speeches ("We know that the white man does not understand our ways. . . . His appetite will devour the earth and leave behind only a desert. . . . If all the beasts were gone, men would die from great loneliness of spirit, for whatever happens to the beasts also happens to man. All things are connected. Whatever befalls the earth befalls the sons of the earth.") were ghostwritten by the white missionaries who accompanied Chief Seathl on his lecture tour.

9   *The Malay Archipelago*, 552.

John van Linschoten gives these names in 1598, and tells us that no one has seen these birds alive, for they live in the air, always turning toward the sun, and never lighting on the earth till they die; for they have neither feet nor wings. [An observation due to the fact that the feet and wings of the birds of paradise skins sent to Europe had been removed.][10]

In the crowded market of Biak, Irian Jaya, I visited the Pusaka ("heirloom") Art Shop. In the dusty, ill-lit confines I politely examined souvenir axes and Chinese export porcelain before asking: "Do you have any birds of paradise?"

Abdul Karim, the proprietor, unlocked a desk in the rear of the store and took out three skins – two of the lesser birds of paradise, *Paradisaea minor*, and a skin of the king bird of paradise, *Cicinnurus magnificus*, a small white-bellied male with a ruby head and two distinctive tail "wires," each tipped with a green feathered disc. Prices for the skins, which are from protected species: around US$20, before bargaining.

Wallace described the *Cicinnurus magnificus*.

By the Malays it is called 'burong rajah,' or king bird, and by the natives of the Aru Islands 'goby-goby.' This lovely little bird is only about six and a half inches [seventeen centimeters] long, partly owing to the very short tail. The head, throat and entire upper surface are of the richest glossy crimson red, shading to orange-crimson on the forehead, where the feathers extend beyond the nostrils more than half-way down the beak. The plumage is excessively brilliant, shining in certain lights with a metallic or glassy lustre. The breast and belly are pure silky white, between which color and the red of the throat there is a broad band of rich metallic green. . . . These plumes are concealed beneath the wing, but when

---

10 Ibid.

the bird pleases, can be raised and spread out so as to form an elegant semicircular fan on each shoulder. But another ornament still more extraordinary, and if possible more beautiful, adorns this little bird. The two middle tail-feathers are modified into very slender wire-like shafts, nearly six inches long, each of which bears at the extremity, on the inner side only, a web of an emerald-green color, which is coiled up into a perfect spiral disc, and produces a most singular and charming effect. . . . It is tolerably plentiful in the Aru Islands . . . and in every part of New Guinea which has been visited by naturalists.[11]

About the time Wallace was traipsing around here, milliners in the UK imported thousands of birds of paradise to make fashionable hats. Today you see stuffed birds of paradise ensconced in glass display cases in the better homes of Jakarta's nouveau riche. Birds of paradise are so valuable that some rural churches have been constructed with money earned by selling birds of paradise, contributed by heaven-seeking Papuan parishioners.

Are these Four Modern Religions – Government, Evangelical, Consumer, Nature Conservation – Four Horsemen of the Apocalypse? Or are they four cardinal directions that provide positive direction for people's lives? Wallace thought they were a constructive force.

The missionaries, however, have much to be proud of in this country. They have assisted the Government in changing a savage into a civilized community in a wonderfully short space of time. Forty years ago the country was a wilderness, the people naked savages, garnishing their rude houses with human heads. Now it is a garden.[12]

---

11   Ibid., 560–1.
12   Ibid., 261.

Four Modern Religions, as primal in their own way as fire, water, earth, air. What they have in common is sanctimony – their proponents know best.

But will they have a lasting impact? I wonder. People get tired of being lectured to. The Four Modern Religions are smug and self-righteous, full of self-serving posturing. They're irritating and boring. Like Cindy Lauper sang, "Girls just wanna have fun."[13]

I thought the Nature Conservation-Religion *had* Zakarias. He seemed so intense and committed, the way he showed me his caterpillars and spouted the conservation gospel.[14]

But clearly the soul is a complicated organ, and in this case the Consumer-Religion was stronger than the Nature Conservation-Religion. The day I was leaving Minyambou, I sought out Zakarias

---

13 WWF missed a chance to reach new audiences. In 2002 WWF – World Wide Fund for Nature – won a trademark dispute with WWF – World Wrestling Federation (which was forced to change its name to WWE – World Wrestling Entertainment). WWF (nature) had as spokespeople earnest, but boring, biologists and economists and politicians. The other WWF had Hulk Hogan, Macho Man, and a television audience of maybe one third of America and Canada, not to mention millions of people in faraway places like Malaysia, who take great pleasure in watching overweight, rude, ill-mannered white people body slam each other into oblivion. I suggested, to no avail, that WWF (nature) should sponsor a fluffy black-and-white wrestler called the Panda, tag-teamed with the Game Warden. And their opponents could be the Poachers from Hell, who could carry Kalashnikovs, just like Zambian elephant poachers, and who could threaten the Panda and the Game Warden with intricate and almost invisible wire snares. The Poachers from Hell could bribe the referee, just as their real-life namesakes bribe local law-enforcement agents. My attempt to reach the redneck market failed, and WWF (nature) is stuck with the rich, earnest, devoted, sanctimonious yuppified greenies, similar to the missionaries Wallace encountered.

14 The Nature Conservation-Religion has picked up numerous tips from the Evangelical-Religion about how to sell End of the World As We Know It myths. In the past forty years we have seen, and believed, dire predictions based on Acid Rain, the Population Bomb, Mass Species Extinction (in WWF we employed the metaphor that our earth is like a plane and the rivets in the plane are species. The plane can still fly if it loses one, two, maybe a dozen rivets/species. But soon the plane/earth will reach a critical point where the structural integrity is gone and, bingo, end of plane/earth), and Climate Change. The way to avoid such calamities was always the same: fund expert groups, stage big meetings, and hire experts to write academic papers. And pay me and my colleagues to generate public awareness about these looming tragedies.

to say goodbye. He admired my watch. Seeing that I wasn't about to give it to him, he offered me a trade: my Casio for a bird-of-paradise skin.

I said a prayer for all of us.

Washington, D.C., United States
United States Beetles are the most common forms of life on earth. Why are there so many?
No one is quite sure. How many are there? Plenty. Why did they so enthrall Wallace?
Just because. These specimens are from Wallace's personal collection, housed in a specially built
Victorian cabinet now owned by a Washington, D.C. lawyer.

Photo: Robert E. Heggestad

III

PASSION

SHIVA'S BEACH –
LATE AFTERNOON

Pulau Enu, Aru Islands, Indonesia

Just before rose-colored fireworks.

Alfred, I walk along this beach of life and smell death.

Like a dung beetle I am drawn to the rotting carcasses and bleached dog-sized skulls of green turtles, who have been slit open by fishermen desirous of the two hundred or so eggs in the reptile's egg cavity – fishermen either too impatient or too greedy to be satisfied with catching fifty or so eggs as they plop out during the normal laying cycle. The tasty turtle flesh has been left uneaten and has begun to rot; the only part used is the stomach, which makes a fine bait.

Earlier today the research group I was with had chased reputedly vicious Indonesian fishermen who came from Sulawesi and were laying nets to capture green turtles in the waters of this unguarded nature reserve. From a distance of a hundred meters we saw that their boat was full of live turtles, perhaps a hundred of the animals, all destined for Bali. Another Western conservationist and I urged the Indonesian captain to give chase. The Indonesian captain made a half-hearted attempt, but his heart wasn't in it. "Those men are armed and dangerous," said a frustrated Ating Sumantri, who was in charge of the Indonesian government's efforts to conserve sea turtles. "We don't have any soldiers, no weapons."

Just then Fata, an Indonesian game warden, jumped overboard and swam ashore to rescue the turtles that had been abandoned on the island when the poachers first saw our boat. Fata flipped over eight of the one hundred kilogram (two hundred and twenty pound) animals and watched them escape into the sea. Then three grounded poachers – who had been left on the island when their boat first spotted us and took off – chased him. Fata himself had to escape into the woods until we could rescue him.

What is a turtle worth? Worth getting stabbed for? Worth shooting someone for?

Later, in Bali, I wanted to know just how important turtle meat is in that island's Shivaistic Hindu culture. This was not merely being environmentally-politically correct. It's also good conservation to understand what emotional and spiritual values lie behind what seems, to outsiders, to be senseless consumption – some eighteen thousand turtles a year, according to one estimate.

"Turtle meat adds something to our ceremonies," explained I. B. Pangdjaja, head of public relations at the Bali governor's office.

"But it's not essential to the religious ceremony?" I asked.

"Like you eating turkey at Thanksgiving. Except it makes you strong."[1]

Odd, isn't it? Transported to Bali for satay, or worse, slit open for their eggs, and left to die on the beach. And then, against all odds, life goes on – more turtles come ashore to lay their eggs. Because we will stay on Pulau Env this particular night, the bad guys will stay away, and just maybe tonight's crop of eggs will hatch. Shiva thrives on contradictions. Do you need to destroy before you can create?

Shiva dances on a beach of skulls
Ecstatic
Life breathes below

---

1   Ask five Balinese about why they eat turtles and you'll get half a dozen answers. One good friend, a Hindu priest, argues that killing a turtle is a good deed, since it releases the animal's soul to reincarnate as a higher being. Another friend, with Balinese royal blood, says he has asked numerous holy men about this, and they couldn't find any religious reasons for eating turtle at ceremonies. "Anyone who tells you eating turtle is part of the religion is talking bullshit," he says.

AN INORDINATE FONDNESS FOR BEETLES

Gunung Mulu National Park, Sarawak, Malaysia

Why are there so many critters? And why do some folks spend their lives collecting and naming them? Could this be the fast track to immortality?

Before Wallace took off for Asia, he spent hours in the Natural History Museum in London taking notes of insects, birds, and mammals he was likely to encounter. But what about the yet-to-be-discovered species that obviously were not on display? He knew he would discover new species, and the only way to distinguish a new species is by comparing it to a known species. Out of necessity Wallace became a competent field taxonomist, and he relied on books and reports written by other scientists. Two volumes that he lugged around were C. L. J. L. Bonaparte's *Conspectus Generum Avium* (Leiden 1850), an octavo volume of some eight hundred pages containing all the known species of birds, and A. Boisduval's equally substantial *Histoire Naturelle des Insectes* (Paris 1836), which described all the known species of the *Papilionidae* and *Pieridae* families of Lepidoptera.

Increasingly, scientists eager to catalog things turn to local people for help. During boozy rice wine evenings in Iban longhouses in Sarawak, when the world took on a softer glow, I would turn the conversation toward bird omens. "This bird does this," one man might say, only to be contradicted by his wife. Then a neighbor would chip in, followed by his brother-in-law. After an hour's spirited discussion, we might agree on which bird is a bad omen for building a new longhouse. Then a couple of bottles of *tuak* later someone would re-open the discussion with a contradictory opinion. I cheated though. I *knew* which were the Official Iban Bird Omens. The list – along with the Iban and Latin names, a description of the call, and the prohibitions that result from sighting each bird – was published in a much-quoted article by J. D. Freeman (who spent far longer on his research than I did) that appeared in the *Sarawak Museum Journal.*

"Seek local wisdom" seems to be the operating principle for many PhD candidates. This tactic is fun, but researchers need to bear in mind that sometimes locals will give visitors the answer they think the scientists want to hear, and sometimes they'll bluff the visitors because they don't want to lose power by giving away information. I realize that some of the questions I asked my Iban friend would seem just as ridiculous if the situation were reversed and an Iban visiting me in America had asked: "How many races of people live in New York? How many cars are there? How many husbands did Liz Taylor have?" The answer to each of the above would be the same as if I had asked an Iban how many different fruits an orangutan eats. *Banyak.* Many.

How many ways are there for someone to become immortal? If you were Verdi, you could write an opera. If you were Faust, you could make an unsavory deal. Wallace has several claims to immortality – his theory of evolution by natural selection, his work in biogeography (and the naming of the Wallace Line after him), and the numerous new species he discovered, which were also named after him.

Besides having kids, the easiest fast track to immortality is to get something named after you (and hope that it is not a "synonym:" a species thought to be new but which, in fact, had already been described and named by someone else – a fate that happens to about three thousand "new" species annually).

According to the rules, the discoverer of a new species cannot name the plant or animal or bacteria after himself or herself. And so, since the beginning of taxonomic classification, people have named creatures after loved ones or have had beasts named in their honor. Wallace so honored the White Rajah of Sarawak.

> This species [Rajah Brooke birdwing butterfly], which was then quite new, and which I named after Sir James Brooke, [Wallace called it *Ornithoptera Brookeana*, now *Trogonoptera brookiana*] was very rare[1] . . . [and] one of the most elegant species known.[2]

Olaf Rudbeck gave Carl Linnaeus his first job. In thanks, Linnaeus saw to it that Rudbeck became a flower, *Rudbeckia hirta*, the American black-eyed susan. Linnaeus wrote to his professor: "So long as the earth shall survive, and as each spring shall see it covered with flowers, the *Rudbeckia* will preserve your glorious name."

Hugh Hefner, of *Playboy* fame, paid a bundle to have an endangered subspecies of marsh rabbit named after him: *Sylvilagus palustris hefneri*.[3]

---

1 *The Malay Archipelago*, 49.

2 Ibid., 48.

3 Wikipedia has a page devoted to creatures named after celebrities (who compiles this stuff? Bless them). Some highlights: *Agra schwarzeneggeri* a species of carabid beetle from Costa Rica with a bicep-like middle femora. Frank Zappa has at least three creatures bearing his name, including a jellyfish. George W. Bush, Dick Cheney, Donald Rumsfeld, and Darth Vader have beetles named after them. Adolf Hitler has a blind cave beetle from Slovenia, while SpongeBob SquarePants has a musky-smelling fungus from Malaysia. Mozart, Beethoven, John Lennon, Mick Jagger, Keith Richards, Sid Vicious, and Freddy Mercury all have their creatures, as do Buddha and

Sir Stamford Raffles, credited as being the founder of modern Singapore, was honored to have the world's largest flower named after him: *Rafflesia*.[4] The victory was perhaps Pyrrhic, since the parasitic *Rafflesia* is also the world's smelliest flower, sometimes referred to as the "stinking corpse lily."[5, 6]

I checked how Wallace rates in the taxonomic naming business. Just as no one has a definitive idea of how many species there are, no one can tell us how many species Wallace discovered, nor how many are named after him. Nevertheless, English ornithologist P. L. Sclater calculated Wallace found 212 new species of birds in the Malay Archipelago. When Wallace couldn't classify the specimens himself he asked others to handle the taxonomy; those colleagues honored him by naming seven species of birds *wallacii*, a number only equalled by eminent ornithologists Sclater and Coenraad Jacob Temminck. These include the mound-making scrub hen *Megapodius wallacii* and Wallace's standardwing bird of paradise *Semioptera wallacii* from the Moluccas. Darwin, in spite of his finches, has only one bird named in his honor: *Nothura darwinii*, a ground-nesting tinamou bird from the Andes in South America.

What is it about this boyish need to collect and put things into order?

Confucius (feathered dinosaur). A spider has been named after the baseball pitcher Dizzy Dean; it uses a sticky ball on the end of a thread to catch its prey. Marilyn Monroe is honored by *Norasaphus monroeae*, a fossil trilobite with an hourglass-shaped glabella, while Greta Garbo has a wasp described as "a solitary female."

4   This is a genus containing numerous species; a higher honor than having a single species named after you.

5   There is a historical precedent to name unattractive plants after enemies. Johann Siegensbeck denounced the prominent botanist Linnaeus as "lewd" and "loathsome" so Linnaeus retaliated by dubbing an "unpleasant small flowered weed," commonly called St Paul's wort, *Sigesbeckia orientalis*.

6   And newly named species can reflect a scientist's frame of mind: Terry Erwin, whose specialty is ground beetles of the genus *Agra*, named one very difficult species *Agra vation*. Wasp expert Paul Marsh was about to retire and named his last new species *Heerz lukenatcha*.

I was introduced to Henry Walter Bates. . . . He asked me to see his collection, and I was amazed to find the great number and variety of beetles, their many strange forms and often beautiful markings or colouring, and was even more surprised when I found that almost all I saw had been collected around Leicester [England], and that there were still many more to be discovered. If I had been asked before how many different kinds of beetles were to be found in any small district near a town, I should probably have guessed fifty or at the outside a hundred, and thought that a very liberal allowance. But I now learnt that many hundreds could easily be collected, and that there were probably a thousand different kind within ten miles of the town. . . . I therefore obtained a collecting bottle, pins, and a store-box; and in order to learn their names and classification I obtained, at wholesale price through Mr. Hills bookseller, Stephens 'Manual of British Coleoptera.'[7]

Darwin had a similar desire to study nature, which infuriated his self-righteous father, who bellowed, "You care for nothing but shooting, dogs, and rat-catching, and you will be a disgrace to yourself and all your family."

Towards the end of his life, Darwin reminisced about the buzz of collecting, noting, "I feel like an old war-horse at the sound of the trumpet when I read about capturing of rare beetles . . . it really almost makes me long to begin collecting again."

Swedish botanist Carl Linnaeus was to taxonomy what Brigitte Bardot was to the bikini.

One might argue that nature, by definition, is chaotic and disorderly. But Linnaeus strove for structure and logic; he was

---

7   *My Life*, Vol. 1, 237.

frustrated by the chaos in which mushrooms were mushrooms. Some were tasty, some were hallucinogenic, and some would kill you, but they were all mushrooms. Linnaeus lamented that there was no common, easy-to-use, universal system of nomenclature for different species, citing the case of the common tomato, which was described as *Solanum caule inermi herbaceo, foliis pinnatis incises* – the solanum with the smooth stem, which is herbaceous and has incised pinnate leaves.

Linnaeus's innovation was the currently used system of classifying organisms, a system that now includes kingdom, phylum, class, order, family, genus, and species. Think of a social structure, with kingdoms, provinces, cities, towns, villages, neighborhoods and individual houses. Or consider a pyramid, with the kingdom (plant or animal) as the base. In particular, Linnaeus's structure for genus and species names – what we commonly call binominal nomenclature (people are of the genus *Homo*, of the species *sapiens*) – is universally used. Hence: *Felix domestica* (the house cat) or *Lycopersicon esculentum* (the aforementioned tomato).

Linnaeus's early efforts resulted in the 1735 publication of *Systema Naturae*, an eleven-page pamphlet in which he grouped animals into the categories of Quadrupedia (four-footers), Aves (birds), Amphibia (including reptiles), Pisces (fish), Insecta, and Vermes (worms and other hard-to-categorize slimy creatures). But by the time he died, Linnaeus's *Systema Naturae* had grown to some three thousand pages containing classifications for roughly 7,700 plants and 4,400 animals. Jean-Jacques Rousseau said of him: "I know no greater man on earth."

In Genesis 2.20 it is written: "And Adam gave names to all cattle, and to the fowl of the air, and to every beast of the field."[8] Linnaeus famously thought of himself as the second Adam. *"Deus creavit, Linnaeus disposuit"* (God created, Linnaeus organized), he liked to say. The frontispiece of his *Systema Naturae* depicts its author in the Garden of Eden, evidently applying binominal nomenclature to all the creatures of Creation.

---

8   Which would make taxonomy the world's oldest profession.

I can't help smiling when I imagine Wallace setting out for a day of collecting, carrying bulky and comically cumbersome equipment that appears to be comprised mainly of dangling gadgets, but which are undoubtedly essential tools.

> My equipment is, a rug-net, large collecting-box hung by a strap over my shoulder, a pair of pliers for Hymenoptera, two bottles with spirits, one large and wide-mouthed for average Coleoptera, &c., the other very small for minute and active insects, which are often lost by attempting to drop them into a large mouthed bottle. These bottles are carried in pockets in my hunting-shirt, and are attached by strings round my neck; the corks are each secured to the bottle by a short string.[9]

Lots of scientists collect. Not all scientists catalog. Taxonomy is meticulous, painstaking, anal work, more suited to the geek than the swashbuckler.

But basic taxonomy is an almost primal practice.

There certainly is evidence that boys like to collect and classify. As a kid I could name every new model of car, every player on the 1955 Brooklyn Dodgers – Duke Snider, Pee Wee Reese, Jackie Robinson, Roy Campanella – every Roman coin in my collection. I was taxonomically inclined as a child, but as I grew up I lost the knack for cataloging my world. But Wallace never lost it.

We are all taxonomists, and we constantly sort our lives. We keep the toothpaste separate from the yogurt. We keep files. And we organize stuff. It's a gradient actually, the point when an accumulation of stuff becomes a collection, when a collection becomes an obsession. For most of us, that transition is normal

---

9   Letter concerning collecting in Si Munjon Coal Works, Borneo, April 8, 1855.
    Zoologist 13, no. 154 (August 1855): 4805.

and usually fun. For Wallace, the classifying of things was one of his *raisons d'être*.

Unlike many taxonomists, however, Wallace was able to extrapolate from the specific to the universal. In a letter to Henry Walter Bates, with whom Wallace explored the Amazon and Rio Negro rivers, Wallace indicated that his attention to detail was merely a stepping stone to something much bigger.

> After referring to a day spent in the insect-room at the British Museum on my way home, and the overwhelming numbers of the beetles and butterflies I was able to look over, I add: 'I begin to feel rather dissatisfied with a mere local [UK] collection; little is to be learnt by it. I should like to take some one family to study thoroughly, principally with a view to the theory of the origin of species.[10]

Wallace wanted to study each little detail, and from that intense scrutiny of bricks, try to imagine the cathedral – the symphony of life in the grandest sense.

But I'm also uncomfortable with Wallace's approach. By giving every little thing a name he separates himself from it. In a way, by naming things he *owns* them, which makes it impossible to be *one* with them. Edward O. Wilson, a Harvard professor generally acknowledged as the "father of biodiversity" for his efforts in making the general public aware of the variety of life and the need to protect this complexity, understands full well this need for people to recognize their unity with nature – he calls it "biophilia."

But maybe I'm not giving Wallace enough credit.

> I have, indeed, materials for a life's study of entomology, as far as the forms and structure and affinities of insects are concerned; but I am engaged in a wider and more general study – that of the relations of animals to space and time,

---

10 *My Life*, Vol. 1, 246–7.

or, in other words, their geographical and geological distribution and its causes.[11]

I'm a simpler boy than Wallace. I don't feel this need to classify each beetle, just as I try not to dissect each emotion. Perhaps my approach is the more juvenile and I'm simply locked into the gee-whiz stage, the state of mind where you lie on your back on a clear summer's night and wonder whether another boy, even if he is green with tentacles, might be lying on his back on a planet orbiting one of those distant specks of light and thinking similar thoughts of wonder.

Alfred Russel Wallace was expanding the frontiers of knowledge. But he probably could never imagine the extent of nature's diversity. It's a staggeringly large number, subject to interpretation and debate.

The question is simple: How many different species are there on earth?

The answer is equally straightforward: We don't know. Not by a long shot.

Harvard biologist Edward O. Wilson notes that we know roughly how many stars there are in the Milky Way: 10^{11}. We know the mass of an electron: 9.1×10^{-31}. "But how many species of organisms are there on Earth?" he asks mischievously. "We do not know, not even to the nearest order of magnitude."

Scientists estimate that there could be three million species on earth. Or there could be one hundred million. Nobody knows and nobody is likely to know in the near future.[12]

---

11 Ibid., 368.

12 I find the question of how many species there are endlessly fascinating, a bit like "How many angels dance on the head of a pin?" A 2011 study by Boris Worm of Dalhousie University in Nova Scotia and Camilo Mora of the University of Hawaii estimated there are 8.7 million species on the planet, plus or minus 1.3 million. In 1988 Robert May, an evolutionary biologist at the University of Oxford, estimated there are ten to fifty million species of land animals alone. Other estimates have ranged from as few as three million to as many as one hundred million. And we have only just begun to catalog the hard-to-see, unsexy creatures. The Mora and

Those huge numbers conceal gaping holes in our knowledge. Of those three to one hundred million species, scientists have named just 1.4 million species.[13] Consider for a moment that number. One point four million. Of those more than fifty percent are insects and forty percent of those are probably beetles. Beetles are the most common form of life on earth.

Increasingly I've been trying, not too successfully, to achieve a Zen mode where I divest myself of "things." I seek to be unencumbered, to be burdened by a minimum of possessions and details. Wallace, however, thrived on details; he defined his success, in large part, by sheer volume.

> [Bacan island] was a glorious spot, and one which will always live in my memory as exhibiting the insect-life of the tropics in unexampled luxuriance. The following notes . . . may be interesting to entomologists. October 15th, 33 species of beetles; 16th, 70 species; 17th, 47 species; 18th, 40 species; 19th, 56 species – in all about a hundred species, of which forty were new to me.[14]

Is this normal, Wallace's need to define himself by the number of collecting boxes he lugged around?

> When I arrived at the mines [in Sarawak] . . . I had collected in the four preceding months 320 different

Worm study estimates there are 660,000 species of fungi on earth, but other studies suggest the number may be as high as 5.1 million fungi species. And microbiologists are confident their tiny life forms will dwarf the diversity of animals, since a single spoonful of soil may contain ten thousand diffferent species of bacteria, many of which might be new to science.

13 And even that number, 1.4 million, is a rough estimate. The exact number of named species probably ranges from 1 million to 1.8 million, since some species have more than one name, usually because more than one person has described it.

14 *The Malay Archipelago*, 330.

kinds of beetles. In less than a fortnight I had doubled this number, an average of about 24 new species every day.[15]

How does one calculate the number of species on Earth when there is no master database? That's where Terry Erwin comes in.

Erwin works for the Smithsonian Institution in Panama. He had a simple but revolutionary idea that Wallace would have loved – he put a sheet on the ground and fogged rainforest trees with an insecticide. Being eco-politically correct, he used a pyrethrin-based insecticide that was not toxic to birds and mammals, thereby sparing himself the wrath of cuddly huggy animal lovers. Over three seasons of fogging *Luehea seemannii* trees, a tropical cousin of the linden, he counted a remarkable total of some 1,200 beetle species. Then, using some basic algebra, he extrapolated himself into the scientific headlines by declaring that the world might be home to more than 30 million insect species.[16]

Is Erwin right? I have no idea. But I find his calculations interesting. First, his work highlights the fact that while we know most of the birds and mammals, we are grossly ignorant about other forms of life, particularly the microscopic creatures and the creepy-crawlies.[17]

---

15 Ibid., 48.

16 Biologist Robert May describes Erwin's chain of logic (and assumptions): "First, [Erwin] needed to know how many of the beetle species he collected live specifically on *L. seemannii*, as opposed to being distributed across many kinds of trees. Erwin guessed that around 20 percent of the herbivorous beetles (the largest group in his sample) are specialized to each tropical tree species. On that basis, he estimated that one kind of tree holds an average of 160 species of canopy beetle.
"Second, Erwin inferred the plenitude of all insect species from the species density of canopy beetles. Forty percent of known insects are beetles; if this proportion applies in tropical tree canopies, then 400 kinds of canopy insects occupy each tree species.
"Third, Erwin supposed that the canopy contains two thirds of the insect species on the tree, implying a total of 600 insect species on every variety of tropical tree. Finally, he cited a widely accepted estimate that the earth supports 50,000 species of tropical trees. Multiplying 600 insect species times 50,000 tree species yields 30 million kinds of insects. The number of all species worldwide would obviously have to be much larger still."

17 We tend to overemphasize the charismatic megavertebrates – the tigers, pandas,

Biologist Robert May adds that, "Researchers currently uncover only about three to five new bird species a year. A similar situation holds for the 4,000 or so species of mammals, although on average about 20 species and one genus are discovered annually. About half of those are truly undiscovered species (mostly rodents, bats or shrews), whilst the others result from reclassifications of old species based on updated biochemical findings."[18]

New species turn up in strange places. Ecologist Mark van der Wal highlighted this when, in February 1991, he found two species of bats that were new to science and one that had only been described once. Interestingly, van der Wal did not make his discoveries while sloshing through isolated caves. Instead, he found these new bat species during just three visits to the market in Kotamobagu, North Sulawesi, where the flying mammals are regularly eaten.[19]

Similarly, Wallace enjoyed a bit of serendipity regarding some of his discoveries.

> One of the most curious and interesting reptiles [actually it is an amphibian] which I met with in Borneo [Sarawak] was a large tree-frog, which was brought me [sic] by one of the Chinese workmen. He assured me that he had seen it come down, in a slanting direction, from a high tree, as if it flew. On examining it, I found the toes very long, and fully webbed to their very extremity, so that when expanded they offered a surface much larger than the body. . . . As the extremities of the toes have dilated discs for adhesion, showing the creature to be a true tree-frog, it is difficult to imagine that this immense membrane of the toes can be for the purpose of swimming only, and the account of the

---

whales, and gorillas – but mammals represent just one quarter of one percent of all recorded species. The tiny critters are much more numerous.

18 Each year more than fifteen thousand new species are described.

19 van der Wal subsequently became famous, not for his new bat species but for surviving, with his pregnant girlfriend, a long and harrowing stint at the hands of Irianese kidnappers on the Indonesian half of New Guinea.

Chinaman that it flew down from the tree becomes more credible. This is, I believe, the first instance of a 'flying frog,' and it is very interesting to Darwinians, as showing that the variability of the toes, which have been already modified for purposes of swimming and adhesive climbing, have been taken advantage of to enable an allied species to pass through the air like the flying lizard. It would appear to be a new species of the genus Rhacophorus,[20] which consists of several frogs of a much smaller size than this, and having the webs of the toes less developed.[21]

Wallace-related serendipity struck Washington, D.C. lawyer Robert E. Heggestad.

In 1979, Heggestad, just out of a midwestern law school and having recently moved to the nation's capital, stopped by an antique store in Arlington, Virginia, looking for carpets. "The carpets weren't interesting," Heggestad recalls, "but before I left the dealer said 'How about a cabinet instead?' "

Heggestad examined an antique rosewood cabinet, as big as an old console-style TV.

"Nice furniture," Heggestad said.

"Aren't you curious about what lies inside?" prodded the dealer.

The cabinet's twenty-six originally hermetically sealed, pine drawers contained butterflies, moths, beetles, birds, dragonflies, spiders, grasshoppers, flies, shells, and botanical specimens — some 1,700 specimens in total. Heggestad had no idea what to make of this cabinet of natural cornucopia.

Heggestad bought the cabinet for US$600, paying in six installments. "Good decision," he says.

Heggestad became curious and learned that the cabinet contained Wallace's personal collection, including the only extant

---

20 Today identified as *Rhacophorus nigropalmatus*.

21 *The Malay Archipelago*, 49–50.

specimens collected by Wallace prior to his 1848 trip to South America, the only Wallace collection of British butterflies and moths, and the only Wallace collection of pods, seeds, wood specimens, and shells.

The cabinet survived several moves, and in each apartment Heggestad showed it off to visitors as a "show and tell piece," until a friend in the museum world said, "this belongs in a museum."

Indeed. David Grimaldi, a curator at the American Museum of Natural History in New York says: "the cabinet is a national treasure." David Furth, collections manager at the Smithsonian Institution's entomology department notes: "It's not just what we call an 'oh my' collection with pretty and big and bizarre creatures. This is as close as a modern scientist can get to looking at the world through Wallace's eyes."

The big mystery is how did the cabinet wind up in suburban Virginia?

The Virginia dealer had bought the cabinet from Anthony Juliano III from Drexel Galleries in Philadelphia, who purchased the collection in 1964 at an unclaimed baggage sale.

But before that? We can only speculate.

Perhaps Wallace took the cabinet with him on his year-long American lecture tour[22] in 1886 and 1887, and he either sold the collection, gave it away, or lost it.

Or the collection never left England, and it was sold by Wallace's descendants.

And then abandoned, to be bought at an unclaimed baggage sale.

I'm continually astounded by the joy some scientists exhibit when they are asked to describe a new specimen. It's quite wonderful, like a wine connoisseur describing a Grand Cru Burgundy (rich tannins, hint of elderberries and old sneakers, lingering aftertaste of stale marijuana smoke and hot fudge).

---

22   During which he was guided through a redwood forest by John Muir.

In the Aru Islands I asked botanists Hubert Turner and Hans P. Nooteboom to describe *Acanthus ilicifolius*. The root of this plant is used by cavorting men as a syphilis treatment the morning after visiting the whores in Dobo the night before. To me, it's an attractive bush, with holly-like leaves and thorns. But to Hubert Turner and his colleague Hans P. Nooteboom, it was a scientific challenge, and they had as much fun determining an accurate botanical description of the plant as some people have playing chess or completing a crossword or fishing for bass.

"It's obviously a perennial herb, glabrous, mangrove," Turner started.

"Obviously," Nooteboom said. "Let's look at the leaves. Opposite, narrowly elliptic, slightly to deeply incised, spiny at end of nerves."

And so it went. The stem is "spiny and lenticellate," the inflorescence "spike."

They got out the magnifying glass for the flower and decided, with as fervent a discussion as two boxing fans arguing whether Muhammad Ali in his prime could beat Mike Tyson, that what I called a "pretty purple and white flower" in reality has "one bract and two bracteoles. Zygomorphic, four sepals and imbricate, four petals, connate, into a flag, with an adaxial slit."

I watched, frankly fascinated. While both Nooteboom and Turner were good-natured men, they had seemed rather quiet. I hadn't come across this side of the two botanists in which they dissected that poor plant with the gusto of a chef trying to reverse-engineer a rival's signature dish.

They moved on to a trickier bit, the petal. "Broadly ovate, style one, stigma apical, minutely two lobed, margins entire, whitish base, purplish-blue at apex, stamens 4, adnate to corolla, alterni-petalous, dorsi-ventrally," Nooteboom observed. "Filament flattened, anthers basifix, opening introrse with longitudinal slit, margins fimbriate, ovaries superior, one ovule locule, placentation basal ascending."

"That's quite obvious in basal placentation," Turner said. Nooteboom nodded.

They got out the Swiss army knife for a dissection of the fruit. "Fruit capsule, seeds flattened and cordate, testa wrinkled, cotyledones erect, laterally beside each other."

And that's the plant that cures the clap.[23]

Today there's big money to be made in biodiversity.

When I was in Yap, a tiny Pacific island best known (if it is known at all) for its giant donut-shaped stone money, I went diving with Japanese researchers looking for marine creatures that could be used to develop new biological anti-fouling agents to replace toxic, barnacle-resistant paints, bacteria that "eat" spilled oil, phytoplankton that fix large quantities of atmospheric carbon dioxide, and unusual pharmaceuticals. Thomas Veach Long II, chairman and president of Maricultura, an American biotechnology company engaged in marine research, says that any of these categories could ultimately be worth US$5 billion a year.

That enormous figure, of course, refers to the commercial potential. But does a species have any value per se? What's a new beetle worth?

---

23   In our sloppy world, where few people pay attention to punctuation or spelling, it's reassuring that scientists take such great care in describing new species. Here's how Peter Ng described, in a scientific journal, a new species of freshwater crab (*Parathelphusa reticulata*) found in Singapore:

Parathelphusa reticulata. Diagnosis – Carapace transverse, smooth; gastric and branchial regions distinctly swollen, surfaces appearing evenly convex. Live coloration reticulate brown and orange for adults, distinctly spotted in juveniles; fingers of larger male chela bright orange, those on smaller male chela and female chelae, especially the dactylus, often pigmented black. External orbital angle broadly triangular, almost truncate; outer margin almost straight or convex. Epibranchial teeth directed forward. Anterolateral regions with few striae. Suture between male second and third sternal segments straight in adult males; distinct marginal notch present between third and fourth segments. Carpal and meral spines of chelipeds often reduced in larger specimens; fingers of larger male chela strongly curved, with distinct gape between them when closed. Ambulatory legs with distinct subterminal spines on meri of first three pairs, meri of last pair usually without subterminal spines. Lower margin of fourth male abdominal segment slightly concave in adults; seventh segment subequal to half length of sixth. GI stout, straight, directed upwards, outer margin of NG: Parathelphusa reticulata 243 proximal part of subterminal segment straight, not distinctly cleft at proximal part of outer margin, tip sharp, opening very small. G2 with long flagellum, almost as long as basal segment.

George Plimpton hosted an auction at the Yale Club that tried to sell the opportunity to name new species of frogs, plants, beetles, and butterflies. An unnamed beetle went for a bargain $1,000, with proceeds going to the Wildlife Conservation Society of Tanzania, which protects biodiversity in the country where the new and nameless creatures originated.

But otherwise, the celebrity auction was a flop. I think the problem was obtuse marketing. The organizers told potential bidders that they could "name a species." But the organizers might have done better if they had offered bidders a chance at immortality, à la Hugh Hefner and his rabbit.

There is immortality to be gotten by naming things. And there is transcendence to be obtained by observing how these creatures simply *are*.

One night at Gunung Mulu National Park in Sarawak, I leave the comfort of my campsite and wander into the rainforest. I stand still. The orchestra of a thousand prima donnas warms up, playing a symphony without a score. There's the drunken digital alarm clock, the doorbell from hell, the electronic washboard, the Star Trek fire engine, and the windup barking dog.

I ignore the mosquitoes and think of the tribe in Irian Jaya where boys attach a string to large humming beetles. By holding the beetles near their mouths, by modulating their exhalations, like blowing over the top of a bottle, the boys create an eerie music.

The scratching insect marimbas are met by hesitant trumpet blasts, a plaintive microwave buzzer is answered five minutes later by a lonely player in a symphony the next swamp over. Each insect and bird, frog and monkey plays to its own rhythm, ignoring melody, waiting for the tuning to end and the song to begin. The flutes from heaven kick in, and the percussionists from paradise join in with muffled whacks. A little night music becomes a whole lot of night music. What do they tell us? A celebration? Fears? Look at me. Enjoy me. Unseen, the bats silently cruise and pick out the unnamed creatures in the band.

No doubt Wallace enjoyed the same nocturnal invertebrate symphony. And he probably would have chuckled at the comments of the nineteenth-century British biochemist J. B. S. Haldane, an ardent Marxist who quit England for India, who was once approached by a distinguished theologian to ask what inferences one could draw about the nature of the Creator from the study of His Creation. Haldane replied, with his usual terseness, that, "God has an inordinate fondness for beetles."

THE ORGASMIC BUTTERFLY

Sanur, Bali, Indonesia

Drinking in a quiet bar in Bali, watching the world's greatest
dragueur, a Balinese guy with a ponytail and a great line,
convince two Australian nurses that their lives will be worthless
unless they make love with him.

Semantics can be funny. What did Wallace mean when he wrote
that "pure sensualism [is] the most degrading and most fatal of
all the qualities that tend to the deterioration of races and the
downfall of nations." And would he have argued that negative
"sensualism" is different to the ecstatic way he wrote about
capturing new butterflies and beetles, using expressions like
"pleasurable excitement" and "trembled with excitement?" Is
this all sublimation for passions unsaid?

I don't know what it is about Asia, whether it's the spicy goat
meat, or the sweaty climate, or the *jamu* medicinal herbs,
but there is musk in the air. It is an atmosphere infused with
pheromones, quite unlike anything I've felt anywhere else. Sex
is in the air as much as the scent of jasmine.

Iwatch the world's greatest *dragueur* at work and can't help but think of the Vogelkop gardener bowerbird.

I am sitting in a small restaurant in Sanur, one of the quieter resort areas of Bali, watching a guy named Made (say MAH-day) charm two holidaying Australian nurses.

I recall a trip to New Guinea in search of a glimpse of how the male of another species gets the girl.

I am in the Arfak Mountains of the Indonesian province of West Papua. My guide is Hangei Ullo, who has an uncanny resemblance to American actor Bill Cosby. He wears a Duran Duran T-shirt and a safety pin in his left ear (useful for removing thorns from his feet). Papuan Punk. It's raining, cold, and slippery. The narrow path has become a stream of muddy brown water, I slide back one step for each two and climb by grabbing roots. It is miserable, aching work and I love it. Near the top of a ridge, at about 1,400 meters (4,600 feet), we find the bower of the Vogelkop gardener bowerbird, *Amblyornis inornatus* (Schlegel), a dramatic meter-tall [yard-tall] maypole construction of sticks and twigs. In front of the bower, on two flattened areas like the terraces of a California split-level condo, the bird has placed some fifty candyapple-colored seeds, a pile of iridescent black beetle exoskeletons, a flattened dark-blue ABC battery case, and some light-blue wool thread. Some observers have seen bowers displaying carefully laid-out film containers, bottle tops, and a baseball-style cap.[1]

This is the avian equivalent of a Porsche or a ski chalet in Vail or an Armani suit, the method the male bowerbird uses to attract a female. Most male birds, particularly the gorgeous birds of paradise, which share this forest, use the glory of their own plumage to attract females. By contrast, the male of the Vogelkop gardener

---

1   In *The Malay Archipelago*, Wallace mentions the bowerbird only in passing, in a discussion of the distribution of birds. He also never mentioned another curious resident bird of New Guinea, the pitohui, whose skin and feathers contain powerful neurotoxic alkaloids, similar to those produced by some Colombian poison dart frogs. In a twist of symbiosis that probably would have amused Wallace, the birds do not produce the batrachotoxin poison themselves; it likely comes from the *Choresine* genus of beetles, part of the bird's diet. And equally surprising, Wallace sailed near Komodo and was apparently unaware of the existence of the giant lizards called Komodo dragons.

bowerbird, a species found only east of the Wallace line and only in the misty Arfak Mountains, is an unexciting brown with little sex appeal on his own. He needs to advertise.

The first European to see the extraordinary bower of this bird was the Italian naturalist Odoardo Beccari in 1872. His disclosure that this plain-colored bird built "an elaborate house of sticks with a front garden on which were arranged ornaments" was a sensational revelation rivaling the initial discovery of birds of paradise.

There's no accounting for what looks sexy in birds or in people. When I was staying in Sangburnih, in northern Bali, I played volleyball every afternoon with a bunch of Indonesian Army Special Forces, the Green Berets of Indonesia. As we went down to the river to bathe one evening, one of the soldiers, a virile guy about twenty, touched my silver and black chest hair. He wasn't gay, but I nevertheless stared at him and told him not to do that again. He seemed confused; this was simply a normal and friendly Southeast Asian gesture of same-gender tactility.

"Where can I buy the medicine to grow chest hair?" he asked.

"Hey, if I had the medicine I'd use it on my head, wouldn't I?" I joked.

He was not convinced there was no medicine.

"Why do you want chest hair?" I asked.

He made several universal gestures of sex and power. What is it with body hair? Some Jungian collective unconscious throwback to our hirsute pre-human ancestors?

Wallace noted cultural differences about the perceived value of facial hair.

> Most Europeans, being gifted by nature with a luxuriant growth of hair upon their faces, think it disfigures them, and keep up a continual struggle against her by mowing down every morning the crop which has sprouted up during the preceding twenty-four hours. Now the men of

Mongolian race are, naturally, just as many of us want to be. They mostly pass their lives with faces as smooth and beardless as an infant's. But shaving seems an instinct of the human race; for many of these people, having no hair to take off their faces, shave their heads. Others, however, set resolutely to work to force nature to give them a beard . . . . [One] man had succeeded, by assiduous cultivation, in raising a pair of mustaches which were a triumph of art, for they each contained about a dozen hairs more than three inches long, and which, being well greased and twisted, were distinctly visible (when not too far off) as a black thread hanging down on each side of his mouth.[2]

I think Wallace missed the point. For many Indonesians, body and facial hair equals sexual power. Indonesia seems locked in a teenage testosterone fog. Indonesians do it, often stutteringly and clandestinely, whenever possible. But more often they talk about doing it. They pretend they are doing it. They imagine doing it.

By contrast, I marvel at America's schizophrenia about sex. Americans insinuate and smirk, but they are remarkably hypocritical about sex – remember the sanctimonious uproar when Janet Jackson had a brief wardrobe malfunction and a bit of her breast was exposed during a broadcast of the Super Bowl? Straight-laced Wallace might have joined the furor.

Pure sensualism [is] the most degrading and most fatal of all the qualities that tend to the deterioration of races and the downfall of nations.[3]

Indonesians are oriented toward performance, and the search for magic sexual medicine permeates Indonesian commerce. In a herbal drug store in Surabaya I did some comparison shopping and

---

2   *The Malay Archipelago*, 478.

3   "Human Selection." *Fortnightly Review*, n.s., 48, no. 285 (September 1890): 329.

sought the advice of the women behind the counter.

"How's this?" I asked, holding up a pack of Kim Loo Tan Forte High Potency tablets (made by Kong Huat Tong Co., Ipoh, Malaysia), which boasted: "A decided advantage over a number of similar preparations of quack reputation."

"It's okay," the sales ladies giggled, not used to this kind of questioning.

Not convinced, I read the label of Nanbao Super Capsules, from China National Chemicals Import and Export Corp, Tientsin. "Ever fills you with the sap of youth," the label boasted. It is effective in treating "renal inadequacy, deficiency of active aspect of an effective position, impotence, ejaculation praecox, psychasthenia, decline of memory, lumbago, leg weakness, wetness and coldness in the kidney, wet dream, sexual excess, decline of sexuality, palpitation of heart, premature senility, inborn deficiency and others of sexual involution." Primary ingredients: testes of donkey and dog.

The women gave me a thumbs up. I asked them how they knew which preparations were the most effective. "Customers report back," they ambiguously replied.

But the most popular sex tonics are numerous Indonesian herbal medicines, called *jamu*. Unlike traditional medicine in many countries, *jamu* is often manufactured in modern factories under supervision of the Ministry of Health and advertised with modern packaging and publicity. Single doses cost less than a Coke. I like to drink it at upper-class *jamu* stands, where it is mixed in a blender with *beras kencur*, honey, and the yolk of a raw duck egg. It tastes like sweetened cigarette butts.

The saleswomen, a twentysomething called Tati and an older woman who more formally identified herself as Ibu ("mother") Suryono, offered mixed opinions about the efficacy of Jamu Kuat Pria (literally "strong man" – there isn't much subtlety in *jamu* brand names), whose pack illustrates an upraised fist in a power salute. It promises "improved manhood, vitality and lust of young or old man."

"How about this?" I asked, showing them a pack of Jamu Pria Perkasa-Piskal 17 featuring a kitschy photo of a cool dude dressed in a Western jacket, wearing dark glasses and a white

Panama hat. Thumbs down.

Jamu Sehat Perkasa, which, like all *jamus*, is required by law to list its herbal ingredients (*Zingiberis rhizoma* 25%, *Coriandri fructus* 5%, *Curcumae rhizoma* 40%, *Isorae fructus* 10%) is "good for men who feel weak, short of breath and who suffer from backaches. It enhances the sexual relationship between husband and wife through the man's revitalized virility." Tati, the younger saleswoman, acknowledges that this is the brand her husband uses. "How's your relationship?" I asked. "Not bad," she said, straight-faced.

A package of *pasak bumi* (literally "the earth shakes") features as its main ingredient the plant of the same name: *Eurcomae* [sic] *longifolia radix* [sic, correct name: *Eurycoma longifolia*]. One package shows a shirtless man flexing his muscles.

Pasak bumi, called *tongkat Ali* in Malay or "Ali's walking stick," has been the subject of extensive mythology and research. Sam Teng Wah and Chan Kit Lam, of the Universiti Sains Malaysia in Penang, Malaysia, isolated about a dozen compounds from the single deep taproot of *Eurycoma longifolia* Jack (Simaroubaceae family), a subspecies, and found several have anti-malarial properties, or act as an anti-pyretic and hypothermic when inoculated into febrile and normal mice. "Unfortunately, none [of the compounds] as yet could be tied to the alleged increase in male libido arising from regular consumption of the root extracts," the scientists report. The sales ladies disagreed with the Malaysian scientists. Does *"pasak bumi"* get the job done? *"Bagus,"* they agreed. Bloody good.

I tell the women that Ketut Santya, a *dukun* medicine man in Sangburnih, Bali, said that *pasak bumi* is for malaria and makes a lousy aphrodisiac. The women shrug. For sex, Santya recommends the patient drinks a concoction of coconut, egg yolk, turmeric, honey, and then eats durian. "But to be really strong," he says, find the common shrub *jambu biji*, with a stem that flows and wiggles in the water current. *"Gini gini,"* he says, making an easily understood motion, which implies the consumer of the plant will wiggle in the same way.

Wallace never wrote specifically about sex or romance, and there's no reason why he should have. He was, after all, a Victorian scientist writing a serious travel book.

Yet, Wallace sublimated his passion by describing butterflies and birds with gushing Mills and Boon-like breathlessness.

He had bird passion in Malacca.

> Handsome woodpeckers and gay kingfishers, green and brown cuckoos, with velvety red faces and green beaks, red-breasted doves and metallic honey-suckers, were brought in day after day, and kept me in a continual state of pleasurable excitement.[4]

And butterfly passion in Sulawesi.

> On our way back in the heat of the day I had the good-fortune to capture three specimens of a fine Ornithoptera, the largest, the most perfect, and the most beautiful of butterflies. I trembled with excitement as I took the first out of my net and found it to be in perfect condition. The ground color of this superb insect was a rich shining bronzy black, the lower wings delicately grained with white, and bordered by a row of large spots of the most brilliant satiny yellow. I gazed upon my prize with extreme interest, as I at first thought it was quite a new species. It proved, however, to be a variety of Ornithoptera remus, one of the rarest and most remarkable species of this highly esteemed group.[5]

Not to mention *more* butterfly passion in Bacan.

> The beauty and brilliancy of this insect are indescribable,[6]

---

4   *The Malay Archipelago*, 40.

5   Ibid., 225.

6   Wallace was describing a new species of birdwing butterfly, more than eighteen centimeters (seven inches) across the wings, which are velvety black and fiery orange.

and none but a naturalist can understand the intense excitement I experienced when I at length captured it. On taking it out of my net and opening the glorious wings, my heart began to beat violently, the blood rushed to my head, and I felt much more like fainting than I have done when in apprehension of immediate death. I had a headache the rest of the day, so great was the excitement produced by what will appear to most people a very inadequate cause.[7]

And *still more* butterfly passion in Dobo.

I had the good-fortune to capture one of the most magnificent insects the world contains, the great bird-winged butterfly (Ornithoptera poseidon). I trembled with excitement as I saw it coming majestically toward me, and could hardly believe I had really succeeded in my stroke till I had taken it out of the net and was gazing, lost in admiration, at the velvet black and brilliant green on its wings, seven inches across, its golden body, and crimson breast. It is true I had seen similar insects in cabinets, at home, but it is quite another thing to capture such one's self – to feel it struggling between one's fingers, and to gaze upon its fresh and living beauty, a bright gem shining out amid the silent gloom of a dark and tangled forest. The village of Dobbo held that evening at least one contented man.[8]

Max van Bloey is one of the finest field botanists in the world, having an encyclopedic knowledge of plants, ranging from the flora of Tahiti to the flora of the Indian subcontinent. He is also

---

7   *The Malay Archipelago*, 342.
8   Ibid., 434.

one of the most charming travel companions one could wish for.

We were together in Aru, and one afternoon he came back to our base camp beaming.

"What's up?"

"New species."

"What is it?"

Max gave me the sample, and showed me his notebook.

"No. 6511. STRONGYLODON? [he used the indication "?" because he was not sure of the identification, since the genus is not recorded from Aru] liana, infl. caulifloris and on young twigs, small flowers, and pods, flower orange, pods inflated, ripe dehiscent red/black, slide."

I asked him how he felt at the moment of discovery.

"It was pure luck that I found the Strongylodon. I was very excited, I recognized it immediately, and it almost made me jump up and down."

His feelings in one word?

"Ecstasy. I know *exactly* how Wallace felt. I don't think you can explain this kind of feeling to someone who is unfamiliar with biological exploration. It's something more than just satisfaction or just pleasure."

"Max, is it as good as sex?"

Max thought a moment.

"I'd say it was comparable to very good sex . . . and there's no disease."[9]

I was swimming in a tidal pool in the Galapagos Islands with several fur seals. A pelican feather floated on the surface, and I grabbed it and dove down about a meter. I let the feather loose, and it started to float toward the surface. As I reached to get it, a fur seal flashed in and captured it in her mouth. She swam a couple

9   Alas, Max's passion had a limited shelf life – upon consulting the taxonomic library at his university in the Netherlands, he found that the plant he thought he had discovered wasn't a new species after all.

of meters away and released it, like a dog releasing a ball with the expression "let's play." I swam to the feather and just as I made a grab for it, the fur seal swooped in again and played keepaway. This went on for about five minutes until I was exhausted and freezing. I've never since had an experience quite like that, to play with a wild animal.

It's been said that Joseph Conrad modeled the naturalist Stein in *Lord Jim* on Wallace (just as Arthur Conan Doyle modeled the naturalist Stapleton in *The Hound of the Baskervilles* on Wallace).[10] Historian Lloyd Fernando writes: "Through Stein's [Wallace's] orgasmic taxonomic discoveries, Conrad illustrates the gap between notions of human idealism and sordid reality. Pointing to a specimen in his collection, Stein rhapsodizes on the giddy excitement he had felt on capturing it, and adds, 'Look! The beauty – but that is nothing – look at the accuracy, the harmony. And so fragile! And so exact! This is Nature – the balance of colossal forces.' Wallace's activities as a collector have here inspired Conrad's metaphor for creative tension between human aspirations and intrinsic human grossness. 'Man should not struggle to climb into the air, for he will surely fall back to the earth,' Stein says. 'He should rather, with the delicate exertion of hands and feet, make the dirt base keep him up.' "[11]

I sit in Agung's Cafe in Sanur, a simple open-air place with rattan chairs, some potted palms, a few *Barong* masks. A Balinese guy in

---

10 Arthur Conan Doyle also referred to Wallace, and his friend Henry Bates, in *The Lost World*. Besides being an admirer of Wallace, Conan Doyle was also a strong believer in spiritualism and noted that "an invisible and friendly presence" that provided him with literary advice was the ghost of Wallace.

11 As science writer David Quammen said: "Wallace was a man of crotchety independence and lurching enthusiasms. If he hadn't existed, it would have taken a very peculiar Victorian novelist to create him."

a puffed white shirt with bunched cuffs, trendy black pants, and ponytail, sings terribly and plays guitar even worse. He knows only the first line of dozens of songs: "I'm leaving on a jet plane . . . dum dum de dum de dum de dum."

Two Australian girls sit nearby. They are intensive care nurses from Sydney, Jackie and Betina. Jackie: blond, oval face, Betina: short curly hair, both normally attractive. I order *gado-gado* and a beer, having been writing all day and needing food but not necessarily company. The singer strums his basic three chords, "No woman no cry . . . dum dum dee dum dum." Made enters, and the mood changes. He is solid, ridiculously handsome, with the best set of teeth this side of a Pepsodent commercial. A smile to seduce Mother Theresa. Made casually takes the guitar from the performer and sings a few songs. Not that he knows too many more lyrics than the other guy, but Made's style is first rate. And he is cosmopolitan. He could be the owner; he works the room like Toots Shor. He goes from table to table. He talks about the time he had dinner with Mick Jagger in Ubud, his surfing experiences, his trips to Australia where he stayed with a well-known publisher, his trips to Europe. He banters with a Swiss couple using a few words of German; he explains he was the guest of one of Zurich's most famous chefs. He eventually moves over to the Australian's table, next to mine, and says to Betina: "Give me your hand." And she gives it. He massages her hand, a sensual thing. He massages hard, but she likes it and soon enough her eyes close and she is in her own world. Later he does Jackie's. "Much stress." But she too relaxes. Once in a while he will give her a hug, a peck on the cheek. She does not object. I am at an adjacent table, and somehow I fall into conversation with Made. All the time Made is massaging the girls' hands, he continues to talk with me. We discuss the *banjar* system of irrigation, wind surfing, and Mick Jagger's wedding. Made recounts how, as a kid, he used to sell postcards on the beach and brags about his love for blue marlin fishing. The night wears on. How I envy people who can play guitar and sing. I'm just a spectator tonight. No one moves, nowhere else to go at 1:00 a.m. The Aussie girls move off with Made to a disco, and then, I have no doubt, one or both of them will sleep with him. I don't begrudge any of them anything. Tonight I'm happy alone and get on my mountain bike and head home, slaloming around sleeping dogs.

THE LAST PERKENIER

Banda, Moluccas, Indonesia

How could one now ignored spice have generated such mayhem?

Wallace made three quick visits to the Banda islands, of one or two days each, in December 1857, May 1859, and April 1861.

While Banda had a few curious creatures, Wallace had time to shoot just eight different birds. He instead focused on the scenery and the dynamics of Dutch colonial rule in what he called "the chief nutmeg-garden in the world."

For thousands of years, Arab, Malay, and Chinese traders, along with Portuguese, Spanish, British, and Dutch mercenaries and navies, visited the Spice Islands – the traders to negotiate, the Europeans to conquer and manage. Wallace's visit to Banda triggered him to provide some of his most inconsistent ruminations on the relative merits of the European colonial systems versus self-government.

Roughly during the period that Wallace visited the Spice Islands, American spice traders from Salem, Massachusetts, had entered the game that had been the comfortable preserve of the Dutch, French, and British. And, in 1860, a free-trade agreement was finalized between Britain and France, which sparked off successive agreements between other countries in Europe. The colonial world, built on economic monopolies, was shifting.[1]

I seek out places with evocative names and history – Makassar, the Irawaddy, Dehra Dun, Gilgit, Kuching, Palembang, Siem Reap, Ayutthaya, Kathmandu, Malacca, Waltzing Banana Island. It was natural that I wanted to visit Banda. Indonesia has no shortage of evocative places, but Banda is surely near the top. Adored by scuba divers, revered by history buffs, appreciated by photographers who like to look at its volcano and crystalline waters, cherished by romantics for its isolated location and friendly folks, the Banda islands are on the radar of travelers who generally prefer to fly beneath the radar.[2]

I sought out the last *perkenier* of Banda.[3]

In 1992, when I took a tiny boat from the main island of Banda Neira to the adjacent island of Banda Besar, I found Wilhelm "Benny" van den Broecke sitting on his porch, as if he had been expecting me.

In Benny's living room hung a famous and valuable painting of Benny's ancestor, Pieter van den Broecke,[4] who came to Banda with

1 And the economic cartels were giving way to government control. In 1858 the British government took direct control of India from the British East India Company, and in 1863 France conquered southern Vietnam.

2 Visitors to Banda have included Princess Diana, Mick Jagger, and Jacques Cousteau.

3 Although widely used in Dutch, Indonesian, and English history books and articles, the Dutch term *perkenier* rarely appears in dictionaries of those languages. It is roughly equivalent to the English term "planter" or "estate manager," but only in the context of nutmeg and other spices grown by Dutchmen in eastern Indonesia.

4 Pieter van den Broecke's life was as colorful as his portrait. A Dutch cloth merchant, while in Mocha, Yemen, he drank what he described as "something hot and black, a

Jan Pieterszoon Coen and became the Dutch East India Company (VOC) administrator in the Banda islands. The 1663 painting, by Frans Hals, shows a prosperous and smiling large-nosed burgher with untidy hair, a long moustache, and a pointed and waxed "van Dyke" beard, wearing a brown velvet shirt that is decorated with lace on the wrists and collar. He has the look of a mischievous seventeenth-century man-about-town.

Benny, by comparison, is a sixtysomething, skinny, unglamorous man of mixed ancestry (his mother was Indonesian, father Indonesian-Dutch). On his aging skinny legs he wears worn brown socks and faded blue scuba-diving booties. He remembers better times.

I soon learned that in order to understand Benny, I had to understand his ancestor Pieter van den Broecke. And that meant understanding nutmeg, a now insignificant commodity that changed the world.

Wallace wasn't particularly impressed by the people of Banda.

> The natives of Banda are very much mixed, and it is probably that at least three-fourths of the population are mongrels, in various degrees of Malay, Papuan, Arab, Portuguese, and Dutch.[5, 6]

He felt they were an unremarkable lot until the good offices of the Dutch came to their aid.

coffee." He was one of the first Europeans to describe societies in West and Central Africa and to develop trade strategies for commerce along the African coast. After capturing a Portuguese ship in 1611, he brought a cargo of some 30,000 kilograms (65,000 pounds) of ivory to Amsterdam (if the 30,000 kilogram number is accurate, this represents some 2,500 African elephants).

5   *The Malay Archipelago*, 297.

6   Wallace wasn't the first European to disparage the residents of Banda. Early-sixteenth-century Italian traveler Lodovico de Varthema found the islands "savage" and the people "like beasts . . . so stupid that if they wished to do evil they would not know how to accomplish it."

There is nothing very remarkable in them. They are Malays – Mohammedans, but retaining many pagan customs and superstitions. They are very ignorant, very lazy, and live almost absolutely on rice alone, thriving upon it, however, just as the Irish do, or did, upon potatoes. They were a bad lot a few years ago, but the Dutch have brought them into order by their admirable system of supervision and government.[7]

I wonder what Wallace would have made of Benny.

Nutmeg today has become a novelty spice, used sparingly by Americans to flavor eggnog and pumpkin pie.[8, 9]

But in its heyday, nutmeg (along with cloves from Ternate, where Wallace had his base camp) was the holy grail of merchants and conquerors.

It has all the attributes of a precious commodity – it was scarce and therefore ridiculously expensive. It came from a distant land whose location was a closely guarded secret. To obtain the spice a merchant (or country) had two choices – pay an exorbitant amount for delivery at home – a price involving a cut to a dizzying number of anonymous traders and merchants. Or send out navies and merchantmen and administrators to largely uncharted and dangerous waters to try to find, and then to manage, and finally to control, the source of the fruit. This was a high-risk high-reward pastime.

And to make nutmeg even more tantalizing, it came from just one tiny island group in the back-of-beyond.

---

7   *My Life*, Vol. 1, 381.

8   The English word "nutmeg" comes from the Latin *nux*, meaning nut, and *muscat*, meaning musky.

9   Nutmeg is commonly used in various cuisines: in an iced dessert in Penang, a jam in Indonesia, and as a flavoring in Mughlai, Dutch, Middle Eastern, and Japanese cuisines. Mark Pendergrast, in his history of Coca-Cola, leaked a copy of the soft drink's closely guarded formula; nutmeg is one of the secret ingredients.

Those beautiful but almost impossible to find islands, of course, were Banda. Rarely has such a tiny piece of real estate had such a major impact on world history.

Nutmeg had a reputation for some two thousand years, during which Chinese, Malay, and Arab traders sent small quantities of the spice to Europe.

In the first century AD, Roman author Pliny speaks of a tree bearing nuts with two flavors.[10] In the sixth century, nutmegs were brought by Arab merchants to Constantinople and twelfth-century Holy Roman Emperor Henry VI had the streets of Rome fumigated with nutmegs before his coronation. In the fourteenth century, half a kilogram of nutmeg cost as much as three sheep or a cow.

Nutmeg, *Myristica fragrans*, has been used in medicine since at least the seventh century. In the nineteenth century it was used as an abortifacient, which led to numerous recorded cases of nutmeg poisoning.[11] During the Elizabethan period, frightened lords and ladies in England sought nutmeg as a cure for the plague. More mundanely, it was widely used as a flavoring, general medicinal tonic, and preserving agent.

I asked Benny to show me the fruit that caused such a fuss.

He handed me an apricot-sized fruit. On breaking the fibrous outer shell, I saw a bright red filigree with the consistency of electrical tape surrounding a shiny black nut. The filigree is the mace; the nut is the nutmeg.

The mace is left to dry in the sun.

The nutmeg is roasted for a week on the second floor of a heating shed near Benny's house, producing a sweet and musky incense-like smell.

I then asked Benny about the bloodshed and mayhem this attractive fruit has caused. He had no recourse but to point to the portrait of his distant ancestor of fourteen generations earlier, Pieter van den Broecke.

---

10 The nutmeg seed and its outer, filligree-like encasement called mace.

11 Although used as a folk treatment for various ailments, nutmeg has no proven medicinal value today.

Pieter van den Broecke came to Banda in 1621, with Jan Pieterszoon Coen, and was appointed administrator of the region.

That sounds innocent enough, but there are blood and guts in the story.

Jan Pieterszoon Coen is one of the poster boys of All-Time Bad Colonialism. He was the first governor-general of the VOC (Vereenigde Oost-Indische Compagnie, the Dutch East India Company) who, in 1621, was given the job of enforcing the Dutch monopoly of Banda's spice trade, a task he did with gruesome brutality and arrogance (and, one might assume, with the cheerleading support of Pieter van den Broecke and other administrators).

In 1621 well-armed Dutch soldiers landed on Banda Neira island. The Bandanese *orang kaya* (literally "rich men" who were the local authorities) were forced at gunpoint to sign an unfeasibly arduous treaty, one that was in fact impossible to keep, thus providing Coen with an excuse to use superior Dutch force against the recalcitrant Bandanese. The Dutch quickly noted a number of alleged violations of the new treaty, in response to which Coen launched a punitive massacre. Japanese mercenaries were hired to deal with the *orang kaya*, forty of whom were beheaded with their heads impaled and displayed on bamboo spears. In addition, it is suggested that perhaps fourteen thousand people out of an estimated total population of fifteen thousand were killed by Dutch muskets and Japanese swords, making the seizure of Banda one of the most brutal commercial takeovers in history. The Dutch subsequently resettled the islands' nutmeg plantations with imported slaves, convicts, and indentured laborers. The VOC directors in Amsterdam later concluded that Coen should have acted with greater moderation, but nevertheless awarded him a bonus of three thousand guilders for his commercially valuable services.

Thus began, under the flag of commerce and later under direct government rule, more than three hundred years of Dutch colonial control of the Spice Islands.

Wallace was a cheerleader for the Dutch system, if not the Dutch people.

> Personally, I do not much like the Dutch out here, or the Dutch officials; but I cannot help bearing witness to the excellence of their government of native races, gentle yet firm, respecting their manners, customs, and prejudices, yet introducing everywhere European law, order, and industry.[12]

He felt that the Dutch had a national obligation to maintain economic domination. At the time of his visit the Dutch monopoly of the spices was under threat, a situation that Wallace said "appears exceedingly injudicious and quite unnecessary."

> A small country like Holland can not afford to keep distant and very expensive colonies at a loss; and having possession of a very small island where a valuable product, *not a necessary* [sic] *of life*, can be obtained at little cost, it is almost the duty of the state to monopolize it. [italics Wallace][13]

Wallace, who generally rooted for the little guy, ignored the brutal history and defended the Dutch colonial mentality and strategy, arguing that abolishing Dutch control of the nutmeg trade would "injure the natives."

> Nothing is worse and more absurd than the sneering prejudiced tone in which almost all English writers speak of the Dutch government in the East. It never has been worse than ours has been, and it is now very much better;

---

12 *My Life*, Vol. 1, 382.

13 *The Malay Archipelago*, 295.

and what is greatly to their credit . . . they take nearly
the same pains to establish order and good government
in those islands and possessions which are an annual
loss to them, as in those which yield them a revenue. I
am convinced that their system is *right* in principle, and
ours *wrong* . . . there is a strong party against the present
system, but that party consists mostly of merchants and
planters, who want to get the trade and commerce of the
country made free, which in my opinion would be an act
of suicidal madness, and would, moreover, seriously injure
instead of benefiting the natives. [italics Wallace][14]

And while he vocally praised the Dutch colonial system, he
heartily disparaged the British.

The Dutch system attempts to supply this missing link
[a paternalistic, almost feudal government], and to bring
the people on by gradual steps to that higher civilization
which we (the English) try to force upon them at once.
Our system has always failed. We demoralize and we
extirpate, but we never really civilize.[15]

Curious as Wallace's opinions are, he came up with knicker-
twisting logic to defend the Dutch colonial philosophy as a way
to generate even more profits to the colonizers. Wallace suggested
a reversal of the commonly understood colonial mentality in
which the colonies are producers of goods and raw materials for
sale and benefit of the specific colonial power in Europe. Instead,
Wallace predicted that after a period of improved living conditions
and income, colonial populations would have sufficient means to
become *consumers* of European goods.

Under such a system [good roads, strict justice towards

---

14 *My Life*, Vol. 1, 382.

15 *The Malay Archipelago*, 206.

the natives, introduction of a good system of cultivation as in Java, production of sheep, horses, and wheat] the natives would soon perceive that European government was advantageous to them. They would begin to save money, and property being rendered secure, they would rapidly acquire new wants and new tastes, and become large consumers of European goods. This would be a far surer source of profit to their rulers than imposts [sic] and extortion, and would be at the same time more likely to produce peace and obedience, than the mock-military rule which has hitherto proved most ineffective.[16]

This Pollyannaish viewpoint eventually came partly true. Today, well after the colonial era, independent Indonesia (and Malaysia, Singapore, and Vietnam) eagerly consume Western frivolities like McDonald's, Louis Vuitton, and the Spanish La Liga.

Two of the most important diplomatic treaties of the early colonial period were the 1494 Treaty of Tordesillas (which split the world into a half "owned" by Spain, and a half "owned" by Portugal), and the 1667 Treaty of Breda, a complicated treaty involving England, the United Provinces (Netherlands), France, and Denmark. As part of this treaty, England, which had control over one of the Banda Islands but little else in the region, traded the tiny island of Run, part of the Banda group, to Holland in exchange for the Dutch territories in the New World. One of the Dutch territories in New Netherland, a region that includes the current Mid-Atlantic states, was New Amsterdam, later known as

---

16 Ibid. Wallace, skeptical that the Dutch and Portuguese would invest sufficiently or bring in non-corrupt managers, even presages the Timor conflict. "To inaugurate such a system would, however, require an immediate outlay of capital, which neither Dutch nor Portuguese seem inclined to make, and a number of honest and energetic officials, which the latter nation at least seems unable to produce; so that it is much to be feared that Timor will for many years to come remain in its present state of chronic insurrection and misgovernment."

Manhattan.

But the troublesome English didn't go quietly into that dark night.

During the Napoleonic Wars, the English took back temporary control of the Banda islands from the Dutch. Being skilled horticulturalists, as well as clever businessmen, the English liberated a bunch of nutmeg trees from Banda and transplated them to their own colonial holdings elsewhere,[17] notably Grenada.[18]

Another blow to Dutch hegemony of the nutmeg trade occurred during the period 1769–70, when French horticulturalist and administrator Pierre Poivre (what an appropriate name for a spice smuggler) smuggled seeds of nutmeg and other spices from the Indies for replanting in Mauritius and the Seychelles.

Although their monopoly had been chipped away, the Dutch continued to retain control of the Spice Islands until World War II.

After decimating Banda's population, Jan Pieterszoon Coen divided the productive land of approximately half a million nutmeg trees into sixty-eight smaller estates. These land parcels were then handed to Dutch planters. With few Bandanese left to work them, slaves from elsewhere were brought in. Now enjoying control of the nutmeg production, the VOC paid the *perkeniers* 1/122 of the Dutch market price for nutmeg. Nevertheless, the *perkeniers* still profited immensely and built substantial villas with opulent imported European decorations, such as the once glamorous but now run-down 1718 villa in which Benny lived.

In the heyday of nutmeg production in pre-independence

17 This botanical piracy was a very British form of colonial economic warfare – in 1876 the British sabotaged the Portuguese monopoly on rubber when Henry Wickham stole seventy thousand wild rubber seeds from Amazonian Brazil. The seeds were planted in London's Kew Gardens. Only 2,800 germinated but that was enough – the resulting domestic seedlings were sent to British colonies in Ceylon and Malaya, where they thrived.

18 The national flag of Grenada, adopted in 1974, shows a stylized split-open nutmeg fruit. Today, Indonesia produces some seventy-five percent of the world's nutmeg, Grenada twenty percent.

Indonesia, Benny's family had a one hundred-hectare (thirty-acre) plantation, but after independence the government "stole" much of it, leaving Benny with only twelve hectares and a few thousand trees. To add insult to injury, Benny noted that the price of nutmeg and mace had crashed because Indonesia didn't support independent farmers like himself. The quality of nutmeg and mace from Grenada is better than that grown in Banda, he said.

"In 1958 there were thirty-four *perkenier*," Benny said. "Now it's only me."

Des Alwi, often described as the unofficial king of Banda, whom I had known since the 1970s and who died in 2010, was a larger-than-life character, a non-stop raconteur, and a tireless promoter of his home.

He was also an Indonesian freedom fighter rebelling against Dutch rule.

It's possible that Alwi would not have become an Indonesian revolutionary hero, except for a quirk of history that has the satisfying ring of cosmic justice.

As a young boy growing up in isolated Banda, Alwi was taken under the wing of two prominent Indonesian rebels who had been exiled by the Dutch to Banda to keep them out of politics. Mohammad Hatta, who, after independence, became the first vice president of Indonesia, and Indonesian intellectual Sutan Sjahrir, who became the country's first prime minister, saw promise in the young and outgoing Alwi and helped foster in him a gift for diplomacy, self-confidence, and a thirst for independence that stood him in good stead later in life.[19]

The few times I had met Alwi, it was early in my time in Indonesia, and I didn't know the right questions to ask him. If I could visit with him now I would ask: "Do you think all this fuss and bloodshed was worth it just to control a few pungent spices?"

---

19 Benny had pointed out the irony that the Dutch had inadvertently "united" Indonesia by getting everyone to speak Bahasa Indonesia.

Wallace's argument in favor of colonialism becomes schizophrenic and confused. As he did throughout *The Malay Archipelago*, Wallace predicts a utopia where everyone knows what is right and wants to do the right thing, so that "all laws and all punishments shall be unnecessary." Seemingly going against his earlier statement about the positive affects of colonialism, Wallace detours and promotes "self-government" as the "perfect social state."

> What is this ideally *perfect social state* toward which mankind ever has been, and still is tending? Our best thinkers maintain that it is a state of *individual freedom and self-government*, rendered possible by the equal development and just balance of the intellectual, moral, and physical parts of our nature, – a state in which we shall each be so perfectly fitted for a social existence, by knowing what is right, and at the same time feeling an irresistible impulse to do what we know to be right, that all laws and all punishments shall be unnecessary. In such a state every man would have a sufficiently well balanced intellectual organization to understand the moral law in all its details, and would require no other motive but the free impulses of his own nature to obey that law. [italics added][20]

So, where did Wallace stand? Rarely has Wallace's thinking been so convoluted – he seems to argue for both colonialism *and* self-rule. He criticized the "religious world and philanthropists" who encouraged "equal political and social rights." He seemed to suggest that inequality and animosity is the default status for relations between Europeans and Asians.

> One set of influences and one trend of opinion, most prevalent in the Colonies, leads to the belief that the

---

20 *The Malay Archipelago*, 596.

natives are the predestined servants or serfs of the whites, and sees no reason why they should not for ever be thus treated, kept in their place by force if necessary, and denied all the rights of freemen or of equals. On the other side we have the religious world and the philanthropists at home who have always exerted themselves to convert the natives to Christianity, to educate them, to force upon them our complex civilisation, and to claim for them, though rather half-heartedly, equal political and social rights. These persons almost ignore the antipathies and ingrained prejudices which everywhere manifest themselves where white and dark races are forced to live together, and which even the loudly proclaimed belief in the brotherhood of man, the equality of rights and the teachings of Christianity, are powerless to overcome.[21]

I've been fascinated by volcanoes since forever, and I wanted to climb Gunung Api (literally "mountain of fire"), which sits on its own island, just across the harbor from Banda Neira.

Wallace prosaically described Gunung Api.

> The volcano, forming a nearly perfect cone, the lower part only covered with a light-green bushy vegetation . . . there is a slight hollow . . . from which constantly issue two columns of smoke. . . . A white efflorescence, probably sulphur, is thickly spread over the upper part of the mountain. . . . The smoke unites as it rises, and forms a dense cloud.[22]

Gunung Api isn't terribly high, just 667 meters (2,188 feet), and the ascent takes a hot, tiring two and a half hours through scrub

---

21 "The Native Problem in South Africa and Elsewhere." *Independent Review* 11, no. 38 (November 1906): 176.

22 *The Malay Archipelago*, 293.

and over scree.

From the summit I saw the things that make Banda special.

The nutmeg plantations.

The coral reefs that lure divers to Banda.

> With water so transparent that living corals and even the minutest objects are plainly seen on the volcanic sand at a depth of seven or eight fathoms.[23]

And the hamlet of Banda Neira, peacefully going about its business, with its main architectural feature, the pentagon-shaped fort.

> The little town, with its neat red-tiled white houses and the thatched cottages of the natives, bounded on one side by the old Portuguese fort.[24]

But as I rested on the edge of the summit and caught my breath, two things in particular stood out.

The first was the sight of Run island in the distance. A tiny, isolated speck of land that, as they say about a great boxer, fought above its weight. I later took a small boat to Run, just to be able to say I went there. I visited a small village, where people were friendly but didn't talk much about the island's place in history. I wanted to go for a swim and a stroll around the beach. My boatman was in a hurry to return to Banda Neira. "Storm's coming," he mumbled. "And anyway there's not much here."

The second memory was the presence of the volcano itself, which last erupted in 1988.

Wallace was fascinated by the power, often lurking beneath the surface, of volcanoes. He knew full well that Indonesia is the most

---

23 Ibid.

24 Wallace is wrong. The fort he saw in 1857 was constructed by the Dutch in 1611; it was an important defensive structure overlooking the bay of Banda Neira. Then, and now, it's called Fort Belgica; at that time "Belgium" was used as the Latin name for the whole of what are now the Netherlands and Belgium.

volcanically active place on earth, and Wallace, like most visitors, waxed eloquent about the volanoes' physical power to destroy and the power they have to drive men to poetry.

> It is only when actually gazing on an active volcano that one can fully realize its awfulness and grandeur. Whence comes that inexhaustible fire whose dense and suphureous [sic] smoke for ever issues from this bare and desolate peak? Whence the mighty forces that produced that peak, and still from time to time exhibit themselves in the earthquakes that always occur in the vicinity of volcanic vents?[25]

In a way Wallace's soppy ode-to-a-volcano resonates with his various "orgasmic butterfly" passages. He stops short, however, of invoking Shiva and the lovely Asian cyclical logic that volcanoes erupt and thereby both cleanse and destroy, with the end result being an even more fertile environment where life can flourish. Volcanoes are the Asian epitome of dynamic opposites – male-female, yang-yin, sun-moon, day-night, dry season-rainy season, and the ultimate set of antagonists: good-evil. Volcanoes kill, but then life returns in even greater fecundity. But that's *my* ode-to-a-volcano. Wallace saw all volcanoes as striking symbols of impermanence in structures where we expect solidity.

> The inhabitant of most parts of Northern Europe sees in the earth the emblem of stability and repose. His whole life-experience . . . teaches him that the earth is solid and firm, that its massive rocks may contain water in abudance, but never fire. . . . A volcano is a fact opposed to all this mass of experience, a fact of so awful a character that, if it were the rule instead of the exception, it would make the earth uninhabitable; a fact so strange and unaccountable that we may be sure it would not be

---

25 *The Malay Archipelago*, 293.

believed on any human testimony.[26]

After climbing the volcano I took a stroll into the village of Banda Neira. I was tired, sweaty, in search of a cold drink. A young girl, maybe ten years old, smiled at me – probably with pity that a foreigner would come all the way to Banda to exhaust himself climbing a volcano – and offered a greeting I hadn't heard before in Indonesia: "Hello, friend."

26 Ibid., 294.

UP AGAINST THE WALL, COLONIALISTS

Aru Islands, Moluccas, Indonesia

Can men with bows and arrows control their destiny?

Alfred Russel Wallace was in Sarawak when Prince Diponegoro died in 1855, a prisoner in Makassar. Born in Yogyakarta, Indonesia, Diponegoro had led a brave but ultimately unsuccessful rebellion against the Dutch, in which the Dutch lost fifteen thousand men, and the Javanese, despite their belief that Diponegoro's hair and magic *kris* would protect them from Dutch bullets, lost some twenty thousand soldiers. During the brutal five-year war, from 1825 to 1830, another one hundred and fifty thousand to two hundred thousand peasants died from the cholera epidemics and starvation that ravaged the countryside.

Diponegoro's power was based on the popular belief (which he no doubt encouraged) that he was the long-expected *Ratu Adil* ("the Just King"), who would lead the people out of their misery and usher in a golden age of plentiful harvests, freedom from taxes, and boundless fertile land to be divided among his followers. He was ultimately tricked into imprisonment and died in captivity. A routine autopsy by the Dutch surgeongeneral reported that Diponegoro bore no scars whatsoever, even though many witnesses noted that he had been shot in battle at least five times.

Undoubtedly, Wallace must have heard this story, but it is equally likely that he was too busy preparing for his own possibly life-threatening adventures to devote too much thought to a Javanese prince.

What could be more exciting than being with men who could walk into the forest wearing just enough to cover their manhood, encumbered only by handmade bow and arrows, accompanied by just a couple of dogs, and return home an hour or two later with a deer? Where in the world are people still so free of constraints?

Ecologist Mark van der Wal and I met such self-sufficient folks on the island of Aru. We were with a combined Universitas Pattimura/European Commission/Aidenvironment project to collect data on biodiversity in the Moluccas and to prepare management plans for conservation efforts. We were working, sure. But it still had a bit of the frisson of the ultima Thule that Wallace encountered.

Mark and I spent a few nights in Jirlai village, a neat community where people had basic consumer goods but little direct contact with the cosmopolitan world of the rest of Indonesia.

We were staying with a family and asked the men of the household, Ely and Yos, how they made money. They explained they sell birds of paradise, birds' nests, and deer jerky. Had they lived on the coast, their products-for-sale would have been sea cucumbers and sharks' fins. They rely on nature, and two of their main sources of cash – the birds of paradise and the swiftlets that create birds' nests – are protected or vulnerable species. In both cases, they make their living by flogging the same commercial wildlife as their ancestors did during Wallace's time in the 1850s.

How ironic. *We* envy people like Ely and Yos for their simplicity. *They* envy us for our possessions. I thought of theologian Thomas Berry's comment that the future belongs not to those who have the most, but to those who need the least. I bet Ely and Yos wouldn't agree. They only see the present. And in the present, the person with the most toys wins.

Had they noticed a reduction in birds or fish or big mammals?

"Yes. There are fewer birds' nests to collect now," the two men told me.

"But why?"

"We collect the nests three or four times a year, so there are fewer swiflets, of course."

"What if you only collect nests twice a year? What if you set up some kind of control system?" I asked.

"Yes! *Sasi*," they said, referring to a traditional control of harvesting natural resources. But they gave me looks that said it will never work. "The problem is, if we don't take them, someone else will."

"Who?"

"Outsiders."

Which hasn't changed much since Wallace was here.

> The trade carried on at Dobbo [Dobo, still the only town in Aru] is very considerable. This year there were fifteen large praus from Macassar, and perhaps a hundred small boats from Ceram, Goram, and Ké [Kei]. The Macassar cargoes are worth about £1000 each, and the other boats take away perhaps about £3000 worth, so that the whole

exports may be estimated at £18,000 per annum.[1]

Same game. The tragedy of the commons. It's a vicious cycle. Wherever local people aren't in control of their resources, nature gets hammered. This is the essence of the conservation problem.

The common, politically correct image of indigenous people is that they live in perfect harmony with surroundings. In the forest of Aru, Mark van der Wal and I, needing a vitamin C fix, had asked Ely if there were any edible leaves.

"What kind?" he asked.

"Like the ones we had yesterday," we said.

Ely went away for the afternoon. That night he cooked up a potful of leaves, probably thinking it doesn't take much to keep two Europeans happy. The next day, while out walking, we came upon a tree, maybe ten meters (thirty feet) tall, about twenty-five centimeters (ten inches) in diameter, that had recently been chopped down. "What happened here?" we asked. "You wanted vegetables," Ely answered, plucking some withering leaves from the fallen tree. We were incredulous. "Never mind," he said, allaying our doubts. "The deer like these leaves. We'll go hunting here tomorrow."

Around the fire we got to talking about abstractions.

"What's the most important thing to give to your children?"

"*Sayang,*" Ely and Yos answered. Love and attention. "And education."

"Are you people more like the (Malay-race) Javanese or the (Austronesian) Papuans?" I asked.

"Papuan," they agreed.

---

1   *The Malay Archipelago*, 485.

"I see lots of Javanese in the towns," I said, expecting to provoke an anti-Javanese response. "Javanese settlers move to Irian Jaya for transmigration. Javanese run the government."

"We need more education," they answered warily.

"Why don't you have better schools?" I asked, recognizing I was treading on sensitive ground.

"The Javanese want to keep us stupid," they eventually said.

"And the future? What about your son, Ely? Will he grow up to be an engineer, or governor of the province?"

Ely and Yos were silent. I pushed. Is there an Arunese equivalent of the American dream in which any child can grow up to be Abraham Lincoln?

"The boy will probably grow up to be like us," they finally admitted.

"And his world?"

"More people. Too many people fishing with nets. Fewer fish, fewer oysters. Fewer birds of paradise."

Ely and Yos then asked me what I thought would happen to nature.

I felt strangely close to these men. I told them how they face the same problems as other rural people in South America and Africa and all over Asia. How rich countries, like mine, could afford anything they wanted, and how less rich countries, like theirs, survived by providing these luxuries. I told them about birds of paradise feathers being in demand a century ago for ladies' hats.

They were too poor to offer me tea.

We talked about the need for a Ratu Adil, a just leader. How local people, like Ely and Yos, know full well how to maintain wildlife populations but don't have a chance because the global marketplace forces them into rapidly depleting their birds' nests. If Ely and Yos don't make money from nature then someone else, an outsider, will. To me it was clear. Don't give outsiders a chance to get rich, I said. They listened quietly.

I thought I should tell them about UNPO, the Dutch-based Unrepresented Nations and Peoples Organization, that fights for Mapuches from Chile, Crimean Tatars, Kurds from Iraq, and Mons from Burma. Raise your voices, I wanted to say. And if that doesn't work, well, get tough.

Then I stopped. I sounded like Che Guevera. Like a college student of the late sixties. Rebel. Take control of your destiny. Peasants of the world arise. I was, God help me, paternalistic. I sounded like Wallace did when he got on one of his soapboxes.

> During many past centuries, of oppression and wrong there has been an ever-present but rarely expressed cry for redress, for some small instalment of justice to the down-trodden workers. It has been the aspiration alike of the peasant and the philosopher, of the poet and the saint. But the rule of the lords of the soil has ever been so overwhelming and punishment so severe, that the born thralls or serfs have rarely dared to do more than humbly petition for some partial relief; or, if roused to rebel by unbearable misery and wrongs, they have soon been crushed by the power of mailed knights and armed retainers.[2]

"Ely, have you ever heard of Diponegoro?" I asked.

He hadn't, but he had heard of the ongoing Papua independence movement, fueled partly because local people are angry that the Javanese have taken the natural resources of their land without benefit to the local folks.[3, 4] He was hesitant to talk too openly, even though we were in the middle of the forest. I was a foreigner, who had metaphorically parachuted into his closely structured world. I too felt somewhat awkward. What was I opening up? Surely thoughts and ideas can't hurt him?

"Wouldn't you be happier being in control of your resources?"

---

2   "Economic and Social Justice," 166.

3   On the outer islands of Indonesia the omnipresent and disliked-to-varying-degrees Javanese are sometimes referred to as *coklat Belanda*, or "brown Dutchmen," in reference to their colonial mentality.

4   I'm reminded of Napoleon's observation that "God is on the side of the heavy artillery."

I asked. With each question Ely became increasingly withdrawn. To me the conversation was a mischievous intellectual exercise, like asking, in the late sixties, whether we should take over the university president's office. To Ely, however, this talk was conspiratorial and not at all in the spirit of Indonesia's national feel-good philosophy of Pancasila.

My half-hearted encouragement that Ely and Yos take control of their resources is unlikely to bear fruit. But throughout Asia local people are fighting bloody and ongoing eco-wars over who owns natural resources.

In far-eastern Indonesia, where Ely and Yos live,[5] a relentless rebellion pits local Papuans (Austro-Malayan in Wallace's terms) against Javanese (Indo-Malayan). The Papuans are angry that the "foreign" Javanese are stealing natural resources that should be under local control.

Sometimes these eco-wars become horrific. A friend sent a gruesome photo of an Asian girl, maybe six years old, lying on the ground, her arms splayed at impossible angles. Her dress is hiked up, and her head is tilted from her body, like a broken puppet's. On closer examination I can see that her head has been sliced off and not too carefully placed near her neck.

This nameless girl was beheaded during the 2001 massacre of some five hundred settlers from the arid island of Madura, which lies just off the coast of Java, by gangs of the indigenous residents of Indonesian Borneo (Kalimantan), collectively called Dayaks.

---

5   Indonesian geographic names and boundaries are sometimes complex. All of the Indonesian (western) half of the island of New Guinea, including neighboring islands like Aru, where Ely and Yos live, was formerly part of the large Irian Jaya province. The eastern part of the island of New Guinea is the sovereign nation of Papua New Guinea. Irian Jaya has subsequently been separated into two newly named provinces: West Papua and Papua (motto: *Karya Swadaya* – "Work with One's Own Might").

The killings were ethnic-specific – all of the victims were Madurese; the Dayak marauders, who had the support of their community leaders, left their Javanese and Balinese immigrant neighbors untouched.

What could spark such hostility?

One of the oft-ignored underlying triggers of communal violence such as this is the fight for control of a people's natural resources.

John Walker, a lecturer in politics at University College, the Australian Defence Force Academy, said of this massacre: "Far from having its origins in ethnicity,[6] the present killings in Central Kalimantan, like those in western Kalimantan in 1998–9, reflect deep conflict over natural resources."

In the Borneo scenario, the Indonesian government encouraged farmers from the overpopulated islands of Java, Bali, and Madura to "transmigrate" to lesser populated outer islands such as Borneo and New Guinea. The new settlers – there were some one hundred thousand Madurese in Kalimantan at the time of the massacres, many have since left or been evacuated – were encouraged to cut down the forests and make farms. Businessmen and military leaders from Java, encouraged by government policies and a laissez faire attitude toward environmental protection, denuded the rainforest for timber and to make way for oil palm plantations. The hitch was that the forests traditionally belonged to local people such as the Dayaks who lived, to varying degrees, in some kind of harmony with nature. But as John Walker adds: "Indonesia does not guarantee indigenous people's rights over land." The Dayaks were left disenfranchised and land-poor.

Michael Dove, a professor at Yale University, added: "For three decades, the indigenous Dayak have seen their natural resource base steadily eroded. Vast amounts of Dayak lands and forests have been destroyed or appropriated for logging concessions, rubber and oil-palm plantations, pulp plantations and transmigration sites."

---

6   I don't buy that ethnicity wasn't a factor – the Madurese have a reputation in Indonesia as being aggressive and *kasar* ("rough") and they undoubtedly clashed with similarly headstrong Dayaks.

Riska Orpa Sari, a Dayak woman who wrote *Riska: Memories of a Dayak Girlhood*, said the current conflict is based on control of the forests. "For centuries, our needs and rights have been denied by the government," she said.

"A flow of human beings has been sent like cattle to Kalimantan. Thousands of hectares of lush rain forest have been clear-cut to fill the need for land for the newcomers [and] the source of life for the Dayak and many rare species of wildlife is intensively cut and timbered," she wrote.

"So, betrayed and exploited, the anger exploded. Being used, neglected and ignored left our people bitter. Vengeance emerged. The need to defend our land has come to the surface, the need to take our land and natural world back."

While recognizing that the causes of violent conflicts around the world are complex and involve economic, ethnic, racial, religious, and political zealots, the fight for control of nature has been one of the most important but frequently overlooked root causes of bloody ethnic and political conflicts.

In 1998 I visited a group of Kenyah in a settlement called Tanah Merah (Red Earth), upriver from Samarinda in Kalimantan. Although they loosely fall under the heading of "Dayaks," they are a different tribe to the folks who slaughtered Madurese and had no role in the gruesome violence. Ironically, these Kenyah were also internal transmigrants, having been resettled several decades ago from their traditional homes further upriver. I stood on a hilltop with Pak Pajan, the village chief. I had just spent a few hours with him in old growth forest, where the air was cool underneath the forest canopy and ripe with the scent of growth and decay. It was perhaps five degrees Celsius (eight degrees Fahrenheit) hotter outside the shelter of the forest, and the barren neighboring slopes, upon which would be planted agro-business monocultures of eucalyptus or acacia, seemed to stoically wither under the equatorial sun. Pak Pajan's people, part of a tribe of some forty thousand found mostly in Borneo's highlands, practice shifting cultivation and rely on the forest for food, shelter, and as the foundation of their cultural heritage. But the Kenyah were being smothered by land-hungry immigrants and government plantation schemes that wipe out rainforests. Pak Pajan did not speak about wild rebellion or head-hunting, but clearly he was a troubled man, caught in a Borneo squeeze-play. I wonder what his flash point would be? I sensed he would agree with Riska Orpa Sari, who said: "I know that the Dayak people want to live in peace with nature. We are the people of the forest. We do not make peace with people who destroy our home."

In Aru, Mark and I had much to admire, much to consider. We had seen lots of other wildlife products. In Dobo, which is in the running for the most miserable town in Indonesia, we had seen rare parrots half hidden away in the back of restaurants, available for a price. In the Aru village of Sia, friendly kids offered to sell us cassowary eggs, crocodile skins, and dugong teeth. I admired a small green parrot that a happy young boy offered, only US$5, a bargain, and a protected species. I was with Timo, one of the lesser lights of the Indonesian Department of Nature Conservation in the Ministry of Forestry. "Don't worry," Timo said, thinking my desires were similar to his. "I can arrange a letter for you if you want to take the bird out of the country." A problem that Wallace obviously didn't worry about.

> I could hardly have torn myself away from Aru had I not
> obtained specimens [of birds of paradise].[7]

But Mark and I, like Wallace, were desperate to find birds of paradise in Aru. For three days we had camped by a tiny river, amusing ourselves by wading through waist-deep streams that

---

7   *The Malay Archipelago*, 466.

flowed through long black caves, netting bats, going hunting, eating freshly roasted venison with our hands, and, in general, doing boys' stuff. Except, we were on "mission," a word concocted by people like me to try to convince the stay-at-home secretaries that we really were working. Our lofty goal: to learn how people relate to their environment.

We had seen much, but had not seen a bird of paradise. Sure, we had heard them, but it's not the same. I asked Ely how they hunt them, expecting him to use a technique similar to that on the distant island of Bacan, off Halmahera. There, a local version of Papageno showed me how he used a live cockatoo or parrot as a decoy to attract wild birds to a tree limb coated with sticky resins. Ely said no, we use these, and he showed me an arrow whose head was a blunt wooden plug.

His weapon, and his description of the hunt, were identical to Wallace's experiences.

> When they are in full plumage, the males assemble early in the morning to exhibit themselves. This habit enables the natives to obtain specimens with comparative ease. As soon as they find that the birds have fixed upon a tree on which to assemble, they build a little shelter of palm leaves in a convenient place among the branches, and the hunter ensconces himself in it before daylight, armed with his bow and a number of arrows terminating in a round knob. A boy waits at the foot of the tree, and when the birds come at sunrise, and a sufficient number have assembled, and have begun to dance, the hunter shoots with his blunt arrow so strongly as to stun the bird, which drops down, and is secured and killed by the boy without its plumage being injured by a drop of blood. . . . The rest take no notice, and fall one after another till some of them take the alarm.[8]

---

8   Ibid., 555–6.

Three days and no birds of paradise. We took long walks along the river. We cut up a mosquito net to fashion an inefficient net with which to catch crayfish. We waded through rivers in caves, catching bats that bounced into us, obviously having failed Sonar 101. Our flashlights also caught glimpses of spooky white fish in this dark cave river, and we flailed around like schoolboys trying to catch some in our mist net that was designed for nocturnal bats. Ely, seeing what we were after, borrowed a flashlight and disappeared into the depths of the cave. He came back with two small fish that he had speared. We were overjoyed, thinking that these *must* be new species.[9] We were somewhat less amused when they arrived on our dinner plates a couple of hours later, grilled. We explained to Ely that we actually wanted to pickle them in alcohol, and we went back the next day to fish again.

Finally, on our last morning, during our walk out of the forest, we saw a tree full of birds of paradise. There were well over a dozen, their calls somewhere between a squawk and a honk – call it a squank. One male was displaying, his yellow and white tail feathers startlingly gaudy and dramatic. This was the great bird of paradise, one of just two birds of paradise species found on Aru.

> The Great Bird of Paradise is very active and vigorous, and seems to be in constant motion all day long. It is very abundant, small flocks of females and young males being constantly met with. . . . Their note is, "Wawk-wawk-wawk-Wok, wok-wok," and is so loud and shrill as to be heard a great distance, and to form the most prominent and characteristic animal sound in the Aru Islands.[10]

Timo, the Department of Nature Conservation official who offered to get us an export permit for an endangered parrot, gazed up at the birds and said he wished that he had a gun. We said that we thought his department was supposed to conserve things. Our

---

9   They weren't.

10   *The Malay Archipelago*, 466.

comments didn't seem to change his mind, and he made irritating shooting gestures and popping noises. Earlier in the trip I had asked him what he thought should be done to conserve Indonesia's forests. "Wah, *sousa*," he said, rolling his eyes. Difficult. I gave him an easier question. "Well, what should be done to save turtles?" This really *was* easier, since Timo had been with us for two weeks while we had chased turtle poachers and where everyone, Indonesians and Europeans, talked turtles nonstop. He even had been present at a four-hour group discussion, held in Indonesian, where everyone aired his and her opinions about turtle conservation. "Wah, *payah*." *Really* difficult, he said, raising his gaze as if searching for heavenly inspiration.

But I wasn't about to let Timo shatter the moment. I gazed upward, as Wallace did.

> The birds had now commenced what the people here call their 'sácaleli,' or dancing-parties, in certain trees in the forest, which are not fruit trees, as I at first imagined, but which have an immense head of spreading branches . . . giving a clear space for the birds to play and exhibit their plumes. On one of these trees a dozen or twenty full-plumaged male birds assemble together, raise up their wings, stretch out their necks, and elevate their exquisite plumes, keeping them in a continual vibration. . . . The bird itself is nearly as large as a crow, and is of a rich coffee-brown color. The head and neck is of a pure straw yellow above, and rich metallic green beneath. . . . At the time of its excitement, however, the wings are raised vertically over the back . . . and the long plumes are raised up and expanded till they form two magnificent golden fans, striped with deep red at the base, and fading off into the pale brown tint of the finely divided and softly wavings points. . . . When seen in this attitude, the bird of paradise really deserves its name, and must be ranked as one of the

most beautiful and most wonderful of living things.[11]

We watched the birds of paradise for half an hour. Mark and I remember this as a profound experience. Ely and Yos waited patiently until we had gazed our fill. Timo, realizing he couldn't shoot the birds, wandered about and made his popping noises, bored.

> One of my objects in coming to the far East was accomplished. I had obtained a specimen of the King Bird of paradise (Paradisea regia), which had been described by Linnaeus from skins preserved in a mutilated state by the natives. I knew how few Europeans had ever beheld the perfect little organism I now gazed upon, and how very imperfectly it was still known in Europe. The emotions excited in the minds of a naturalist who has long desired to see the actual thing which he has hitherto known only by description, drawing, or badly-preserved external covering, especially when that thing is of surpassing rarity and beauty, require the poetic faculty fully to express them. The remote island in which I found myself situated [Aru], in an almost unvisited sea, far from the tracks of merchant-fleets and navies; the wild luxuriant tropical forest, which stretched far away on every side; the rude uncultured savages who gathered round me – all had their influence in determining the emotions with which I gazed upon this "thing of beauty." I thought of the long ages of the past, during which the successive generations of this little creature had run their course – year by year being born, and living and dying amid these dark and gloomy woods, with no intelligent eye to gaze upon their loveliness – to all appearance such a wanton waste of beauty.[12]

---

11 Ibid., 466–7.

12 Ibid., 448.

Funny, isn't it. Take three people and plant them under a bird of paradise tree. One person will look at the birds and see a meal, another will, like Wallace did, wax eloquent and just about have an orgasm, while a third will mentally calculate how much it's worth stuffed.

I tried for a final time to instigate Ely to revolt. "*You* should be controlling these birds of paradise." As soon as I said it, we both knew it was unlikely. Without saying a word, we looked at Timo and then looked back at each other in understanding. Timo, who was not-from-there, nevertheless had access to this forest, and, via his government job, some authority, which he could leverage into bribes in exchange for turning a blind eye to trading in birds of paradise. If push came to shove, it would be the Timos of the world who got control of the birds of paradise. I looked at Ely standing there in his shorts , holding his bow and arrows and remembered our conversations about his needing money to send the kids to school. I then looked up at these beautiful, valuable birds. It's easy to paraphrase Keats, I thought, if you can afford a Nikon around your neck.

A RENOIR IN THE ATTIC

Bukit Timah Nature Reserve, Singapore

New species in urban Singapore? Who would have thought?

Alfred Russel Wallace arrived in Singapore on April 20, 1854 after a three-month voyage in first class aboard a Peninsular and Oriental steamer. Pirates generally ignored the European vessels sailing in the Straits of Malacca but had no compunction about attacking Asian craft – in 1854 it was estimated that only half the Asian craft succeeded in reaching Singapore.[1] Wallace used Singapore as a base for several of his travels during his eight years in the Malay Archipelago, making four trips to the island, a presence surpassed only by his time in Ternate, where Wallace lived for many months and where he visited five times. Singapore during the Victorian era was alive with commerce and society. The year Wallace arrived, so did thirteen thousand Chinese immigrants, many of them dangerous men – rebels and refugees from the civil war raging in southern China. The Crimean War broke out in 1854, jolting Singapore merchants out of their complacency, since they felt the country's

---

1   In 2010 the Straits of Malacca still accounted for forty percent of all global pirate incidents.

defenceless prosperity could make her an attractive target of Russian warships.[2]

More than half the Chinese adults in Singapore were opium addicts, and there were so many foreign prostitutes that *The Straits Times* newspaper complained that there were almost as many whores as respectable women among the European female population. The first telegraph line was laid between Singapore and Batavia (present-day Jakarta) in 1859, the year Singapore's first dry dock was built. The commodity exchange listed opium (Straits $385 per chest), ebony, and Turkey red chintz. The P&O fare from Singapore to Southampton was Straits $600. Wallace wrote: "I quite enjoy being a short time in Singapore again. The scene is at once so familiar and yet so strange. The half-naked Chinese coolies, the very neat shopkeepers, the clean, fat, old, long-tailed merchants, all as pushing and full of business as any Londoners. After two years in the East I only now begin to understand Singapore, and to thoroughly appreciate the life and bustle, and the varied occupations of so many distinct nationalities on a spot which a short time ago was an uninhabited jungle."[3]

Today, Singapore remains a regional *entrepot*, and the country's Changi Airport and Keppel Harbour are arguably the best in the world. I first visited Singapore in 1970 on R&R from Sarawak, where I served in the Peace Corps. I stayed at cheap (and noisy) Chinese hotels on Beach Road. After the Peace Corps I lived in Singapore for three years and subsequently, while I lived in neighboring Indonesia, I must have visited the country on business and pleasure perhaps a hundred times. I went to Singapore to produce my advertising films and write

2   One result of the war was Tennyson's poem "The Charge of the Light Brigade," published the year Wallace arrived in Asia.

3   *My Life*, Vol. 1, 348.

catchy jingles. I went to Singapore when I got fed up with the noise and hassles and corruption and nonexistent telephones of Indonesia. I went to Singapore because Jakarta at the time was a funky backwater with no supermarkets and Singapore was the place to stock up on cheese and Oreos. I went to Singapore because it worked (according to my world view) and Jakarta didn't. And surprisingly to my friends, I went to Singapore to enjoy easy access to a small chunk of intact tropical rainforest.

Singapore would seem to be an odd place to seek nature. In spite of being the greenest city-state in the world, Singapore's nature is more often perceived to reside in giant airport aquariums and air-conditioned gardens in hotel lobbies than in natural rainforests, coral reefs, and mangroves. The common thinking is that most of Singapore's wildlife has been replaced by public housing and highways, and that's partly true, but the reality, like most things in life, is more nuanced.

The bad news: since Stamford Raffles established modern Singapore in 1819, the country has lost more than ninety-nine percent of its original vegetation due to construction of housing, roads, reservoirs, and military facilities. Of one hundred and eighty-three species of birds known or presumed to be breeding in the republic since 1940, thirty-nine have become extinct and forty-one resident species are considered to be at risk. Some sixty percent of all the country's coral reefs have been seriously damaged.

The good news: Singapore is still home to more than forty thousand wild, native, non-microbial species, according to *Singapore Biodiversity*, a new comprehensive study of the country's natural resources. David Bellamy, a noted English conservationist, pointed out that the number of plant species growing in Singapore's Bukit Timah Nature Reserve is more than that in the whole of North America. New species are being found regularly.

I went looking for Wallace in Singapore.

Reassuringly, the view that delighted Wallace in 1854 hasn't changed that much.

> The island of Singapore consists of a multitude of small hills, three or four hundred feet high, the summits of many of which are still covered with virgin forest.[4]

The heartening thing is that amidst the construction one can *still* see wooded hills from the top of Bukit Timah (Hill of Tin)[5] – at 163 meters (534 feet), Singapore's highest peak.

> The vegetation was most luxuriant, comprising enormous forest-trees, as well as a variety of ferns, caladiums, and other undergrowth, and [an] abundance of climbing rattan palms.[6]

The forests form the country's central catchment area, protected because the Singapore government doesn't want to lose its water supplies. As it is, Singapore is forced to import forty percent of its water from neighboring Malaysia, which puts the proud Singaporeans in a potentially precarious position. Singaporeans don't like to be beholden to anybody.

Bukit Timah Nature Reserve today is a protected area, and along with the Nee Soon swamp forest is a key oasis for biodiversity. Even though the reserve encompasses an area of less than one percent of Singapore's original rainforest cover, it is home to fifty percent of all the island's native flora and fauna. The reserve is as spic-and-span as most everything else in this efficient mercantile nation. Wallace had his base nearby.

4   *The Malay Archipelago*, 35.

5   A misleading name, since the area was never mined for tin; granite was quarried there.

6   *The Malay Archipelago*, 36.

> The mission-house at Bukit-tima was surrounded by
> several of these wood-topped hills, which were much
> frequented by wood-cutters and sawyers, and offered me
> an excellent collecting-ground for insects.[7]

Wallace never mentioned at which Catholic mission he stayed.
I discussed this question with D. H. "Paddy" Murphy, a biologist
at the National University of Singapore, and we decided Wallace
had probably stayed at Saint Joseph, founded in 1846 and which
today is a spacious and airy church, constructed in a Spanish style
but with a Chinese-style roof.

> I lived . . . with the missionary at Bukit-tima . . . where
> a pretty church has been built, and there are about 300
> converts.[8]

I asked Augustine Tay, the Chinese parish priest at St. Joseph's,
if there was any documentation on Wallace's visit. "No, never heard
of the guy," the priest said. "There's no history of this parish. People
aren't interested in history. You know they wanted to throw away
this beautiful wooden paneling from the old church?"

The Chinese priest lived a pretty middle-class life, at least
based on what I could see in his sitting room. His minor modern
comforts contrasted with the hair-shirt approach of the priest with
whom Wallace stayed.

> One secret of the success of these [Jesuit] missions is the
> rigid economy practiced in the expenditure of the funds.
> A missionary is allowed about £30 a year, on which he
> lives in whatever country he may be. . . . The natives,
> seeing their teachers living in poverty and with none of
> the luxuries of life, are convinced that they are sincere in
> what they teach.[9]

7   Ibid., 35.

8   Ibid., 34.

9   Ibid.

My friend at Bukit-tima was truly a father to his flock.
He preached to them in Chinese every Sunday. . . . His
house was open to them day and night. If a man came to
him and said, 'I have no rice for my family . . .' he would
give him half of what he had in the house, however little
that might be. If another said, 'I have no money to pay my
debt,' he would give him half the contents of his purse,
were it his last dollar. The result was that his flock trusted
and loved him, for they felt sure that he was their true
friend, and had no ulterior designs in living among them.[10]

I was about to go. "Wait," the priest said. "I have a 'spare tire' from
the period your English friend was here." Spare tire? He rummaged
in a back room and presented me with a corroded horseshoe. "I'll
bet your friend used this."

Wallace was as happy in Bukit Timah as a dung beetle in an
outhouse.

Insects were exceedingly abundant and very interesting,
and every day furnished scores of new and curious forms.
In about two months [in Singapore] I obtained no less
than 700 species of beetles, a large proportion of which
were quite new.[11]

Almost all these [beetles] were collected in one patch
of jungle [in Singapore], not more than a square mile in
extent, and in all my subsequent travels in the East I rarely
if ever met with so productive a spot.

10 Ibid., 35.

11 Singapore-based biologist Ian Turner estimates Singapore's potential insect species
at between ten thousand and seventy-three thousand. Local entomologist D. H.
Murphy estimates that Bukit Timah alone might contain ten thousand species of
beetles, two hundred species of ants, and two hundred species of cockroaches.

This exceeding productiveness [at Bukit Timah] was due in part no doubt to some favorable conditions in the soil, climate, and vegetation, and to the season being very bright and sunny, with sufficient showers to keep every thing fresh. But it was also in a great measure dependent, I feel sure, on the labors of the Chinese wood-cutters. They had been at work here for several years, and during all that time had furnished a continual supply of dry and dead and decaying leaves and bark, together with insects and their larvae. This had led to the assemblage of a great variety of species in a limited space, and I was the first naturalist who had come to reap the harvest they had prepared.[12]

I find it reassuring that Singapore still has some nature left.

One morning I trekked through the Nee Soon swamp forest, important to Singapore's multi-tasking technocrats because it serves double-duty as a water catchment area and as an army training ground. Carsten Huttche, a graduate student at the National University of Singapore, was looking for leaf monkeys, which, because they have little direct impact on Singapore's trade balance, are considered irrelevant by some of the country's leaders. The scientific community, however, was concerned because a poacher had recently captured one of the rare primates from this forest. The poacher would have made a couple of thousand dollars by selling the animals, had he not been nabbed by the authorities.

We didn't see leaf monkeys that morning, but we got a feel for this forest, which seems to survive under a constant shadow of destruction. The forces of modernization in Singapore are generally more powerful than the voices of environmental probity. A new freeway was going to be constructed through Nee Soon until the small but vocal band of Singapore nature lovers raised their

---

12 Ibid., 36.

voices and stopped the construction.[13] The truncated section of the elevated highway has since grown over and "greened" itself.

The well thought out protests of a bunch of modern conservationists are a far cry from Wallace's trepidation about being attacked by a tiger.

> There are always a few tigers roaming about Singapore, and they kill on an average a Chinaman every day, principally those who work in the gambir plantations. . . . We heard a tiger roar once or twice in the evening, and it was rather nervous work hunting for insects among the fallen trunks and old sawpits, when one of these savage animals might be lurking close by, waiting an opportunity to spring upon us.[14]

Our greatest danger that morning was walking too close to the Singapore Army firing range at Nee Soon. But Wallace had to watch out for other perils.

> Here and there, too, were tiger-pits, carefully covered over with sticks and leaves, and so well concealed, that in several cases I had a narrow escape from falling into them. They are shaped like an iron furnace, wider at the bottom than the top, and are perhaps fifteen or twenty feet deep [six meters], so that it would be almost impossible for a person unassisted to get out of one. Formerly a sharp stake was stuck erect in the bottom; but after an unfortunate traveller had been killed by falling on one, its use was forbidden.[15]

---

13 Peter Ng thinks part of the problem is that "engineers and managers don't realize that a particular patch of forest or wetland is important for natural heritage – to them, all forests are equal and represent unused land that can be developed. If they are prewarned, they can often help mitigate such developments."

14 *The Malay Archipelago*, 35.

15 Ibid.

Later, we walked up Bukit Timah hill, along a path Wallace perhaps used (but which today is cemented, like a sidewalk) looking for beetles. I scraped the bark off a fallen log and saw a bore hole. From deep within the log I heard a soft squawk, squawk, like a muffled rubber duck. I keep on chopping with my Swiss army knife until I could see a critter's head. Using two sticks, chopstick style, I pulled the beetle out. Not expecting to collect, I had no container. I put the insect into my front pocket, and whenever the cloth pressed against my chest the beetle would emit a soft screech. This was one of my first tropical beetles, and I was desperate for it to be a new species. Not likely, said Paddy Murphy back at the university. It was a longhorn beetle, *Batocera albofasciata*. I checked the book. "Probably the commonest species of a large and important genus . . . when held in the hand, will stridulate with shrilling noises continuously until it is set free."

During one of my visits to Singapore, in 1993, the nation's scientific community was abuzz with reports that an "AIDS tree" was growing in the intact rainforest occupying a corner of the Singapore Botanic Gardens.

It's a complicated story. Exploring in Malaysian Sarawak, a researcher from the U.S. National Cancer Institute took samples from a tree identified as *Calophyllum lanigerum var austrocoriaceum* as part of a routine search for plants with chemical compounds that potentially could be used to treat cancer and AIDS. The plant proved active in laboratory tests, but when the scientist returned to Sarawak a year later he found that the site had been cleared for logging and his "medicinal" tree was gone. Quick off the mark, Tan Wee Kiat, then executive director of the Singapore National Parks Board, which manages the Singapore Botanic Gardens, told the American scientist that the tree was relatively common in Singapore. The story even made CNN. "How exciting that biodiversity still exists in Singapore," the scientists cheered. "How wonderful that we can make some money to pay for nature conservation," the National Parks Board said. As it turned out, the Singapore variety of the tree fizzled out in lab tests, and the tree was subsequently found in many other places in Sarawak. Attempts to develop a viable pharmaceutical from the tree are still going on. The dreamers carry on looking for new things. The businessfolk continue to buy resources from everywhere and anywhere. Immortality for some comes from making a discovery, for others from making a killing.

But biodiversity is in everyone's backyard, and surprises can be found in the most unlikely settings. In Singapore researchers can kiss their spouses goodbye early in the morning (maybe even have time to take the kids to school), drive to within a few kilometers of their research site, spend the day in the forest, and be home in time to enjoy dinner and watch the football on TV.

I find it inspiring that more than a hundred species that are completely new to science have been discovered in Singapore in the last few years, including new species of moss, fungi, lichens, fishes, nematodes, spiders, mites, harvestmen, wasps, beetles, bugs, flies, shrimps, barnacles, and crabs.

Peter Ng, a professor at the National University of Singapore and director of the Raffles Museum, is the Indiana Jones of Singapore.[16] He has a knack for finding new creatures amidst the urban sprawl.

Peter Ng recounts some of the discoveries he and his students have made while shuffling through the rainforests of the country's interior and the mangroves of the coast. Several of these creatures are not simply new to Singapore – they're new to science.

"We've found a snapping shrimp that doesn't snap," Ng explains of a rare freshwater variety of crustacean. "It was sitting there for donkey years, unnoticed. One day, just by luck, we were out sampling and this popped into the net."

---

16 He prefers to compare himself to a Don Quixoteish "hunter killer."

Ng explains that "another time we found another shrimp, a pinkish, semi-transparent, very small fellow. We could easily have overlooked it – it digs deep holes in banks of streams, you have to bash the bank and chase it out. But this creates a mess – you get lots of leaves and even then you'll probably miss it unless it moves. And then, even if you see it you think it's a juvenile. It's probably restricted to the small stretch of stream where the water flows quickly."

Imagine a small stretch of a small stream of a small forest in a small industrialized country (Singapore is only one-third the size of Greater London and only two-thirds the size of Hong Kong), with a population density four times greater than New York, and you begin to get an idea of how impressive these discoveries are.

"One fellow found a new catfish in the catchment area, a black and yellow clown catfish," Ng said. "It's a bit of a joke to find one more new fish in this small area."

Ng and his colleagues discovered four new freshwater crab species in Singapore waters. One of his fondest discoveries is a new freshwater prawn, *Caridina temasek*, which he found in a one-kilometer- (0.6-mile-) long stream that flows near the Singapore Island Country Club, the nation's premier golf course. The prawn's diminutive size – similar to a grain of rice – may work in its favor in food-crazy Singapore. "This prawn would probably taste great when fried with eggs," Ng said, "but since it is so small, it would take quite a number of them to make one omelette."

Ng's "all-time favourite" discovery came in 1990. In 1988 he wrote a book on the freshwater crabs of Peninsular Malaysia and Singapore, in which he recorded five true freshwater crab species from Singapore, including two endemics.[17] "I was pretty confident I had found all the freshwater crabs there were to find on such a small island with so little forest," Ng says. "But in 1989 a student, Kelvin Lim,[18] showed me a photograph of a crab from a small

---

17 The number keeps growing. In 2012 Ng notes that there are six species of true freshwater crabs in Singapore, and he named four of them. Of these, three are found *only* in Singapore.

18 Kelvin Lim himself is a bit of a rare creature. Although he was an Arts undergraduate,

patch of swamp forest in the center of the central catchment, from an area I had sampled before. The animal looked rather odd, with a rather unusual color pattern, but I was rather sure of myself then and dismissed it merely as an extreme variant of a common species found there, *Parathelphusa maculata*. Some months later, I got a specimen of this 'variant' myself and doubts began to surface in my mind about its presumed identity. But the specimen was a juvenile, and I had to get an adult specimen to be dead sure that it was a new species. Kelvin and I subsequently visited the swamp many times, often in the middle of the night, to find this elusive animal; we even sacrificed our New Year's Eve in 1990 in an attempt to find specimens. They are so secretive. By day, they hide in deep burrows in soft mud and are virtually impossible to dig out. The adults only come out in total darkness in the middle of the night, especially during moonless nights, and even then, they crawl slowly in shallow streams, underneath very dense leaf litter. This behavior, coupled with their well-camouflaged color patterns, makes them almost impossible to see. We finally learned how to catch them, though, by grabbing any clump of submerged leaves that moved. As it turned out, I had been wrong. It was a separate species after all, and to beat everything, it was new to science. I named it *Parathelphusa reticulata* for its beautiful carapace pattern. Moreover, this species was endemic to Singapore. As later studies showed, it is found only in a five-hectare (five-acre) patch of swamp in Singapore and nowhere else on this planet. This is a reasonably large crab. So if something like this could have been missed for so long, heaven knows what else we are still ignorant of in the catchment area. This experience was a humbling one for me – I'll never again be complacent about biodiversity, even in Singapore."

To me, this is akin to finding a Renoir in the attic.

---

he was a keen amateur naturalist and volunteered to work at the university museum. Peter Ng notes, "We later appointed him as curator for fish. Imagine asking the dean of science that you want to hire a Bachelor of Arts graduate to a science curatorship. My dean thought my head of department and I were mad – but this guy was good and he got the job. He is now collection manager, has written dozens of articles and books about Singapore's biodiversity, and he even obtained an MSc in systematics of catfish."

I asked Peter Ng whether the Bukit Timah Nature Reserve is the same today as in Wallace's day?

"Wallace was surprised that in such a small area he could collect so much stuff," Ng explains. "Remember, even in Wallace's time, Bukit Timah was just a bit of a forested island surrounded by development, although the pressures today are obviously much greater."

Nevertheless, Bukit Timah's ecology has changed during the ensuing 150 years, according to Ng. "If Wallace came back today he'd find a different composition of insects. Bukit Timah is smaller today than it was in Wallace's time. The forest is gradually dying and the National Parks Board is studying ways to keep it alive."

Ng argues that Bukit Timah is too small to be sustainable. He tells his students: "Bukit Timah forest is in deep shit . . . it's like a loved one in ICU in hospital . . . it is very hard to keep alive without substantial human intervention, technology, and a lot of attention."

In conservation, size matters.

Just as it's impossible to determine how many species there are, scientists can only offer educated guesses at how big a patch of rainforest needs to be to survive. The Minimum Critical Size of Ecosystems project in the Amazon led the way in scientific studies of what happens ecologically to fragments of huge rainforests. But what about a tiny forest like Bukit Timah that is surrounded by human stuff?

Ng says that "ecologists argue that for a rainforest patch to be self sustaining and able to survive, it needs several thousand hectares. But Bukit Timah is *only* fifty hectares or so – and it suffers from too much usage, wind effect, alien species, drying out, inability to spread seeds, and so on. The forest has changed a lot: there are no more top predators, etc. Messy. Another challenge is that it is cut off from the rest of the secondary forest catchment by a highway – and isolated all round by commercial developments and roads. And it doesn't have sufficiently powerful champions. So to keep it alive for the long term we need 'active intervention' or it cannot survive long. It needs human attention and money."

Is Peter Ng a realist or a Chicken Little-type warning of catastrophe that might never happen?

"My colleagues from National Parks think I am too cynical. Maybe, but I am also a realist with a touch of sentimentality. We must try. Not trying is surrendering. I do not like to surrender."

He might have quoted Wallace.[19]

> If this is not done, future ages will certainly look back
> upon us as a people so immersed in the pursuit of wealth
> as to be blind to higher considerations. They will charge
> us with having culpably allowed the destruction of some
> of those records of Creation which we had it in our power
> to preserve; and while professing to regard every living
> thing as the direct handiwork and best evidence of a
> Creator, yet, with a strange inconsistency, seeing many
> of them perish irrecoverably from the face of the earth,
> uncared for and unknown.[20]

"We have no choice," Ng said. "Death for Bukit Timah is *not* an option for a much cherished loved one."

---

19 Wallace was referring to the "extinction of the numerous forms of life which the progress of cultivation invariably entails." Although Wallace's recommendation was "that in all tropical countries colonised by Europeans the most perfect collections possible in every branch of natural history should be made and deposited in national museums, where they may be available for study and interpretation," his eloquent plea has been adapted as a call to arms for nature conservation worldwide.

20 "On the Physical Geography of the Malay Archipelago." *Journal of the Royal Geographical Society* 33 (1863): 234.

Sarawak, Malaysia
The rural people of Sarawak face paternalistic and greed-driven efforts to take their ancestral land
and convert the forests into oil palm plantations.
Photo: Paul Sochaczewski

IV

TRANSFORMATION

Shiva's Beach – Night

Pulau Enu, Aru Islands, Indonesia

With stars that make me wish I was a poet.

Tonight I wander the beach on the windward side, sand gritting my contact lenses, looking for the tractor-like tracks that mean a meter-long turtle has visited the low dunes to lay her eggs.

It is a night with stars like I've rarely seen, and I half expect you to appear out of the shadows, gaunt and curious and quietly eager to join me as I examine small piles of sand that indicate one of these turtles has laid her eggs below the high water line, where they are certain to become water-logged and spoiled.

It isn't easy to find her original hole since the turtle camouflages her cache by shuffling sand in a wide area.

I finally unearth her sixty eggs, slimy with turtle juices, and transplant them into another hole I dig a few meters further inland, safe from the high tide.

Shiva dances
To music wild
Does the breeze whisper?
Hope will come with the dawn

THE MAN WITH PINS
IN HIS LUNGS

Kotamobagu, northern Sulawesi, Indonesia

After dinner, chatting with a man who speaks with Moses.

Wallace spent June through September 1859 in the Minahasa region of northern Sulawesi, then called Celebes. The island, shaped like a malformed orchid, occupies a curious middle position between two biogeographic realms. By studying the unusual fauna of the island, the world's eleventh largest, Wallace concluded that "while [Celebes] is poor in the actual number of its species, it is yet wonderfully rich in peculiar forms." As usual he used specific observations to illustrate broad theories, writing "the amount of individuality in the productions of a district will be to some extent a measure of the time that district has been isolated from those that surround it. Judged by this standard, Celebes must be one of the oldest parts of the Archipelago. It probably dates from a period not only anterior to that when Borneo, Java, and Sumatra were separated from the continent, but from that still more remote epoch when the land that now constitutes these islands had not risen above the ocean." But Wallace observed people as well as butterflies. He noticed that the people of northern Sulawesi had skin tones that "approached the fairness of a European," and "highly peculiar" mental and moral characteristics since "they are remarkably quiet and gentle in disposition, submissive to the authority of those they consider their superiors, and easily induced to learn and adopt the habits of civilized people." Near the city of Manado, Wallace marveled at the fine coffee plantations and how the "paternal despotism" of the Dutch had helped the local people become "the most industrious, peaceable, and civilized in the whole Archipelago," thereby making "some progress toward a higher social state."

In Southeast Asia, there is general agreement that the prettiest girls come from Chiang Mai in Thailand, Baguio in the Philippines, and Manado in Indonesia. Not coincidentally, those regions produce people with the fairest complexions of their respective countries, and Thais, Filipinos, and Indonesians will not hesitate to explain that "fair equals beautiful." Those three regions have also become important tourist destinations – in Manado's case because tour operators have begun offering diving holidays on the nearby coral reefs at Bunaken. Manado itself is a rather boring, rather Protestant town, where people energetically do the right thing. The houses are neat, the people are bright, the gardens are lush and, alas, most of the beautiful women seem to have been of export quality and therefore sent by the Manado tourist office strategists to distant Jakarta to fuel the reputation of the city as a place of beauties. Is there excitement in northern Sulawesi? A while ago a few visionaries announced optimistic plans to establish an international (Alfred Russel) Wallace University, a center of learning dedicated to the study of natural history and sustainable development. The project came to naught. The region boasts an exotic cuisine, featuring spicy dog, spicy bat, and spicy bear. And Mandao is famed for mystics, acclaimed to be among the most powerful in Asia.

We were eating lunch in a simple *warung* outside Bogani Nani Wartabone National Park in northern Sulawesi – this group I'm with can't go an hour without a food break – and over the grilled fish I started asking about spirits.

This is not a normal question for a foreigner, but the people I was with tolerated my sometimes arcane interests. Endie, a sophisticated woman active in Indonesian conservation decided she could trust me and told us a curious story.

Endie's father was a senior official in the Indonesian customs service. Suddenly he fell ill, and for three years he passed blood in his urine. The eerie thing was that this only happened when he was in Indonesia. When he went overseas for treatment, doctors in Singapore, Taiwan, and Belgium found his urine was normal; once he returned to Indonesia the blood returned. The doctors were baffled. One day, when it was clear he was dying, his assistant came to the house and announced: "My mother, who is a *dukun* (shaman or medium) told me to come."

The younger man explained that he wanted Endie's father's job, and to get it had put a spell on the man, the materials for which included the boss's picture, a small *kris*, some rice husks, palm fibers, needles, and a shroud. By way of explaining his strange confession to the sick old man, he added: "My mother says I must confess that I put a spell on you in order to cleanse my soul."

The young man came from Aceh, in north Sumatra, a land of strange happenings, Endie said, which made it easier for the family to understand his aggressive behaviour.

Endie and her siblings asked her father whether they should take revenge. "No," he answered. "God will decide his fate." Her father died three days later. The murderer, if such he may be called, got the coveted job, but was arrested four months later for corruption.

I asked Endie what she made of all this. "I used to not believe in this mumbo-jumbo," she said. "I do now."

She asked me what I made of it. "If I believed that the man actually did put a spell on my father, then I would have taken revenge. That's the Western approach. An eye for an eye and all that."

Endie shook her head. "No. Let it be. The account will even out by itself."

Even though he seldom wrote about bizarre tales in *The Malay Archipelago*, Wallace was constantly confronted by things that go bump in the night. Sometimes he took a wise-guy approach to such stories.

> I was rather surprised one evening to hear the following curious fact stated; and as it was not contradicted by any of the persons present, I am inclined to accept it provisionally, as a contribution to the natural history of the island. A Bornean Malay who had been for many years resident here said to Manuel [an assistant], 'One thing is strange in this country – the scarcity of ghosts.' 'How so?' asked Manuel. 'Why, you know,' said the Malay, 'that in our countries to the westward, if a man dies or is killed, we dare not pass near the place at night, for all sorts of noises are heard, which show that ghosts are about. But here there are numbers of men killed, and their bodies lie unburied in the fields and by the roadside, and yet you can walk by them at night and never hear or see any thing at all, which is not the case in our country, as you know very well.' 'Certainly I do,' said Manuel; and so it was settled that ghosts were very scarce, if not altogether unknown in Lombock [Lombok]. I would observe, however, that as the evidence is purely negative, we should be wanting in scientific caution if we accepted this fact as sufficiently well established.[1]

This single passage is the only mention of the spirit world in

---

1   *The Malay Archipelago*, 171.

The Malay Archipelago. I've often thought it odd that Wallace didn't mention other strange happenings. I say this for two reasons. The first is that throughout the Malay Archipelago people need very little encouragement to start telling ghost stories. Sitting around the campfire he must have heard strange tales every night. The second is that in later life he was not shy at all about experimenting with, and writing about, spiritualism, seances, and other practices that risked his scientific credibility.

Here's my theory: While in England, and then in the Amazon, Wallace developed an interest in the supernatural. He learned mesmerism (hypnotism) in 1844, ten years *before* leaving for Asia, and said of his controversial talent:

> I thus learnt my first great lesson in the inquiry into these obscure fields of knowledge, never to accept the disbelief of great men or their accusations of imposture or of imbecility, as of any weight when opposed to the repeated observation of facts by other men, admittedly sane and honest. The whole history of science shows us that whenever the educated and scientific men of any age have denied the facts of other investigators on *a priori* grounds of absurdity or impossibility, the deniers have always been wrong.[2]

Most likely Wallace's interest in the occult blossomed while he was in Southeast Asia, and the challenge of trying to figure out what wasn't-meant-to-be-figured-out-using-Aristotelean-logic was actually one of the reasons he stayed in Asia as long as he did. But he refused to mention the black arts in the book. No doubt this was for the same reason he chose not to mention personal passion – except for his headache-inducing butterflies. Did he feel that to discuss the occult world of *djinns* and *dukuns*, *pawangs* and soothsayers, would have somehow lessened the value of *The Malay Archipelago* and turned it from a scholarly travelogue into a lesser work?

---

2   "Notes on the Growth of Opinion as to Obscure Psychical Phenomena During the Last Fifty Years." *Religio-Philosophical Journal*, n.s., 4, No. 15 (1893): 440–441.

I think of Wallace during this northern Sulawesi trip. I'm traveling with friends from the Wallacea Development Institute, an organization set up by a group of well-placed Indonesians to promote sustainable development in the region they define as Wallacea – basically everything between Borneo, Bali, and Irian Jaya. I am watching, with a fair amount of bemusement, their efforts to develop a private Wallace University. They are Wallace's biggest fans in a country that has forgotten him. Although public awareness of his name is not that of McDonald's or Nike, he has spawned a modest intellectual cottage industry. The *warung* in which we sit is near the research station where, in a few weeks, the group will stage a symposium on Biodiversity in Wallacea. We eat curried chicken with our fingers and trade ghost stories. The group finds both habits – my ignoring the fork and enquiring about spirits – somewhat unusual in a foreigner.

We fall into a pattern of "I'll tell you my strange story if you'll tell me yours." Yan Mokoginta, a member of parliament and a major landowner with holdings several hours north, tells of his aunt, Sabina, who sometimes goes into a trance to find rare medicinal plants, which are much-prized by traditional healers. This is a surprising skill since during non-trance periods she can barely distinguish a pumpkin from a pineapple. While in a trance, however, she wanders off into the forest, which is why her family is reluctant to let her practice her quest at night.

We talk about how Manado is famed for black magic, and someone jokes that Yuli, the attractive trophy wife of a much older senior government official, both of whom are traveling in our group, resorted to *"Guna-guna di pakai oleh isteri muda."* The understanding is that Yuli got her husband by putting a powerful spell on her paramour, a typical tactic employed by young gold-digging women. There was some nervous laughter, but Yuli and her husband didn't deny it.

My turn. I tell of meeting the late Sultan Hamengkubuwono IX and asking him about his relationship with Nyai Loro Kidul (also spelled Nyi Roro Kidul), the Queen of the Southern Ocean, the mythical nature spirit whom the sultan considered to be his ancestor. Every June 21, on the sultan's birthday, he made the nineteen-kilometer (twelve-mile) trek to the dangerous surf on the slate-gray southern coast of Java. At the site of his ancestor Senopati's rendezvous with Loro Kidul, the sultan presented an offering to the mermaid queen that included a full set of women's clothing and his own nail and hair clippings.

Sultan Hamengkubuwono IX told me that during the Indonesian fight for independence he fasted for two weeks in order to meet Loro Kidul in a vision. "I saw her, *Eyang* – I call Loro Kidul *Eyang* ("grandmother") – seated behind two of my newphews." Those two newphews died within the week, he said.

This was a critical period for Indonesia, when difficult decisions were being made about when to fight and when to negotiate. The Dutch ruled all but the seven percent of Java that was governed, under contract, by the Javanese royal houses of Solo and Yogyakarta. The negotiations between Hamengkubuwono IX and the Dutch were long and difficult. According to the sultan, the crucial moment came when Loro Kidul told him, "Give them their contract, because soon they will go home."

My friends were entranced. They hadn't heard this story before. I took advantage of their intense interest to spoon some *rendang* beef onto my rice.

"The sultan told me he wasn't worried," I said. I asked him why and he explained that "One night during the Dutch occupation I, and others as well who were living in the *kraton* [palace], heard people moving noisily about, as if wearing armor. The soldiers of Loro Kidul were protecting the *kraton*."

All of us around the table accepted that the mysterious soldiers were simultaneously mystical *and* real. None of my friends doubted for a minute that the sultan had heard warriors milling about. The sultan felt secure and signed the contract, but to this day has never read it, having been reassured by Loro Kidul that the Dutch were on their way out and that the contract was irrelevant. Her predictions came true: a year later, the Japanese invaded Indonesia and evicted the Dutch.

I asked the sultan how a man with a Dutch university degree, a former minister of defence and vice president, a man who spoke Javanese, Indonesian, English, Dutch, and German, a cosmopolitan man in all senses, could believe that he is descended from a mermaid. He offered a typically oblique Javanese response. "Every year on my birthday, people go into the sea to make offerings to her – they go in up to their necks yet nothing happens to them in spite of the sharks and strong currents. The genuine offerings – my fingernails and hair – are accepted by her, but the old clothes people offer her wash back to shore."

I was skeptical. "What is real and what is imagination?" I asked.

"When I was four years old I was already living with a Dutch family, so my brain is in some ways a Western brain," he concluded. "You make a mistake, however, if you insist on a Western answer. Many things happen which can't be explained in a logical way."

We order more Coke. One of my hard-to-break American habits is that I only enjoy Coke with lots and lots of ice, and then I enjoy it immensely. Indonesians, like Americans, understand ice (Europeans don't). The *warung* owner places a bowl of ice chunks on the table.

Yan's turn. His daughter is a physician. She had a patient who complained of severe chest pains and bloody coughs. An X-ray showed that the patient's lungs were filled with needles, a common mystical condition that is often cited when people trade stories about voodoo-like spells. Yan's daughter told the man that there was nothing she could do for him and suggested he see a *dukun*, a local wizard. The man with needles in his lungs went for a *dukun* treatment and returned a few weeks later, feeling just fine. The second X-ray showed nothing in his lungs.

When I heard this I shuddered, as Wallace probably did when he said: "I have heard of strange phenomena but many accounts [seem] too wild and *outre* to be anything but the ravings of madmen." But this is a *doctor*. With X-rays!

Endie, a woman in our group, wants to know more about Loro Kidul and Sultan Hamengkubuwono IX. The Mermaid Queen and the Prince. Both evoke the essence of being Javanese, and Endie's curiosity is a subtle reminder that all but two (Yan and me) of the seven people around the table come from Java, the center of Indonesia's power.

I continue the story, explaining that K. R. T. Hardjonagoro, a senior advisor to the royal family of Solo, which claims an even more direct line of descent from Loro Kidul, told me that "in 1966 Sultan Hamengkubuwono attended the opening of the Samudra Beach Hotel, on Java's southern coast. The night before the opening a local *lurah* (village headman) asked for an audience with the sultan. The old headman told the prince that he had had a dream the previous night in which an old lady demanded her offerings. She was dressed in green, which is Loro Kidul's color.

"The sultan thanked the stranger but explained that he would not make an offering since he was attending the hotel opening in his capacity as minister of defence, not as sultan, and he wanted to separate the affairs of the state from the mystical duties of the palace," Hardjonagoro said. "I was outside, near the pool, when the sultan said goodnight to the well-meaning old man," Hardjonagoro said. "Shortly thereafter I heard the sound of a locomotive. The noise increased until it sounded like ten locomotives were coming towards the beach-front terrace where we were enjoying the hotel's hospitality. A ten-yard-high tidal wave erupted from the sea, which had been calm. It washed away the hotel's buffet table and soaked all the visitors. Some trees were knocked down."

"What did the sultan do?" I asked.

Hardjonagoro looked at me kindly, as if taking pity on me for asking such a stupid question.

"The sultan changed into his royal garments and made the appropriate offerings to Loro Kidul. The sea was calm once again."

My friends momentarily stopped eating.

"The story continues," I said, reaching for the vegetables cooked in coconut milk. "The hotel room in which Sultan Hamengkubuwono made peace with the Mermaid Queen, number 308, is today kept locked and reserved only for her. And another room is kept for her at the Ambarrukmo Palace Hotel in Yogyakarta, near Gunung Merapi, the volcano that is her terrestrial home, so she has a comfortable place to stay when she decides to visit."

As we got into the cars, Yan took me aside. "Come to my family's house. There is someone you should meet."

Once Wallace returned to England his interest in the spiritual world blossomed. He "came out of the closet" in 1865, just three years after returning from Asia, and adopted "spiritualism." This was a brave move for a scientist. A year later he wrote "The Scientific Aspect of the Supernatural," and in 1875 published *On Miracles and Modern Spiritualism*. Charles H. Smith, a history professor at Western Kentucky University who maintains the most complete website devoted to Wallace's writings and life, notes with an even tone that "Wallace's association with spiritualism has generally been regarded as his greatest intellectual inconsistency." Actually, lots of people thought he was nuts. "A little probing, however, reveals that there is considerably more intellectual content to spiritualism than a simple belief in disembodied spirits," Smith concludes. Even Carl Jung noted that Wallace's interest in mesmerism, phrenology, seance, and spirit manifestations merited praise for "having thrown the whole of [Wallace's] authority on to the side of non-material facts, regardless of . . . the cheap derision of [his] contemporaries; even at a time when the intellect of the educated classes was spellbound by the new dogma of materialism, [Wallace] drew public attention to phenomena of an irrational nature, contrary to accepted convictions." Smith notes that Wallace felt that the use of spiritualism must be integrally connected to mankind's spiritualization (i.e. intellectual/moral evolution) in a world that, in his terms, "is really but one of the stages in an endless career."

Of particular interest to me in northern Sulawesi was Wallace's thinking on the possibility that the soul survives after death.

Man is a duality, consisting of an organized spiritual form, evolved coincidently with and permeating the physical body, and having corresponding organs and development. . . . Death is the separation of this duality, and effects no change in the spirit, morally or intellectually.[3]

And Wallace was convinced that such spirits can be contacted.

Spirits can communicate through properly-endowed mediums.[4]

Yan Mokoginta invited me for dinner at his brother's house. The family has large landholdings in this part of northern Sulawesi, but the house is simple, Indonesian middle class. Stone floor, whitewashed walls. Plastic flowers. Brown upholstered furniture. Straight curtains over the doorways – red and grey leaf pattern. Two paintings hang on a far wall, fish and reindeer, in dull colors.

We are four – Yan, a family friend named Sukardi, and Yan's brother, Usman Mokoginta, who has a long face like a seal's, with slicked-back hair. Casually, Usman he tells me he sees two other men in the room. I see nothing, but Usman assures me that he sees a big man with a long white beard and long white hair, who wears a white wool cap, jacket, and tie.

Another man has a black jacket and tie, a big man, bald. Usman asks if this could be my father. "No," I answer. "My father was short and had all his hair."

"Then they must be *jaga*," he decides. Guardians.

I have been to see numerous fortune tellers, mystics, prophets, and holy men. Usually I feel neutral in their presence. I am curious but not a believer. I wait to hear what they have to say. I am cynical;

---

3   "A Defence of Modern Spiritualism," Pt. 2. *Fortnightly Review* 15, No. 90 (1874): 801.

4   Ibid.

I am strong.

Tonight I am apprehensive, in spite of the inaccurate supposition Usman has just made. My posture is twisted. I try to center myself. My body remains off balance. I taste my lunch.

I was sitting with my back to the doorway. I turn around just in time to see a man poke his head in the front door, then withdraw it. In that instant I felt frightened, partly because of his unusual entrance, but more because of what I saw. The man, whose name I learn later is Mansur, has a generous moustache, wavy black hair, and a mischievous smile. He enters the room and we shake hands. He reminds me of a man I never met. He resembles my Pavarotti-resembling grandfather, whom I know only from a single photo.

After dinner we go into a smaller room, a bedroom. An international tennis match being played in distant Jakarta, several thousand kilometers and a time zone away, is on the television in another room – Carl-Uwe Steeb is beating Michael Chang.

The room is hot and crowded. We sit on the floor. My back hurts, and I lean against a bedpost.

Mansur – the man who reminds me of my never-met grandfather – sits cross-legged. He bends forward, puts his right hand to his forehead, then thrusts out his hand. At that moment Sukardi, who is the medium, suddenly shivers, pounds his chest, hits his forehead with a fist, shakes the fist, and makes an abrupt rowing motion. He hunches his shoulders and resembles a bear. His hands shake. He points to a spot next to me. "Your father. He's there. Small body." I look at Sukardi's eyes. They protrude like those of an ornamental goldfish.

Wallace wrote:

> The universal teaching of modern spiritualism is that the world and the whole material universe exist for the purpose of developing spiritual beings – that death is simply a transition from material existence to the first grade of spirit-life – and that our happiness and the degree of our progress will be wholly dependent upon the use we

have made of our faculties and opportunities here.[5]

"Your father is very clever, likes to write," Yan says, trying to translate. Yan has trouble following, since Sukardi speaks partly in Bahasa Mongondow, a rarely heard archaic local tongue.

Sukardi hunches again, a stylized movement that reminds me of Javanese *wayang wong*, where men dance like wooden puppets. He reaches to shake each of our hands.

"You've made contact with your father three times," he says. What am I to make of this?

> The present life will assume a new value and interest when men are brought up not merely in the vascillating and questionable *belief*, but in the settled, indubitable *conviction*, that our existence in this world is really but one of the stages in an endless career, and that the thoughts we think and the deeds we do here will certainly affect our condition and the very form and organic expression of our personality hereafter. [italics Wallace][6]

He said I've contacted my father three times. This is true if I consider that I had visited three other mediums who claim to have made contact with him. But otherwise Sukardi is a bit of a psychic wash-out.

But I play along, wondering what is the correct question when enquiring of a dead relative?

Instead of asking what the weather's like in heaven, or if there are pretty girls up there or how's the food, I ask my father, rather feebly in retrospect, if he is all right.

Sukardi speaks with a gruff, theatrical voice. Mixed in with the words are many guttural, animal-like sounds. "He's a writer, like you."

No, I think. You're wrong. He's not a writer, like me. He's a

---

5 "Spiritualism." In *Chambers's Encyclopaedia*, 1892, London and Edinburgh: William & Robert Chambers, Ltd., 648.

6 Ibid.

dreamer, like me.

> What more natural than that [the spirits] should wish,
> whenever possible, to give some message to their friends,
> if only to assure them that death is not the end, that they
> still live, and are not unhappy. Many facts seem to show
> us that the beautiful idea of guardian spirits is not a mere
> dream, but a frequent, perhaps universal reality.[7]

I ask about a man called David, without explaining who he is.
"He is smart. Do whatever you feel is right. Your father will
help."
"What will happen to my son?"
"He will be like you."
I am not sure this is a good thing.

Sukardi has been giving me vague answers, and I am full yet
unsatisfied, the Chinese dinner syndrome in a spiritual context. I
reflect on the strange circumstances that brought me here. I had
met Yan Mokoginta in Jakarta more than a year earlier, through Russ
Betts, head of WWF in Indonesia. I was interested in Yan's work in
developing the Wallace University. Since then we had lost contact.
Then, I ran into Mokoginta at the Ujung Pandang (Makassar)
airport. The circumstances were serendipitous. I had planned to
fly on a Sunday from Denpasar to Manado and then take a local
bus down to Bogani Nani Wartabone National Park. My flight had
to transit through Ujung Pandang. A friend convinced me to leave
on the Monday instead. Yan was on a Monday flight from Jakarta
to Ujung Pandang, which connected to my flight. His destination?
Manado and then Bogani Nani Wartabone National Park. He was
traveling with Gunawan Satari, the number two man in the Ministry
of Research and Technology, and officials of the Indonesian Red

---

7   "Miracles and Modern Spiritualism." *Light*, No. 806 (1896): 276.

Cross, the British Council, and the Wallacea Development Institute. They were preparing a workshop on biodiversity in the Wallace region. They invited me to join them for the recce and to come back for the workshop several weeks later. Coincidence? Destiny?

"Your son is in Java," Sukardi says, taking a guess.

"Yes."

"Jakarta."

Not really. He is in Bogor, forty-five minutes away. Close enough.

"You've never met him."

I sit stunned. This man has no way of knowing that. He has no business in knowing that. I stare at the man with Marty Feldman eyes, legs folded, shoulders hunched like a Neanderthal, speaking an ancient language. He's been giving me softball answers and then comes out and tells me I've never seen my son, a situation which I will change in a few weeks. He grunts. My spine feels like a pretzel.

"What about *jodoh*?" What is my fate?

"You have two destinies. Romance and work. You have success in both, but need great patience."

More softball answers. "My mother?"

"Sick." He makes asthma sounds, massages his leg.

I explain she's dead.

Sukardi extends his hand and, acting as medium, conveys my parents' love to me. Sukardi and I are both shaking. "They protect you."

He closes his eyes and shudders. His body relaxes and he "awakes" from the trance. He does not remember the previous half hour and asks what happened.

Later, I ask Mansur how he got his gift. He explains he has only had it for two years, since he was forty. He had had a dream in which he was fighting against many people, when the "force" came to him and he was able to vanquish his enemies. Now, whenever he is in trouble he listens to a voice that tells him what to do. I think of Sultan Hamengkubuwono IX and Loro Kidul. How reassuring to have a guardian angel, or a mermaid queen, looking after you. I am reminded of Wallace's comment.

> If there be a spiritual world, if those whose existence
> on earth has come to an end still live, what is more
> natural than that many spirits should be distressed at the
> disbelief . . . that so widely prevail[s] with respect to a
> future life. . . . What more natural than that they should
> wish . . . to give some message to their friends, if only to
> assure them that death is not the end, that they still live,
> and are not unhappy. Many facts seem to show us that the
> beautiful idea of guardian spirits is not a mere dream, but a
> frequent, perhaps universal reality.[8]

Before we leave, Yan disappears with his brother into another room. I assume they are talking about family matters. Back in the car, however, Yan tells me what his brother said.

"Remember the man my brother saw protecting you at the beginning of the evening? The big man in white?"

I remember.

"That was Moses. Moses protects you."

I don't know what to make of that. I don't want to hurt Yan's feelings, but I also have trouble taking this too seriously. I am well over the brush with discomfort I had fifteen minutes earlier and back to my normal skeptical self. Again, someone (or something) gives me the wisdom to shut up.

"My brother also saw Moses protecting me," Yan says. "We both have a task. You are Jewish. I am Muslim."

"And what is the task?" I ask.

"Peace in the Middle East."

"Yan, I can't get away. I have a book to write," I protest, trying to lighten the mood.

"Not now. You don't have to go now. The time will come," Yan says. "But that was Moses."

---

8   Ibid.

SCUBA DIVING FROM
REALM TO REALM

On the Ocean Floor, Komodo National Park,
Indonesia

*Shallow seas gave Alfred Russel Wallace key ideas about the
movement of people and animals.*

It is not coincidental that both Charles Darwin, on his Beagle
voyage, and Alfred Russel Wallace, on his Asian travels, carried
Principles of Geology by Charles Lyell. When Wallace sent his
Ternate Paper to Darwin, he requested that if Darwin felt the
paper had merit he should pass it on to Lyell. Why was Lyell
so important? One reason, of course, was Lyell's status in the
British scientific establishment. And through his writings, Lyell
offered the naturalists a solid scientific foundation on which
to develop evolutionary theories. Sagely refusing to speculate
on the origins of the earth, and thereby avoiding the wrath
of creationists, Lyell argued that the earth has been shaped
from the beginning by uniform forces still at work – erosion,
accumulation of sediment, earthquakes, and volcanoes – and
that those forces created environments in which new species
emerged and others became extinct. Both Darwin and Wallace
recognized that changes in physical habitats had a major
influence on species diversity and evolution. Darwin mentions
this in the very first sentence of *The Origin of Species*: "When

on board H.M.S. 'Beagle,' as naturalist, I was much struck with certain facts in the distribution of the organic beings inhabiting South America, and in the geological relations of the present to the past inhabitants of that continent."

Wallace developed similar observations while in the Amazon and in Indonesia, and his contributions to a discipline now termed biogeography, although less recognized, can be considered as important as his ideas about natural selection and evolution.

I learned to scuba dive in downtown Jakarta, in a public pool in the middle-class neighborhood of Cikini. The bottom of the pool did not reward close examination, but the experience did get me a diving certification and thereby entry into the Nusantara Diving Club. At that time, in the early 1970s, Indonesia was a more laissez-faire place than it is now, and on several occasions we chartered Indonesian navy and police boats for our weekend jaunts to the Thousand Islands just outside Jakarta harbor. Usually we had to hide below decks while our gun boat left sight of land, playing a silly charade to obfuscate the fact that fifty pleasure-trippers were paying the captain a chunk of cash to use the armed forces' boat.

Jakarta harbor then was littered with rubbish and dead rats. The coral reefs of the Thousand Islands forty years ago were okay in spots, but even then they were getting hammered by careless anchoring, dynamite fishing, and uncontrolled exploitation of coral for road construction and to make terrazzo flooring tiles. Today, the Thousand Islands have been turned into a weekend holiday getaway. You can still get a tan at the Thousand Islands, part of which is now a national park, but you might have trouble seeing coral or manta rays or sand sharks or turtles. For diving, people fly to the other side of Indonesia – Manado or Flores or West Papua.

I sit on the sandy ocean floor in about twenty meters (sixty-five feet) of tepid water and try to stay calm as a group of manta rays swim over, next to, and in front of me. I slow my breathing, not wanting my bubbles to disturb the huge fish, but they pay me no mind. They remind me of Darth Vader creatures, black on top, pale below, as wide as cars, slim as a flat-screen TV, with whippy tails that add another few meters, swimming with an unwordly grace. It is an "oh my god" moment for me, and I only leave my sandy seat after the rays depart and my air supply is low. My dive buddies and I swim to the waiting liveaboard dive boat, have a quick shower, change into shorts and T-shirts, and enjoy a few cold beers before a delicious dinner, followed by more beer while sitting on the roof of the boat watching the tropical night sky. Then to bed in an air-conditioned cabin, listening to Beethoven on my iPod.

I was scuba diving in Komodo National Park. This is the Far East of Indonesia, a country similar in width to San Francisco to New York. Eastern Indonesia is the equivalent of America's Far West during the nineteenth century – a vaguely uncomfortable, vaguely alien, and difficult-to-get-to place seldom visited by the sophisticated and much more numerous people living on the western islands of Sumatra, Java, Bali, and Sulawesi.

Two reasons for mentioning this incident.

The first is the observation that if I had an unlimited supply of scuba tanks, I could have scuba dived along the sea floor all the way from Komodo to New Guinea to Australia in the eastern part of Indonesia, without ever going deeper than forty meters (one hundred and thirty feet). And I could have done a similar long-distance submarine trek from Bali to Java to Sumatra to Malaysia in the western part of the country. But such a journey would be impossible in the middle of Indonesia, along the transition region called Wallacea, where the ocean is substantially deeper.

The second reason is to imagine how much Wallace would have enjoyed the comfort of such a liveaboard dive boat.

Wallace did his collecting on land, but the seas were of paramount importance to him. The ocean was his highway from one island to another – on arrival at a coastal village he quickly headed into the interior where the beetles, birds, and butterflies lived – land-based critters he understood. He was less comfortable with the creatures, and personality, of the sea.[1]

While Wallace was in the Amazon and Rio Negro in Brazil, he collected, and sketched, numerous river fishes. But in the Malay Archipelago he chose to focus on land-based life forms. When he did describe natural productions of the sea, it was usually in terms of a commodity (as when he wrote about sea cucumbers) or as a simple observation, like a couple of lines scribbled on a postcard.

> [In Ambon harbor] the clearness of the water afforded me one of the most astonishing and beautiful sights I have ever beheld. The bottom was absolutely hidden by a continuous series of corals, sponges, actiniæ, and other marine productions of magnificent dimensions, varied forms, and brilliant colors. . . . For once, the reality exceeded the most glowing accounts I had ever read of the wonders of a coral sea. There is perhaps no spot in the world richer in marine productions, corals, shells, and fishes than the harbor of Amboyna [Ambon].[2]

For the most part, Wallace had miserable experiences in small boats. Most of the time Wallace's sixty sea journeys were largely miserable, dangerous, exhausting, and costly.[3]

Wallace describes the worst of his Asian sea journeys, which

1   After his near-fatal experience in the Atlantic Ocean on his return from Brazil, Wallace promised: "Fifty times since I have left Para have I vowed if I once reached England, never to trust myself more on the oceans. But good resolutions soon fade."

2   *The Malay Archipelago*, 301.

3   No doubt his dislike of the sea was intensified after he had drifted for ten days in a lifeboat in the Atlantic after the ship he was sailing on from Brazil to England caught fire.

was aboard a boat he commissioned and designed, with a crew he recruited himself.

> My first crew ran away in a body; two men were lost on a desert island, and only recovered a month later after twice sending in search of them; we were ten times run aground on coral reefs; we lost four anchors; our sails were devoured by rats; our small boat was lost astern; we were thirty-eight days on a voyage which should not have taken twelve; we were many times short of food and water; we had no compass-lamp owing to there being not a drop of oil in Waigiou when we left; and, to crown all, during our whole voyage from Goram by Ceram to Waigiou, and from Waigiou to Ternate, occupying in all seventy-eight days, all in what was supposed to be the favourable season, we had *not one single day of fair wind*. [italics Wallace][4]

Only once did he have (relative) comfort.

> I have never, either before or since, made a twenty days' voyage [Ujung Pandang to Kei to Aru] so pleasantly, or perhaps more correctly speaking, with so little discomfort. This I attribute chiefly to having my small cabin on deck, and entirely to myself, to having my own servants to wait upon me, and to the absence of all those marine-store smells of paint, pitch, tallow, and new cordage, which are to me insupportable. Something is also to be put down to freedom from all restraint of dress, hours of meals, etc., and to the civility and obliging disposition of the captain. . . . The crew were all civil and good-tempered, and with very little discipline every thing went on smoothly, and the vessel was kept very clean and in pretty good order, so that on the whole I was much

---

4   *My Life*, Vol. 1, 370–1.

delighted with the trip, and was inclined to rate the luxuries of the semi-barbarous prau as surpassing those of the most magnificent screw-steamer, that highest result of our civilization.[5]

When I lived in Jakarta, I shared a boat with two friends, Randy, a banker, and David, a market researcher. Knowing more about packing a picnic lunch than the workings of an outboard, we were at the mercy of our boat boy Abdul, who worked concurrently as boat boy for a dozen other small pleasure boats moored at the Police Harbor, most of which were nicer, better maintained, and whose owners paid him more money.

On weekends we would putter out to one of the nearby islands for some diving and, toward the end of the afternoon, find that we couldn't start the damn engine, no matter how hard we pulled the cord and how loudly we cursed. Our reputation for having to be towed back in did not enhance our invitations to women to join us on our pleasure cruises.

It was therefore with mixed feelings that I received the following message from a colleague at the advertising agency where I worked. It arrived as I was shooting a particularly troublesome commercial featuring white angora cats that were supposed to be cute and cuddly but threw up whenever the studio lights were turned on. "Paul, please call David urgently," the note began. "Your boat sunk. Have a nice day."

David, the world's best salesman, then did the impossible. He sold the boat, sight unseen, to a newly arrived American businessman, convincing the guy that with this boat he could enjoy spectacular tropical delights, not the least of which would be having lissome Indonesian ladies willing to rub suntan oil on his body. Somehow (I think Randy called in some favors from the Chinese businessmen to whom he loaned money at the bank where he worked), someone

5   *The Malay Archipelago*, 431.

dredged the boat, washed away the gunk, removed the dead wildlife, and tuned up the engine. Last I heard, the American paid Abdul a real salary and was happy with his purchase.

For Wallace, the presence of shallow seas in the Western (the Sunda Shelf) and Eastern (Sahel Shelf) halves of Indonesia, separated by a deep trough in the middle, was a key to island biology. His observations of sea levels, plus observations of the flora and fauna on different islands, led Wallace to elaborate on the distinction between Western and Eastern Indonesia; this demarcation was later dubbed the Wallace line by Thomas Huxley. Wallace wasn't the first observer to note the differences, and he was quick to give credit to another scientist.

> It was first pointed out by Mr. George Windsor Earl, in a paper read before the Royal Geographical Society in 1845, that a shallow sea connected the great islands of Sumatra, Java, and Borneo with the Asiatic continent, with which their natural productions generally agreed; while a similar shallow sea connected New Guinea and some of the adjacent islands to Australia, all being characterized by the presence of Marsupials. . . . Notwithstanding important differences between us, to him undoubtedly belongs the merit of first indicating the division of the Archipelago into an Australian and an Asiatic region, which it has been my good-fortune to establish by more detailed observations.[6]

Wallace, using extensive biological evidence that he alone was in a position to compile, was the first to put meat on the bones of the East-West differentiation. Here's where Wallace's knowledge of taxonomy was applied to something grander than identifying new species.

---

6   Ibid., 20–1.

It is certainly a wonderful and unexpected fact, that an accurate knowledge of the distribution of birds and insects should enable us to map out lands and continents which disappeared beneath the ocean long before the earliest traditions of the human race.[7]

There is now a Club Med on the beach at Kuantan, Malaysia, and the exotic aromas of Bain de Soleil and Camembert hang heavy in the afternoon glare. The picture-book beach is well sheltered to avoid outraging the conservative sensitivities of devout Muslim villagers who do not understand the importance of a good suntan to an upwardly mobile vacationer's well-being.

This beach was high and dry as recently as ten thousand years ago. In fact, much of the South China Sea didn't exist in those days, and it would have been possible to walk from Kuantan to Kuching, Bangkok to Brunei, or Singapore to Surabaya. During the most recent ice age, at its coldest just eighteen thousand years ago, the low temperatures locked up so much water in the polar regions that the tropical sea level was lowered by some 115 meters (377 feet), exposing dry land where today the shallow South China Sea protects colorful coral gardens.

But the low sea level was just part of the long cycle of shifting coasts. When the great polar ice caps melted, as they have some twenty times over the past two million years, the subsequent raising of the sea flooded much of the land, isolating the large islands of Borneo, Sumatra, and Java, along with thousands of smaller islands. Today the sea level is about as high as it has ever been, and Southeast Asia has only half as much land as it had when the poles were at their iciest.

Part of the diversity of wildlife in the region is due to this cycle of sea level changes. The animals isolated on each island evolved new characteristics and, in some cases, became new

---

7 Ibid., 29.

species. Then the cycle repeated itself, the ice caps refroze, the sea levels dropped, and land bridges were recreated. New migrations took place, followed in turn by yet another sequence of isolation and evolution. The smaller, rapidly reproducing mammals were particularly malleable; each of the larger offshore islands has its own forms of rats, squirrels, tree shrews, and mouse deer.

An understanding of geology led Wallace to the concept of what later was dubbed the "Wallace Line."

> We can draw a line among the islands, which shall so divide them that one-half shall truly belong to Asia, while the other shall no less certainly be allied to Australia. I term these respectively the Indo-Malayan, and the Austro-Malayan divisions of the Archipelago.[8]

Wallace went further still. He was intrigued that large islands (in this case, Borneo and New Guinea), which lie at similar latitudes and which both have vast expanses of forest, mangrove, coastal, and mountain ecosystems, *should* have similar life forms. But they don't. Again, he attributed these differences to the respective locations of these gigantic islands on opposite sides of the Wallace line.

> Borneo and New Guinea, as alike physically as two distinct countries can be, are zoologically wide as the poles asunder; while Australia, with its dry winds, its open plains, its stony deserts, and its temperate climate, yet produces birds and quadrupeds which are closely related to those inhabiting the hot, damp, luxuriant forests which everywhere clothe the plains and mountains of New Guinea.[9]

8   Ibid., 21.
9   Ibid., 27.

Wallace's conclusion, obtained after studying thousands of specimens and consulting geology texts, was that island Southeast Asia should be divided as follows:

> West – which Wallace called the *Indo-Malayan* region, comprising Peninsular Malaysia (and therefore the Asian mainland), Sumatra, Java, Bali, Borneo, and the Philippines. Here Wallace found tigers, monkeys, and wild cattle; hornbills, bears, and squirrels; barbets, fruit thrushes, and woodpeckers.
>
> East – which Wallace called the *Austro-Malayan* region, comprising eastern Molucca, Seram, New Guinea, and Australia. Here Wallace found marsupials, birds of paradise, large flightless birds like cassowaries, and brush turkeys, but no monkeys, cats, sheep, or wild cattle.
>
> Center – a curious transition zone, later dubbed *Wallacea*, comprising Sulawesi, Ternate, and western Molucca, with elements of both West and East, and with specific life forms found nowhere else. Here Wallace found:[10] megapodes (ground-nesting birds), babirusa (literally pig-deer), anoa (a dwarf buffalo), numerous tarsiers and macaques, as well as several marsupials that reflect the Austro-Malayan region.

My friends Lily and Farquhar have a splendid house outside Ubud, in the center of Bali, and one afternoon we sat in their garden and gazed at the intricate basket-like nest of a streaked weaver bird that had made its home in a nearby clump of bamboo. As we sipped gin and tonics we recalled that Wallace too observed weaver birds in Bali, but notably did *not* see them in Lombok, just twenty-four kilometers [fifteen miles] to the east.[11]

---

10 A stunning sixty-two percent of Sulawesi's mammals and thirty-four percent of the birds are endemic.

11 The Lombok Strait is forty kilometers [twenty-five miles] wide at its northern end

In so well-cultivated a country [Bali] it was not to be expected that I could do much in natural history, and my ignorance of how important a locality this was for the elucidation of the geographical distribution of animals, caused me to neglect obtaining some specimens which I never met with again. One of these was a weaver bird with a bright yellow head, which built its bottle-shaped nests by dozens on some trees near the beach. It was the Ploceus hypoxantha, a native of Java; and here, at the extreme limits of its range westerly.[12]

Weaver birds, Wallace knew, were common throughout the lands to the west of Bali: Java, Sumatra, the Malay Peninsula. The strait between Bali and Lombok, although superficially similar to dozens of other straits in Indonesia, must nevertheless represent a significant natural barrier that separated two major realms of nature, he reckoned.

On crossing over to Lombock [Lombok], separated from Bali by a strait less than twenty miles wide [thirty-two kilometers], I naturally expected to meet with some of these birds again; but during a stay there of three months I never saw one of them, but found a totally different set of species, most of which were utterly unknown not only in Java, but also in Borneo, Sumatra, and Malacca.[13]

The Lombok Strait, one of the most accessible demarcations of the Wallace Line, is today a major tourist route where several times a day a modern hydrofoil zips across the 250-meter- [820-feet-] deep strait.

The great contrast between the two divisions of the Archipelago is nowhere so abruptly exhibited as on

and eighteen kilometers [eleven miles] wide at its southern end.

12   *The Malay Archipelago*, 162.

13   Ibid., 211.

passing from the island of Bali to that of Lombock, where
the two regions are in closest proximity. In Bali we have
barbets, fruit-thrushes, and woodpeckers; on passing
over to Lombock these are seen no more, but we have
abundance [sic] of cockatoos, honeysuckers, and brush-
turkeys, which are equally unknown in Bali, or any island
further west.[14] The strait here is fifteen miles [twenty-
four kilometers] wide, so that we may pass in two hours
from one great division of the earth to another, differing
as essentially in their animal life as Europe does from
America.[15]

It's interesting that Wallace chose birds to make his point about
the West-East boundary; he also noted that birds can indicate when
the islands separated from the mainland.

Birds offer us one of the best means of determining the
law of distribution; for though at first sight it would
appear that the watery boundaries which keep out the
land quadrupeds could be easily passsed over by birds,
yet practically it is not so. . . . As an instance, among the
islands of which I am now speaking, it is a remarkable fact
that Java possesses numerous birds which never pass over
to Sumatra, though they are separated by a strait only
fifteen miles wide, and with islands in mid-channel. Java,
in fact possesses more birds and insects peculiar to itself
than either Sumatra or Borneo, and this would indicate

14 There are variations, of course, and this is not a perfect science. While Bali is
"connected" to Java in broad biogeographic terms, both being part of the (Western)
Indo-Malayan realm, the strait between Java and Bali is sufficiently wide and
sufficiently old so that differences abound. American evolutionary biologist Philip
Darlington noted that "Many groups of mammals that reach Java do not reach
Bali, such as hairy hedgehogs, flying lemurs, lorises, gibbons, flying squirrels, some
other genera of rodents, the Asiatic wild dog, weasels, badgers and otters, leopards,
rhinoceros, chevrotains, and probably wild buffalo. Bali does not share the main
part of the Javan mammal fauna. Mammals that do extend (from Java) to Bali but not
to Lombok include a tree shrew, two monkeys, a scaly anteater, two squirrels, the
leopard cat, and the tiger."

15 *The Malay Archipelago*, 25–6.

that it was earliest separated from the continent; next in organic individuality is Borneo, while Sumatra is so nearly identical in all its animal forms with the peninsula of Malacca that we may safely conclude it to have been the most recently dismembered island.[16]

While I theoretically *could* scuba dive from Singapore to Kuching on the island of Borneo it is more comfortable to take a ship. I remember fondly my journey in 1970 aboard a freighter that carried goods across the South China Sea. I was one of just a handful of passengers and I had the time during the three-day crossing to complete work on a play that I was certain would win me the Pulitzer Prize.

In the mid-1990s I wanted to take a similar cruise and called the twenty-odd shipping companies that ply the Singapore–Kuching route. They each told me the same thing. The small passenger-carrying freighters were history. If I wanted to sail to Borneo it would have to be inside a container.

---

16 Ibid., 24.

SERENDIPITY AND DRAGONFLIES

Sangburnih, Bali, Indonesia

In a simple country temple, overlooking the shore where Wallace made landfall.

Alfred Russel Wallace had no intention of going to Bali. He visited the island (landing in Bileling, now Buleleng) in June 1856 simply because the ship he was taking to Sulawesi ("the Kembang Djepoon [Rose of Japan], a schooner belonging to a Chinese merchant, manned by a Javanese crew, and commanded by an English captain") stopped there. He spent just two days in Bali (and gave the island just two pages in *The Malay Archipelago*), less time than most modern tourists, but managed to see enough (and shoot sufficient quantities of birds) to determine that Bali's biogeographic position formed the eastern boundary of the Indo-Malayan realm that includes Borneo, Java, Sumatra, and the Malay Peninsula. During his subsequent visit to Lombok, just several kilometers to the east, Wallace found completely new forms, which indicated that the narrow but deep straits he had sailed formed a natural boundary between two distinct biogeographic realms. "[Bali and Lombok] are the only islands of the whole Archipelago in which the Hindoo religion still maintains itself," he wrote, "and they form the extreme points of the two great zoological divisions of the eastern hemisphere; for although so similar in external appearance and in all physical features, they differ greatly in their natural productions."

While living in Jakarta, a weekend break in Bali was never enough, but better than nothing. Dubbed by tourism promoters as the "island of the gods," Bali never failed to entrance me. Was it the green of the rice paddies? The surf at Kuta? The dingaling of the gamelan? The magic-mushroom omelettes? The best thing was that many of my trips were for business since one of my advertising clients was the Hotel Bali Beach Intercontinental, the first, tallest, and by far the ugliest hotel built on the island (paid for partly by Japanese war reparations). After the eight-story Bali Beach was built, Balinese officials declared that no subsequent construction would be allowed on the island that was taller than a coconut palm. While working on this book I spent half a sabbatical year at the Bali complex in Sanur of my artist friends Didier, Brent, Leonard, and Tom. It was the most sybaritic period of my life. Early in the morning I would sit on the terrace of the thatched-roof cottage, eating mango, gazing into the lily ponds.

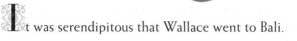

It was serendipitous that Wallace went to Bali.

> It was after having spent two years in Borneo, Malacca, and Singapore that I made a somewhat involuntary visit to [Bali and Lombok] on my way to Macassar. Had I been able to obtain a passage direct to that place from Singapore, I should probably never have gone near them, and should have missed some of the most important

discoveries of my whole expedition to the East.[1]

My friend Vithal Rajan tells me that things do not happen accidentally. And Bali seems to be the place for unlikely but nevertheless fruitful events. Like the time I met Made Murni while walking along the main Kuta-Seminyak road in Bali. She was a secretary for a small garment export firm, but that stifling afternoon she was in front of the factory/office doing a bit of gardening. It took me about five minutes to get past the tiring Indonesian queries ("You speak Indonesian!") to the point where I decided I could entrust her with my interest in the arcane and mystical.

"My brother can help you," she offered. North. Outside Singaraja. As it turned out her village was just a few kilometers from the location where Wallace made landfall in Bali. We agreed that I would return the next day at which time she would give me a letter.

I was skeptical she would have it ready, having been burned too many times by Indonesian promises built on honey. But I was wrong. Not only did she have a letter ready but she had written instructions on how to get to her tiny village.

I was traveling rough and cheap, with no map, deliberately, and only had a vague idea where I was headed. The roads became smaller, the villages poorer, the traffic lighter, the stares more frequent. The money taker of the last of the five *bemo* rides that hot day knew Made Murni's family. Riding jauntily on the small truck, half in, half out of the open side door, he asked me where I was from, and I told him, as I had told twenty other people that day.

The most striking feature of the countryside of northern Bali is how lush it is. To be sure, much of the green is cultivated, as Wallace remarked:

> I was both astonished and delighted; for as my visit to
> Java was some years later, I had never beheld so beautiful
> and well cultivated a district out of Europe. A slightly
> undulating plain extends from the sea-coast about ten or

---

1   *The Malay Archipelago*, 160.

twelve miles inland, where it is bounded by a fine range of wooded and cultivated hills. Houses and villages, marked out by dense clumps of cocoanut palms, tamarind and other fruit-trees, are dotted about in every direction; while between them extend luxuriant rice-grounds, watered by an elaborate system of irrigation that would be the pride of the best cultivated parts of Europe.[2]

While it's true that much of Bali's forests have been converted to agriculture, I was reassured to see expanses of natural forest in the region of Sangburnih, where Made Murni's family lives.

I wanted to explore the forest, but we never got further than talking about it. I suspect this was because Made Murni's brother Surata, who became my guide and host and adopted younger brother, either didn't want me to go, or didn't want to go himself, or didn't know the path (his official excuse), or whatever.

But it worked out okay. Serendipity is a funny concept. If I hadn't walked down the street in Kuta that afternoon . . . if I hadn't stopped to talk to Made (following our ten minutes of conversation I never saw her again; she disappeared like a forest nymph) . . . if I hadn't followed a hunch . . . if I hadn't abandoned the idea of exploring the forest and gone with the flow in Sangburnih I would have missed one of the most sublime places of my voyage.

Surata and I took a *bemo* to a nearby *kampong*, and we sat around a while talking boy talk that characterizes Indonesia as much as fried bananas and population pressure. We shot the breeze and checked out the talent. "He's my darling," Surata would announce about every thirty seconds as a stream of female "relatives" strolled around.

"*She*, Surata," I would correct.

"Yes. *She* is my beautiful love," he would giggle as girl after girl sauntered by. (I perfectly understand Surata's heightened testosterone level. Noel Coward was one of many visitors to comment on the attractiveness of Balinese women. Of their bosoms he wrote: "Their longitude and latitude/Have come to be a platitude.")

---

2   Ibid., 161.

We got a couple of young boys to show us the way to the top of the *pura* on the hill behind Desa Lebah. An easy twenty minute walk.

As temples go, this *pura* is definitely blue collar. Small, not terribly elaborate, isolated. I climbed the final set of stairs, made a *namaste* and entered to see a wooden carved deer head, which looked like a happy-face reindeer. I looked around and finally decided that this place was too precious to share. I realize that this sounds too precious to write, but sometimes, when I find a special place, I go into Greta Garbo mode. I asked Surata and the boys to go on ahead. I would follow shortly.

Indonesians hate to leave foreigners alone. Partly it is because they are frightened to be alone themselves, and they project this fear onto others ("You're not frightened to sleep alone?"). Partly it is that they take seriously the responsibility of looking after a guest. And I think there is a third explanation, which is that they think that Europeans are clumsy, ignorant, innocent children who, instead of safely scampering down the hill to the village like any four year old, will take a wrong turn, break a leg, be attacked by demons, scramble over the watershed, and wind up, days later, crippled, angry, and broke in distant Denpasar. How would Surata explain that to the police?

How could I get Surata to leave me alone? I told him a half-truth, that I wanted to pray. That made sense, although prayer is not something for which a Balinese requires solitude. Nevertheless, Surata did leave me alone, and I am grateful.

Imagine the setting. The temple, like all Balinese temples, faces inland, the direction the Balinese call *kaja*, toward the mountains. The good gods live in the inland volcanoes; the bad ones reside in the sea, a direction termed *kelod* in Bali, one reason most Balinese have never learned to swim.[3] Wallace too had noted the danger of the Balinese ocean.

---

3   Hawaii has similar terms, but with opposite implications. The term *mauka* indicates the direction inland, toward the mountains, the dangerous realm of Pele, the unpredictable goddess of volcanoes and destruction. The sea, however, toward the direction the Hawaiians call *makai*, is positive to the Hawaiians. Hawaiians, after all, are seafaring Polynesians, the folks who invented surfing and catamaran dinner cruises.

I felt considerably relieved when all my boxes and myself
had passed in safety through the devouring surf, which
the natives look upon with some pride, saying that 'their
sea is always hungry, and eats up every thing it can catch.'[4]

It seems logical that a truly dangerous surf evolves negative
spiritual attributes. I looked to the dangerous *kelod* north and saw
several kilometers of villages, the plains, and, in the distance, the
angry demon-filled sea. To the *kaja* south lay reassuring mountains,
garlanded with forests that provided water to the fruit trees growing
half way up the slope and to the rice paddies nestled at the base of
the hills. I counted at least five stages of rice cultivation in an area
of less than a square kilometer. A farmer with two golden brown
cows, which Wallace noted are "descended from the [wild] Bos-
banteng of Java," ploughed the grey mud. How wonderful that this
drab dirt color would be transformed into the emerald green of rice.

Wet rice is a particularly human invention. It is one of the four
major "eco-revolutions" that has transformed the shape and style
of Asia, and in Bali it relies on intricate networks of terraces and
cooperative irrigation. The terraces, in fact, may be among the
most memorable aspects of Balinese scenery.

> The whole surface of the country is divided into irregular
> patches, following the undulations of the ground . . . each
> of which is itself perfectly level, but stands . . . several
> feet above or below those adjacent to it. Every one of
> these patches can be flooded or drained at will by means
> of a system of ditches and small channels, into which are
> diverted the whole of the streams that descend from the
> mountains. Every patch now bore crops in various stages
> of growth . . . of the most exquisite green tints.[5]

Conservationists can be hard-nosed realists and sometimes try

---

4   *The Malay Archipelago*, 163.
5   Ibid., 161.

to put a monetary value on nature by calculating "environmental services." Trees equal water equals food. That's pedantic economics, but it sells, at least in certain conservation quarters. But sitting up in that modest temple I recognized that there might be more to nature than that. Yes, from the interior god-blessed *kaja* mountains comes fertile volcanic ash and water which makes agriculture possible.

But from the *kaja* mountains also comes the blessings of good spirits.

The lush and mysterious forests that enchanted me were designated as nature reserves by the government but are managed by the people. And I think that people look after nature for both pragmatic (water) and spiritual reasons. It didn't take long before I stopped mentally calculating stream flows and the rupiah value of constant water and sought a different arithmetic. I wanted to use the sacredness of the place to see myself, and I began a series of meditation and breathing exercises I had learned in Hawaii.

I entered my own little world, feeling quite pleased with myself and satisfied that the day had turned out so rich. I explored a tiny corner of the cosmos that day, up there in the temple of trees in northern Bali. But my reverie didn't last long. In my heightened emotional state I had neglected to notice that I had been sitting on a red ant track. The insects pulled me back smartly from the path to Nirwana.

Wallace was a magnet for serendipity.

Arnold Brackman, a Wallace biographer and cheerleader of the theory that Darwin cheated Wallace out of fame and glory, tells of an event that occurred when Wallace was eighty-five and living in England. Wallace had received a bag of orchids from a colleague working in South America. Out of the sack dropped three beetles, which turned out to be rare species that were not even in the vast collection of the British Museum (Natural History). Brackman also writes that shortly thereafter, just before Christmas, "Wallace made the evening round of his orchid rooms. Suddenly a large insect flew by him and settled on a workbench. Its lower wings were brilliant orange, the upper, brownish-orange." Brackman goes on to quote Wallace (in a letter to his son Will): "At first I thought it was a butterfly that mimicked a moth, but I had never seen anything like it before." The insect, which had been hidden in a chrysalis on an orchid, turned out to be a strange South American moth, which indeed does resemble a butterfly. Like the beetles a few days earlier, it too was missing from the British Museum's collections. James Marchant, Wallace's friend and admirer, later wrote, "It was certainly a strange . . . coincidence that these creatures should find themselves in Wallace's greenhouse, where alone they would be noticed and appreciated."[6]

I had my own bit of Wallace-related serendipity in Kuching, Sarawak. I went into an antique shop along the Main Bazaar in Kuching. I started to chat with the proprietress named Diana, an Iban, who informed me that her father was Sarawak's first chief minister. I explained that I wanted to look for the site of James Brooke's cottage at Peninjauh where Wallace and Brooke's assistant Spencer St. John spent a week. "Uncle Ho would be interested in going with you," she said. Then, almost as if the gods had been watching, Uncle Ho, a prominent local historian, walked into the shop. Although in his seventies Ho An Chon was full of energy and insights. We drove to a small village at the base of what Wallace described as a "very steep pyramidal mountain of crystalline basaltic rock . . . covered with luxuriant forest." We asked a few people whether anyone might be able to show us the path and were directed to a house in the middle of the *kampong*. The man we had been instructed to see turned out to be a former classmate of Ho's whom he had not seen for some thirty years. He took us up a little-used path, and we followed Wallace's landmarks – "face of precipices, slippery paths, cool spring under an overhanging rock." Not only did we find the spot where James Brooke's cottage

---

6   The Natural History Museum has more than 28 million insects in its collection from
     all over the world, but entomologists were bewildered when a tiny red-and-black
     bug appeared in the museum's own gardens in 2007. The taxonomists were unable to
     classify the creature, about the size of a grain of rice, which was initially found on the
     museum garden's plane trees and which has since been spotted in other London parks.

had been, but, amazingly after 140 years, we found remains of the belian ironwood foundation posts. This was where Wallace set out a lamp to collect moths, and "on good nights I was able to capture from a hundred to two hundred and fifty moths, and these comprised on each occasion from half to two-thirds that number of distinct species."

After brushing off the ants I noticed different energies. On the (not so good) *kelod* ocean side I heard sounds associated with people: distant roosters, gamelan music, motorcycles. On the (good) *kaya* mountain side I heard birds and crickets and the gentle sound of dozens of tiny man-made waterfalls as water flowed among the rice terraces. Of greater interest was that on the good *kaja* mountain side I watched hundreds, perhaps thousands, of golden dragonflies that hovered nearby, insect Tinkerbells telling me that the forest, holy or otherwise, is special.

This, to me, is a sacred place. I'm not sure what the parameters of "sacred" are, but, like pornography, I know it when I see it.

The origin of most sacred groves is lost in time. One morning in Switzerland, Vithal Rajan, chairman of the Deccan Development Society in India and then director of the Education and Ethics Program for WWF International, and I took a coffee break in a local patisserie. Over *pain au chocolat* I asked him how sacred groves might have started.

"You find sacred places everywhere," he explained. "Stonehenge, the Aboriginal songlines. They're the meeting place of culture and nature."

This clearly was not going to be a one-minute answer, and we ordered *chaussons aux pommes*. Rajan walked me through the Hindu/Buddhist philosophy that life consists of three parts – *artha*, which is the husbanding of wealth and physical comfort; *kama*, the search for aesthetic, sexual, and physical knowledge; and *dharma*, the acknowledgement of justice, peace, and spiritual harmony. Above these precepts sits *moksha*, liberation or nirwana, which comes once you understand the linkages between the physical and the spiritual and natural worlds.

I must have looked bewildered. Rajan and I considered sharing a chocolate eclair, but it was approaching lunch time. Like a true teacher, Vithal Rajan re-framed the argument. "Let me put it another way. Modern science recognizes two basic forces – matter and energy. Asian philosophy adds a third power – consciousness. And one of the ways this third force is represented is through the sixth sense – feminine intuition, or communication with animals and forest spirits or other seemingly 'unscientific' phenomenon. Sacred groves combine the pragmatic and the spiritual. Don't ask only Western questions."

This to me is ridiculous. How can I avoid asking logical Western questions? I was born in Brooklyn, not Bombay; my favorite participant sport is softball. I *liked* algebra.

I was reminded of another time a wise man told me not to get too caught up in a Cartesian view of the world. The man was the late Sultan Hamengkubuwono IX, a former vice president of Indonesia, a man with a Dutch university degree, a powerful and kind man who was born to accept the fealty of dozens of millions of Javanese. Unlike many royals he had earned respect to accompany the common person's devotion, partly due to his diplomatic courage during Indonesia's war of independence from the Dutch. I had asked the Sultan how such a common-sense man – he had also held positions as minister of finance and later, of defense – could pay homage every year to a mermaid – Nyai Loro Kidul, the legendary Queen of the Southern Ocean – to whom he attributes the founding of his royal line and who, incidentally, he also attributes the wise advice that helped him defeat the Dutch. He told me: "part of my brain is a Dutch brain, part is Javanese. You're trying to explain a Javanese situation by asking a Western Cartesian "yes or no" question. You either accept it or you don't. But don't try to analyze it." He hadn't quoted Shakespeare, but he might as well have. He had given me the Javanese equivalent of "There are more things in heaven and earth, Horatio/Than are dreamt of in your philosophy."

Wallace must have met people like Sultan Hamengkubuwono IX. Did he discuss philosophy with them or limit his conversations to pragmatic issues like whether they would rent him a house?

Wallace had his reasons for whatever he did. Everybody makes his own movie. Life is the illusion of reality. Smoke and mirrors.

Which is what the Balinese understand so well. Reality that isn't quite what it seems. Sultan Hamengkubuwono IX might as well have quoted the Balinese, who distinguish between *sekala*, that which you can sense, and *niskala*, that which can only be felt within.

Actually the *sekala-niskala* dichotomy was explained to me by a Balinese friend I had met in a curious manner. A few years ago I had rented a motorcycle from the Balinese family who owned the *losman* in which I was staying. I had gone to the Bali Hyatt in Sanur to meet a friend and when I was ready to leave found that the helmet, which I had naively left on the handlebars, was gone. I complained, somewhat loudly and aggressively, as much to make a point as to get the incident out of my system. The person who calmly bore the brunt of my spleen venting was Ida Bagus Gede Jika, a security officer who had just come on duty. He muttered "Javanese," the folks that Balinese like to blame for the island's petty crime and bad habits, and explained to me that there was nothing he could do. He implied that I was silly for believing that smiling happy-to-see-you Bali was still inhabited only by innnocent people.

I cooled down, and we got to talking. He told me he had an art shop nearby. I went there the next day. Jika is a painter and a student of Balinese culture. "I'm a Brahmin; I *have* to know the rituals," he said.[7]

Jika and I sat in the garden of his studio in Sanur, and I admired

---

7   Later in life Jika went through a rigorous process of purification and study to become a Brahmin priest.

a painting that he said represented the creation.[8] Contrary to my preconceptions about how the origin of life should be portrayed, there was no organic tidal soup, no bubbling high-pressure underwater geothermal vent, no omnipotent bearded old man discharging the electricity of life. Jika had instead painted a turtle and two snakes.

"What do you think the creation was, anyway?" he laughed. "In the beginning there was absolutely nothing. I think your bible agrees with us on that. But then a universal serpent named Antaboga appeared, which in turn created the cosmic turtle we call Bedawang. Look at the painting. On the turtle's shell are two coiled snakes, Nagas, and together they form the foundation of the world. The island of Bali rests on the turtle, which floats on the ocean."

I told this story to Vithal Rajan, back in Switzerland. He listened carefully, not surprised, not making a judgement. I waited for deep advice, which he is prone to give.

"We won't solve the turtle riddle without some external input. Let's go to the restaurant across the street and see what they have for lunch," Rajan suggested. "Everybody needs to eat."

---

8   Not everyone is enamored by the fact that almost every Balinese is skilled in one art or another. Noel Coward, who visited Bali with Charlie Chaplin, wrote in the complaints book of a Denpasar hotel:
   "As I said this morning to Charlie
   There is *far* too much music in Bali,
   And although as a place it's entrancing,
   There is also a *thought* too much dancing.
   It appears that each Balinese native,
   From the womb to the tomb is creative,
   And although the results are quite clever,
   There is *too much* artistic endeavour."

In Search Of The (Not Quite) Lost Tribe Of Giant White Cannibals

Bobale Island, off the coast of Halmahera, Indonesia

Swatting mosquitoes in a neat, stifling village, waiting for the wind to calm down so we can take a boat to look for crypto-Europeans.

Wallace's knowledge of the "natural productions" of "the large and little known island" of Halmahera (then called Gilolo) initially came secondhand, since he had dispatched "first my boy Ali, and then my assistant, Charles Allen, who staid two or three months each in the northern peninsula, and brought me back large collections of birds and insects." Wallace eventually went to Halmahera, where it is likely he had his famous malaria fever and conceived the Ternate Paper (see chapter "Ten Pages that Shook the World"). Although he moved his camp several times he found the collecting only moderately interesting and focused equally on the people, declaring that he "had discovered the exact boundary-line between the Malay and Papuan races, and at a spot where no other writer had expected it."

Halmahera is shaped – similar to its large and more well-known western neighbor Sulawesi – like a malformed orchard. It's a big, four-tentacled, New Jersey-sized island and an underachiever in terms of visitors and economic development. But in recent years timber operations have cropped up, presenting the usual threats to the biodiversity of the island. My interest in Halmahera was its position in the transition zone of Wallacea. The island lies midway between the Indo-Malayan (Western) region and the Austro-Malayan (Eastern) region, and, like Sulawesi to the west, Halmahera has natural varieties found nowhere else. That includes varieties of people who are neither Malay nor Papuan, a form of racial "missing link."

I quest for things that probably don't exist.

Some folks look for remains of the biblical ark. Others seek Atlantis, or dinosaurs in the Congo. I have searched for, and found, creatures as unlikely as white elephants and Hobbits, and places as unlikely as Hanuman's mountain and Waltzing Banana Island.

But the quest that eluded me was the admittedly Quixotic search for a tribe of giant white cannibals called the Togutil. It is a happy coincidence that these crypto-humans are said to live in the region that Wallace had decided was the border between the Malay races of the Indo-Malayan (Western) realm and the Papuan races of the Austro-Malayan (Eastern) realm.

Ted Danson, a white comedian in love with black comedian Whoopi Goldberg, was accused of being politically incorrect when he donned blackface at a Friar's Club roast in honor of Goldberg, a significant free spirit herself. He was roundly criticized and noted wearily: "I have people who call me a nigger lover, and now I have people who call me a racist pig. So . . . I've got a little balance."

Balance. And separations. And racial stereotypes. Describes Halmahera pretty well.

Wallace was as interested in different races of people as he was curious about different varieties of beetles. And just as he divided "natural productions" into distinct West-Middle-East groupings, he observed similar dividing lines for the two primary races, going against the "one race" hypothesis of the time.

> Before I had arrived at the conviction that the eastern and western halves of the [Malay] Archipelago belonged to distinct primary regions of the earth, I had been led to group the natives of the Archipelago under two radically distinct races. In this I differed from most ethnologists who had before written on the subject, for it had been the almost universal custom to follow William von Humboldt and [Augustin] Pritchard in classing all the oceanic races as modifications of one type.[1]

Wallace mapped the racial dividing line and noted that Halmahera sits in the center of the line dividing the Malayan (West) and the Papuan (East) races, just as clearly as the line dividing zoological diversity.

> If we draw a line commencing to the east of the Philippine Islands, thence along the western coast of Gilolo [Halmahera], through the island of Bouru [Buru], and curving round the west end of Flores, then bending back by Sandalwood Island to take in Rotti [Roti], we shall divide the Archipelago into two portions, the races of which have strongly marked distinctive peculiarities. This line will separate the Malayan [West] and all the Asiatic races, from the Papuans [East] and all that inhabit the Pacific; and though along the line of junction intermigration and commixture have taken place, yet the division is on the whole almost as well defined and strongly contrasted, as is the corresponding zoological division of the Archipelago, into an Indo-Malayan and

---

1   *The Malay Archipelago*, 30.

Austro-Malayan region.[2]

He saw the racial line as being as distinct as the similar zoological lines which he identified through his study of birds and animals.

> It is important to point out the harmony which exists between the line of separation of the human races of the Archipelago and that of the animal productions of the same country. . . .The dividing lines do not, it is true, exactly agree; but I think it is a remarkable fact, and something more than a mere coincidence, that they should traverse the same district and approach each other so closely as they do. If, however, I am right in my supposition that the region where the dividing line of the Indo-Malayan and Austro-Malayan regions of zoology can now be drawn, was formerly occupied by a much wider sea than at present, and if man existed on the earth at that period, we shall see good reason why the races inhabiting the Asiatic and Pacific areas should now meet and partially intermingle in the vicinity of that dividing line.[3]

He speculated that the same geological upheavals were responsible.

> [Since] man coexisted with extinct quadrupeds, and has survived elevations and depressions of the earth's surface to the amount of at least several hundred feet, we may consider the effects of the breaking up or re-formation of continents, and the subsidence of islands, on the migrations, the increase, or the extinction of the people who inhabited them.[4]

---

2   Ibid., 592.

3   Ibid., 594.

4   "On the Varieties of Men in the Malay Archipelago." 1863. In *Report of the Thirty-third Meeting of the British Association for the Advancement of Science*: 210.

Wallace cataloged the two human races with a similar alacrity to the distinctions he made between different species of birds of paradise.

> Observation soon showed me, however, that Malays and Papuans differed radically in every physical, mental and moral character; and more detailed research, continued for eight years, satisfied me that under these two forms, as types, the whole of the peoples of the Malay Archipelago and Polynesia could be classified.[5]

Foreign travelers visiting strange countries invariably tried to describe the strange people they encountered, generally using their own experiences and prejudices as benchmarks. These descriptions in the past have tended to be refreshingly politically incorrect. Consider how the eighteenth-century taxonomist Carl Linnaeus distinguished these varieties of man:

Wild Man: Four-footed, mute, hair.

American: Copper coloured, Choleric, erect. Hair black, straight, thick; nostrils wide, face harsh, beard scanty, obstinate, content free. Paints himself with fine red lines. Regulated by customs.

European: Fair, sanguine, brawny. Hair yellow, brown, flowing; eyes blue; gentle, acute, inventive. Covered with close vestments. Governed by laws.

African: Black, phlegmatic, relaxed. Hair black, frizzled; skin silky; nose flat; lips tumid; crafty, indolent, negligent. Anoints himself with grease. Governed by caprice.

---

5   *The Malay Archipelago*, 30.

It would have been fascinating if these early anthropologists had asked the people themselves how they describe themselves. But Wallace, like other explorers, considered himself an expert and neutral observer and came up with his observations – which compared the Malay with the Papuan – using terminology that resonated with his descriptions of wildlife.

> [The] Malay is of short stature, brown skinned, straight haired, beardless, and smooth bodied; the Papuan is taller, is black skinned, frizzly haired, bearded, and hairy bodied; the former is broad faced, has a small nose and flat eyebrows; the latter is long faced, has a large and prominent nose, and projecting eyebrows.[6]

Wallace expanded his observations from physical characteristics into describing general personality traits.

> [The Malay is] bashful, cold, undemonstrative, and quiet; the Papuan is bold, impetuous, excitable and noisy; the former is grave and seldom laughs; the latter is joyous and laughter-loving; the one conceals his emotions, the other displays them.[7]

He was equally brutal in describing the Malays and Papuans he met.

> In character the Malay is impassive. . . . His feelings of surprise, admiration, or fear, are never openly manifested, and are probably not strongly felt. . . . The higher classes of Malays are exceedingly polite, and have all the quiet ease and dignity of the best-bred Europeans. Yet this is compatible with a reckless cruelty and contempt of human life, which is the dark side of their character.[8]

6   "Varieties of Men," 204.

7   *The Malay Archipelago*, 590.

8   Ibid., 586–7.

The moral characteristics of the Papuan [show him to be] impulsive and demonstrative in speech and action. His emotions and passions express themselves in shouts and laughter, in yells and frantic leapings. Women and children take their share in every discussion. . . . Of the intellect of this race it is very difficult to judge, but I am inclined to rate it somewhat higher than that of the Malays, notwithstanding the fact that the Papuans have never yet made any advance toward civilization. . . . The Papuan has a greater feeling for art than the Malay. In the affections and moral sentiments, on the other hand, the Papuans seem very deficient. In the treatment of their children they are often violent and cruel; whereas the Malays are almost invariably kind and gentle, hardly ever interfering at all with their children's pursuits and amusements . . . the harsher discipline of the Papuans may be chiefly due to that greater vigor and energy of mind which always, sooner or later, leads to the rebellion of the weaker against the stronger – the people against their rulers, the slave against his master, or the child against its parent.[9]

And the giant white cannibals called the Togutil I was searching for? Wallace never met them; if he had they surely would have merited an opinionated paragraph or two.

What is physical beauty? Women and men all over the world decorate their body, or modify their physical appearance, in order to be attractive. In previous generations women of the Katchin tribe in Burma elongated their necks with rings, Kenyah women in Sarawak extended their earlobes with brass weights, while the men of the tribe liked to stick clouded leopard teeth through their ears.

9   Ibid., 589.

Women in America dye their hair blue; others, worldwide, have boob jobs or facelifts. Tattoos. Scarring. Body building. Dieting. Gorging. All self-induced cosmetic changes based on the standards of a particular society. Wallace wasn't shy about opining on who was attractive.

> On the whole the Malays are certainly not handsome. In youth, however, they are often very good-looking, and many of the boys and girls up to twelve or fifteen years of age are very pleasing. . . . I am inclined to think they lose much of their good looks by bad habits and irregular living.[10]

I wonder what would happen if Wallace had shown a picture of a "good-looking" Malay youth to an Australian aborigine, or to a sophisticated Italian, or to a Masai tribesman? Would there be agreement on which people were physically "beautiful" and which were "ugly?"

One of my advertising clients made a successful product that I had been unfamiliar with before I came to Asia. Hazeline Snow whitening cream, which was first introduced in 1892. Rub it on and that rustic dark skin tone is supposed to lighten a shade or two.[11] The reason for the product's success is obvious; in many parts of Asia there is a general acknowledgement that the prettiest women in each country are those with fair skin. These pale beauties come from Manado in Indonesia, from Chiang Mai in Thailand, from Baguio in the Philippines. White is beautiful.

The inhabitants of Minahasa [northern Sulawesi] differ

---

10 Ibid., 586.

11 Many companies make similar products with brand extensions that include, in Thailand, concoctions to lighten a woman's armpits and, in India, to lighten women's private parts.

much from those of all the rest of the island, and in fact from any other people in the Archipelago. They are of a light-brown or yellow tint, often approaching the fairness of a European; of a rather short stature, stout and well-made; of an open and pleasing countenance, more or less disfigured as age increases by projecting cheekbones; and with the usual long, straight, jet-black hair of the Malayan races. In some of the inland villages, where they may be supposed to be of the purest race, both men and women are remarkably handsome; while nearer the coast, where the purity of their blood has been destroyed by the intermixture of other races, they approach to the ordinary types of the wild inhabitants of the surrounding countries.[12]

Racial stereotypes work both ways, but the ones that are strongest originate, no surprise, from the dominant group. In the Asian context, the stereotype of the dark, Negroid Papuans as ugly and backward is promoted by the dominant lighter-skinned and Mongolian-featured Malays, who favor a "European" look. In 1526 Jorge de Meneses was the first European to visit New Guinea. He asked his Malay crew what to call the strange dark, curly haired people he encountered. "Orang Papuwah," his crew replied in the Malay language. Frizzy-haired men. By being blown off course, the first Portuguese governor of the Moluccas thereby earned the honor to name the inhabitants of the island and, by inference, an entire race.

Wallace remembered well his first contact with Papuans.

I now had my first view of Papuans in their own country . . . the people I now had an opportunity of comparing side by side [Malay and Papuan] belonged to two of the most distinct and strongly marked races that the earth contains. Had I been blind, I could have been certain that these

---

12 *The Malay Archipelago*, 249–50.

islanders were not Malays. The loud, rapid, eager tones, the incessant motion, the intense vital activity manifested in speech and action, are the very antipodes of the quiet, unimpulsive, unanimated Malay. These Ké [Kei] men came up singing and shouting . . . and on coming alongside, without asking leave, and without a moment's hesitation, the greater part of them scrambled up on our deck just as if they were come to take possession of a captured vessel. Then commenced a scene of indescribable confusion. These forty black, naked, mop-headed savages seemed intoxicated with joy and excitement. . . . Our crew [of Malay origin], many of whom had not made the voyage before, seemed quite scandalized at such unprecedented bad manners, and only very gradually made any approach to fraternization with the black fellows. They reminded me of a party of demure and well-behaved children suddenly broken in upon by a lot of wild, romping, riotous boys, whose conduct seems most extraordinary and very naughty.[13]

Wallace described the racial and behavioral difference between the Malay and Papuan races. But he asked a more subtle question that was identical to the conundrum that led him to theorize a line (and transition zone) separating the nature of Western and Eastern Indonesia. Is there a clear geographic line that separates the two races or is there an intermediate zone? And, Wallace added, if there *is* a racial transition zone, who are the people who straddle this racial divide?

In the country round about Sahoe [on Halmahera] . . . there is a large population of indigenes, numbers of whom came daily into the village. . . . A careful examination

---

13 Ibid., 420–1.

convinced me that these people are radically distinct from all the Malay races. Their stature and their features, as well as their disposition and habits, are almost the same as those of the Papuans; their hair is semi-Papuan – neither straight, smooth, and glossy like all true Malays' [sic], nor so frizzly and wooly as the perfect Papuan type, but always crisp, waved, and rough, such as often occurs among the true Papuans, but never among the Malays. Their color alone is often exactly that of the Malay, or even lighter. Of course there has been intermixture . . . but in most cases the large, somewhat aquiline nose, with elongated apex, the tall stature, the waved hair, the bearded face, and hairy body, as well as the less reserved manner and louder voice, unmistakably proclaim the Papuan type. Here then I had discovered *the exact boundary-line between the Malay and Papuan races, and at a spot where no other writer had expected it.* [italics added][14]

I think I too have found the line between the Malay and Papuan races. Not too far from where Wallace put it, actually.[15] It's in a tiny village called Daru, near Kao, in Halmahera. I had taken the ferry from the island of Ternate to the mainland of Halmahera. I got on a jammed minibus that blasted the whiny *dangdut* music so beloved by rural folk and bounced a few hours up the east coast of the northern "petal" of Halmahera. I was waiting for a boat to take me to Bobale island and got talking.

"Hey guys, what race are you?" I asked diplomatically.

"*Suku Boeng,*" they answered. I had never heard of the Boengs, but since there are perhaps a thousand language groups in all of Indonesia (about one sixth of the world's languages are spoken in these seventeen thousand islands), I didn't feel particularly ignorant.

I looked at the faces. Unlike Malays or Papuans, the Boeng

14   Ibid., 323.

15   Of course in today's fluid world people move around freely, and it's quite ridiculous to try to determine a clean boundary line that separates the races. Nevertheless, it's a fun exercise that points out that Wallace had it pretty much right.

people had slightly grey or slightly brown eyes. Their hair was somewhere between frizzy and straight. The men had more facial and body hair than Malays, less than Papuans.

"We're different to people from Ambon, or Papuans, or Malays," one man told me, not seeming to mind my questions.

In fact they looked more like Dravidians from South India than Indonesians, a point Wallace alluded to.

> The people [of Sahoe, on Halmahera] are like the Timorese, with frizzly or wavy hair, and of a coppery-brown color. The better class appear to have a mixture of some superior race, which has much improved their features. I saw in Coupang [Kupang, Timor] some chiefs from the island of Savu, further west, who presented characters very distinct from either the Malay or Papuan races. They most resembled Hindoos, having fine well-formed features and straight thin noses, with clear brown complexions. As the Brahminical religion once spread over all Java, and even now exists in Bali and Lombock, it is not at all improbable that some natives of India should have reached this island, either by accident or to escape persecution, and formed a permanent settlement there.[16]

Relicts of an Indian civilization? That's exactly what I found in Halmahera, a thousand kilometers (621 miles) north of Wallace's observations in Timor. Neither Papuan nor Malay. I saw one woman who had a Roman nose. Nine out of ten men sported luxuriant moustaches, a favorite affectation of Malays. The faces were generally long or oval, rarely round. I wondered about all the theories of people migration. Had I stumbled on a lost tribe of refugees from the subcontinent?

Wallace pointed out the need to examine physical evidence *and* what he termed "natural character."

---

16 *The Malay Archipelago*, 195.

Writers on the races of mankind have too often to trust to the information of travellers who pass rapidly from country to country, and thus have few opportunities of becoming acquainted with peculiarities of national character or even of ascertaining what is really the average physical conformation of the people.[17]

He warned against too-quick conclusions.

Such [instant experts] are exceedingly apt to be deceived in places where two races have long int ermingled, by looking on intermediate forms and mixed habits as evidences of a natural transition from one race to the other, instead of an artificial mixture of two distinct peoples.[18]

After a short walk I arrived at the beach. There was no harbor – half a dozen small boats had been dragged on to the shore. A shifty-eyed man named Manuel motioned me to his outboard engine-powered boat – a step up from a dugout, a step below a seaworthy craft. His boat was the only game in town, and for a fee that I considered expensive he took me to Bobale. The ride was uneventful, but I was uncomfortable with Manuel who had an oily look that shuttled between a scowl and obsequiousness.

On Bobale I asked about race.

"Our skin is *sawo matang*," the residents of Bobale island agreed, referring to the golden-brown tone of ripe sawo fruit, that most Malay-race Indonesians consider as the best way to describe their complexion. By comparison, they wasted no time in agreeing that my skin color was clearly "white," even though I had the tan of my life.

---

17   Ibid., 439.

18   Ibid.

"*He* has curly hair," one man said, pointing to his friend. "He must be from Ambon." Everybody laughed.

"And *he* has straight hair," the curly-haired man added in retort. He then forgot the punch line.

"Then *he* must be from Jakarta," I said, to help him out.

Laughter. "Jakarta. That's right."

"And from where do *you* originate?" I asked some others.

"We are from Tobelo," they told me, referring to a town further up the coast. But none of them knew in racial terms where their people originally came from. Call it lack of curiosity or lack of historical knowledge; Wallace found a similar pattern.

> Of an evening [in Aru] the men, having got over their first shyness, began to talk to me a little, asking about my country . . . and in return I questioned them about any traditions they had of their own origin. I had, however, very little success, for I could not possibly make them understand the simple question of where the Aru people first came from. I put it in every possible way to them, but it was a subject quite beyond their speculations; they had evidently never thought of anything of the kind, and were unable to conceive a thing so remote and so unnecessary to be thought about as their origins.[19]

I told the folks of Bobale theories of how the Malay race originated in southern China, how early Indonesians settled the Pacific, and how Indonesians also settled Madagascar. In turn they told me an even stranger racial story.

I doubt Wallace would have had a good explanation to account for the existence of the Togutil. My friends on Bobale island told me about these strange people – tall, broad-shouldered Europeans

19 Ibid., 459.

who live deep in the mountains of Halmahera. These misplaced white men have small waists, blue-grey eyes, and sunburn easily because of their pale skin. They wear loincloths but are otherwise naked. The Togutil eat raw meat, and their only hunting technique is for a man to fling a stone with his foot, a procedure none of the fishermen from Bobale could demonstrate.

Amazingly, the folks in Bobale explained it's not all that difficult to visit the Togutil. All I had to do was take a boat across the bay to Dodaga on the northeastern "petal" of Halmahera, then walk seven kilometers (four miles) to the sixty-family Togutil settlement at Kampong Rica Rica Ino. There was a path. No, they had never gone there. "Have others visited these strange crypto-people?" I asked, thinking I might be stumbling on to a group akin to Pakistan's fair-skinned, blue-eyed Kalash people, who claim to be descendants of Alexander the Great.

"An American man studied them some time ago," my host Pak Paspalangi said, recounting an urban legend he completely believed. "He returned to American and came back to Indonesia some time later with an American woman whom he wanted to mate with a Togutil man."

"What happened?"

"The Togutil ran away."

"We Orang Tobelo wouldn't run away," another man said to general laughter.

There is an orphaned branch of science called crypto-zoology, which studies creatures that exist in the wrong place or time. A dinosaur surviving today in Scotland or the Congo would fit the crypto definition, as would any of the "snowmen of the jungle" who inhabit various rainforests in Southeast Asia.[20] The Togutil people definitely sounded crypto, and I itched to visit them.

Paspalangi, the village headman, said that the only boat belonged to shifty-eyed Manuel, who had agreed to take me over for about $50, then bring me back a couple of days later.

"Isn't there another boat?"

---

20   See chapter "Tears for Tosca."

Turned out there *was* a smaller boat, owned by a man named Yunos, which I could have chartered for half that price. I asked Paspalangi to book it – we would leave at first light. I passed the afternoon snorkeling with the men from the village as they spearfished on a coral reef nearby, which was rapidly being depleted of anything they could eat or sell. Paspalangi took me to the other side of the island to see a Japanese bunker left over from the war. I sat on Bobale's white sand beach and watched the sun set in colors I had not seen since a lost weekend in 1969 when, with the help of recreational chemicals and Iron Butterfly, God's palette had exploded into my brain, perhaps causing, some might say, permanent neuron displacement.

The next morning the sky was grey, the seas were rough, and Yunos's small outboard didn't start. "Can't the guy borrow another engine?" I asked. "The only other engine on the island is Manuel's," Paspalangi explained.

I sensed that Yunos was afraid to go out in this weather, sensible enough for him, but I was on an adventure, and with limited time. I was apprehensive to go into open water in Yunos's small boat.

That left Manuel, with his smirk and too-expensive boat.

I felt the same apprehension about being ripped off that Wallace felt in Sarawak.

> The next morning at daybreak I came to the place [where he had shot an orangutan], and found that the mias was evidently dead, as his head was visible in exactly the same position as before. I now offered four Chinamen a day's wages each to cut the tree down at once, as a few hours of sunshine would cause decomposition on the surface of the skin; but, after looking at it and trying it, they determined that it was very big and very hard, and would not attempt it. Had I doubled my offer, they would probably have accepted it, as it would not have been more than two or three hours' work, and had I been on a short visit only I would have done so; but as I was a resident, and intended to remaining several months longer, it would not have

answered to begin paying too exorbitantly, or I should
have got nothing done in future at a lower rate.[21]

Manuel agreed to make the trip, but I decided against it. Based
on . . . nothing really. Just a visceral distrust of the guy; I didn't
want to be in his care in his boat on the open sea. So I declined.
Perhaps a stupid self-defeating decision. Perhaps if I had gone
with Manuel I would have met the Togutil, become an adopted
member of the clan, and learned to kill wild animals and enemies
by hurling stones at them with my feet. Or perhaps if I had gone
with Manuel we would have capsized and died.

What was almost a classic trip turned out to be a non-trip. The
Orang Togutil would have to continue waiting for me.

Basically, I got zapped. As I suspect my friends and I got zapped
a few months later. We were in Aru, and Max, one of the botanists,
had lost his notebook. Word came back that someone had found
it, and we took our small boat and went back to the village where
the finder lived. We were ashore for about an hour. The village
was friendly and interesting, and boys offered to sell us protected
parrots and cassowary eggs. When we returned to the river bank, we
found that our boat was stuck in the sand, a victim of the outgoing
tide. "Bad luck," someone from the village said. "Bad seamanship,"
I argued. "Shit, that's just plain dumb," one of the Dutchmen said,
with a little bit of justification since just two nights earlier the
Dutchman had been forced to spend the night in the village when
exactly the same stupid thing had happened with the same boat
and the same crew. We managed to rock the boat off the sand and
take our leave. All the way back to our base camp, we Europeans
grumbled, "Why couldn't *they* have merely moved the boat to the
center of the river when they saw the tide was going down?"

Westerners in Asia constantly invoke the "we" versus "them"

---

21   *The Malay Archipelago*, 62.

didactic, often to question the logic (or lack thereof) of decisions "they" have taken. And I'm sure that the situation is true in reverse and that our Asian hosts invoke a similar "we" versus "them" mindset.

But, if the stereotypes are to be believed, this lack of ability to think like us betrays a good humor that is all too missing in our Western society.

> The striking contrast of character between these people [Papuans] and the Malays is exemplified in many little traits. One day when I was rambling in the forest an old man stopped to look at me catching an insect. He stood very quiet till I had pinned and put it away in my collecting-box, when he could contain himself no longer, but bent almost double, and enjoyed a hearty roar of laughter. Every one will recognize this as a true negro trait. A Malay would have stared, and asked with a tone of bewilderment what I was doing; for it is but little in his nature to laugh, never heartily, and still less at or in the presence of a stranger, to whom, however, his disdainful glances or whispered remarks are less agreeable than the most boisterous open expression of merriment.[22]

Some foreigners today go out of their way to try to understand whichever Asian society they live in. And, of course, there is a vast cultural difference between the sophisticated people that foreigners meet at work and the poorly educated rice farmer. The time is long over when whites would carry on as did one of Joseph Conrad's white characters in *An Outcast of the Islands* – set in Indonesia – who married a brown woman: "He loved to breathe the coarse incense they offered before the shrine of the successful white man; the man that had done them the honor to marry their daughter, sister, cousin. . . . They were a numerous and an unclean crowd, living in ruined bamboo houses, surrounded by neglected compounds. . . . He kept them at arm's length . . . having no illusions as to their

---

22 Ibid., 430.

worth," Conrad wrote. "He saw them as they were – ragged, lean, unwashed, undersized men of various ages, shuffling about aimlessly in slippers, motionless old women who looked like monstrous bags of pink calico stuffed with shapeless lumps of fat. . . . They wanted much, but he could give them all they wanted without ruining himself. In exchange he had their silent fear, their loquacious love, their noisy veneration. It is a fine thing to be a providence, and to be told so on every day of one's life."

It is interesting (and far too rare) when an Indonesian gives his version of a reverse stereotype. Historian Ong Hok Ham described a "gargantuan" colonial *rijsttafel* served at the Hotel des Indes in Batavia (Jakarta): "A Dutch gentleman, usually dressed in a white suit, would sit in front of his plate of rice and the multitude of other dishes consuming glass after glass of beer. Afterwards, overly satisfied and drowsy, the perspiring Dutchman would slump into the comfortable chairs."

The common refrain by folks throughout Southeast Asia is that a foreigner "can't understand my country." Just as Wallace dubbed the tribal folks he met "savages," all Asian cultures, including "polite" Southeast Asian cultures, have terms to describe foreigners, for people who are different in skin color or language or dress or religion. Sometimes the term is neutral, describing an "other," but usually it equates with "strange/stranger," which equates with "someone different to the standard." The term can very easily become caustic and unpleasant. Nevertheless, being called an "other" is a reality of venturing in a strange land where the visitor is invariably an object of curiosity. Because I am white and Anglophone, when I travel in Asia I am treated a certain way. Sometimes with undeserved deference. Sometimes with taunts. Often with inflated prices. Constantly, I'm sure, with behind-my-back gossip.

Few places in Asia have as ingrained an "us" and "them" mentality as Thailand, a country where folks brag that they have never been colonized and where the subtext is usually "no foreigner can understand "Thai-ness." This attitude came to the fore when chef David Thompson, owner of Michelin-starred Thai restaurant Nahm in London, decided to open a branch in Bangkok, vowing to serve authentic and historically accurate Thai food. Some Thai socialites were aghast, others gave him grudging credit. From my point of view (but what do I know, I'm not Thai), Thompson has done Thai cuisine a huge favor. He speaks and reads classical Thai, has a library of hundreds of books, recipes, and menus from centuries past. He is a historian as well as being a talented chef. He discovers recipes and tastes that other Thai chefs have not investigated. Good for him.

The Thai term for a European foreigner is *farang* (and the term is used exclusively for white folks; there are other terms for Chinese or Japanese or Africans or Arabs). In Thailand, as in virtually every culture, the term "foreigner" equates with "an other," which equates with "strange/stranger," which equates with (usually negatively) "someone different to the standard."

Thais say *farang* to your face; they say it *sotto voce*; they growl it when they don't like your driving; as you pass in the street, they say it out loud and point at you and instruct their toddlers in the use of the term. Some Europeans don't mind and use it to describe themselves. I mind a lot. Thais will argue over whether it is used pejoratively. Sometimes I gently scold Thais for what I consider an insensitive use of the word (a very un-Thai action on my part.) Certainly not all Thais are racist, and not all Thais use the term pejoratively. But of course it is pejorative, because it says "you are different."

This is a universal experience – every language and culture has its own jokes and slurs based on gender/ethnicity/social class/fashion sense/religion. Everybody knows what they are, and most people avoid using them in proper company.[23] The term *farang* isn't in that nasty, hateful category. Nevertheless, the *Bangkok Post* ran a column written by Pichaya Svasti, who argued that the phrase is

---

23 I'm reminded of the Bedouin proverb: "I against my brother/I and my brother against our cousin/I, my brother and our cousin against the neighbors/All of us against the foreigner."

not intended to hurt or belittle. But I wonder. Surely Khun Pichaya has visited Europe and the United States. Did people in Europe point at her in the street and mutter, in full hearing, "Asian?" Did mothers point her out to their wide-eyed children and teach them the word "Oriental?" I doubt it happened, but if it did how did she feel about being so singled out?

Since my first visit to Bobale I spent ten years regretting my decision not to stay longer in Halmahera and search for the elusive Togutil. But info was scanty.

Nevertheless, with the help of friends who work for BirdLife International, which is hoping to establish North Halmahera's first national park in the deep forests occupied by the three thousand or so Togutil, my friend Bill and I ventured into the far end of this rarely visited island.

It wasn't all that hard, actually. Starting from the volcano-dominated island of Ternate (historically famous as the origin of cloves and Wallace's base camp, we took a few journeys in open boats to reach the depressing dusty frontier town of Subayim on Halmahera. We then climbed on the back of motorcycles for a dusty hour, then walked for another forty-five minutes.

We came to a small village of twenty-five families, and the Togutil were sitting around, as if waiting for us. Right away it was clear that this wasn't the wild lost white tribe.

Albertus Paspalangi, my fisherman friend on Bobale, is a coastal "lowlander." Although he certainly isn't rich, he has a nice house, he follows a monotheistic religion, he speaks the national language, he sends his kids to school, he has electricity and a TV, and he knows the names of Indonesian politicians and pop stars. He's never been to the interior forests of Halmahera and has no interest in doing so. To him, the interior is a place of jungle and potential danger.

Given the chance for a holiday, there's no question he'd head for a city like Ternate and not to inner Halmahera.

He's not at all an evil man, but the dismissive tone he used when he described people living in the hills ("*they* are rough and dangerous.") perpetuates a "we" versus "them" attitude that has been at the root of brown-brown discrimination, which has existed since city-states were created.

The same dynamic is at work in regard to destruction of nature – American (white, educated, well-dressed, Christian) pioneers "conquered" the west by decimating (brown, pagan, dangerous) Indians and, by extension, (wild, dangerous) wildlife; today's American leaders propose to drill for oil and "conquer" the Arctic Wildlife Refuge in Alaska for the benefit of people in the cities. And throughout the tropics, governments and entrepreneurs feel little remorse in "conquering" the wilderness – whether that wilderness consists of forest-dwelling people or tropical forests.

Perhaps this "we" versus "them" arrogance toward wilderness partly stems from man's need-fear relationship with nature.

On the one hand, we need nature. We come from nature; we are part of nature. This connection is very deep, very ancient, very Jungian in its impact on our collective unconscious. Our very earliest ancestors, well before the development of agriculture and writing, before the wheel and fire, when people fought animals for carrion, found shelter in the forests and opportunity in the plains. They understood, at least unconsciously, the cycles of rain and drought. Our ancestors came from nature; nature was part of them. This may explain why today the presence of green scenery slows our blood pressure and relieves stress. It might explain why people working in bleak, anonymous offices nurture houseplants to brighten things up, and why people recover faster when their window has a view of a park (curiously, even having a photograph of nature in the hospital room speeds healing compared to a barren wall).

But what about the fear? We define ourselves partly by what we are not. We are no longer "savages" who coexist with animals; we are civilized; we have left the darkness. Our ancestors learned to use plants for medicine, build complex shelters, and, after much trial and error, to dominate nature by mastering fire, making metal tools, growing crops, and domesticating other animals. We became the masters of the universe. We have civilization, language, Michelangelo and Michael Jackson and Michael Jordan. We have ploughs and guns, bicycles and cellphones. Many of us have been imprinted by one of the three strict paternalistic monotheistic desert religions that put a lot more emphasis on us having "dominion" over nature than on, say, the Buddhist approach of living in "harmony" with nature. That's why we're uncomfortable when "undisciplined" nature ventures too close. We tend our gardens and kill crab grass to "manage" nature. That's why the Balinese file the teeth of their preadolescent children – so that the child does not have pointy, animal-like cuspids. That's why most first- and second-generation urban people, like those you'll find in Jakarta, will look at me askance when I explain that I'm going into the deep forests. I'm likely to get a response like: "Ugh, full of snakes!" or "No electricity," or "Go shopping in Singapore instead." It's all a way of saying "the forest is alien, it's dangerous, it's filled with people having strange animistic beliefs who worship spirits that reside in the trees and streams and volcanoes." There are creatures in the deep wilderness (think *yeti*) that will tear off your head. We're afraid of looking too deeply into the mirror and seeing our wild side.

This is near the core of our schizophrenic relationship with nature. *We need nature but we fear it.* We're part of nature, but we want to dissociate ourselves from anything too wild. On one side we have what could be termed a female-yin approach to nature: we are part of the global scheme of things, the interwoven tapestry of life – mysterious, complex, sharing, questioning, supportive, fertile. On the other hand we are very male-yang: logical, goal-driven, suspicious of outsiders, confident, potent. Conquerors.

Physically the Togutil looked similar to other Indonesian hill tribes, although considerably poorer and less sophisticated. They certainly had a simple life – few people in their tiny community spoke Indonesian, they didn't grow rice, they hunted for deer and wild pigs with simple bows and arrows. A couple of the older men wore loincloths, but most wore shorts and T-shirts. But the Togutil weren't totally out of the mainstream – Christian missionaries had built a small chapel in the village.

More dramatically, the Togutil were neither white nor tall nor nasty. They could not throw stones with their feet. They seemed quite happy for us to spend a few days with them.

I went for a walk with one of the older Togutil, Pak Pisondolo, curious to see how he hunted with just a handmade bow and arrow.

Pisondolo was born in 1957 but looked ancient – short and skinny, with a wispy beard, wearing a loose loincloth made of faded and torn batik held in place by a strip of rattan, his wide calloused feet never encumbered by shoes.

We heard the distinctive whoosh of a pair of Blyth's hornbills in flight, one of the many protected birds in these forests. They were safe from Pisondolo's simple bamboo arrows, which are accurate only at short range because they have no fletching to guide them in flight.

We tried to tread softly, but of course no deer or wild pig in its right mind would hang around when it heard clumsy Europeans stumbling through the forest. Realizing there was little need to keep quiet, I asked Pisondolo about the legends that his people were tall, white, and fierce.

"Oh, that's not us," he said. "You want the Orang Lingon. But be careful. Those guys are mean. Very *galak*. Fierce. Eyes like sharks. Powerful magic. They eat people raw."

My informant on Bobale had clearly sent me to the wrong isolated tribe.

Pisondolo explained that the Lingon made themselves hard to find and lived in the deep forest without fixed settlements.

Would he be willing to take us to look for them?

Pisondolo shook his head no. "Those Lingon are really savage."

Helping Our Poor, Brown, Naked Cousins

Gunung Mulu National Park, Sarawak, Malaysia

In a crude shelter in the rainforest near a Penan camp.

Wallace never made it this far upriver. During the fifteen months he stayed in Sarawak he had no need to go more than a few days journey from the town of Sarawak, today called Kuching. While the beetle-collecting was terrific, he missed meeting some of the most interesting tribes living in the interior. He did, however, make cogent observations of the Iban (Sea Dayak) and Bidayuh (Land Dayak) people he encountered: "They [he was referring to the various indigenous people he met, loosely grouped together as Dayaks] are more communicative and lively than the American Indians [from the Amazon and Rio Negro], and it is therefore more agreeable to live with them. In moral character they are far superior to either Malays or Chinese, for though head-taking has been a custom among them, it is only as a trophy of war. . . . One wet day I got a piece of string to show them how to play 'scratch [cat's] cradle', and was quite astonished to find that they knew it better than I did and could make all sorts of new figures I had never seen."

My first encounter with the Penan ethnic group was in 1969. We were at the beginning of a two-day, twenty-five-kilometer (fifteen-mile) walk from Long Atip to Long Seridan, splashing along a clear stream, when we turned the corner and met a family of five Penans. They stood there quietly, one wearing a loincloth, the others shorts and worn sarongs. Obviously they had heard us stomping along and were curious. We gave them some rice, cigarettes, and tinned food. We invited them to lunch; they did not accept. They walked away quietly.

During those admittedly idyllic days my longhouse friends and I would throw a circular fishing net into rivers and come up with more than enough fish for dinner. We would go out at night to hunt wild boar and more often than not return with a hairy wild pig on our shoulders. Jungle gibbons hooted their morning call behind the longhouses.

Today such a scene would be unlikely. For a start, the rainforests are largely gone, victims of rapacious timber operations, which open the land for conversion to oil palm. The rivers run dirty and dangerous with silt and debris from land clearing. And the Penans are mostly resettled into dismal government resettlement communities.

I was looking at my photographs of semi-nomadic Penans, taken next to a small river more than forty years ago. They were simple people, suspicious, isolated and naive, but sophisticated in their own way. I didn't know what questions to ask them. I was so naive that I didn't stop to imagine that the scene – "natural" people, unblemished rainforest – wouldn't continue for the foreseeable future.

Looking at those photos, I thought about the challenges of

writing my novel *Redheads*. One non-negotiable writing guideline kept springing into my mind. *Without conflict you have no story*. This is what I call in my writing workshops the Nancy Reagan Principle ("Just say no to drugs"). Without a "no," without a problem, without a Nancy Reagan, you don't have a story. Otherwise, it's like Joe Frazier fighting Muhammad Ali without a winner and loser. Stories, at least good stories, must have a hero and a villain.

And what a wonderful cast can be found in the real-life drama that is Sarawak. In this corner, the "good" guys: the downtrodden, simple, innocent, loved-by-the-media Penans, and Bruno Manser, the polite Swiss rebel with nerves of steel.

And wearing the black hats are Abdul Taib Mahmud, Sarawak chief minister,[1] Mahathir bin Mohamad, former Malaysian prime minister, and James Wong Kim Min, Sarawak's former minister of tourism and local government.

Gentlemen, start your engines.

At the heart of the Penan problem lies several emotional conundrums. Can (and should) societies evolve? Who (if anyone) has the right/responsibility to construct a fair development model for the downtrodden? Is there a gracious way to deal with irritating involvement by outsiders? Is civil disobedience the best way to achieve social change? How can people without a voice learn to sing?

Both Charles Darwin and Alfred Russel Wallace toyed with the concept that later became known as "social Darwinism:" the idea that societies and civilizations evolve according to the

---

1   After years of amassing a multi-billion dollar fortune by raping and pillaging Sarawak's forests, Taib Mahmud and his family are coming under intense moral, political, and legal scrutiny. One result of the increased pressure: In a May 2011 letter to the Bruno Manser Foundation, the president of the Swiss Federation Micheline Calmy-Rey advised that she has forwarded information about Taib Mahmud's assets in Switzerland to the regulatory body FINMA (the Swiss Financial Market Supervisory Authority) for investigation. The Swiss president made it clear that the country's authorities take extremely seriously the concerns that have been raised internationally about Taib Mahmud's profiteering from timber corruption and are unhappy that such assets may have been invested in Switzerland.

principles of evolution, with the implication that the highest form of advancement is some form of European society.

This concept has been at the heart of considerable colonial excess, and, taken to its frightening extreme, is the essence of eugenics and ethnic cleansing.

The Penan ethnic group face significant social and cultural pressures. Once semi-nomadic hunter-gatherers, today most of the several thousand remaining Penans live unsettled lives in government-enforced settlements.

The Penans, who are generally described by their supporters as "shy, gentle, and living in harmony with nature," are potent symbols of modern-day brown-brown colonialism.

The Penans are a problem the Sarawak government wishes would go away. The Penan plight illustrates one of the biggest challenges in development thinking today – how to deal with indigenous people who, by definition, are different from (and considered lesser than) the folks in power.

The bad guys in this saga, according to most Western observers, are Sarawak Chief Minister Abdul Taib Mahmud and other senior state and federal officials who either own or grant or encourage timber concessions. Westerners contend that these timber operations, the first step in converting land to oil palm plantations,[2] destroy the Penans' forest homeland. Joseph Conrad's observation that "the conquest of the earth mostly means taking it away from those who have a different complexion or slightly flatter noses than ourselves" is giving way to a brown-brown arrogance with a more nuanced dynamic.

The corollary is that the Malaysian government is criticized for being guilty of "cultural genocide," for encouraging the Penans to quit the forest and settle in longhouses.[3] I asked Alfred Jabu, who

2   Wetlands International, a Dutch-based NGO, charges that Malaysia is destroying its tropical rainforest at a rate three times faster than the rest of Asia combined. The group predicts that such "expansion of oil palm plantations may lead to the complete loss of [rainforests] by the end of this decade [2019]."

3   Anthropologist Wade Davis said of the Penans: "Within a single generation a way of life, morally inspired and inherently right, was being crushed just as the forest in which they were born was being crushed."

is deputy chief minister of the Malaysian state of Sarawak and who is a member of the indigenous Iban tribe (numerically the largest ethnic group in the state) why he was so concerned about changing Penan lifestyles. He answered: "To give them the chance to enjoy the same benefits other Malaysians have."

This refrain is repeated whenever I spoke to someone involved in "developing" their less fortunate (and always more isolated) brethren: "We want to help them enjoy the fruits of our development." It's *in loco parentis* and it's sanctimonious and the worse thing about it is that many of these individuals do so with the humorless, almost evangelical drive that comes from knowing that they are following an "absolute right."[4]

---

4   Who has the blueprint for social change? I consulted James Wong Kim Min, who was concurrently the Sarawak state minister of tourism and local government and one of the state's biggest timber tycoons.

Referring to Bruno Manser, the Swiss who was living with the semi-nomadic Penans and encouraging them to demand protection for their forest home, Wong said: "I met with Bruno's Penans in the upper Limbang [River]. I asked the Penans, who will help you if you're sick? Bruno?" Here, Wong laughed. "The Penans now realize they've been exploited. I tell them the government is there to help them. But I ask them how can I see you if you've blocked the road that I've built for you?"

I asked if he had a message for his critics.

"If [theWest] can do as well as we have done and enjoy life as much as we do then they can criticize us. We run a model nation. We have twenty-five races and many different religions living side by side without killing each other. Compare that to Bosnia or Ireland. We've achieved a form of Nirwana, a utopia."

I explained my experience with Penans who had been encouraged by generous government incentives to resettle into longhouses. How their natural environment had been hammered, how their faces were devoid of spirit and energy, how they had seemingly tumbled even further down the Sarawak social totem pole.

In reply, Wong lectured me, as I have been lectured by numerous Asian officials when I raised similar concerns. In effect, he said "We just want our cousins, the naked Penans, to enjoy the same benefits we civilized folk enjoy."

"We are very unfairly criticized by the west," Wong added. "As early as 1980 I was concerned about the future of the Penans."

He read me a poem he had written:

"O Penan – Jungle wanderers of the Tree
What would the future hold for thee?....
Perhaps to us you may appear deprived and poor
But can Civilization offer anything better?....
And yet could Society in good conscience
View your plight with detached indifference
Especially now we are an independent Nation
Yet not lift a helping hand to our fellow brethren?
Instead allow him to subsist in Blowpipes and clothed in Chawats [loincloths]
An anthropological curiosity of Nature and Art?

Wallace bought into the unquestioning Victorian belief in a higher social order, a continual march toward "true progress."

> We most of us believe that we, the higher races, have progressed and are progressing. If so, there must be some state of perfection, some ultimate goal, which we may never reach, but to which all true progress must bring us nearer.[5]

Wallace tried to explain his ideal social state in terms of an overriding moral law.

> What is this ideally perfect social state toward which mankind ever has been, and still is tending? Our best thinkers maintain that it is a state of individual freedom and self-government, rendered possible by the equal development and just balance of the intellectual, moral and physical parts of our nature, – a state in which we shall each be so perfectly fitted for a social existence, by knowing what is right, and at the same time feeling an irresistible impulse to do what we know to be right, that all laws and all punishments shall be unnecessary. In such a state every man would have a sufficiently well balanced intellectual organization to understand the moral law in all its details, and would require no other motive but the free impulses of his own nature to obey that law.[6]

The reality is that the Penans of the "noble savage" variety live

---

Alas, ultimately your fate is your own decision
Remain as you are – or cross the Rubicon!"

5   *The Malay Archipelago*, 596.

6   Ibid.

a rugged, unhealthy existence. Should they be denied health care, education, sanitation, and the opportunity for economic as well as social advancement?

There is ample sanctimony on both sides. Some Westerners are happy to let the isolated folk like the Penans continue to run around with infections, tattoos, and ringworm, just as long as they continue to wear loincloths and use a blowpipe to get dinner. We feel better by having primitive cousins, somehow reassured that there are still people in this world living a Rousseau-like existence.

Bruno Manser told me that one of his biggest frustrations was that the Penans were so shy and so used to being isolated and downtrodden that they could not speak out forcefully to protect their forests. This is changing, slowly, as more and more Penans become educated, as they receive encouragement from other (more sophisticated) Sarawak tribal groups, as they see they really have no choice but to speak out. Defensive Sarawak state officials blame the federal government for the problem of forest destruction, noting that since ninety-five percent of the state's substantial oil revenue (and eighty-five percent of the natural gas income) goes to federal coffers, Sarawakians have no choice but to earn money from natural products, of which timber and oil palm are by far the most profitable.

Compounding the issue is the fact that Malaysian officials have major chips on their shoulders at what they consider Western bullying. Dr. Mahathir bin Mohamad, the former Malaysian prime minister, had this testy exchange of correspondence with young Darrell Abercrombie from Surrey, England.

Using his best penmanship, the boy wrote: "I am 10 years old and when I am older I hope to study animals in the tropical rain forests. But if you let the lumber companys [sic] carry on there will not be any left. And millions of Animals will die. Do you think that is right just so one rich man gets another million pounds or more. I think it is disgraceful."

The prime minister replied on August 15, 1987: "Dear Darrell, It is disgraceful that you should be used by adults for the purpose of trying to shame us because of our extraction of timber from our forests.

"For the information of the adults who use you I would like to say that it is not a question of one rich man making a million pounds. Every tree that is extracted creates jobs for at least ten poor men who support probably ten wives and thirty children. In addition the rich man pays 40% in income tax. Without this rich man not only will the Government get no tax but there will be no logging and numerous people will be jobless. Additionally the rich man reinvests his money or simply spends it. No matter whether he invests or just spends money a lot of people will benefit, people who otherwise would be very poor. The tax the Government collects will provide education, health and other services also for the poor.

"The timber industry helps hundreds of thousands of poor people in Malaysia. Are they supposed to remain poor because you want to study tropical animals? Is your study more important than filling the empty stomachs of poor people? Are Malaysians expected to lose millions of pounds so that you can study animals?

"When the British ruled Malaysia they burnt millions of acres of Malaysian forests so that they could plant rubber. The timber was totally wasted because in those days nobody wanted Malaysian timber. Millions of animals died because of the burning. Malaysians got nothing from the felling of the timber. In addition when the rubber was sold practically all the profit was taken to England. What your father's fathers did was indeed disgraceful.

"If you don't want us to cut down our forests, tell your father to tell the rich countries like Britain to pay more for the timber they buy from us. Then we can cut less timber and create other jobs for our people.

"If you are really interested in tropical animals, we have huge National Parks where nobody is allowed to fell trees or kill animals. In any case we don't cut all the trees when we do logging in the forests. Only marked mature trees are cut. We also do reforestation.

"I hope you will tell the adults who made use of you to learn all the facts. They should not be too arrogant and think they know how best to run a country. They should expel all the people living in the British countryside and allow secondary forests to grow and fill these new forests with wolves and bears etc. so you can study them before studying tropical animals.

"I believe strongly that children should learn all about animals and love them. But adults should not teach children to be rude to their elders.

"Sincerely, Dr. Mahathir bin Mohamad."

Some people might consider this letter a bit of overkill, or at least messy public relations. Dr. M, as he is known, perhaps saw his missive to his young idealistic pen pal as a warning shot over the bow of Western public opinion.

The Penans, and other native groups of Sarawak, have erected a series of blockades to stop timber operations. Hundreds of people have been jailed as a result. In retaliation there are reports of Penan women being raped, of Penans being denied hospital care.

The situation for the Penans and the forest they live in became even more complicated by the presence of a Swiss named Bruno Manser, who lived with the Penans for some four years.[7] According to his fans, Manser was a modern-day Robin Hood, a true eco-hero, one of the few men who really lived his ideals. Forsaking clean, efficient, and boring Switzerland for the wilds of Borneo, Manser endured a fugitive life in the jungle, where he encouraged the tribal Penan people to protest government-sponsored logging. During his tenure (coincidentally he claimed), the Penans and other indigenous groups in Sarawak began blockades of logging

---

7   Manser disappeared in mysterious circumstances in Sarawak in May 2000 and is presumed dead, having failed, in his own admission, to either stop the forest destruction or to convince the Penans to continue the high-visibility, high-risk political actions he promoted. For a fictional account of a similar scenario, see my novel *Redheads*.

operations.[8, 9]

For the Malaysian authorities, the Penans are a public relations headache. *Perkasa*, the magazine of the Sarawak Timber Industry Development Corporation ran a special piece, "Focus on Penan Development Programmes" in December 1992. The article featured a large photo of a smiling, barechested Penan elder showing Dr. M a traditional musical instrument. Dr. M, wearing an impeccable white safari suit, examines the instrument while his wife and Sarawak Chief Minister Taib Mahmud look on. Everyone looked happy, but something was wrong with the photo, and it took me a while to figure it out.

Alfred Jabu would have used this photo as evidence that the Penans who have been settled into simple longhouses near Gunung Mulu National Park are happy. "They have 22 acres [nine hectares] of terraced padi, which provides enough rice for a whole year,"

---

8   Mahathir bin Mohamad, perhaps welcoming the chance to face a tougher pen pal than young Darrell Abercrombie, also took on Bruno Manser. The two met at the 1992 Earth Summit in Rio de Janeiro, a meeting preceded by six months of private correspondence in which Mahathir was unapologetic, threatening, and sarcastic. He began a March 3, 1993 letter to Manser: "If any Penan or policeman gets killed or wounded in the course of restoring law and order in Sarawak, you will have to take the blame." Mahathir added: "It is the height of arrogance for you to advocate that the Penans live on maggots and monkeys in their miserable huts. . . . What right have you to condemn them to a primitive life forever?" Manser was more conciliatory and acknowledged that many industrialized nations are guilty of "injustice" and have even committed "genocide" against many indigenous peoples. But he also denounced the alleged arrests and beatings of 452 *bumiputras* (literally "sons of the earth" and generally used to describe Malays who receive preferential treatment in Malaysia; Manser is tauntingly including the Penans in this affirmative action group) by the authorities since 1987 for opposing the logging companies. Manser charged that people who are already suffering from the destruction of their food supplies from logging have been detained for months without trial. "Is this respect?" he asks Mahathir. "Is this allowing them to choose their own destiny?"

9   Bruno Manser was a keen letter writer and often sought tactical advice from friends. In 1998 Manser wrote to Anthony and Gita Brooke, whose ancestors were the White Rajahs who ruled Sarawak, telling them "I have decided to jump into Kuching with a parachute (the Malaysian/Sarawak Flags) at Hari Raya Haji, to hand myself to the authorities and draw attention to the Penans' pleas – and as a surprise. If you have any recommendation helping for success – plese [sic] let us know, how to touch Taib's heart [Sarawak Chief Minister Abdul Taib Mahmud, whom many hold accountable for forest destruction]. Anthony and Gita advised that "the heart of one person can only be touched from within the heart of another, lightly, lovingly and without forcefulness." Manser, ignoring the bathos, said "I will listen to my heart [and] apologising by giving a white lamb to the Chief Minister and his wife in confidence."

he told me. "They grow plenty of vegetables, fruits, papaya and pineapples, which they sell to tourist resthouses. We are teaching them to cultivate mushrooms."

Alfred Jabu is smart enough to know that the mushroom metaphor works both ways – a Penan mushroom farmer might well have thought: "They keep me in the dark, feed me shit, and eventually I get sliced up and wind up in the soup." I reexamined the photo and recognized that the seemingly happy Penan indeed had what we call a "shit-eating grin." The loinclothed Penan's face was in rictus. He appeared terrified.

The article applauded the success of the Prime Minister's scholarship scheme for Penans, which "reflected the seriousness of the government to bring the Penans to the mainstream of development." An official quoted in the article was happy to note that there was a noticeable improvement in the sanitary condition of the village, "and now, some of the Penans even have modern houses."

In the article the government is candid: "The short term projects are implemented in the form of minor rural projects which actually are hand-outs given to meet the basic requirements of the community. A typical Penan Service Centre established close to Penan settlements caters to the basic needs of the community, and includes primary school, clinic, and an agriculture station. So far six service centres have been planned, by end of 1991 two had been completed.

"It is clear that the Penans do not want to stay in the jungle forever and that they do want a change in their way of life and to have access to modern facilities and services. This is evidenced by the fact that every time a government officer visits a Penan settlement, the villagers would not fail to give a list of requests which contains all sorts of modern items such as outboard engines, rice-mills, electric generators, building materials, schools and clinics.

"In trying to bring development to the Penans, the state government realises that the Penans are a simple people and that an overnight change is not possible. Although the government has been generous in providing the Penans with facilities and services, care has also been taken to ensure that the Penans will not be overdependent on the government so that they will not expect handouts all the time. . . . Penans will be trained to stand on their own and learn to face the challenges of modern living like other Malaysians."

Alfred Jabu added the final proof that the Penans are happy. "They have a Penan elder as spokesman. He lives in a big house and drives a Mercedes."

This kind of attitude is anathema to northerners, who view the Penans (and other indigenous people) with much the same rose-colored vision as they do wildlife. "We must not let the elephant/tiger/orangutan/Penan die. Save them for future generations." Northerners see the Penans, and similar isolated groups, as a cause célèbre, as a form of ideal that has ceased to exist elsewhere. Wallace wrote in a similar vein.

> Here [Aru], as among most savage people I have dwelt among, I was delighted with the beauty of the human form – a beauty of which stay-at-home civilized people can scarcely have any conception.[10]

We in the North *want* the idea of noble, naked savages.

> What are the finest Grecian statues to the living, moving, breathing men I saw daily around me? The unrestrained grace of the naked savage, as he goes about his daily occupations, or lounges at his ease, must be seen to be understood; and a youth bending his bow is the perfection of manly beauty.[11]

---

10 *The Malay Archipelago*, 467.

11 Ibid.

The origin of the word "savage" comes from the Latin *silvaticus*, which means woodland, with the implication that it is something inherently rural, isolated, and perhaps mysterious and evil and therefore to be avoided.[12] But what a word to stir us from our boring civilized existence. What connotations, what Rousseau-tinged dreams. One of the great ironies is that Sarawak officials are not above manipulating this interest in the noble savage, and tourism officials promote the "cultural experience" of spending a night in an Iban longhouse with the "children of headhunters."

One of the first words a visitor learns in Sarawak is *"ulu,"* Malay for the upper reaches of a river. It refers to far more than geography. To many people it describes a way of life that gets more primitive, alien, and unattractive the farther inland you go. *Ulu* is a concept that depends on your perspective. To the urbane businessman in Kuching, the people who live in communal longhouses thirty kilometers away are country bumpkins, regardless of the fact that they too may speak English and have electricity, running water, and television. The perceived difference between "us" (civilized and modern and handsome) and "them" (none of the above) gets wider the farther upriver one goes. It is considered "modern" to live in an apartment building with one family perched on *top* of another. Lay the apartment building on its side with up to fifty individual apartments sharing a common porch and sitting *next* to each other and you get an "old-fashioned" longhouse.

The differentiation between "us" and "them" is an age-old phenomenon. In Southeast Asia, it stretches back to the prehistoric movements of people, adding complexity to the term "melting pot."

The Penans are Proto-Malays, people who came overland from northwest India or Burma some seven thousand years ago. They were once the most sophisticated people in the forest, and

---

12 There are countless criteria for demonstrating civilized versus savage. Homer, in *The Odyssey*, used the art of bread-making as the criteria for distinguishing civilized folks from savage barbarians.

perhaps even pioneered domestication of plants. They since lost the skills of agriculture and have largely reverted to hunting and gathering, probably when pushed into the isolated hills by the Deutero-Malays who came from southern China and who now are the dominant people of Southeast Asia. In a state with dozens of tribes, the Penans, who have a rightful claim to being the true "sons of the soil," are at the bottom of the pecking order.

What should an outsider make of all this? The Malaysian attitude – and you find exactly the same attitude in Indonesia – could be mistaken for brown-brown colonialism where "*we*, the people in power, know what's best for *you*, our poor rural relatives."

Wallace seemed to take both sides of the argument. On the one hand he sided with the "help our poor naked brown cousins to develop" attitude of Malaysian officials.

> Can it be right to keep a number of our fellow creatures in a state of adult infancy, of unthinking childhood?[13]

But on the other hand Wallace's description of the Uaupés Indians sounds just like the kind of Western romanticism that Dr. M railed against when he argued that "[Europeans] would like the Penans in Sarawak to live below subsistence level . . . [and] to use blowpipes for them to gawk at. The Penans are not a showpiece," he argued, "neither are they there for the Europeans to do their anthropological theses on; they need to live like human beings."

> [I had] my first meeting and living with man in a state of nature – with absolute uncontaminated savages! They had nothing that we call clothes; they had peculiar ornaments, tribal marks, etc.; they all carried weapons or tools of

---

13 *A Narrative of Travels on the Amazon and Rio Negro, With an Account of the Native Tribes, and Observations on the Climate, Geology, and Natural History of the Amazon Valley.* 1870. London: Macmillan & Co., 83.

their own manufacture; they were living . . . many families together . . . but, more than all, their whole aspect and manner were different – they were all going about their own work or pleasure which had nothing to do with white men or their ways. . . . In every detail they were original and self-sustaining as are the wild animals of the forests, absolutely independent of civilization, and who could and did live their own lives in their own way, as they had done for countless generations before America was discovered.[14]

A student of Machiavelli or Dick Cheney might see a different motive in all this brotherhood business. The simple fact is that if the Malaysian leaders and business magnates succeed in taking the Penans out of the forest, then they will have neatly eliminated one of the major hurdles against uncontrolled forest exploitation – first cutting the forest for timber, then establishing plantations of either pulpwood or palm oil.

In Sarawak I visited a semi-settled Penan group upriver from Belaga, near the Rajang River. They lived in a basic, run-down longhouse. There was litter, indicating that they had some cash and that they had yet to learn (or care) that Coke cans are not biodegradable. They had more *things*, but not, as far as I could see, more joy.

I also stayed with several semi-settled Penan groups in ulu Bintulu. They reminded me of kids on summer holiday, just hanging around their huts, showing off tattoos of naked women and helicopters. Several men wore sports shorts and T-shirts. They spoke the national language, more or less. During that particular trip it became apparent that while the Penans were getting the

---

14 *My Life*, Vol. 1, 288.

publicity, the real issue was that many of the rural people – not just the Penans but also other ethnic groups with considerably more political muscle – were similarly fighting the timber operations. Logging was ruining hunting and fishing; it was dangerous, and loggers desecrated tribal burial grounds. Equally important: much money was being made from timber, but little was going to the locals. I flew over the state and saw large chunks of barren land that had recently been forest.[15] I walked along logging roads that were dust bowls in the dry season and mires in the wet. When I bathed in the rivers in front of longhouses, I had to wear gym shoes to protect myself from sharp debris. I walked along paths where I had once seen gibbons and now saw tractors.

The last time I visited with Penans I was with a man named Jim, who had been one of my guides during a climb to the limestone pinnacles that form one of the Gunung Mulu National Park's most dramatic features. He lived in one of the longhouses that Alfred Jabu considered such a success. The longhouse was similar to army barracks or timber camp housing, with tin roofs that amplified the heat, making the residences uninhabitable during the day. The Penans I saw were listless, with vacant eyes. True, they now had access to basic health care and simple schools, but it seemed as if all the energy had been sucked from their thin frames. At that time, the only lightness came when I asked for a blowpipe lesson, and the Penans laughed at my incompetence.

So, I suppose I live up to Dr. M's image of an unrealistic, dreaming Westerner. Boys are dreamers. Bruno Manser was a dreamer. Alfred Russel Wallace was certainly a dreamer. Darrell Abercrombie may indeed grow up to be a dreamer, but he has already tasted the bitter pill that dreamers of all ages encounter: confusion and disillusionment.

The paranoid Sarawakians figure there is no place for dreamers, or even objectivity, when confronted with the Penan/logging issue. I wrote a chapter on Malaysia's natural wonders for a coffee table book, *Malaysia: Heart of Southeast Asia*, the coordinator of which was

---

15   According to the Bruno Manser Foundation, more than seventy percent of Sarawak's rainforest has been cut during the past twenty years.

Marina Mahathir, the prime minister's daughter. At an editorial committee meeting we asked the Malaysian advisors how candid we should be about environmental issues in Sarawak. "Tell the truth," they insisted. Easy for them to say – they were from Peninsular Malaysia, not from the distant and relatively independent state of Sarawak.

Someone (not me) wrote a photo caption in the book that really annoyed Sarawak state officials: "A logging road [not unlike the fictional one I describe in my novel *Redheads*] snakes along a once forested ridge in Sarawak. Gunung Mulu [the national park as well as the mountain] in the background is now an island of green in a battlefield of dust and chainsaws." Another caption referred to "once crystal-clear waters" which "have become choked with mud and debris washed downstream from logging areas. The rivers have been further polluted by oil, chemicals and other industrial and human effluent from timber camps located at the headwaters of many major river systems. This pollution has been a major source of conflict between Sarawak's lucrative logging industry and the native population." Aside from the "crystal-clear waters" (most tropical rivers, except those *very* far upstream, are naturally muddy from silt), these captions are accurate. They were also inflammatory, and the Sarawak chief minister, who was going to launch the book in Kuching the day after the prime minister launched it in Kuala Lumpur, declared that he was instead going to ban the book. This led to a hectic bit of publishing diplomacy for poor Marina, and ultimately a compromise was reached. The edition to be sold in Sarawak would be reprinted, at significant expense, with the inflammatory photos and captions replaced by shots of people weaving baskets and giving each other tattoos. The irony is that six months after publication, Kuching's two leading bookshops – at the Sarawak Museum and the Kuching Hilton Hotel – were blithely unaware of the affront to the state, and both proudly sold the original version of the book with the inflammatory photos and captions.

COME IN RUBBER DUCK

Morowali, Sulawesi, Indonesia

In a village where children are gleefully shouting
"Rubber Duck, Rubber Duck!"

The white-brown interface (not to mention white-brown intercourse) has been around since white folks first met brown folks. Wallace's comments on this dynamic seem to foretell the cynicism of Kipling's famous poem "The White Man's Burden," which he penned in 1899 on the occasion of America taking possession of the Philippines.

> Take up the white man's burden—
> The savage wars of peace—
> Fill full the mouth of famine,
> And bid the sickness cease;
> And when your goal is nearest
> (The end for others sought)
> Watch sloth and heathen folly
> Bring all your hope to nought.

A cartoon I use in my writing workshops to convey the importance of point of view shows a native American in a dugout canoe approaching his village. On the high seas in the background can be seen three ships, similar to those in which Columbus sailed. The headline reads: "1492: Further evidence that history is a matter of perspective." The guy in the canoe (yes, he's wearing feathers) says to his compatriots: "Hey guys, I just discovered Europeans."

Since people first started to travel outside their home villages, the notion that "they" are different to "us" has been a universal constant. The "others" might look different, speak a strange language, pray to a different god, eat curious food (frogs legs! durian! oysters! termites!). They might be welcoming, urbane, generous. Or not. Wallace constantly had people looking over his shoulder.

> When I sat down in the afternoon to arrange my insects, the house was surrounded by men, women, and children, lost in amazement at my unaccountable proceedings; and when, after pinning out the specimens, I proceeded to write the name of the place on small circular tickets and attach one to each, even the old kapala [headman], the Mohammedan priest, and some Malay traders could not repress signs of astonishment.[1]

They amaze us. We amaze them. What a wonderful world.

Derek Jackson, or, as he preferred to be called, Major (Retired) Derek Jackson, was the leader of the Sulawesi leg of Operation Drake, a 1980 British scientific expedition that roughly retraced

---

1   *The Malay Archipelago*, 330.

Sir Francis Drake's circumnavigation of the world four centuries earlier. Over five hundred people took part in the project designed to give hundreds of international Young Explorers a chance, as their patron HRH Prince Charles explained, to experience "some of the challenges of war in a peace-time situation."

I joined Op Drake, as it was called, in Morowali, eastern Sulawesi, where we helped prepare a management plan for a proposed nature reserve. A group of eight of us planned an expedition to a "wild Wana" village that ostensibly had never been visited.[2] After trekking a couple of days we reached the outskirts of the "wild Wana" village. We asked if we could enter, and we were cautiously, but politely, received.

The Wana proudly showed off their possessions: a ceremonial cap made of monkey hair, a blowpipe, a homemade harpoon, and goggles for fishing in the nearby Morowali River. They played a guitar-shaped instrument they called a *ukelili*, which may be proof that Hawaiian is the closest thing we have to an international language. They had idiot children, probably from inbreeding; goiters, probably from lack of seafood; and malaria, which I caught. A woman with safety-pin earrings cooked rice, and we brought out some tinned food as our contribution to lunch. We asked an old man if we could borrow his machete.

"What for?" he asked.

"To open this can of sardines."

Silly foreigners. "You don't need a *parang*." He reached up into the thatched roof of his shelter, pushed aside some deer skins, and proudly showed us a sardine key.

"Where did you get that?" we asked as he deftly opened the tin.

"Operasi Drek," he replied, using the Indonesian pronunciation of Operation Drake. Our own fellow expedition members had discovered these isolated savages a few weeks before we had.

---

2   Op Drake publicists, including Derek Jackson, had a penchant for hyperbole. On an earlier leg of the expedition he had announced on the BBC World Service that his team had "discovered" a totally isolated tribe in Papua New Guinea that somehow spoke six languages.

Logistics for Op Drake were a continual problem. We sat aboard our Mother Ship, the brigantine *Eye of the Wind* for four days in Kendari harbor while Major (Retired) Derek Jackson engaged in – as he described them – "headman to headman" talks with various government officials in an effort to purchase gas, water, and other supplies.

Soon, a more substantial logistical problem arose. Operation Drake required a supplementary boat to ferry people the one hundred and twenty kilometers (seventy-five miles) from base camp to the nearest airport at Kendari. The *Eye of the Wind* was too big, too slow, and, in any case, was needed for continuing a fruitless search for dugongs. I joined Major (Retired) Derek Jackson on a Zodiac trip to visit the tiny fishing village of Bungku in order to negotiate the use of an alternate vessel.

Our group was welcomed by the headman's wife, who explained her husband was at a meeting. She asked in Indonesian: "Are you in a hurry?"

Jackson replied, using Indonesian journalist Rudy Badil as an interpreter: "No. Tell her we'll be patient, like their culture demands."

The headman soon arrived, accompanied by assorted assistants, one of whom was smoking his clove cigarette in a holder carved from a dugong tusk. This was noted by Derek, who was stopped from commenting only after an icy glare from Badil. "Please down," the host headman requested in English, pointing to some worn chairs.

Jackson was in his element now, speaking headman to headman. "We'd better beat around the bush for ten minutes," he mumbled. "This is a lovely village you have here, sir. Beautiful children."

Dozens of bright young faces peered in through every available window and door. It was a mass of youthful humanity, both noisy and claustrophobic. "When a white man comes it's a circus," Jackson observed, as did Wallace.

I was obliged to stay [in the village], as my men wanted
to return and others could not possibly go on with me
without the preliminary talking. Besides, a white man
was too great a rarity to be allowed to escape them, and
their wives would never have forgiven them if, when they
returned from the fields, they found that such a curiosity
had not been kept for them to see. On entering the house
to which I was invited, a crowd of sixty or seventy men,
women, and children gathered around me, and I sat for
half an hour like some strange animal submitted for the
first time to the gaze of an inquiring public.[3]

Captain Anna Stasiuk, who was seconded, like many of Op
Drake's directing staff, from the British army, went outside to radio
the *Eye of the Wind*. She was a robust woman, prone to wearing a
minimum of clothing, and she attracted a large and intensely curious
crowd as she made radio contact with the brigantine. "Eye of the
Wind, come in. This is Rubber Duck," she shouted, referring to
the Zodiac's call name.

"Come in, Rubber Duck, we read you."

Back in the house, the visiting headman presented the host
headman with an Operation Drake badge, asking Rudy Badil
to explain that Jackson had smaller badges to give to the other
gentlemen, but that this particular headman's badge was the best.
"It gives him face," Jackson explained. "That's very important."

Jackson sat down, smiling, after the presentation. Badil said,
"Normally you shake hands." Still smiling, Jackson rose again to
do as local custom demanded.

Down to business. After explaining that he was a major (he
neglected to mention retired), Derek Jackson informed the host
headman that the Indonesian colonel in charge of security for
Op Drake and the British defense attaché planned to visit the
expedition's base camp.

"Say, I've got an idea," Jackson said, smiling. "Perhaps they would

---

3 *The Malay Archipelago*, 78–9.

like to visit this beautiful village of yours. I can suggest that."

Smiles all around, tempered by concern. Visiting dignitaries expect free hospitality.

"And it would really impress these important people if they could travel in a boat from this attractive village of Bungku," Jackson continued. More smiles. They sensed money and pride. An unbeatable combination.

"We would be delighted if we could use a Bungku boat. Naturally we'll pay for it." No question now about the sincerity of the smiles.

"And perhaps the Bungku boat could leave a day earlier and make a short detour to our Ranu base camp. Then it could carry about twelve people, including some *very important* UN officials, down to Kendari, where the colonel will arrive."

Op Drake's headman then offered 280,000 "rue-pie-ahs" for the charter. Never mind that he mispronounced the name of the national currency. The host headman agreed, as undoubtedly they are taught to do in headman school.

Half the morning had gone by, and it was time to leave. "Tell him we'd like to walk around the village," Jackson said to Badil. "That way we don't have to say we want to go." Our group strolled around the neat community, followed by hordes of youngsters shouting: "Rubber Duck! Rubber Duck!"

Alfred Russel Wallace didn't hesitate to poke fun at himself.

> If they had known a little more about the ways and opinions of white men, they would probably have looked upon me as a fool or a madman, but in their ignorance they accepted my operations as worthy of all respect, although utterly beyond their comprehension.[4]

Wallace endorsed the idea that a white-brown relationship was

---

4   *The Malay Archipelago*, 329–30.

similar to that of master and pupil.

> Now, there is not merely an analogy – there is in many respects an identity of relation between master and pupil or parent and child on the one hand, and an uncivilized race and its civilized rulers on the other. We know (or think we know) that the education and industry, and the common usages of civilized man, are superior to those of savage life; and, as he becomes acquainted with them, the savage himself admits this. He admires the superior acquirements of the civilized man, and it is with pride that he will adopt such usages as do not interfere too much with his sloth, his passions, or his prejudices. But as the willful child or the idle schoolboy, who was never taught obedience, and never made to do anything which of his own free will he was not inclined to do, would in most cases obtain neither education nor manners; so it is much more unlikely that the savage, with all the confirmed habits of manhood and the traditional prejudices of race, should ever do more than copy a few of the least beneficial customs of civilization, without some stronger stimulus than precept, very imperfectly backed by example.[5]

It's curious how different Europeans act when they are posted to Indonesia. Some go troppo – they bizarrely pretend they are locals by insisting on using an inordinate number of Indonesian words when speaking with foreign friends, traveling on cheap transportation, abstaining from air conditioning, and doing whatever else they think lower class local folks do. Some foreigners stay pretty much themselves – by far the sanest strategy. And then there are the colonialists-in-spite-of-themselves. I've seen many nice, sensitive people come out to Asia from the United States and Europe. They land in Jakarta and catch arrogance faster than

---

5   *The Malay Archipelago*, 262.

diarrhea. Somehow they pick up on the perceived vibes that Asians respect them simply for their whiteness. With whiteness comes perceived intelligence, stature, and wisdom. With whiteness comes expected leadership. And some whites wallow in this seduction.

Westerners, particularly folks who consider themselves sensitive and culture-friendly, invade villages, homes, and ceremonies to witness, and sometimes participate in, local rites. Asian tourists are more restrained. What would happen if a group of Malaysians show up, unannounced, at a West Virginia homestead? "We're from the Authentic Redneck Appalachia Tours and Travel Company and were headed for an incest ceremony over in the next county, but they didn't want us," the tour group leader says. "Well, we asked those fine folks where else we could see inbreeding and black lung disease and ramshackle housing and cute naked children with worms, and they sent us over here. Do you mind if we stay a few days, eat your simple food, and drink lots of your moonshine without paying a penny? Great! By the way, do your dogs make doo-doo on the front porch? We definitely want dog doo-doo. You say we can use the outhouse if we don't mind running a free-range pig gauntlet? Terrific. Hey, I see you've got lots of old refrigerators for the kids to play in!"

The U.S. Peace Corps gave me the opportunity to live globally. However well-intentioned the program might be, it smacks of white-brown arrogance. Why do we send young U.S. Peace Corps volunteers, like me, to Asia, but Asians never send volunteers to help Americans? I'd like to see some Bhutanese community development experts do something constructive in south central Los Angeles. Send Borneo Iban community reforestation experts to help grow town parks in Detroit. Encourage Thai Buddhist monks to teach locals to sanctify old growth trees in Washington and Oregon.

I was at an international biodiversity workshop in Bogani Nani Wartabone National Park in Sulawesi. The "secretariat" was in the so-called lab, a run-down facility with broken sinks, chipped white tiles, and cracked white counters. I walked in one morning and found a stunning variety of moths and beetles that had been attracted by the lights burning all night. I thought of Wallace having written:

> As soon as it got dark I placed my lamp against the wall, and with pins, insect-forceps, net, and collecting-boxes by my side, sat down with a book. Sometimes during the whole evening only one solitary moth would visit me, while on other nights they would pour in in a continual stream, keeping me hard at work catching and pinning till past midnight. They came literally by thousands. On good nights I was able to capture from a hundred to two hundred and fifty moths, and these comprised on each occasion from half to two-thirds that number of distinct species. Some . . . would settle on the wall, some on the table, while many would fly up to the roof and give me a chase all over the veranda before I could secure them.[6]

The mellifluously named Bogani Nani Wartabone National Park was a great place for moths, but a lousy environment in which to seek consensus. The workshop was not going well. Ian Swingland, the Englishman running the exercise, had waited until the sixth day of a seven-day symposium to tell the participants – Indonesians and foreigners from about ten countries – that President Soeharto himself wanted the group to make specific recommendations in the form of an Action Plan. Wanting to do his duty, and perhaps sensing that there might be a consulting contract for him somewhere down the line if the recommendations were accepted, Swingland had written a draft Action Plan. I was asked to edit it. I read the structureless platitudes, worse than UN-ese, and told him that there

---

6   Ibid., 95–6.

was just one specific recommendation in the fifteen single-spaced pages and that was hidden in para 3, page 6. If I was a decision-maker I'd throw this draft back at the creators.

Swingland went back to the group. The scientific symposium had turned into a political mud wrestle. We spent half an hour debating one word: "destruction." I forget the specific reference, but it was something innocuous like "bad management and greed contribute to destruction of nature."

At least the foreigners thought it was innocuous. The Indonesians and the Malaysians in attendance said nothing, but thought otherwise. We voted. The term "destruction" was accepted. Twenty minutes later someone came back to the troublesome word. Ian Swingland blew up. "We already covered that!" I watched, fascinated by the dynamics at play. "Do we vote to say what we mean or do we want to alter it to consider local sensitivities?" he asked, thereby doubly insulting his Indonesian hosts – first by voicing the uncomfortable truth and second by making them uncomfortable by insisting on a second vote, which goes against the Indonesian policy of *musyawarah*, in which you bore your opponent into consensus. "Destruction" passed a second time. Then somebody said "Do we really want to say 'greed?' How about 'inadequate legal and social parameters?' "

Swingland had twelve hours to get the Action Plan ready, along with a Declaration, various appendices, and a Memorandum of Understanding between his research institute and the government. About half a dozen symposium participants, mostly all European, were busy in the makeshift office, typing away.

He wanted to print the drafts. Anita, an Indonesian who worked at the British Council and who had been typing for days, looked at me and mouthed the word "trouble." The printer cartridge was out of ink; no one had thought to bring a replacement. Six computer "technicians" brought over from distant Manado were smirking in the corner, smoking clove cigarettes and watching the white man fume. Finally one of them tried to drip fountain pen ink into the empty cartridge through a straw.

"No, the ink is OK," Swingland said to Anita, the only

Indonesian in the inner sanctum. "He just put the cartridge in wrong. Could you please tell him that, Anita."

She did. The technician continued his drip feed.

"No, the problem is the paper. He has to put the paper in *this* way. No, *I'll do it*." Swingland pushed the technician aside.

"Why didn't anyone think of getting extra cartridges?" Swingland fumed, by now trying to fill the printer cartridge by dripping ink from a straw. "Explain to him I'm just tired, and I've got so much to do. This is very important. The president of the republic asked for it. I haven't slept for two days."

In the meantime, a gentleman named Dr. Hakim, a senior official of one of the two host ministries, which had been bickering behind the scenes, popped in to our war room to say goodbye. His departure was unexpected, and he got in his car to leave for Manado, seven hours away.

Meanwhile, Swingland asked: "Anita, how are we going to get thirty copies of the Action Plan for this afternoon?"

Fifteen minutes later, Swingland realized that things were not going to get better without some executive decisions: "Anita, you may have to go to Manado," he said finally. A car was commandeered. Just as Anita was leaving she discovered that one crucial diskette was missing. For reasons that were never made clear, but likely involved inter-ministry rivalry, Swingland decided that the diskette was "inadvertently" taken by Dr. Hakim. "Catch up with him and get it back, please Anita."

Indonesian women are portrayed as being soft and gentle. They are, but they are also hard as nails. Anita took off after Dr. Hakim. Frustrated because her driver was too cautious, she took over the wheel and quickly caught Dr. Hakim in a "Nixon," as she later described it. He sheepishly handed over the diskette.

Ternate, Indonesia
A street mural painted by schoolchildren featuring Wallace, with the
Indonesian message: "Let's protect and care for the beautiful city of Ternate."
Photo: Paul Sochaczewski

V

RETURN

SHIVA'S BEACH –
SOMEWHERE IN THE WORLD
THE SUN IS SHINING

Pulau Enu, Aru Islands, Indonesia

Is it really darkest before the dawn?

A shooting star. I can never think of a wish fast enough, and the opportunity for good luck goes up in flames, as it were.

Too easy to get depressed, thinking about the unlikelihood of achieving conservation.

Too easy to get bogged down in reflection.

I feel like a teenager on a blind date. If Alfred was here, would we get along? Would we have the same sense of humor? Would I be awed? Would I try to impress him with my amusing traveler's tales?

And what if – it's possible – he was boring?

Damn these stupid turtles. Why did God, or that special force or "different agency" or whatever weasel words Wallace used, why did that unfathomable but all-knowing Power make turtles so complicated? It could have been easy. Sure, they're reptiles, and they have to lay eggs to reproduce. But so do crocodiles, and you don't hear of people stealing crocodile eggs. Maybe the Power could have arranged it so that the eggs of the sea turtles taste bad to predators. Wallace could have figured out an explanation of why that fitted in with natural selection.

Darwin's theory was cleaner. Natural selection, all the way. Wallace fudged, fiddled, and got his knickers in a twist. There's no good American way to say that.

He was cursed with a free-range brain, like the more expensive chickens in the supermarket. He saw one side of an issue then called in what I call the Nancy Reagan "no" words – however, but, nevertheless, in spite of – to say "maybe there's another way to look at this."

But sometimes he was so damn sure of himself. He "knew" that spirits exist. Should have been a Sunday morning televangelist.

I put my ear to the sand, like the storybooks say the American Indians (or Native Americans or whatever) used to do to track deer. Is that a scratching I hear? Is that a baby turtle boxing his way out of his shell, trying to climb over his brothers and sisters and claw his way through half a meter of sand to reach the surface? What a tough way to begin life. But maybe that just makes the little critter tough enough to survive the rest of life's challenges.

Shiva is god, is he not?
Like so many of his kin
The trident smites both ways
Gleaming, nevertheless

WOMEN ON TOP

Sangburnih, Bali, Indonesia

Dancing the Balinese version of the hula in front of several hundred very amused villagers with a girl whose goal in life is to make me look like a rut-obsessed goat.

During Wallace's time in Southeast Asia the women's rights movement was stirring:

1848 – The world's first women's rights convention is held in Seneca Falls, New York; a Declaration of Sentiments and Resolutions sets the agenda for the women's rights movement that followed.

1848 – The state of New York allows separate economy and independence for married women.

1850 – Iceland grants legal majority for (unmarried) women, followed by Denmark (1857), Sweden (1858), Norway (1863), Finland (1864), and Italy (1865).

1851 – Guatemala: Women who fulfill the demands of personal economic wealth are granted citizenship.

1851 – Elizabeth Smith Miller appears in "Turkish trousers," soon to be known as "bloomers," named after Amelia Jenks Bloomer[1] who in 1849 publishes *Lily*, the first prominent women's rights newspaper.

1855 – Lucy Stone becomes first woman on record to keep her own name after marriage, setting a precedent among women who are consequently known as "Lucy Stoners."

1859 – The birth rate continues its downward spiral as reliable condoms become available.

You heard this one? A guy appears moody. His wife asks: "What's wrong, honey?" "Nothing," he replies, and continues to read the paper. She makes herself miserable considering all the options: "He's sick and isn't telling me. He's having an affair and isn't telling me. He doesn't like my new hairstyle and isn't telling me." She calls up her girlfriends to discuss. She can't sleep. She considers marriage counseling. Or maybe plastic surgery. The guy also can't sleep. "Four-putt on the 18th? Who in the world four-putts?"

It's tough, this business of gender models and gender expectations. How much is biological, and how much is social? Men and women show varying metabolic action in different parts of the limbic system: for men it's a more primitive region of the limbic system related to direct action, and for women the metabolic activity is higher in the cingulate gyrus, a more recently evolved part of the limbic system associated with symbolic action. This could be biological proof of something most men face daily – women want to talk about feelings, men want to either jump into the hot tub, go for a run, or speculate on Michael Jordan's comeback.

---

1   She was also an early fan of the vulcanized rubber girdle.

"It's going to be a wild night," Surata says, jiggling his hips and practicing his moves. "Lots of hot *gadis*."

The idea of hot "virgins" on a steamy Balinese night intrigues me, and we walk a kilometer down the road to a village *joged* performance.

I buy us both a few numbered tickets at about twenty-five cents a throw. If our numbers are called we will have the chance to go on stage and make fools of ourselves.

We are attending an event that is a competition by two groups of young women (with bands) to see which team can do a better job of pseudo-seducing testosterone-charged young men.

"I want to dance with *him*," Surata oozes as the first dancer wiggles on to the stage. I correct his pronoun. "I want to dance with *her*," Surata says and watches transfixed as the dancer gyrates her hips and wraps a sash around the clove-cigarette-dangling, faux-Levis-clad Balinese boy who is lucky enough to be the first victim. Surata stares at his tickets – numbers 17–23; surely he will be called next. The lucky young man sways in rhythm with the *gadis* on stage, a member of the Joged Dwi Tunggal group from Desa Suwug, supported by a gamelan orchestra in green shirts and blue sarongs and gold sashes. Her job, and that of her sister dancers and male band members, is to be more provocative, outrageous, and intimidating than the girls and boys of the opposing team, a group wearing yellow shirts and gold sarongs that bills itself as Joged Tumpul Sar from Desa Depaha.

I ask Surata why this old dance tradition still has so much force.

"*Joged* can never be lost here," he explains, referring to the sensuous dance movements so popular in Indonesian villages. "If no one dances *joged* then people will start to die, one every two days." He was very exact.

I ask for his proof.

Silly foreigner, his face says. "Seven years ago they stopped dancing and some people died. Then they started *joged* again. And today, well, we're all here."

It was a battle of the bands, with the percussionists waving their drumsticks like mock rifles, and the crowd loved it. Musicians jump and shout; one percussionist plays tiny cymbals in his mouth while he simultaneously pounds a conga drum behind his back.

"Why is this so popular?" I ask, but it is a silly question. It is sex, of course.

As it happens, my number is called early. I dance with a beautiful twentysomething virgin (hey, give the girl the benefit of the doubt) wearing a red and purple sarong. She performs an Asian Salomé with her sash, which she then wraps around my neck and proceeds to entice me with a sort of Balinese Lambada. I had already seen a few other boys dance, and I make the expected mock passes and mildly suggestive gestures. The crowd, as might be expected, seeing a balding uncoordinated white man up on stage, goes wild. After five minutes the virgin gets bored, and we rather chastely thank each other, and I find Surata, who is pleased that I have had my turn, but a touch jealous.

In *joged* the woman calls the shots. Does this have any relevance for the real world?

Are Balinese women more highly evolved than the men?

Wallace thought a lot about how society evolves.

> There are certain stages through which society must pass, in its onward march from barbarism to civilization.[2]

That may or may not be true. But assuming that society does evolve and that the social evolution is "positive," what is the mechanism? It's not unlike the question Wallace posed for himself about the animal world, the answer in that case was natural selection, a passive process. But women are not passive; they take certain actions that affect whether and where they pass on their genes.

---

2   *The Malay Archipelago*, 264.

There may be an orangutan precedent here.

Conservation scientist Michael Kavanagh alerted the world to the fact that female orangutans seldom get pregnant from rape, which happens rather frequently, but readily get pregnant from mutually agreed sex. One reason, according to Kavanagh: female orangutans only experience orgasm during mutually pleasurable sex, rarely during rape, and that contractions of the female's uterus during orgasm suck the semen in the direction of the egg that is waiting to be fertilized.[3] So, females – well, female orangutans – can more or less control whether they're having a good time and, by extension, decide whether they're willing to have an orgasm and get pregnant.

What are female humans able to do?

For a start they often actively decide by whom they will get impregnated.

In academic terms, this is "modified female choice," which generally occurs whenever a young woman follows the admonitions of her relatives to marry a Chinese/Catholic/Brahmin/doctor/chief's son/whatever. It's old hat (which isn't to say that women aren't as capable as men of making stupid reproductive decisions).

What *is* new is the commercialization of evolutionary choice in the form of "boutique" sperm banks. These facilities provide a service to progeny-challenged couples but can also provide the delivery mechanism for an experiment in social engineering to "improve" the race and reverse a trend that Wallace noticed.

It is notorious[4] that our population is more largely

---

3   Another thing about orangutans is that they are the Kama Sutra cognoscenti of the primate world; and it seems that the most reproductively successful orangutan mating is that in which the male practically lies on his back in the tree branches. The female then straddles him and thrusts up and down until they are finished. It is not known whether the female orangutan then calls up her girlfriends to question where this relationship is going or if the male orangutan calls out for a pizza.

4   I find this a curious statement. First, Wallace uses the emotive (and imprecise) term

renewed in each generation from the lower than from the middle and upper classes.[5]

The Rodeo Drive version of such a facility was The Repository for Germinal Choice, which billed itself as "an activity of the Foundation for Advancement of Man." A winner of a Rolex Award for Initiative, the Repository was widely referred to as the Nobel Sperm Bank since it included Nobel laureates and other "superlative donors."[6] Although donors were anonymous (and unpaid), one donor went public: inventor of the transistor William B. Shockley, controversial for his theory that blacks are genetically inferior to whites.

I wrote to the Repository's founder Robert Graham on WWF letterhead, and we corresponded for a while. I was fishing for information (and maybe an invitation to donate); he was fishing for a prince, writing: "I have long admired the thinking of the Duke of Edinburgh (WWF's international president at the time), as well as his splendid physical presence, and should be glad to consider him as a donor if he were willing." I sent the letter to Prince Philip at Buckingham Palace. Don't know if he forwarded a condom filled with royal sperm.

Even without the Duke of Edinburgh, women in need of high quality sperm had a dizzying array of options offered by the Repository. Donor no. 28, for example, was "voted the best-looking man in his [university] department." He sails and hikes. He twice scored 800, the highest possible, on the mathematics section of the Scholastic Aptitude Test. Minor drawback: "Slight haemorrhoids." Or they could choose Donor no. 13, a Nobel laureate in science. "Imaginative, persevering. A shy man, with one of the sweetest natures I have ever known," according to Graham.

"notorious" to describe a reality. More important, he misses the point: the "lower classes" might indeed propagate in greater numbers than "middle and upper classes," but the "middle and upper classes" nevertheless retain the power.

5   "Human Selection," 325.

6   The Repository closed in 1999, two years after the death of its creator; 218 children had been born under its auspices.

Or, if myopia and dental malocclusion are not handicaps, Donor no. 27 offered "Remarkable intellectual ability (professor of mathematics), excellent character and health, and high fertility." He is tall (6' 1"), dark brown curly hair (no balding!), has a good sense of humor, enjoys playing with children, and is blessed with an IQ of 206 measured at age eight.

Roald Dahl employed a similar concept in his novel *Uncle Oswald*, where an attractive female sperm-obtainer named Yasmin used a "Sudanese fly" aphrodisiac to collect sperm from James Joyce, Giacomo Puccini, Henry Ford, Claude Monet, and even asexual George Bernard Shaw, for resale to upwardly mobile would-be mothers.

Robert Graham based the Repository's efforts on the warnings of the late Nobel Laureate Hermann Joseph Muller, who wrote: "If the human species was to keep from regressing, natural selection had to be replaced with artificial selection." Muller, a geneticist, theorized that a special sperm bank could "conserve intelligence." He also thought that his creation of the Repository was more significant than the research on mutations that won him a Nobel Prize.

Clearly, not everyone thinks that Graham's idea is terrific. Ann McMillan Nunes, of Santa Clara, California, describes herself as "the product of a 'Nobel sperm bank,'" where the donation came directly from her father (Edwin McMillan, winner of the 1951 Nobel Prize for chemistry) to her mother. "I am reasonably smart and reasonably happy, but I am not smarter, richer, or happier than anyone else," she says. "What bothers me about the sperm bank idea is that I fear women will believe that obtaining Nobel genes for their children is more important than having a father present when their offspring are growing up. In my case, it was not my father's Nobel prize that brought joy to my childhood but his presence. He was always there, sharing his wit and humor, giving me things to think about, and listening when I had something to say. It was my father, not his genes, that made my childhood special."

Meanwhile, back at the *joged*, Surata keeps glancing at his tickets, numbers 17–23, like an addicted bingo player down to his last card. He appraises every virgin who comes on stage and finds each one more ravishing than the previous: *"He* is my darling,* Surata exclaims. Again, I correct his choice of personal pronouns. "He, no, I mean *she* is very so much beautiful."

Wallace pointed out that:

> The wealth and knowledge and culture of *the few* do not constitute civilization, and do not of themselves advance us toward the 'perfect social state.' [italics Wallace][7]

Like Alfred Russel Wallace, Robert Graham too was more concerned with bigger social issues than the happiness of the individual. He noted that social change does not necessarily correlate with social improvement. Graham (selectively) quoted French historian Alexis de Tocqueville, who said that the French revolution was a "new and terrible thing whose toughest agents are the least literate and most vulgar classes," and he quoted American historian, eugenicist, and anti-immigration advocate Lothrop Stoddard who said that the Russian revolution was "a persecution of the intellectuals." These types of social movements, he said, reflect "an evolutionary phenomenon in which intelligence – the quality that enabled man to prevail throughout the earth – now tends to lead to massive extermination of those who possess it most fully. Here is radical selection leveling downward to the level of the masses; working almost exactly contrary to natural selection," leading if not arrested, he speculates, to "a quick reversion of the whole species back to the brute state."

Is there a "brute" state? Is there a "higher" state? Wallace seems to anticipate Maslow's hierarchy of needs as elements in social evolution.

---

7   *The Malay Archipelago*, 598.

These people [Dayaks in Sarawak] have passed beyond that first stage of savage life in which the struggle for existence absorbs the whole faculties, and in which every thought and idea is connected with war or hunting, or the provision for their immediate necessities. These amusements [playing "cat's cradle"] indicate a capability of civilization, an aptitude to enjoy other than mere sensual pleasures, which might be taken advantage of to elevate their whole intellectual and social life.[8]

I suggest to Surata that he go to the side of the stage and talk to the girls, but he demurs. The dancing virgins are probably of his modest social class, but for whatever reason he prefers to wait for his number to be called, which will result in a few moments of excitement, followed by a longer period of frustration.

Perhaps Robert Graham would have done better to concentrate on physical beauty rather than on intelligence. Studies of the Halo Effect show than beautiful people are more successful than the rest of us. Beautiful people are better at coping with lower back pain, and people in the U.S. and Canada who are considered "very attractive" earn five percent more on average than those with "average" looks.

This "beautiful sperm" concept could develop in two ways.

The first would be branded sperm. For women with tight budgets, the sperm could be generic, like simply packaged supermarket canned peas. Or it could be celebrity sperm, sold at a premium and promoted with the verve of celebrity perfumes. The market research would be fascinating. Of course, men are complex, and a good-looking man might also be a talented cook, a clever tax accountant, a sublime horseman, a gifted car mechanic – but what

---

8   Ibid., 99.

criteria *really* matter to a woman shopping for good sperm? Would the female customers choose a celebrity donor based on a primary attribute (good looks, academic achievement, leadership, athletic prowess), or would she seek someone more rounded, with perhaps more subtle attributes such as (difficult-to-quantify) qualities like morality, sense of humor, generosity. I'd love to do the advertising for celebrity sperm. "Give your kid a headstart in becoming a really rich captain of industry!" could work for Donald Trump Sperm™. "Sensitive yet funny, highly successful intellectual!" (John Updike). "Courageous, and he weaves his own clothes!" (Mahatma Gandhi). "Able to endure decades of humiliation and hardship then reach the world stage wearing a just-ironed batik shirt!" (Nelson Mandela). "Able to use his mind control to fight Himalayan winters, and then to stick the needle into the occupying Chinese!" (Dalai Lama). "Sublime control of his finely tuned body – too bad about that heart attack mid-orgasm!" (Bruce Lee).

The other direction, which also has been tried, is outright social genetic engineering on a major scale, as in Aryan Nazis and dozens of other scary social/cultural/religious movements. What if a society permitted only men who resembled, physically and intellectually, say, Wilt Chamberlain, to mate with only women who are like Venus Williams? That society would turn out quite different within a few generations to one whose ideal genetic role models were, say, Woody Allen and Golda Meir.

Wallace reacted with indignation to a similar proposal suggested by philosopher Hiram M. Stanley that "artificial selection [is essential so that] the drunkard, the criminal, the morally weak should never come into society."

> Of this proposal . . . nothing can possibly be more
> objectionable . . . it is quite certain that any such
> interference with personal freedom in matters so deeply
> affecting individual happiness will never be adopted by

the majority of any nation, or if adopted would never be submitted to by the minority without a life-and-death struggle.[9]

While Wallace saw problems with the human race, he saw a different solution, one involving socialism and education and women's choice in an ethos of "freedom and human dignity." Just as the eugenicists suggested that the human race can be improved by selective breeding, Wallace manipulated the concept of natural selection in a more benign direction, arguing: "For the first time in man's history, 'selection of the fittest' may be ensured by more powerful and effective agencies than the destruction of the weak and the helpless."

Wallace was conscious of the likelihood that a concept as explosive as "survival of the fittest" would be abused, and he took great pains to point out that humanity's care of the sick and weak was an evolutionary *strength*, because it kept us moving forward, morally, if not always physically.

> Exceptionally great and good men are always produced in sufficient numbers. We do not need more of these so much as we need less of the weak and the bad. This weeding-out system has been the method of natural selection, by [one in] which the animal and vegetable worlds have been improved and developed. The survival of the fittest is really the extinction of the unfit. In nature this occurs perpetually on an enormous scale. Under our hitherto imperfect civilisation this wholesome process has been checked as regards mankind; but the check has been the result of the development of the higher attributes of our nature. Humanity – the essentially *human* emotion – has caused us to save the lives of the weak and suffering, of the maimed or imperfect in mind or body. This has to some extent been antagonistic to

---

9   "Human Selection," 328–9.

physical and even intellectual race-improvement; but it has improved us morally by the continuous development of the characteristic and crowning grace of our human, as distinguished from our animal, nature. [italics Wallace][10]

But what about the morality and good behavior of "simpler" societies than ours?

Now it is very remarkable, that among people in a very low stage of civilization, we find some approach to such a perfect social state. I have lived with communities of savages in South America and in the East, who have no laws or law courts but the public opinion of the village freely expressed. Each man scrupulously respects the rights of his fellow. . . . In such a community, all are nearly equal. . . . All incitements to great crimes are thus wanting, and petty ones are repressed, partly by the influence of public opinion, but chiefly by that natural sense of justice and of his neighbor's right, which seems to be, in some degree, inherent in every race of man.[11]

I'm not convinced that the human race is getting better. I think there are wonderful things about people and I think there are miserable things just alongside.

I think people have *always* speculated that the next "new age" would be better than the one we now have, that in the future people living in the "Age of Aquarius" or the next millennium, or after they did EST, or after having read *The Celestine Prophecy* would be, to paraphrase a Gillette razor commercial, "everything a human can be."

I think that's rubbish.

---

10 Ibid., 337.

11 *The Malay Archipelago*, 596–7.

But Wallace was convinced that a better world was coming, a world without excessive consumption, where men and women were equal. He started his argument by noting that women are overworked or forced into "uncongenial marriages."

> Our present phase of social development is not only extremely imperfect but vicious and rotten at the core. How can it be possible to determine and settle the relations of women to men which shall be best alike for individuals and for the race, in a society in which a very large proportion of women are obliged to work long hours daily for the barest subsistence, while another large proportion are forced into more or less uncongenial marriages as the only means of securing some amount of personal independence or physical well-being.[12]

He objected to a Martha Stewart-like extravagantly consumeristic society and the working conditions of the period.

> Let any one consider, on the one hand, the lives of the wealthy as portrayed in the society newspapers and even in the advertisements of such papers as *The Field* and *The Queen*, with their endless round of pleasure and luxury, their almost inconceivable wastefulness and extravagance, indicated by the cost of female dress and such facts as the expenditure of a thousand pounds on the flowers for a single entertainment; and, on the other hand, the terrible condition of millions of workers – men, women, and children – as detailed in the *Report of the Lords Commission on Sweating*, on absolutely incontestable evidence, and the still more awful condition of those who seek work of any kind in vain and, seeing their children slowly dying of starvation, are driven in utter helplessness and despair to

---

12 "Human Selection," 330.

murder and suicide.[13]

And then he drifts into his familiar Brave New World rhetoric.

> It is my firm conviction . . . that, when we have cleansed
> the Augean stable of our existing social organization, and
> have made such arrangements that *all* shall contribute
> their share of either physical or mental labour, and that
> all workers shall reap the *full* reward of their work, the
> future of the race will be ensured by those laws of human
> development that have led to the slow but continuous
> advance in the higher qualities of human nature. When
> men and women are alike free to follow their best
> impulses; when idleness and vicious or useless luxury on
> the one hand, oppressive labour and starvation on the
> other, are alike unknown; when all receive the best and
> most thorough education . . . then we shall find that a
> system of selection will come spontaneously into action
> which will steadily tend to eliminate the lower and more
> degraded types of man, and thus continuously raise the
> average standard of the race. [italics Wallace][14]

And Wallace prepared a scenario of how it would work, based
on female choice in which the woman refuses the advances of
"idlers" and "drunkards" and "liars." He considered the principle of
female sexual selection under socialism[15] to be his most important
contribution, a considerable claim given his other accomplishments.
His view would no doubt be applauded by modern feminists, indeed
by women worldwide.

---

13 Ibid.

14 Ibid., 330–1.

15 Wallace's embrace of socialism seems paradoxical – he was from a modest, middle-
class family and benefited greatly from being a white man, which in Asia equated
with high social status. And he earned his living selling beetles and birds to rich
collectors in England.

The most careful and deliberate choice of partners for life will be inculcated as the highest social duty; while the young women will be so trained as to look with scorn and loathing on all men who in any way wilfully fail in their duty to society – on idlers and malingerers, on drunkards and liars, on the selfish, the cruel, or the vicious. They will be taught that the happiness of their whole lives will depend on the care and deliberation with which they choose their husbands, and they will be urged to accept no suitor till he has proved himself to be worthy of respect by the place he holds and character he bears among his fellow-labourers in the public service.[16]

Actually, the Asian woman of the twenty-first century *might* have much more say in who she marries, but not for the idealized socialist reasons Wallace suggested.

Quite simply, there are far more boys than girls in Asia. As the world population reached seven billion in 2011, demographers noted a shortage of 160 million women in the region. Many Asian parents prefer male children, and inexpensive prenatal sex-determination technology has led to abortions of female fetuses.[17] This imbalance *could* provide women with a greater say in choosing their breeding partners. Or, it could turn into a social debacle involving mass migrations of men in search of wives, cross-border kidnapping, and forced prostitution and concubinage.

---

16 "Human Selection," 333.

17 Global awareness of the problem of gender inbalance was raised back in 1990 with an article by the Nobel Prize-winning Indian economist Amartya Sen that carried the now famous title: "More Than 100 Million Women Are Missing." Some demographers believe the resulting shortage of adult women over the next fifty years will have as deep and pervasive an impact as climate change. The natural sex ratio at birth is 104–106 males to every 100 females. Today, the figure in India and Vietnam is around 112 boys for every 100 girls; in China it is almost 120–100. The trend is not limited to Asia; in the South Caucasus region, Azerbaijan, Georgia, and Armenia all show birth ratios of more than 115 to 100.

One point on which Darwin disagreed with Wallace was Darwin's idea that "there is a second agency at work in most unisexual animals tending to produce the same effect [natural means of selection], namely, the struggle of the males for the females."

Women's assertiveness takes various forms.[18]

For a start, women are more responsible than men; ask any small local non-governmental organization whether they would prefer to fund projects run by women or men of the village. I'd say the response would be ten to one in favor of the more responsible, less-likely-to-buy-beer-with-donated-money females in the society.

Look around any Asian city, I see an increasing number of women who run businesses, scuba dive and parachute jump, write books, paint, run charities, and raise kids. I'm not saying that the women in Asia have reached égalité and not suggesting that all is rosy, but things certainly are changing, at least in certain circles.

Nevertheless, it's all pretty confusing.

In 2011 women in Malaysia were polarized about The Obedient Wives Club, an international Islamic organization dedicated to teaching wives to be submissive to their husbands. The group's 115-page sex manual, *Islamic Sex, Fighting Against Jews To Return*

---

18 Some women interpret independence as having a right to a lifetime of bad hair days. On a long domestic Merpati flight (the airline's name means pigeon), I left the blue cardboard box containing the remnants of a forgettable lunch on the floor in front of my aisle seat while I got up to walk around the cabin. The stewardess (they don't call them flight attendants in this backward land) saw me place it down, and I watched her walk past the garbage without collecting it. I sat down and nudged the box into the aisle. She walked past. I got my neighbors' boxes and started to build a modest construction of used lunch boxes in the aisle. Eventually the pile got so large that the stewardess had to step over them, but she was damned if she was going to bend down and pick them up. This is a woman with an attitude. Me, too, of course. As we were coming in to land I asked her if I could help her collect the used boxes. She was not amused. I was, though, and remembered a recruitment ad for a competing Indonesian airline I had saved from the 1970s. Their ideal stewardess would be "Unmarried – by showing certificate from the Village head" and having "Good character and not involved in G-30-S/ob [security clearance] production of police certificate." She was also expected to be "Owning good and attractive face, creative and cunning." Those applicants who meet these rigid standards "will be invited to follow a selection of dropping out system."

Islamic Sex To The World, purported to encourage group sex between a man and his multiple wives. The group argues that the sexual submission of a wife to her husband will reduce the likelihood of the husband engaging in adultery; one of the group's leaders publicly suggested that it is a wife's responsibility to perform sex like a "first-class whore." The Malaysian Home Ministry banned the manual, but the mufti of the northern state of Perak offered support for the club's objectives, saying: "Wives must be very obedient to their husbands."

Although they were speaking about Thai women, the Foreign Correspondents' Club of Thailand (FCCT) succinctly summed up the problem affecting many Asian women. "There is a sharp dichotomy in the situation of women in Thailand. While UN indices show progress in terms of gender development and gender empowerment, there is a dark side to the role women play in Thai society," the FCCT wrote. "Women provide much of the waged and unwaged labor that is the foundation of the Thai economy, yet women remain disadvantaged in rewards, ownership, and access to resources. Women also lack many legal rights available to men, and are subject to increasing levels of sexual and domestic violence. Not to mention the commercial sex industry on which Thailand thrives. . . . Thai society reveals a deep hypocrisy over gender roles and expectations."

Wallace clearly wanted to marry and had a clear view of qualities a good wife should possess.

> I believe a good wife to be the greatest blessing a man can enjoy, and the only road to happiness, but the qualifications I should look for are probably not such as would satisfy you [George Silk]. My opinions have changed much on this point: I now look at intellectual companionship as quite a secondary matter, and should my good stars ever send me an affectionate, good-

tempered and domestic wife, I shall care not one iota for accomplishments or even for education.[19]

Wallace went on and on about female choice, but his arguments depend on some alternative and unlikely scenarios. In Wallace's Panglossian world women are financially independent, intellectually stimulated, and might increasingly choose not to marry. In that same ideal world men can release their sexual passion only through marriage, and women who are "weak in intellect" would not marry.

> This improvement I believe will certainly be effected
> through the agency of female choice in marriage. In a
> society in which women were all pecuniarily independent,
> were all fully occupied with public duties and intellectual
> or social enjoyments, and had nothing to gain by marriage
> as regards material well-being, we may be sure that the
> number of the unmarried from choice would largely
> increase.[20]

Wallace envisioned a utopian society where people are honest, loving, and altruistic, and in which women hold the key. It will happen by:

> Encouraging the activity of a still higher human
> characteristic – admiration of all that is beautiful and
> kindly and self-sacrificing, repugnance to all that is selfish,
> base, or cruel. When we allow ourselves to be guided
> by reason, justice, and public spirit in our dealings with
> our fellow-men, and determine to abolish poverty by
> recognising the equal rights of all the citizens . . . to

---

19 *Alfred Russel Wallace: Letters and Reminiscences*, 1916. London: Cassell and Company., Ltd., 87–8.

20 "Human Selection," 335.

an equal share of the wealth which all combine to produce . . . then we may safely leave the far greater and deeper problem of the improvement of the race to the cultivated minds and pure instincts of the Women of the Future.[21]

I fear Wallace's Arcadian optimism was a touch over the moon.

At the fairgrounds Surata waits expectantly every time a number is called. He wants nothing more than to jump on stage and dance with a *gadis*, who will excite him and then reject him in full view of his friends. He watches his friends get called on stage to preen and strut. He rehearses his moves. His seven numbers are never called. All that practice, all that teenage testosterone surge, for nothing. Welcome to the real world, Surata.

---

21 Ibid., 337.

TEN PAGES THAT CHANGED THE WORLD

Ternate, Moluccas, Indonesia

Wallace's eureka moment, triggered by malarial fever, challenged both his ego and the belief systems of many people.

Wallace had two bases in Southeast Asia where he could recover his strength, keep supplies, receive mail, pack and ship his collections, and eat decent food: Singapore and, more importantly, Ternate.

During a malarial fever in February 1858, and perhaps inspired by Ternate's "grand views on every side," Wallace had a breakthrough that explains the mechanism of natural selection. Within two days he had written "On the Tendency of Varieties to Depart Indefinitely from the Original Type" and sent the ten-page paper to Charles Darwin.

Darwin, on receiving Wallace's "Ternate Paper," wrote to his friend, the noted geologist Charles Lyell: "I never saw a more striking coincidence; if Wallace had had my manuscript sketch, written out in 1842, he could not have made a better short abstract of it."

Thus began one of the most curious episodes in the history of science.

The first impression of tiny[1] and isolated Ternate is of a postcard-pretty tropical island, dominated by the cone of spiritually enhanced and sweet-on-the-tongue Gamalama volcano. But the specks of Ternate and nearby Tidore, Moti, Mare, and Makian islands generated mammoth global conflicts in years past since they were once the world's only source of cloves, a commodity desired by the Portuguese as early as 1521, and subsequently fought over by the Spanish and Dutch.

For years the sultan of Ternate, the forty-eighth of his royal line, claimed that a house he owned near his run-down *kraton* (palace) was on the site where Wallace lived. However, more recently the civic authorities have declared that a house a kilometer (0.6 miles) away, in what used to be the European enclave, was actually where Wallace wrote one of the most important intellectual breakthroughs of our time. The newish dwelling constructed on the site is owned by a Chinese trader. Impressed by the regular stream of visitors who come to take photos at the location, he has raised the selling price to an astronomical figure, hampering efforts by the governor to build a visitors' center on the historic site.

We're taught by parents and the media to think "I can do anything." Paradoxically, we're taught by many religions to believe "I am nothing in the overall scheme of things." Our lives are a constant juggling of how we nurture (and control) our egos. How did Wallace deal with these issues of ego and personal worth?

---

1 Ternate is a bit smaller than Manhattan.

It never hurts to have a letter of introduction to the sultan, and I obtained a "please help this strange foreigner" note from Pak Ola, a relative of the sultan of Ternate, whom I met by chance on the ferry from Ternate to Halmahera.

Pak Ola and I had studied a map prepared by Charles H. Lamoureux, director of the Lyon Aboretum in Honolulu, in which Lamoureux described the site of Wallace's Ternate house as being located at 16 Jalan (street) Sultan Hairun. Several days later I went to the specified address. The purported site of Wallace's house is a few steps from the sultan's palace, across the street from the old mosque, a distinctive building with a sharp-edged multi-tiered roof made of rusted red zinc. The house is now occupied by the family of Pak Zainal, a nephew of the sultan.

Two mountain bikes leaned against the weathered timbers. Inside, the walls were whitewashed. Wooden beams supported three-meter (ten-foot) ceilings, which were water-stained and crumbling in places. Out back, near a rusting pickup truck, is a well that corresponds with Wallace's description of "a deep well which supplied me with pure cold water." The house is located "five minutes walk" from the beach, just as Wallace described. Wallace also noted it was "surrounded by a wilderness of fruit trees," but only a few large fruit trees remain, and these are certainly of more modern vintage. The house built on the site, probably of 1930s era, is littered and dirty, but I can imagine that in Wallace's time the much simpler house he built here would have been peaceful and restorative, where he could "return to after my voyages to the various islands of the Moluccas and New Guinea, where I could pack my collections, recruit my health, and make preparations for future journeys."

This is where Wallace had what might be the most famous malaria fit of all time.[2] Most people have nightmares about demons,

2   Or maybe not. His journals do not specifically mention where he was when he wrote the paper; we only know that he mailed it from Ternate (and the date of posting, and the date on which Darwin received it is a key point for conspiracy theorists who

flights of fancy, and great adventures; Wallace's breakthrough dream starred Thomas Robert Malthus.

> I was suffering from a sharp attack of intermittent fever, and every day during the cold and succeeding hot fits had to lie down for several hours, during which time I had nothing to do but to think over any subjects then particularly interesting me. One day something brought to my recollection Malthus's "Principles of Population," ["An Essay on the Principle of Population"] which I had read twelve years before. I thought of his clear exposition of "the positive checks to increase" – disease, accidents, war, and famine – which keep down the population of savage races to so much lower an average than that of more civilized peoples. It then occurred to me that these causes or their equivalents are continually acting in the case of animals also; and as animals usually breed much more rapidly than does mankind, the destruction every year from these causes must be enormous in order to keep down the numbers of each species, since they evidently do not increase regularly from year to year, as otherwise the world would long ago have been densely crowded with those that breed most quickly. Vaguely thinking over the enormous and constant destruction which this implied, it occurred to me to ask the question, Why do some die and some live? And the answer was clearly, that on the whole the best fitted live. From the effects of disease the most healthy escape; from enemies, the

claim that Darwin received the letter earlier than he claimed, thereby giving him time to retrofit Wallace's ideas into his earlier notes). A 2012 paper by John van Wyhe and Kees Rookmaaker dispute that claim, arguing that Darwin received the paper on June 18, 1858, and he wrote to Charles Lyell the same day. Regardless, based on the timelines, it is likely that Wallace had his famous malarial dream while in Halmahera (which was then called Gilolo), not Ternate. Specifically, he was in the village of Dodinga, "Situated at the head of a deep bay exactly opposite Ternate . . . [near a] very small but substantial fort erected by the Portuguese" – which I visited. Wallace does not mention the Ternate Paper in *The Malay Archipelago*, but obliquely refers to his malaria attack while on Halmahera: "I got some very nice insects here, though owning to illness most of the time, my collection was a small one."

strongest, the swiftest, or the most cunning. . . . Then it suddenly flashed upon me that this self-acting process would necessarily *improve the race*, because in every generation the inferior would inevitably be killed off and the superior would remain – that is, *the fittest would survive* . . . . I waited anxiously for the termination of my fit so that I might at once make notes for a paper on the subject. [italics Wallace][3]

Once he got back his strength he got to work and wrote the paper over the next two evenings. Wallace recognized what a significant breakthrough this was, and described his Ternate Paper as "the long-sought-for law of nature that solved the problem of the origin of species."

This, as they say, is eureka time. Archimedes in his bath, Newton under the apple tree. Wallace in a cold sweat.

The BBC made a bad film about Alfred Russel Wallace. Here's how they handled the "malaria fit" apotheosis:

Wallace is lying feverish in bed.

An ethereal woman's voice whispers: "Where do they all come from Alfred? Out of the Ark?"

Wallace, weak, hesitant: "Always where there is a closely related, pre-existing species."[4]

Aggressive male voice: "You still haven't explained how one species can change into another."

Wallace, a bit stronger: "The individual deaths don't matter. It's as Malthus said, but nobody knows the mechanism."

Darwin's voice: "I agree with everything you wrote about the genesis of species, but I would go further, much further."

Wallace, stronger yet: "It doesn't matter as long as some of them

3 *Darwinism: An Exposition of the Theory of Natural Selection With Some of its Applications.* 1889. London and New York: Macmillan and Co., 173.

4 A reference to Wallace's Sarawak Law of 1855.

survive, the strongest ones or the ones that can run fastest, or the ones best fitted to the kind of . . ." At this point Wallace opens his eyes and there is a trumpet fanfare (true). "That's it!!" Wallace calls to his faithful servant Ali: "Pencil and paper!"

Ali sees that his master is still delirious. "No *Tuan*, tomorrow."

Wallace wrote a ten-page paper and mailed it to Charles Darwin in England. He and Darwin had met once, in the insect rooms of the Natural History Museum (then the British Museum (Natural History)), an event Wallace remembered but Darwin couldn't recall. Nevertheless, they became pen pals – Wallace would update Darwin on his adventures in the Malay Archipelago, and Darwin would ask for specimens (skins of unusual Indonesian poultry and bee's combs) and observations (stripes on horses, mating of leopards, parrots that change color after eating fish, and the means of dispersal of animals and plants that inhabit oceanic islands).[5]

Wallace did not keep a copy of his paper.

In his cover letter, Wallace asked Darwin, if he thought the paper had merit, could he please share it with Charles Lyell, Darwin's friend and doyen of the British scientific establishment.

Of course we can never know someone's state of mind except through their actions, but it seems that Darwin, sitting in his home at Down House outside London, was flabbergasted and fearful of losing priority on a subject he had pondered for years. Up to that point Darwin had been studiously collecting evidence on natural selection and what we now term evolution and natural selection but had not published one word on the subject.

On receiving Wallace's Ternate Paper, Darwin wrote to his friend Sir Charles Lyell: "Your words [Lyell had encouraged Darwin to publish his theories earlier] have come true with a vengeance that I

---

5   After the voyage of the *Beagle*, Darwin never again left England. He asked Wallace
     and numerous other correspondents to, in effect, gather evidence for his own
     research. In the specific request for information about animal and plant dispersal he
     was asking for information that Wallace had gathered and filtered through years of
     painstaking collecting and observation.

shd be forestalled. You said this when I explained to you here very briefly my views of 'natural Selection' depending on the Struggle for existence. – I never saw a more striking coincidence. [I]f Wallace had my M.S. sketch written out in 1842 he could not have made a better short abstract! Even his terms now stand as Heads of my Chapters. . . . So all my originality, whatever it may amount to, will be smashed."

Charles Lyell and Joseph Hooker, both at the top of the British scientific food chain, decided to call a special meeting of the Linnean Society to put Darwin's and Wallace's ideas into the public record.

One of the most speculated on and one of the most inaccurately reported events in the history of science was a special meeting of the Linnean Society in London held on July 1, 1858 with one agenda item: the reading of two short contributions by Charles Darwin and a longer, complete scientific paper by Alfred Russel Wallace.

Here's what happened.

Arnold Brackman described the events of July 1, 1858, the date a small audience heard Wallace's Ternate Paper read at the Linnean Society: "Victoria went horseback riding. The steamship *North Star* arrived from New York in eleven days and six hours, a spectacular record. There was the usual trouble in the Balkans, this time between Turks and Montenegrins. In Parliament Disraeli held forth on the 'sewage question,' the pollution of the Thames. Madame Tussaud announced a new full-length portrait of American President James Buchanan. The Royal Italian Opera Company performed von Flotow's *Martha*, with an additional reading by Charles Dickens of excerpts from his works."

Lyell and Hooker wrote a now famous (and vaguely legal-snarky, cover-your-ass-sounding) introductory letter to the meeting: "Two indefatigable naturalists, Mr Charles Darwin and Mr Alfred Wallace . . . having, independently and unknown to one another, conceived the same very ingenious theory to account for the appearance and perpetuation of varieties and of specific forms on our planet, may both fairly claim the merit of being original thinkers on this important line of inquiry."

Lyell and Hooker presented Wallace's paper without asking his permission. And, most importantly, by placing Wallace's paper sequentially *after* Darwin's hastily assembled notes, they relegated Wallace to a perceived supporting role in comparison to Darwin.[6]

J. J. Bennett, secretary of the Linnean Society, read Darwin's and Wallace's contributions to twenty-eight fellows of the society. Darwin's contribution: portions of an unpublished essay Darwin had written in 1844, and a letter summarizing his theory, which Darwin had sent to American botanist Asa Gray in 1857. Wallace's contribution: a completed scientific paper suitable for publication in a serious journal.[7, 8, 9]

Wallace was out of contact and couldn't complain or comment. On July 1, 1858 he was in Dorey [now Manokwari] on the Indonesian side of the island of New Guinea. Charles Darwin –

---

6   Arnold Brackman argues that "academic integrity – and, more simply, what was just fair play and cricket – required that Wallace's Ternate Paper be read without a dropped line, and read first because it presented a total theory. Darwin's extracts (not abstracts, and the distinction is important) should either have served as a footnote or should have been read after the presentation of Wallace's monograph . . . [but] if Wallace's paper should be read first it would dilute Darwin's claim to priority."

7   Many Internet bloggers, even serious reporters and sites that should know better, get it wrong. The Linnean Society website, for instance, refers to "The Darwin-Wallace Paper," and the website of the Natural History Museum misstates that the Linnean Society presentation was a "joint paper." Not true. There was no joint paper, nor were they "co-authors." Wallace's paper was a ready-for-publication academic paper; Darwin's contributions were in the form of notes and ideas. They were presented separately and attributed to their respective authors. But part of the confusion arises from the heading in the published proceedings of the Linnean Society, which states: "On the Tendency of Species to form Varieties; and on the Perpetuation of Varieties and Species by Natural Means of Selection [Lyell and Hooker changed the title of Wallace's paper without asking him and used this revised title as the heading for the entire evening (including Wallace's paper), to position Darwin as the senior author]. By Charles Darwin and Alfred Wallace."

8   Nor were the theories identical; there are at least six striking differences in emphasis, including evidence from domestic or wild animals, competition between separate species vs interspecific competition, the hard-to-dislodge (at least for Darwin) idea of the inheritance of acquired characteristics, and the struggle among males for females.

9   No doubt Wallace could have published the paper in a journal such as the *Annals and Magazine of Natural History*, which had published his Sarawak Law three years earlier.

whose youngest son had just died of scarlet fever and whose daughter Etty, aged fourteen, was very ill with diphtheria – stayed home.

The Linnean Society reading made a modest noise. Thomas Bell, president of the Linnean Society, noted in the 1858 annual report that the year "has not, indeed, been marked by any of those discoveries which at once revolutionise, so to speak, the department of science in which they occur."

Darwin later wrote: "Our joint productions excited very little attention, and the only published notice of them which I can remember was by Professor Haughton of Dublin, whose verdict was that all that was new in them was false, and what was true was old."[10]

The real bang came with the publication of *The Origin of Species*.[11]

Wilma George, lecturer in zoology at the University of Oxford, wrote that "Darwin's fame came not from the appreciation of a new biological theory by a few members of the Linnean Society but from the intelligent reading public. Evolution by natural selection was a revolutionary theory but the public of Victorian England did not read the proceedings of the Linnean Society. It read books. And the readers, shattered by the convincing mechanism for a process which was already a subject of conversation, were troubled by the implications of the theory for the status of man."

Why was Wallace's paper seminal?

10 Darwin biographer Janet Browne thinks the Linnean Society ideas had a greater impact than commonly thought: "The double paper appeared in the Linnean Society Journal (in the zoological section) in August 1858. During the next two or three months it was reprinted either in full or in part in several popular natural history magazines of the day. A number of people made their views known in letters, reviews, and journals. There were more notices than usually assumed."

11 When Darwin's *The Origin of Species* was published in 1859, Wallace was suffering on the distant island of Seram, which made it rather difficult for reporters to contact him for a quote. He couldn't have been more isolated: his crew had disappeared and stolen some supplies, he "found no rare birds or insects," he was sick and yet somehow got up the energy to write a classic description of the process by which the sago palm is transformed into "a thick glutinous mass, with a rather astringent taste," which forms the staple of life in rural eastern Indonesia.

Men of science and philosophy had for centuries pondered an almost primal question: were all of Earth's creatures created by an all-powerful, all-knowing, infallible, definitely male, Christian god, or did some species die out while others were created? Even Darwin's grandfather Erasmus Darwin had opinions on the subject, as did Goethe.

Charles Darwin, like many thinkers of his time, seemed to be convinced that there was a process of change and renewal but he was missing one key element: the mechanism, the trigger that made such a blasphemous series of natural events possible. Wallace provided that key through his description of how "the fittest would survive."

I worked for a now defunct personal development group called Athanor. They ran a workshop called The Event that helped people unblock their lives. It's tough, street-smart, dramatic stuff – they positioned it as a boot camp for your soul. And it's based on the premise that nobody has to be a victim, that all people can take charge of their lives with a bit of insight, a dollop of courage, and a little help from their friends. But before they can build you up they have to tear you down, scrape you raw. I watched the process in others and half-heartedly underwent it myself. I learned that people are similar to watches and Humpty Dumpty – a lot easier to take apart than to put back together.

How different from many Asian philosophies, which teach that the way to get out of a stressful situation is to ignore it, like kids who cover their eyes and say "you can't see me." It's the Western do-it-yourself/anybody-can-be-president approach versus the Eastern meditate-to-clear-your-mind/it-doesn't really-matter-anyway approach.

Wallace was full of contradictions. He was highly spiritual, yet rejected formal religion. His ego was a strange-colored creature indeed. On the one hand he was never shy about taking stands, often very controversial stands, on subjects ranging from vaccination (he was against it) to the Crimean War, to spiritualism, to Edgar Allan Poe (seventeen letters praising and seeking information regarding Poe's authorship of a previously unknown poem, "Leonainie," which Wallace thought "contains the essence of modern spiritualistic teaching."[12] Without stopping for breath he roamed the world intellectually as much as physically and wrote about land nationalization, phrenology, glaciation, the evils of slavery (but the benefits of wise colonialism), government aid to science, climatology, mimicry in insects, land reform, disarmament, the status of teachers, the possibility of life on Mars (no way, he argued), the age of the earth, the causes of the ice age, and even that eternally vexing question of whether the earth is an oblate or prolate spheroid. Wallace was so prolific, and so outspoken, and contributed so much to so many fields that one biographer, Charles H. Smith, considers that focusing just on Wallace's ideas about natural selection represents a limited view when it comes to trying to understand his worldview.

Here's the dilemma for Wallace-watchers. He was frank and outspoken. Yet, on his biggest discovery – the mechanism of natural selection – he seemed to put his ego in storage.

Or did he?

Wallace was on the other side of the world and had no control over events in London. And when he returned to the UK, events had taken their course.

Part of the dynamic was that Wallace wasn't as socially well connected as Darwin; Darwin was at the top of the British totem pole, Wallace was a spear-carrier in the chorus. Wallace lacked Darwin's education and standing in the community, and was just beginning to assert himself in scientific circles.

Did he back out of the fight? Or, seeing the fight had grown too large, did he choose to step aside, adopting what one observer calls a "bamboo strategy." Wimp? Warrior? Sage?

12 The poem turned out to be a hoax, written not by Poe but by a young poet named James Whitcomb Riley. Nevertheless, it has a certain lollipop charm: "Leonainie – Angels named her;/And they took the light/Of the laughing stars and framed her/In a smile of white;/And they made her hair of gloomy/Midnight, and her eyes of bloomy/Moonshine, and they brought her to me/In the solemn night."

During the eight years Wallace was in the Malay Archipelago he wrote two papers – the Sarawak Law and the Ternate Paper – which he recognized, even then, as being of fundamental and landmark importance.

But he only obliquely referred to these achievements in *The Malay Archipelago*.

Here's how he describes the time he spent in Sarawak in February 1855, when he wrote the Sarawak Law.

> The first four months of my visit [following November 1, 1854] were spent in various parts of the Sarawak River . . . [but] this part of the country has been so frequently described that I shall pass it over.[13]

The next paragraph begins "In March, 1855 . . ." So much for the events of February when he took the first steps that changed history and his place in the public mind!

And Wallace was similarly vague about the time he spent on Ternate (or was it Halmahera?) when he wrote one of the most important papers of the century.

Now I could understand this, perhaps, if he had published *The Malay Archipelago* while he was in Indonesia and had not had a chance to learn how his theories had been received. But Wallace completed *The Malay Archipelago* in 1869, *seven years after* he had returned to England. He *knew* the impact his theories had made.

Strangely, here's all he wrote about evolution in *The Malay Archipelago*, which became one of the most popular natural history/travel books of the period.

> Geology teaches us that the surface of the land and the distribution of land and water is everywhere slowly changing. It further teaches us that the forms of life

---

13 *The Malay Archipelago*, 46.

which inhabit that surface have, during every period of
which we possess any record, been also slowly changing.
It is not now necessary to say any thing about *how* either
of those changes took place; as to that, opinions may
differ; but as to the fact that the changes themselves *have*
occurred, from the earliest geological ages down to the
present day and are still going on, there is no difference
of opinion. Every successive stratum of sedimentary rock,
sand, or gravel is a proof that changes of level have taken
place; and the different species of animals and plants,
whose remains are found in these deposits, prove that
corresponding changes did occur in the organic world.
[italics Wallace][14]

That's about all he directly said about evolution in the entire
book. In fact, he obfuscates: "It is not now necessary to say any
thing about *how* either of those changes [geology and forms of life]
took place; as to that, opinions may differ." This seems curious.
Wallace *did* explain how evolution took place. He *did* stick his neck
out. Didn't he feel it would be appropriate in a travel book? Afraid
of losing his readership? Bossed around by the publisher?

Wallace did, however, in *The Malay Archipelago*, go out of his
way to get out of Darwin's way.

From these [cases of protective imitation] it is possible to
deduce a general theory of the manner in which they have
been slowly brought about. The principle of variation
and that of "natural selection," or survival of the fittest,
as elaborated[15] by Mr. Darwin in his celebrated 'Origin
of Species,' offers the foundation for such a theory; and I
have myself endeavored to apply it to all the chief cases
of imitation in an article published in the *Westminster
Review* for 1867, entitled, "Mimicry, and other Protective

14   Ibid., 21–2.

15   Interesting word, perhaps a subtle dig: To "elaborate" means building on what is
     already there.

Resemblances among Animals."[16]

Wallace not only gives *all* the evolutionary credit to Darwin, relegating himself to a deeply secondary status, but he also unfairly limits his own contribution to evolutionary theory to "protective imitation," which is just one aspect of the jigsaw of natural selection.

Wallace became a vocal cheerleader for Darwin.

In a letter to his friend George Silk, written in Ternate in September 1860, shortly after *The Origin of Species* was published, Wallace gushed:

> I have been reading of late two books of the highest interest, but of most diverse characters, and I wish to recommend their perusal to you. They are Dr. Leon Dufour's 'Histoire de la Prostitution' and Darwin's 'Origin of Species'. . . . [Origin] you may have heard of and perhaps read, but it is not one perusal which will enable any man to appreciate it. I have read it through five or six times, each time with increasing admiration. It will live as long as the "Principia" of Newton. It shows that nature is, as I before remarked to you, a study that yields to none in grandeur and immensity. . . . The most intricate effects of the law of gravitation, the mutual disturbances of all the bodies of the solar system, are simplicity itself compared with the intricate relations and complicated struggle which have determined what forms of life shall exist and in what proportions. Mr. Darwin has given the world a *new science*, and his name should, in my opinion, stand above that of every philosopher of ancient or modern times. The force of admiration can no further go!!! [italics Wallace][17]

16 *The Malay Archipelago*, 143.

17 *My Life*, Vol. 1, 372.

Wallace wrote to Darwin:[18]

> You [Darwin] had worked it out in details I had never
> thought of, years before I had a ray of light on the
> subject, & my paper would never have convinced anybody
> or been noticed as more than an ingenious speculation,
> whereas your book has revolutionized the study of
> Natural History, & carried away captive the best men of
> the present Age.[19]

Why did Wallace shrink from the limelight? Why did he retreat
and let Darwin do the heavy lifting?

Wallace took on all manner of less important (and sometimes
stupid) fights, to the extent that Darwin later wrote to him: "I hope
that [by explaining your belief in a spiritual influence to explain
human evolution] you have not murdered too completely your
own and my child."

So why did Wallace opt out of *this* fight?

It is dangerous, but fun, to psychoanalyze a traveling companion.

Wallace's father was a lawyer, rarely solvent, a renegade thinker,
his mother was a bit of a tyrant.[20]

He remembered his childhood, full of boyish angst.

---

18 The two men were keen letter writers – Darwin, for his part, sent or received some
    fourteen thousand letters; by 1857 he was spending a yearly sum on postage and
    stationery that was roughly equal to his butler's annual salary. But Wallace's letter to
    Darwin from Ternate, and the accompanying manuscript of his Ternate Paper, were
    never found in Darwin's meticulously kept files.

19 *Alfred Russel Wallace: Letters and Reminiscences.*

20 Charles H. Smith writes: "Wallace was not 'lower class'; in fact, his parents came from
    quite upstanding stock: his father had been trained and sworn in as a lawyer (but
    because of inherited wealth did not practice), and had reputedly hung around with
    leisure-seekers (and met Beau Brummel) when he was younger; another paternal-side
    relative who died in 1803 had been an Admiral and was knighted. On his mother's
    side some of his relatives had held prominent positions such as architect and town
    mayor. Of course the family did fall on hard times financially, but that is another
    matter."

I was especially sensitive to what all boys dislike – the being placed in any exceptional position, or having to do anything different from other boys. Every time I entered the schoolroom I felt ashamed. For at least twenty years after I left I was subject to frequently recurring dreams of still having to go to school in the hybrid position of pupil and teacher [he was a teacher's assistant], aggravated by feeling myself taller and, at last, a man, and yet suffering over again with increased intensity, the shyness and sense of disgrace of my boyhood.[21]

He was born left-handed but was forced to use his right. He was self-conscious and hated to have attention drawn to him. His mother, unable to afford to buy him new clothes, patched up his jackets like quilts. As a somewhat sloppy boy Wallace used his sleeve cuff to clean his school slate, which so irritated his mother she made calico sleeves. Imagine a hormone-raging adolescent having to wear calico sleeves! He refused, until his mother asked the teacher to *order* him to wear them. This shame in front of the entire class, he wrote later, was "perhaps the severest punishment I ever endured." Wallace specifically used the term "loss of face."[22]

Put another way, Bangkok-based novelist Christopher G. Moore suggests that Wallace had adopted some Asian characteristics and that "his behavior [in relinquishing credit to Darwin] was Asian-like, in that he didn't want to challenge the chain of subjugation."

In his autobiography Wallace complains of his "deficiencies," perhaps as a form of explanation why he never demanded more credit for his theories.

[My deficiencies] have been my want of assertiveness and of physical courage, which combined with delicacy of the nervous system and of bodily constitution, and a general disinclination to much exertion, physical or mental, have

---

21 *My Life*, Vol. 1, 58.

22 Reflecting on his experiences, Wallace wrote many years later, "Even savages often surpass us in [respect for personal feelings, especially those of children]."

caused that shyness, reticence, and love of solitude which, though often misunderstood and leading to unpleasant results, have, perhaps, on the whole, been beneficial to me.[23]

Historian Daniel J. Boorstin writes: "If a Greek dramatist had contrived two characters to show how fate could bring men by opposite paths to the same destination, he could hardly have done better than invent Darwin and Wallace. Darwin, the elder by a dozen years, had been dedicated by his wealthy family to a career in the Church. All his life Darwin did his best to follow Lyell's advice 'never to get entangled in a controversy, as it rarely did any good and caused a miserable loss of time and temper.' Tediously gathering specimens and evidence over two decades, Darwin seemed led to his theory of natural selection almost against his will. The impoverished Wallace, inspired early with a suspicion of religion and all established institutions, was hasty to embrace theories and plunge into controversy. When he was only twenty-two, Robert Chambers' popular *Vestiges of the Natural History of Creation* had converted Wallace to an unshakable conviction that species arose through a process of evolution, and his trip to the Amazon was for facts to convince others. By his later trip through the Malay Archipelago . . . he aimed to gather conclusive evidence. . . . Wallace's essay "On the Law which Has Regulated the Introduction of New Species" (Sarawak Law) was published three years before the paper he sent to Darwin," Boorstin said. "The facts of geographical distribution that provided the cautious Darwin with questions supplied the brash Wallace with answers."

But in his public statements about evolution and natural selection Wallace didn't sound like the "brash" man with the answers. Just the opposite, he hid like a scolded puppy.

---

23 *My Life*, Vol. 1, 225.

What if Wallace's handwritten manuscript of his Ternate Paper had disappeared in transit from Ternate to England and never reached Darwin?

Without Wallace's impetus Darwin certainly would not have been rushed into preparing a hasty presentation for the Linnean Society. Darwin might have prevaricated for decades longer and perhaps never written *The Origin of Species*.

Wallace, however, probably could have more or less replicated the Ternate Paper on his return to the UK. Then, enjoying a higher scientific profile due to his numerous scientific writings and vast collections, he would not have been as insecure, and he might have presented the paper for publication himself.[24]

I'm reminded of other discoveries by several people more or less simultaneously – what writer Malcolm Gladwell calls "multiples."[25]

Contemporary multiples are likely to end up in court.

Jack Kilby and Bob Noyce – one a quiet, deliberate introvert who struggled through college, the other a clever, impulsive extrovert who had been a success at everything he had ever undertaken – independently "invented" the monolithic integrated circuit, or semiconductor chip, the minute sliver of silicon at the heart of computers. They went to court over "ownership" and now, based on the Solomonic wisdom of the U.S. legal system,

---

24 He had already proven his ability to perform similar feats when he wrote two books about the Amazon – *A Narrative of Travels on the Amazon and Rio Negro* and *Palm Trees of the Amazon* – largely from memory after almost all his notebooks and reference specimens had been lost at sea.

25 We generally think of single inventors or discoverers, but many of our most important discoveries were "multiples." Both al-Tusi and Copernicus came up with the idea of how the solar system orbits around the sun, both Leibniz and Newton developed calculus, both Hilbert and Einstein came up with the gravitational field theory, Franklin – independently of Watson and Crick – discovered the double-helix structure of DNA. Scheel and Pristly discovered oxygen, six men invented the thermometer, nine men invented the telescope. And the list goes on.

are referred to as "co-inventors."

Luc Montagnier of the Pasteur Institute in Paris and Robert Gallo of the U.S. National Cancer Institute in Bethesda, Maryland, fought a long and bitter public battle over which one of them first isolated the HIV virus that causes AIDS. At one point Montagnier sued Gallo and the U.S. government. They settled out of court. Science journalist Thomas Bass noted that "As announced at the White House by President Ronald Reagan and French Prime Minister Jacques Chirac, royalties on the AIDS blood test [a by-product of the scientists' research] were to be split between the two countries."

Compare their "dirty laundry" approach with that of the gentlemanly Jonas Salk, who invented the polio vaccine. When reporter Edward R. Murrow asked: "Who holds the patent on this vaccine?" Salk replied: "Well, the people, I would say. There is no patent. Could you patent the sun?"

Maybe *that's* what it means to be a warrior. Strong enough to know who you are, to really understand your strengths and weaknesses so that you do not feel the need for external approval of your actions. "Shambhala," it's called in Tibetan. The sacred warrior.[26]

Perhaps Wallace needed a bulldog like Arnold Brackman by his side. Brackman wrote in *A Delicate Arrangement* "[Wallace] was the victim of a conspiracy by the scientific aristocracy of the day and was robbed in 1858 of his priority in the proclaiming of the theory." As partial evidence Brackman continues: "The guilt-ridden Darwin felt Wallace his moral superior and in a letter as early as April 14, 1869, as if under a compulsion to tell Wallace the truth about the conspiracy and cover-up leading to the Linnean meeting, Darwin wrote in admiration, 'You are the only man I ever heard of who

---

26 Biologist E. O. Wilson made two comments that resonate with Wallace's reticence to take credit: "Scientists most esteemed by their colleagues are those who pass the acid test of promoting new knowledge even at the expense of losing credit for it." And: "It takes a strong man to be gentle."

persistently does himself an injustice and never demands justice.'"

By all accounts it was a strange situation, and emotions (some might say thoughts of larceny) were running high: Leonard Huxley, son of English biologist Thomas Huxley, termed the incident, "This delicate arrangement." Darwin characterized it in a letter to Hooker as "This delicate situation."

Regardless of whether they prove Darwin's intent to cheat Wallace out of priority (or at least deny him due recognition), the Darwin letters provide fascinating glimpses into his thinking.

In a letter to Lyell dated June 25, 1858, shortly after Darwin says he received Wallace's Ternate Paper in the post, Darwin claimed priority, said he was unwilling to act dishonorably, very subtly posited (and rejected) the notion that Wallace might have copied from Darwin (!), and asked Lyell and Hooker to advise him on the best course of action: "There is nothing in Wallace's sketch which is not written out much fuller in my sketch copied in 1844, & read by Hooker some dozen years ago," Darwin wrote. "About a year ago I sent a short sketch of which I have copy of my views (owing to correspondence on several points) to Asa Gray, so that I could most truly say & prove that I take nothing from Wallace. I sh^d. be *extremely* glad **now** to publish a sketch of my general views in about a dozen pages or so. But I cannot persuade myself that I can do so honourably. Wallace says nothing about publication, & I enclose his letter.— But as I had not intended to publish any sketch, can I do so honourably because Wallace has sent me an outline of his doctrine?— I would far rather burn my whole book than that he or any man shd. think that I had behaved in a paltry spirit. Do you not think his having sent me this sketch ties my hands? I do not in least believe that that he originated his views from anything which I wrote to him. If I could honourably publish I would state that I was induced now to publish a sketch (& I sh^d be very glad to be permitted to say to follow your advice long ago given) from Wallace having sent me an outline of my general conclusions.— We differ only, that I was led to my views from what artificial selection has done for domestic animals. I could send Wallace a copy of my letter to Asa Gray to show him that I had not stolen his doctrine.

But I cannot tell whether to publish now would not be base & paltry: this was my first impression, & I sh^d. have certainly acted on it, had it not been for your letter. This is a trumpery affair to trouble you with; but you cannot tell how much obliged I sh^d. be for your advice." [italics and bold Darwin]

After the Linnean Society event Darwin wrote Hooker: "You must let me once again tell you how deeply I feel your generous kindness and Lyell's on this occasion, but in truth it shames me."

In January 1859 Darwin wrote Wallace ("My dear Sir")[27] and baldly disclaimed knowledge and responsibility for the Linnean Society machinations. Darwin not only fibbed about his role, he even had the temerity to imply he was a victim because of his poor health: "I was extremely much pleased at receiving three days ago your letter to me and that to Dr. Hooker," Darwin wrote. "Permit me to say how heartily I admire the spirit in which they are written. *Though I had absolutely nothing whatever to do in leading Lyell and Hooker to what they thought a fair course of action*, yet I naturally could not but feel anxious to hear what your impression would be. I owe indirectly much to you and them; for I almost think that Lyell would have proved right, and I should never have completed my larger work, for I have found my Abstract[28] hard enough with my poor health, but now, thank God, I am in my last chapter but one." [italics added][29]

In the same letter Darwin praises Wallace's "paper" and tries to reclaim the priority territory by reminding Wallace that he had written his notes twenty years earlier. "Every one whom I have seen has thought your paper very well written and interesting. It

27 Over the years the salutations used by Darwin and Wallace became increasingly less formal – Darwin's salutation started as "My dear Sir," then "My dear Mr. Wallace," then "My dear Wallace."

28 A bit disingenuous; the "Abstract" Darwin refers to is *The Origin of Species*.

29 What makes Darwin's denial of knowledge and involvement especially grating is that in his autobiography he admitted his complicity: "The circumstances under which I consented, at the request of Lyell & Hooker, to allow of an extract from my MS, together with a letter to Asa Gray . . . to be published at the same time with Wallace's Essay, are given in the *Journal of the Proceedings of the Linnean Society* 1858, p. 45. I was at first very unwilling to consent as I thought Mr. Wallace might consider my doing so unjustifiable, for I did not then know how generous and noble was his disposition."

puts my extracts (written in 1839, now just twenty years ago!), which I must say in apology were never for an instant intended for publication, into the shade."

Three months later, Darwin, in the postscript of a letter to Wallace dated April 6, 1859, wrote: "You cannot tell how I admire your spirit, in the manner in which you have taken all that was done about publishing all our papers. I had actually written a letter to you, stating that I would not publish anything before you had published. I had not sent that letter to the post when I received one from Lyell and Hooker, urging me to send some M.S. to them, and allow them to act as they thought fair and honestly to both of us; and I did so."

And the one I like the best, for its resonance with Richard Nixon, was when Darwin wrote Hooker in 1859: "I never did pick anyone's pocket."[30]

Darwin's correspondence seems, if not a smoking gun, at least like a kid caught stealing the cookies.

As Wallace said, "Truth is born into this world only with pangs and tribulations."

Wallace continued his self-flagellation late in life. He dedicated *Island Life* in 1880 to "Sir Joseph Dalton Hooker, K.C.S.I., C.B., F.R.S., etc., etc., who, more than any other writer has advanced our knowledge of the geographical distribution of plants, and especially of insular Floras, Dedicate this volume on a kindred subject as a token of admiration and regard." Hooker, of course, was one of the

---

30 This quote has often been taken out of context and does not directly relate to Darwin's actions regarding Wallace. Nevertheless the tone is defensive and intriguing. Darwin was writing on geographical distribution and was "borrowing" material from Hooker. The full quote: "Lastly, I should like particularly to know whether I have taken anything from you, which you would like to retain for first publication; but I think I have chiefly taken from your published works, and, though I have several times, in this chapter and elsewhere, acknowledged your assistance, I am aware that it is not possible for me in the Abstract to do it sufficiently. ("I never did pick any one's pocket, but whilst writing my present chapter I keep on feeling (even when differing most from you) just as if I were stealing from you, so much do I owe to your writings and conversation, so much more than mere acknowledgments show.")

architects of Darwin's takeover of the Linnean Society meeting; he referred to himself as "Darwin's agent" while his detractors dubbed him "Darwin's bulldog."

British philosopher, biologist, and prominent classical liberal political theorist Herbert Spencer (who coined the term "survival of the fittest," based on Wallace's phrase "the fittest would survive") agreed Wallace had been treated poorly. "I regret that you [Wallace] have used the title Darwinism," Spencer complained, "[because] you will, by using it, tend greater to confirm the erroneous concept almost universally current." There was no need to spell out the "erroneous concept" to Wallace.

Perhaps I'm wrong. Perhaps Wallace's ego was sufficiently strong so that he didn't need to see his name in lights. Perhaps he had read Goethe's philosophy in Faust: "No one can take from us the joy of first becoming aware of something, the so-called discovery. But if we also demand the honour, it can be spoiled . . . for we are usually not the first. What does discovery mean, and who can say that he has discovered this or that?"

David Hallmark, an English lawyer who has retraced Wallace's travels in Southeast Asia, feels Darwin was an academic cheat – Hallmark isn't shy about mentioning the loaded word "plagiarist." Hallmark is using specially designed plagiarism software – the kind used to catch deceitful college students – to compare the content and timing of Darwin's and Wallace's writings on natural selection to prove that Darwin was further from the theory than he or his friends wanted to admit, and that by their conduct they failed to give Wallace the credit to which he was due.

Hallmark's *prima facie* case against Darwin is based on facts raised in *Just Before the Origin* by John Langdon Brooks and an academic paper, "Darwin and Divergence: The Wallace Connection" by biologist Barbara G. Beddall, in which she said the only way to resolve the problem is by *fiat*, referring to *fiat justitia*, meaning "let justice be done." In support of his argument, Hallmark notes a number of things, including Darwin's defensiveness in reply to Lyell's criticism that Darwin omitted adequate attribution to Wallace, Darwin's multiple defensive and sensitive comments about the "delicate situation," as Darwin himself described it, his history of obfuscation, and, above it all, his fear of losing "priority" (his life's work had been "smashed"), which was what the entire game was about (according to Darwin's algebra, the more Darwin acknowledged Wallace the less of a genius Darwin would be perceived to be).

But not everyone believes that Wallace had been the victim of an idea-steal.

James Moore, a professor at Britain's Open University and a Darwin biographer, does not think Darwin plagiarized Wallace. Nor does Peter Raby of Cambridge University, who wrote one of the more successful Wallace biographies.

George Beccaloni, a curator at London's Natural History Museum, is uncertain. Beccaloni, who has described himself as "Wallace's Rottweiler" (an allusion to Thomas Huxley, who, as Darwin's champion was called "Darwin's Bulldog") notes: "The question hasn't been resolved about whether Darwin had the idea many years before Wallace, or whether it was Wallace's letter and ideas that provided the missing pieces of the puzzle."

Charles Smith asks: "Did Darwin really steal material from Wallace to complete his theory of natural selection?" Smith's answer: "Maybe, though the evidence is something short of compelling."

Wallace, for his part, maintained a generous front, and his acceptance speech on receiving the Darwin-Wallace Medal from the Linnean Society in 1908 (just five years before his death) praises Darwin's efforts while downplaying his own.

The *one fact* that connects me with Darwin . . . is that the idea of what is now termed 'natural selection' or 'survival of the fittest,' together with its far-reaching consequences, occurred to us *independently*, and was first jointly announced before this Society fifty years ago.

But, what is often forgotten by the press and the public, is, that the idea occurred to Darwin in October 1838, nearly twenty years earlier than to myself (in February 1858); and that during the whole of that twenty years he had been laboriously collecting evidence. . . .

How different from this long study and preparation – this philosophic caution – this determination not to make known his fruitful conception till he could back it up by overwhelming proofs – was my own conduct. The idea came to me, as it had come to Darwin, in a sudden flash of insight: it was thought out in a few hours – was written down with such a sketch of its various applications and developments as occurred to me at the moment,– then copied on thin letter-paper and sent off to Darwin – all within one week. [italics Wallace][31]

The truth? Like all rumors and gossips, like all urban legends and conspiracy theories, the truth is a slippery commodity depending largely on the proclivity and memory of the observer. Did Darwin rip off Wallace? Yes! No!

Don't mess with egos.

The sultan of Ternate is one of four remaining hereditary rulers in Indonesia (there were dozens previously) permitted to retain

---

31 "Acceptance speech," 6–7.

their titles after independence in 1945.[32] The reason behind this dance was that the newly independent post-colonial government recognized the power of the sultans and felt that the best way to nurture them as allies would be to allow them to retain some of their prestige. Although the four sultans acknowledge the pre-eminence of the central government, they still wield (diminishing) power, particularly in acting as intermediaries between the mundane world on earth and the powerful spirits that really control things.

As writer Kal Muller relates, in 1983 Ternate's Gamalama volcano threatened to blow. Sultan Mudafarsa, who was working in Jakarta (in the new Indonesia even sultans have to bring home a paycheck), flew home and took the ancestral crown on a sacred canoe ride around the island. Upon completion of the ceremonial circuit, the volcano quieted.

Sultan Mudafarsa was proud that one of his properties was the site of Wallace's house of discovery. I visited with Pak Zainal, the sultan's relative who lived on the site of "Wallace's home." Pak Zainal sat relaxed, in a white T-shirt and blue shorts, on "Wallace's" back porch. We talked about the historical significance of "Wallace's" house. I asked whether he would be prepared to move if the building could be converted into a national monument. Yes, he said, adding he had already discussed it with the sultan, who had offered to donate the house to the government in order to turn it into a museum.

I suggested this to the British ambassador, and we discussed whether the British Museum might like to get involved.

I went to the district provincial office to see whether I could push this idea along. "Yes, sounds interesting," they said.

I discussed this further with a mid-level executive in the Maluku tourist office in Ternate. I was a foreigner, and he didn't know how much to trust me. "It's a good idea," he said thoughtfully. Then, later that night over a male-bonding meal of goat soup and Guinness Stout, he added: "They'll never do it."

"Why not?"

32 The other remaining rulers are the sultan of Yogyakarta and the Susuhunan (king) of Solo, both in central Java, and the sultan of Aceh in northern Sumatra.

"It would mean tacitly acknowledging the power of the sultan." My tourist office friend explained the history. "Wallace's original house was built on land owned by a sultan a century and a half ago. That house, or at least the site of that house, is currently occupied by the current sultan's family." My friend explained that in Indonesian-speak the sultan would gain a large amount of face by donating the house as a national monument, while the government would lose face. Because of ego, "Wallace's" house remains a comfortable residence for a middle-class Ternate family.

A complicating, indeed a deal-breaking factor is that the sultan's house at 16 Jalan Sultan Hairun almost certainly *isn't* the site of Wallace's house.

On a visit to Ternate in 2009 I asked friends if they could take me to "Wallace's house." We drove in the direction of the sultan's crumbling palace and past the sultan's relative's dwelling, where I had visited several years earlier with Pak Zainal.

"You've gone past it," I said.

"No, it's up here a bit," my friends replied.

They drove a kilometer beyond Pak Zainal's "Wallace house" on Jalan Sultan Hairun and turned up a street that had recently been renamed as Jalan Alfred Russel Wallace. Some two hundred meters (two hundred and twenty yards) from a simple shopping center that was nevertheless the best in Ternate, we knocked on the door of a normal looking dwelling. The Chinese owner was not surprised to see visitors. He let us wander around his cluttered back yard to examine the deep well.

"This is where Wallace's house was," my friend said with certainty. "It matches Wallace's descriptions better than the sultan's house."

I re-examined the evidence.

For a start, Wallace wrote that he "obtained" a house from Mr. Duivbenboden, the self-described king of Ternate and, by implication, lived in the European quarter and not the native quarter.

I brought letters of introduction to Mr. Duivbenboden, a native of Ternate, of an ancient Dutch family, but who was educated in England, and speaks our language perfectly. He was a very rich man, owned half the town, possessed many ships, and above a hundred slaves. He was, moreover, well educated, and fond of literature and science – a phenomenon in these regions. He was generally known as the king of Ternate, from his large property and great influence with the native Rajahs and their subjects. Through his assistance I obtained a house, rather ruinous, but well adapted to my purpose, being close to the town, yet with a free outlet to the country and the mountain. A few needful repairs were soon made, some bamboo furniture and other necessaries obtained, and, after a visit to the Resident and police magistrate, I found myself an inhabitant of the earthquake-tortured island of Ternate.[33]

Wallace referred to a well, but each site has a well that could have been in existence 160 years ago.

[My house had] a deep well which supplied me with pure cold water, a great luxury in this climate.[34]

The most convincing bit of evidence is that Wallace had written:

Just below my house is the fort, built by the Portuguese, below which is an open space to the beach.[35]

And indeed the "new" site is opposite the old Portuguese fort. I asked, naively, why the local government didn't buy the house and turn it into a visitors' center, or biodiversity museum, or

---

33 *The Malay Archipelago*, 312–3.

34 Ibid., 314.

35 Ibid.

something that would be both historically sensitive and educational.

My friend looked at me like I was nuts. "Ever since the historians decided that this was Wallace's house, the guy who owns it had raised his asking price every year. It's now up to about US$350,000, more than you'd pay for a mansion in Jakarta." The devilish combination of Ego and Greed strike again.

Pulau Enu, Aru Islands, Indonesia
A newly hatched baby turtle encounters a turtle skull on Shiva's Beach.
The little critter made it to the sea safely, on his own steam.
And then he began his own hero's journey.
Photo: Paul Sochaczewski

VI

ENLIGHTENMENT

SHIVA'S BEACH – BETWEEN LATE AND LATER

Pulau Enu, Aru Islands, Indonesia

Where have the stars gone?

I stretch; my back aches. What time is it? The battery in my watch is old, and the night-light on my Casio hardly illuminates the dial; I should have traded it to Zakarias for that bird of paradise skin.

I fell asleep during a left brain-right brain shootout. Kill anyone who kills a turtle, my emotional right brain screamed. But then my left brain kicked in and argued that trade is inevitable – people are inherently evil and greedy, aren't they? No, of course not, the right brain said, amazed that the left could be so stupid. In each of us resides a spirituality that can develop provided our better selves are nurtured and encouraged and rewarded.

This unanswerable internal debate mercifully stopped while I dozed in the shelter of a fallen tree.

I wait for turtles. They will come. I scan the beach, trying to decide which direction to walk.

I stand and stretch. A burst of heat lightning screams through the light clouds, and I think I see someone approaching from the far side of the beach. He is a couple of hundred meters away. He carries no flashlight. Must be a poacher who thinks that all the scientists are in bed. I've rarely met such a complacent group – with the exception of Ating Sumantri, the Indonesians in our team are content to tag a couple of turtles each night and head back to the comfort of the camp on the other side of the island.

Okay, if it's a poacher, I'll wait for him. If I catch him and he has turtle eggs – or worse, if I catch him killing a turtle – I'll rugby tackle him and beat him up and be a hero, at least to myself. That is if he doesn't beat me up in the process. Mano a mano.

The stranger is tall, walks with a slight stoop. He moves with some stiffness. Not furtive, as a poacher would be. Just cautious, looking around.

"Alfred? Is that you?"

"Good evening, Paul. It is all right if I address you as Paul?"

"Hello Alfred."

Without another word he sits next to me on the bleached log. For a long moment we stare, in parallel, out toward the sea, a crescent moon illuminating a strip of surf.

"It's been a good trip," I say finally.

"Yes."

We watch phosphorescence dazzle the waves.

"Can I ask you something?" I ask Alfred Russel Wallace. His silence is a yes. "What do you think of this world? Is it what you had expected?"

As an answer Alfred offers a whimsical smile and takes off his tiny John Lennon-like wire-rimmed glasses, similar to those Bruno Manser wore during his four years living with the Penans in the Sarawak rainforest. Alfred wipes them with a handkerchief he takes from his coat. He is dressed in a dark cotton-and-wool jacket, with a linen shirt that once was white. His clothes smell, but he doesn't.

"Where are your boots?" I ask.

"Those heavy leather boots, they were my bane. They became soaked in sea water once too often," he says, offering a modest glimmer in his eyes. "I fed them to the sharks."

We sit silently, watching the stars.

"The Arab astronomers undoubtedly had quite a vigorous imagination in order to visualize animals in the firmament," Alfred says. "I am unable myself to see the images without a book that shows where to connect the lines."

I look for Leo, my constellation. He looks for his, Capricorn. All we can make out is Orion, dominating the equatorial sky. "Don't you get humbled by all the possible worlds out there?" I ask.

"As a young boy I laid on my back, looking at the stars. As I suppose all young boys do. Now I am more interested in what happens here on this planet.

Modern science has discovered some most astounding things. But still, there are things I dare say we will never figure out. Right here."

"Like what?"

"Like the hidden biosphere, deep within the planet, where microbes called hyperthermophiles survive in heat of an extraordinary temperature. Apparently these miniscule natural productions may even constitute a separate kingdom of life."

"Some scientists say that the existence of these hyperthermophiles could change our view of evolution. Does that bother you?"

For the first time, Alfred laughed. "Why should it? Paul, imagine. Do you not think that there is something spectacularly appropriate in the fact that a microscopic, anaerobic, heat-loving microbe that derives its very energy from the most inner core of the earth could teach us more about ourselves?"

"I don't follow you."

"Earlier you asked me about the supernatural force that gives man his unique powers. Perhaps I was a bit hasty. Oh, don't misunderstand my intention. I believe in that force and probably always will. But maybe I was too hesitant in my opinions."

I cannot believe that Alfred Russel Wallace would admit to being hasty about anything, and I prod him to explain his position.

"I tried to separate that 'life force' from religion. I was so bungled about wanting to be provocative, but also afraid of what havoc I might create."

"What are you saying Alfred?"

"That the supernatural force which makes people uniquely human is everywhere. But people get confused, they think I mean religion. People drag their own emotions into the debate. There's no dogma, no ritual. Just natural laws we can't understand. I know most people don't understand that, but it's really as simple as that. People don't need all those symbols and myths."

"You sound like Obi Wan Kenobe," I say. I have to explain the cultural reference.

We watch the sky again. I teach Alfred a few Beatles songs; he is particularly pleased to learn "Yellow Submarine." I see a falling star but am too slow to make a wish.

"I was able to catch that one," Alfred says, as if reading my mind.

"What did you wish for?"

"It would invalidate the wish were I to tell you." After a while he adds, "but it had something to do with television."

"Go on."

"Television, if you think about it, is like this supernatural force. We accept it; we don't usually think about it, but if we did accept its existence then we would have to believe that there is a god. Imagine. Transmitting an image. Unbelievable, really."

"But you believe television exists."

"Of course. I watch it. But I'm blasted if I could explain it to anyone back in the mid-nineteenth century. I might as well try to explain to them about space travel or computers."

"So technology is the new religion."

"No, not by itself. Technology is the cutting edge of religion, the advertising for religion, but not the religion itself."

"So, is there a new religion?"

"Listen Paul. I am merely an unemployed, lonely, and lowly beetle collector. Why are you asking me all these questions about theology?"

"Come off it, Alfred."

He sighs. "I do not understand your world. Life used to be simple. Now people have so much more and appear to be so much less happy."

"Are people really less happy?" I insist. "Haven't people always been frustrated with their work, or their homes, or the way their husbands and wives look in the morning? Isn't the difference now that instead of accepting it, people are encouraged to examine it, and, by so doing, the problems become bigger and more important?"

Alfred scratches his beard, then rubs the bridge of his nose. "What will happen to the turtles?" he asks.

"They'll keep on disappearing," I reply. "But not entirely. Nature is too cunning, and the sea is too large."

"Where do you suppose they go?"

"Just accept it, Alfred. Don't try to question everything. Holoholo e like me ná honu i ka hohonu."

Alfred looks at me. "I collected vocabularies of fifty-seven languages. Yet I do not recognize the words."

"It's Hawaiian. 'Cruise with the turtles into the deep.' Except it sounds better in the original."

"I had better write that down. My memory is not what it used to be."

"Neither is my back," I say, readjusting my position against the fallen tree. Clouds begin to block Orion. "Regrets?"

"A few," he answers. "You know I always felt restricted by those irritating customs and expectations of my age. There were many times, many times, Paul, I wanted to wander off with one of those pretty damsels. Many times I wanted to lend a hand to the farmers building rice terraces. I would have quite liked to have had a go at that joged dance. There were times I wanted to . . . oh well. I did not."

"Would you rather have lived today?"

"No, today I find there is simply too much information. I think I would go crazy as a court jester trying to learn everything. The establishment would try to force me into becoming a specialist, and that would drive me quite mad."

"What do you think will happen to the turtles?" I ask after a while.

"Siapa tahu. I have no idea. I simply wish them well."

"You think they recognize your good wishes?"

He shrugs. "I hope they do. That's the only thing we can hope for. That the turtles, with their reptilian brains somehow have the wisdom to sense our presence and that they sense which people mean well and which people don't."

"That's a funny statement coming from a guy who shot seventeen orangutans, not to mention twenty-four red birds of paradise."

"Times change. People grow up. I would not do that now."

"What would you do?"

"Sometimes you tire me with these questions. But you took me to some places I had never been, so I will answer you. If I could begin again and repeat the voyage, but do so in the present time at the beginning of the twenty-first century, I would be a farmer. I would have an organic farm on the edge of a wilderness. Australia, perhaps, or Brazil. I would seek the company of one good woman who wished to be a devoted wife, and she would bless me with children. Oh yes, I would possess my own plane so I could seek out the company of friends when I choose."

"Will you have a satellite dish to watch football?"

Alfred Russel Wallace laughs. "Of course I will want a satellite dish. We all need some religion."

The sky clouds over, and the dark becomes oppressive. It starts to rain. Small drops, at first. We are old Asian hands. We know what is coming. We sit there on the log in the certainty that within moments the heavens will unload.

I have nowhere else I want to be. Nor, I suspect does Alfred. A particularly big raindrop lands on his right spectacle lens, obliterating his vision. He reaches into his pocket, for his handkerchief, I think. Instead he pulls out two small plastic bags, like the kind you put sandwiches in.

"Put your notebook in this," he instructs, offering me one of the bags.

I do, and he does, and we sit in the rain waiting for turtles.

ABOUT THE AUTHOR

Paul Spencer Sochaczewski is a Bangkok- and Geneva-based writer and writing coach. He is also chairman and creative director of International Golf and Life Foundation, a Swiss-based NGO that promotes environmental and social responsibility in golf.

While with WWF (World Wide Fund for Nature International), Paul created global campaigns to protect rainforests and biological diversity and then developed the WWF Faith and Environment program.

He has written more than 600 by-lined articles for publications including *The International Herald Tribune*, *Wall Street Journal*, *Travel and Leisure*, *CNN Traveller*, *Reader's Digest*, *DestinAsian*, and *Geographical*. He wrote *Redheads*, a comic conservation adventure set in a mythical sultanate on Borneo, *The Sultan and the Mermaid Queen*, which describes rarely written about Asian people, places, and events, and *Distant Greens*, which looks at golf's curious facets. He co-authored two books with Jeff A. McNeely, *Soul of the Tiger: Searching for Nature's Answers in Southeast Asia*, which examines the eco-cultural revolutions that have influenced people-nature relationships, and *Eco-Bluff Your Way to Instant Environmental Credibility*.

Paul wrote about the nature of Malaysia in *Malaysia: Heart of Southeast Asia* and served on the Editorial Advisory Board for the *Indonesian Heritage Encyclopedia*. He was project initiator for *Tanah Air: Celebrating Indonesia's Biodiversity*.

Website: www.sochaczewski.com

The voyages in search of Wallace were taken over a period of some forty years; some information and facts might be dated, but the essence of the stories remains intact.

——————

ACKNOWLEDGEMENTS

Innumerable people have aided and abetted my journey.
Monique, David, and Shynta, who no doubt heard more about this book than they wanted to.
David Hallmark and Bill Stone, who continue to share the journey.
Countless people along the roadside who have taken a few minutes to talk to a stranger and offer an encouraging smile.
And many other friends, in roughly alphabetical order:

Rambli Ahmad
Lesley Luyoh Akah
Douglas Amrine
Robert Basiuk
Baru Bian
Russel Betts
Boedhi Boedhihartono
Intu Boedhihartono
Mike Boon
Ramesh "Zimbo" Boonratana
Lee Wai Ching
James Clad
Aloysius Dris
David Ferdiaz
Shynta Ferdiaz
Sri Indrastuti Hadiputranto
Larry Hamilton
Charles de Haes
Robert E. Heggestad
Brent Hesselyn (RIP)

Ho An Chon (RIP)
Aristedes Katoppo
Ro King
Herschell Gordon Lewis
Margo Lewis
Bruce Littman
Leonard Lueras
Sukianto Lusli
Sangkot Marzuki
Jeffrey A. McNeely
Peter Mikelbank
Kenton Miller (RIP)
Didier Millet
Andrew Mitchell
Yan Mokoginta (RIP)
Rachael Morris
Paddy Murphy
Daniel Navid
Peter Ng
Edgar Ong
Ramsay Ong
Charles Orwin
Bayang Penguang
A.A. Gede Rai
Vithal Rajan
Peter Raven
Gordon Riggle
Sanib bin Haji Said
Dhanapala Samarasekara
Veronique Sandoz
Mimis Sasmoyo
Jeffrey Sayer
Peter Schoppert
Richard Evans Schultes (RIP)
Tony Sebastian
Rebecca de Souza
David Sparkes (RIP)

Farquhar Stirling
David Stone
Dudi Sudibyo
Ating Sumantri
Andy Sundberg
Lee Talbot
Lani Anak Taneh
Ida Pendana Gede Djelantik Putra Tembuku
Annie Teo
Jim Thorsell
Andrew Alek Tuen
Mark van der Wal
Lily Wardoyo
Yeoh Jun Lin

BIBLIOGRAPHY
of works cited in this book

(All by Alfred Russel Wallace)

Books

Alfred Russel Wallace: Letters and Reminiscences. 2 vols. Edited by Sir James Marchant. London: Cassell and Company, Ltd., 1916.

A Narrative of Travels on the Amazon and Rio Negro, With an Account of the Native Tribes, and Observations on the Climate, Geology, and Natural History of the Amazon Valley. London: Reeve & Co., 1853. (reprinted 1870, London: Macmillan & Co.)

Darwinism: An Exposition of the Theory of Natural Selection With Some of Its Applications. London and New York: Macmillan & Co., 1889.

My Life: A Record of Events and Opinions. 2 vols. London: Chapman and Hall, Ltd., 1908.

Social Environment and Moral Progress. London, New York, Toronto and Melbourne: Cassell and Company, Ltd., 1913.

The Malay Archipelago: The Land of the Orang-utan and the Bird of Paradise; A Narrative of Travel With Studies of Man and Nature. 2 vols. London: Macmillan & Co., 1869. (1989 edition, Singapore: Oxford University Press) Citations refer to the Oxford edition.

The Wonderful Century: Its Successes and Its Failures. London: Swan Sonnenschein and Co., 1898.

Articles, Short Pieces, Lectures, Speeches

"Acceptance speech on receiving the Darwin-Wallace Medal." Spoken by the author. July 1, 1908. In *The Darwin-Wallace Celebration Held on Thursday, 1st July, 1908.* Edited by Linnean Society of London. London: Burlington House, Longmans, Green & Co., 1909.

"A Defence of Modern Spiritualism." Pts. 1 and 2. *Fortnightly Review*, n.s., 15 (o.s., 21), no. 89 (May 1874): 630–657; n.s., 15, no. 90 (June 1874): 785-807.

"Economic and Social Justice." In *Vox Clamantium: The Gospel of the People.* By "writers, preachers & workers brought together by Andrew Reid." London: A. D. Innes & Co., 1894.

"Human Selection." *Fortnightly Review*, n.s., 48 (o.s., 54), no. 285 (September 1890): 325–337.

Letter concerning collecting in Si Munjon Coal Works, Borneo, April 8, 1855. *Zoologist* 13, no. 154 (August 1855): 4803–4807.

Letter to Samuel Stevens concerning collecting in Dobbo, Aru Islands, March 10 and May 15, 1857. In *Proceedings of the Entomological Society of London* (*1856–1857*): 91–93. (communicated to the ESL meeting of October 5, 1857)

"Miracles and Modern Spiritualism." *Light*, No. 806 (1896): 298.

"Notes." In *Contributions to the Theory of Natural Selection: A Series of Essays*. London and New York: Macmillan & Co., 1870. (reprinted 1871, with corrections and additions, including notes. London and New York: Macmillan & Co.)

"Notes on the Growth of Opinion as to Obscure Psychical Phenomena During the Last Fifty Years." *Religio-Philosophical Journal*, n.s., 4, no. 15 (September 1893): 229a–230a. (communicated to the Physical Congress in Chicago, August 21–25, 1893. Sent from Parkstone, Dorset, England)

"Observations on the Zoology of Borneo," dated March 10, 1856 (Singapore). *Zoologist* 14, no. 164 (June 1856): 5113–5117.

"On the Law Which Has Regulated the Introduction of New Species, dated February 1855 (Sarawak, Borneo). *Annals and Magazine of Natural History*, 2nd ser., 16, no. 93 (September 1855): 184–196. (Sarawak Law)

"On the Physical Geography of the Malay Archipelago." *Journal of the Royal Geographical Society* 33 (1863): 217–234. (read at the Royal Geographical Society meeting, June 8, 1863)

"On the Varieties of Men in the Malay Archipelago." In the Notices and Abstracts of Miscellaneous Communications to the Sections portion of *Report of the Thirty-third Meeting of the British Association for the Advancement of Science*; held at Newcastle-upon-Tyne in August and September 1863: 147–148. (read at the meeting of Section E, Geography and Ethnology, of the British Association for the Advancement of Science, September 1, 1863)

"Sir Charles Lyell on Geological Climates and the Origin of Species." *Quarterly Review* 126, no. 252 (April 1869): 359–394. (running title for review of Principles of Geology (10th ed.), 1867–1868, and Elements of Geology [6th ed.], 1865, both by Sir Charles Lyell; anonymous, but referred to in My Life [Vol. 1, p. 406])

"Spiritualism." In *Chambers's Encyclopaedia*, vol. 9 of 10. New edition, London and Edinburgh: William & Robert Chambers, Ltd., 1892.

"The Dawn of a Great Discovery (My Relations With Darwin in Reference to the Theory of Natural Selection)." 1903. *Black and White* 25 (624): 78–79.

"The Limits of Natural Selection as Applied to Man." In *Contributions to the Theory of Natural Selection: A Series of Essays*. London and New York: Macmillan & Co., 1870.

"The Native Problem in South Africa and Elsewhere." *Independent Review* 11, no. 38 (November 1906): 174–182.

"What Are Phantasms, And Why Do They Appear?" *Arena* 3, no. 15 (February 1891): 257–274. (reprinted in *Miracles and Modern Spiritualism*, 3rd ed. (January 1896): 255–278)